RONIN RO

HAVE GUN
WILL TRAVEL

THE SPECTACULAR RISE AND
VIOLENT FALL OF
DEATH ROW
RECORDS

Q QUARTET BOOKS

FIRST PUBLISHED IN GREAT BRITAIN BY QUARTET BOOKS LIMITED IN 1998
A MEMBER OF THE NAMARA GROUP
27 GOODGE STREET
LONDON W1P 2LD

COPYRIGHT © BY RONIN RO 1998

A CATALOGUE REFERENCE FOR THIS BOOK IS AVAILABLE FROM THE BRITISH LIBRARY.

ISBN 0 7043 8102 8

PRINTED AND BOUND IN GREAT BRITAIN BY C.P.D. (WALES) LIMITED

For my lovely wife, Susan, and our beautiful daughter, Rachel Ro (Daddy loves you, honey).

"Do not become envious of the man of violence, nor choose any of his ways."
Proverbs 3:31

"ALL THEY FOUND WAS HIS WALLET"

Outside the Los Angeles County Courthouse near Temple Street and North Broadway on Friday, February 28, 1997, three or four teenagers tried to form a "Free Suge Knight" march. They may have hoped to inspire a gathering as large as the one people formed in support of O.J. Simpson, another football player turned defendant, but save for his employees and a few starstruck teens, no one on this street really wanted Suge Knight free. "We been out here for about a half an hour," one young black male told a passerby. "If you want, just pick up a sign." Death Row Records had printed up placards that read IS THIS A BLACK OR WHITE ISSUE? No one lifted any signs.

CEO of Death Row Records, Marion "Suge" Knight was the most intimidating executive the music industry had ever seen, an imposing former bodyguard who stood six foot three inches tall, weighed over three hundred pounds, and stared at people as if measuring them for a coffin.

Inside the courthouse, Suge was to be sentenced for violating probation. In the downstairs lobby, metal detectors blocked every entrance; slit-eyed guards told people to empty their pockets and bags and walk through the detector once more: People in line stared at each other with open hostility, fear, and loathing.

In front of Department 123, on the thirteenth floor, the mainstream media tried their best to avoid the contingent of burly Death Row supporters attending the hearing. Some were members of the Bloods gang, and wore the gang's identifying color: red suits, shirts, markdown slacks, patent leather shoes, and sweatshirts; they wore thick gold chains with medallions fashioned after the label's logo (a man strapped into an electric chair) dangling from their necks. As fearful reporters studied them, Suge's buddies swaggered down hallways, slapped hands, filled the air with muttered curses, and did nothing but fuel law-enforcement rumors that Death Row was an ongoing criminal enterprise. Usually, they did this in their "neighborhood," where terrified neighbors remained indoors and let them control the street.

Death Row singer Nate Dogg, himself exonerated of robbing a Taco Bell restaurant in 1995, stood silent near his girlfriend. In the Los Angeles suburb of Long Beach where Nate grew up, police officers were distrusted and despised. Deputies in beige shirts, green pants, sidearms, and black belts looked just as uncomfortable near this unruly mob, but remained calm. Through gritted teeth they asked the label's supporters to hand over identification, wear laminated passes; sign their names on lists, and stand in line.

The label's supporters were furious; Suge, they felt, was being prosecuted due to his race. In their minds, white law enforcement officials were jealous of Suge's quick and impressive success. More officers arrived to guard the perimeter around the courtroom. One told another it would be a tense day in Department 123.

Before his arrest Suge Knight had helped make his company, Death Row Records, one of the most successful black-owned record labels of all time. In four years the label had sold over eighteen million albums and earned more than $325 million (a record for a rap label); their videos were in "heavy rotation" on MTV, their albums regularly outsold releases by white rock 'n' roll bands, and the label's artists were among the most popular in the world. Some, in fact, had even won Grammy Awards.

As the label continued to grow, rap fanzines promoted Suge as a Robin Hood figure whose goodwill efforts benefited his Compton neighborhood. According to the fanzines, Suge hosted Mother's Day dinners for single mothers, distributed turkeys to poor families on Thanksgiving, provided Christmas toys for needy Compton children, and vowed to create a bus service for women visiting relatives in prison. "While there have been many tales of Knight's, shall we say, *persuasive* way of doing business," *The Source* claimed, "almost equally legendary is his concern and care for his acts, upon whom he is known to lavish cars, homes, alimony payments, back taxes, and, in the case of Snoop and Tupac, Death Row's biggest stars, their freedom."

Away from the lights and cameras, however, Suge's private life had begun to mirror the plots of recent gangster films. As a humble kid in Compton, Suge had befriended classmates in elementary school who would later become gang members; then he played football, and demolished his opponents on the field, using any dirty trick he could get away with; then, when his career as an L.A. Ram ended, he hired himself out as a bodyguard and often beat disorderly clubgoers to a bloody pulp; then he associated with drug dealers and in their presence beat people's faces with enough force to shatter bone; then, during nights on the town, he argued with bouncers and battered them to the point where their spleens were damaged and required multiple surgeries; as label CEO, he threatened his competition with lead pipes, slapped people with pistols, and fired shots at their head; chased people with gun in hand at peaceful music industry conventions and had opponents living in fear that one day Suge would want something they owned. With each violent episode, his legend increased; soon everyone in the recording industry knew: If you offended Suge Knight, no matter where you went, he would find you. Here was a man who settled out of court, who admired frontier justice used during the days of the Wild West. "Everything was so much simpler," he once said. "In those days, what was right was right and what was wrong was handled."

Before Suge entered the West Coast music industry, the very nature of the music West Coast rappers recorded seemed to invite trouble. Instead of using their albums to promote politics, unity, and education, like their East Coast counterparts, West Coast groups glamorized the gang violence plaguing L.A. neighborhoods since the 1920s. Many West Coast rappers promoted the image of trigger-happy gang member—whether they were truly gangsters or not.

As a result, actual gang members decided to test these individuals, to see if they were as tough as they claimed to be on record. After rapper Ice-T (Tracy Marrow) performed at a local high school in 1986, close to one hundred fans surrounded his Cadillac Seville to ask for autographs: Ice-T, a former Crip gang member, happily obliged. To him, it was show business, and stars were expected to mingle with fans. Unfortunately, he was wearing a red outfit that day. Red was the color favored by rival Bloods. "A bunch of Crips chased him down," said a witness.

Kurtis Blow, a harmless Jheri-curled pop rapper, flew in from Queens, New York, in 1986 to perform his radio hit "If I Ruled the World" in a Compton nightclub. Blow was the epitome of the Old School ethic: rappers in fancy outfits, riding in limos, acting like celebrities. "He had on a blue jacket, and people were just getting riled up," said a concertgoer that evening. "All you saw was khakis and red shoes and beanies." The audience was filled with Bloods. By night's end, security guards clashed with local Bloods, who were angered by Kurtis Blow's jacket. The guards put up a valiant fight, but one Blood member managed to sneak a handgun past the club's metal detectors. He fired it at a security guard's chest. Whether the guard survived is unknown. Initially, Blow was terrified, but drawn to the region's climate, he soon relocated to California.

In town to perform at a concert, pop rapper (and future sitcom star) Will "Fresh Prince" Smith was standing in front of a nightclub, when four unknown rappers from Chicago, a group called the Fresh Pack Four, challenged Smith to a battle (a verbal tournament that would determine which rapper had the best lyrics). Smith recorded gentle rap; he never gave an audience reason to dislike, fear, or want to challenge him. Smith agreed to the battle. "Next thing I know," said someone traveling with Smith that day, "I look up and there's like fifty of the biggest Samoans I've ever seen!" Members of the Sons of Samoa gang, affiliated with local Bloods, felt the blue-clad Chicago quartet were nothing but local Crips. "They had no guns, but then a forty [ounce beer] bottle came crashing down on the skull of the guy battling the Fresh Prince—" The Samoans threw one rapper through the nightclub's plate-glass window, then continued charging the group. Fresh Prince wisely ran into the club and hid in a broom closet, where he remained until the Samoans departed.

Then there was the 1986 Long Beach concert, a stop on the Fresh Fest Tour of New York groups and local talent. By now, California rappers knew that local gangs would use any opportunity they could to disrupt concerts. "That was the worst I've ever seen in my life," said KDAY programmer Greg Mack, who also hosted the event. Unaware that the colors red and blue signified affiliation with Crip or Blood gangs, security guards admitted members of rival gangs. As rapper L.L. Cool J tried to perform some of his confrontational rap singles, minor fights erupted in the audience. Then a sea of Crips in blue clothing marched down the aisle, stood directly in front of the stage, and glared at L.L. with murderous intent, challenging him by waving curled fingers that formed letters representing the name of their gang.

While the mood throughout the entire concert was tense, the apotheosis arrived when Brooklyn rap trio Whodini appeared onstage to perform a few gentle rhythm-and-blues-flavored raps. "Then [one gang member] threw this other guy right over the balcony onto the stage while Whodini was performing," said Greg Mack. Security guards rushed the stage to speak with the victim and determine the extent of his injuries. "Next thing you know, a whole section was running: Gangs were hitting people, grabbing gold chains, beating people." Outnumbered, the security guards hid backstage. In the parking lot, beleaguered concert host Mack recalled seeing a Crip "getting his shotgun, getting ready to do God-knows-what. As we were leaving, I saw cop cars and helicopters. On the news, people were leaving all covered in blood." Six people died at the event, and the group Run-D.M.C., who did not perform that evening, were eventually scapegoated for the violence.

Despite the fact that the West Coast music industry was desensitized to violence, Suge Knight managed to up the ante. After bringing L.A. gang members into the recording industry, he led them in a reign of terror that found his goons treating everyone from rival music executives to his own roster of artists like weak inmates in a cellblock.

One *L.A. Times* reporter related the rumor that Suge had a white artist manager kidnapped from an ATM machine in broad daylight. "All they found was his wallet," this reporter confided. "And when they found him four days later, he was walking around the streets naked, in a daze. He was in the hospital and wouldn't admit that Suge was behind it." To this day, the executive denies any of this ever took place.

When young black journalists tried to investigate the rumors surrounding his violent temper, they became victims of it: One incident involved a black writer from *The New Yorker*, who interviewed Suge in his office at the Can-Am [recording] Studios and made the mistake of saying, "C'mon, man. That answer's bullshit!"

Suge yanked the writer from his chair. After dragging him over to a tank where he kept piranha, he said, "How 'bout if my fish eat your fucking face?!" It didn't matter that *The New Yorker* was one of the "important" white magazines and that a negative writeup would surely be seen by many of the law enforcement officials investigating his label. No one got away with insulting him. Once the writer was suitably terrified, Suge tossed him back into his chair and said, "Now rewind your tape and ask me the questions again." The writer got his Dictaphone going, and this time, Suge gave better answers.

So-called "tough" writers always had to meet Suge on his turf, a recording studio deep in the middle of the Los Angeles suburb Tarzana, where you could leave only if someone unlocked the door, if the guards patrolling the premises with sidearms hanging in plain sight decided to let you go; if the Bloods who rapped on the label's albums decided they didn't want to beat the hell out of you after they finished smoking marijuana and drinking tall bottles of malt liquor. When *Vibe* magazine's "tough" writer arrived to meet with Suge, he was greeted by a "big light brown German shepherd rolling on the floor." The writer's Death Row escort sneered, "He won't bother you. He's only trained to kill on command." During the interview, the bellicose canine sat by the writer's chair—baring its fangs and salivating as Suge took offense at one of the writer's queries, cut the interview short, and began to utter threats. And it wasn't just the media that Suge terrorized: This was just the tip of the iceberg. Even well-respected political leaders dealt with his dark side. *Vanity Fair* reported that Al Sharpton and Jesse Jackson arrived at Suge's office to see an assistant mopping up a pool of blood. Suge didn't even bother to explain the grisly sight. "Business dispute," he quipped.

Like John Gotti with his Fourth of July cookouts and fireworks displays, Suge continued to publicly promote the image of street-smart philanthropist. Despite his verbal attacks on New York–based record label Bad Boy Records—in magazine interviews that further divided segments of the black community on the East and West coasts—Suge still found time to appear at the August 29, 1996, ceremony for A Place Called Home, a safe house for youths. At the ceremony, held at Central Avenue and 28th Street in South Central, he stood near Mayor Richard Riordan and other celebrities and announced plans to have Tupac Shakur and other Death Row artists perform at a benefit concert to be held in the first weeks of November at the Shrine Auditorium. The proceeds, he explained, would go to the safe house, which offered alternative schooling for children, dance classes, and Gangsters Anonymous, a counseling service modeled after the 12-step programs used by recovering addicts. Two weeks after this ceremony, Tupac Shakur was gunned down on the strip in Las Vegas. Then, in October 1996, Suge Knight was re-imprisoned: A judge felt Suge had violated probation by participating in the vicious beating and stomping of gang member Orlando Anderson at the MGM Hotel in Las Vegas—an attack that occurred hours before Death Row Records' top draw, Tupac, was murdered in a "payback" drive-by shooting.

By trying to kick Anderson, Knight had violated the terms of the probation he received for another violent incident: In 1992, he pistol-whipped siblings George and Lynwood Stanley after they dared to use the pay phone in Death Row's office: Knight said he was waiting for a call; the aspiring rap duo hung up the phone and were leaving the office; Knight followed with a gun, beat them, forced them to strip naked, then robbed them. Once he was behind bars, like sharks scenting blood, the feds moved in.

Originally, the Federal Bureau of Investigation; the Bureau of Alcohol, Tobacco and Firearms; the Internal Revenue Service, and the Drug Enforcement Agency wanted only to establish that Suge and Death Row were linked to the M.O.B. Piru Blood gang in Compton. But Suge, believing press clippings that called him a "hitman," openly defied the government. Now the government was trying to build a RICO case against Suge and his record label, a tactic usually reserved for use against the Italian Mafia.

Passed by Congress in 1970, the Racketeer Influenced and Corrupt Organizations Act was a legal tool designed by Notre Dame law professor G. Robert Blakey to help law enforcement agencies imprison the hierarchy of organized crime families. The act listed thirty-two specific criminal acts; if an organization was guilty of committing two of them, the government could label the organization a "criminal enterprise" and bring it to an end. Penalties for any racketeer involved with a "criminal enterprise" would be severe; most mobsters convicted for multiple RICO counts received long prison sentences (life without parole, served in maximum security federal penitentiaries).

As the FBI, BATF, IRS, and DEA continued building their joint racketeering case against his record label, claiming that known gang members committed crimes while on his payroll, Suge Knight began to wear the M.O.B. Piru gang's identifying bright red color on magazine covers. "There is no truth to the allegation that I had any knowledge of any crime committed by any of my employees," he claimed. "I don't even know what crimes they are talking about."

When agents said Death Row was financed by imprisoned drug dealers, Suge (who drove around California and Las Vegas in red cars) replied, "If the government is saying that these people gave me the money to start Death Row, they couldn't be more wrong."

When agents claimed that a paper trail leading to Suge's Las Vegas nightclub linked him to organized crime, he said, "If I was part of some so-called organized crime circle, how is it that I ended up getting beat out of my money? These allegations are ridiculous."

Yet, he painted his home, office, and Las Vegas nightclub red. He bought the Compton house he had been raised in and painted that red. He bought a Beverly Hills skyscraper, 8200 Wilshire Boulevard, and quickly hung cherry-red letters out front. He even bought the home that film director Martin Scorsese used as Frank Rosenthal's home in *Casino*, then painted that (and its swimming pool) red. Despite this, Suge maintained that he had no ties whatsoever to Compton, California's, drug-dealing M.O.B. Piru Blood gang.

"This is the most outrageous story I have ever heard," he said from his cell. All the federal investigation would uncover, he predicted, was that Death Row worked hard to produce engaging rap music.

Inside the enormous wood-paneled courtroom on February 28, 1997, six defense lawyers sat at a table and shuffled papers around. Their job would be to convince an angry judge to release Suge. The judge had already told them he was inclined to send Suge, who had eight convictions to his name, to state prison. The defense lawyers had their work cut out for them. Bailiffs shut the doors and told spectators to be quiet.

When Judge Stephen Czuleger entered and sat at his bench high above the chamber, his expression confirmed that it was all over for Death Row. A dark-haired white man with a mustache and a benevolent expression, Czuleger was aware of Suge's violent reputation; he knew that the federal government was investigating his record label, and that Suge flaunted his allegiance to a murderous Compton drug gang: The only man willing to confront the person *Prime Time Live* had recently labeled "the most dangerous man" in the music business, Czuleger shifted in his seat and watched armed guards lead Marion "Suge" Knight, shackled, into the courtroom.

"MOM, ONE DAY I'M GOING TO LIVE IN A HOUSE WITH A SECOND FLOOR AND I'LL HAVE A LOT OF CARS"

Marion Hugh Knight Jr. was born in a downtown Los Angeles hospital on April 19, 1964, to Marion Knight and Maxine Chatman Knight, a hardworking truck driver and his strong-willed wife, who relocated to California from Mississippi to be near other family members and escape the racism prevalent in the South. Upon their arrival, Marion Sr. quit driving trucks and worked as a custodian in UCLA's housekeeping and laundry departments. Maxine, a short, cheerful woman with bleached-blond hair, was hired by an electronics factory and worked on their assembly line.

In 1969 they used their savings to buy a home large enough to hold them, their two daughters, and their youngest child, Marion (called "Sugar Bear" by his father due to a gracious disposition). Married nine years and dreaming of a new life in the land of opportunity, the Knights paid $25,000 for a gray stucco one-story home—with two bedrooms, one bath, barred windows, and a tiny front lawn—in the working-class suburb of Compton.

While Compton had once been as lily white as regions of Mississippi, African Americans who worked for local factories began to buy one-story tract homes in the suburb. Fearing a rise in the crime rate, or lower property values, white neighbors quickly flew to some of the other white suburbs surrounding Los Angeles.

By the time the Knights and their children arrived, street gangs like the Crips and Bloods were on their way to becoming a fact of life. Gangs had been prevalent in California since the 1920s, when they were composed of African American juveniles who had recently arrived in the area from the South; after moving into quarters in downtown Los Angeles, family members and friends banded together and formed groups like the Goodlows, the Kelleys, the Magnificents, and the Boozies, which were involved in everything from armed robbery to prostitution.

Over the next three decades, gang membership swelled; black gangs rose in the Central Avenue section of town and in East Los Angeles. In the 1950s civic leaders tried to stop their expansion by encouraging youth to join car clubs. Many gang members did, and successfully turned the clubs into hangouts for territorial groups like the Businessmen, the Slausons, the Gladiators, and others. At this point the gangs used knives, chains, and bats for weapons, and were involved in petty theft, robbery, and assaults.

In the 1960s car clubs began to vanish: After riots in the Watts section of California in 1965, which started after a police officer arrested someone for drunk driving, street gangs became more organized and political. By decade's end, many gang members were involved with organizations like the Black Panther Party. A year before the Knight family moved to Compton, kids who were too young to participate in the Black Panthers formed their own groups, and one of these—started by fifteen-year-old Fremont High School student Raymond Washington—would become the Crips.

Originally, Washington and buddies like Stanley "Tookie" Williams called themselves the Baby Avenues, in honor of their adult friends and relatives in the Avenue Boys gang. Then Washington renamed his gang the Avenue Cribs and, with a few members, committed a series of robberies and assaults. During this period there was nothing glamorous (or marketable) about the group: They did not have identifying colors; they didn't commit drive-by shootings; they did not decorate the walls in their neighborhood with elaborate graffiti murals; they did not wear handkerchiefs on their faces to disguise their identities—they were just a group of semiliterate teenagers who wore jackets with their school name on the back. They looked like a group of football players off the field, and killed boredom by smoking marijuana, drinking cheap wine, cruising in cars and chasing girls, listening to soul music, and attending parties thrown in neighbors' homes. For money, however, they resorted to petty crime, and it was after one robbery that the group's name changed.

One night, Washington and his Avenue Cribs ran into a group of Asian storeowners. The merchants had left a meeting in one of their stores, where a local policeman provided suggestions on how to safeguard their businesses. Washington and his friends appeared, threatened them with knives and sticks, then took their money. Police arrived after Washington and his buddies fled the scene, to find the merchants trying to explain that, like a cripple, one of the robbers had been carrying a walking stick. Not fluent in English, one victim yelled, *"Crip! Crip!"*

A white crime reporter heard the word and wrote an account about the "Crips" gang; Raymond Washington and his buddies saw the article and enjoyed the attention; they adopted the name and continued robbing and assaulting people; more newspaper stories appeared, and these, in turn, led to more divisions of the new gang—the Eastside Crips, the Westside Crips (formed by Washington's buddy, Tookie), the Compton Crips.

By late 1971 the Avalon Garden Crips and the Inglewood Crips joined forces with other Crip gangs and the Crips expanded into other non-Crip sections of town. More and more established street gangs abandoned their old identifying colors and names and took up the color blue, the badge of honor for the Crips. A unified army, the Crips were now considered L.A.'s most fierce, feared, and famous black gang.

During the summer of 1972, however, Crips from Compton and a gang called the Original Pirus had a conflict. The latter, a group from Piru Street in Compton, were originally members of the Crips. As the Piru Street Crips, they proudly wore the traditional blue bandannas that promoted their Crip status. But the argument with another Compton Crip gang led to the Pirus being beaten in a nasty brawl in which they were vastly outnumbered. As a result, the vengeful Pirus severed all ties with the Crips, turned to a gang named the Lueders Park Hustlers for help, then called for a meeting on Piru Street. Since the Crips had murdered a member of a gang called the L.A. Brims earlier that year, the Brims appeared. Then other gangs that feared the Crips—the Bishops, the Athens Park Boys, and the Denver Lanes. During this historic meeting the gangs tried to decide how best to protect themselves from the Crips and decided to form an alliance. Since Crips had taken to wearing blue railroad handkerchiefs to conceal their identities, the Pirus and these other gangs would instead wear an opposite color, red. They would also call themselves the Bloods after the Vietnam-era slang term for "brother."

When more gangs joined the Bloods, they became L.A.'s second largest black gang. Though outnumbered by Crips three to one, they nevertheless became the Crips' deadliest rivals.

While his family had moved to California from Mississippi—to escape racism and find opportunity—young Suge learned that he lived in one of the most segregated, racist areas in America. At this point, Los Angeles County's 650,000 blacks were hemmed into the south central part of the city; one in four families lived below the poverty line; opportunities for financial improvement were limited; public transportation was bad; the police were brutal, and the crime rate in his Compton neighborhood was high.

At home, Suge's assertive mother spoiled him. She would cook his favorite meals, clean his room, iron his clothes, and shower him with affection. If his grades were bad or if he misbehaved or picked on his sisters, she turned the other way. In Maxine's eyes he could do no wrong. "I would always do anything for him," she remembered. "He could get anything he wanted." His mild-mannered father, a former singer, managed to get a word in edgewise: When he wasn't pushing a mop at his job, he instilled in Suge a love for music and football. Suge's home life, though characterized by struggle, was a stable one. Unlike many of his neighbors, he had two parents present in the household.

But outside his window, gangs were turning Compton into a scale-model Vietnam. In Suge's neighborhood, the Tree Top Pirus—a Blood gang—had to beware of the Southside Crips, the Atlantic Drive Crips,

Kelly Park, Neighborhood Crips, Front 'Hood, and Spook Town, gangs that lived within minutes of his home and assumed he was connected to the Bloods on his street simply because of his address and the fact that once in a while, to stay on their good side, Suge said hello to these gang members.

Even so, as years passed, Suge grew to love the place. "Compton's like the ocean," he would say years later. "It's real pretty, but, anytime, something can happen. Somebody getting eaten. Somebody fightin'. Something's always going on."

At age thirteen Suge was still thin and gawky; he was nervous about running into bullies. And like other teens, he wanted to earn his father's respect. Since Marion Sr. had been a high school football star—he played tackle—Suge figured a career on the field would do the trick. While many of his friends ran the streets, he began lifting weights, focusing on sports, and dreaming about securing an athletic scholarship and landing an NFL contract. After he began to play in local games, nearby Crip gangs would see him on pass-bys—when they'd drive past their enemies' neighborhoods in a car, hunting for a victim. Instead of leaping out of the vehicle to beat him with sticks, bats, or chains, they'd say, "Oh, that's Suge" and continue driving.

By the time Suge reached high school, gang feuds involved guns and drive-by shootings. His friends in the Tree Top Pirus had an established set of rules: Teenagers were being recruited, forced to prove their mettle by fighting other members of the gang. And the gang became even more territorial; his buddies took to carrying weapons and patrolling the block like security guards. On walls they used cans of spray paint to write *TTP*, the initials of the Tree Top Piru gang, marking their territory.

While his friends stirred up trouble, Suge focused on sports and earned a reputation as an athlete, which kept him out of the line of fire. His buddies since elementary school viewed him with pride; they didn't drag him into the gang. "When you're an athlete, gangsters respect you," said record promoter and club owner Bigga B, who later played football with Suge. "All gangsters love sports. They love to come to your games and see you play."

On the field, Suge Knight worked to become unstoppable. His eyes studied opponents while his mind tried to predict their next move. Seconds before they veered to the side, he leaped into position, smashed into them, and headed for the quarterback. From the stands, his mother, father, sisters, and uncles cheered him on. At game's end, after bulldozing his opponents, Suge would cross the field, remove his helmet, and accept compliments and pats on the back; then his eyes would brighten; uncles handed over hot dogs for a reward. His buddies in the Bloods were amazed: This kid who lived on the same street had this incredible talent; he would make it; he wouldn't be out there with them in baggy red clothes, smoking weed and starting trouble.

"By the late '70s," wrote L.A. Weekly reporter Joe Domanick, "Compton's streets were becoming grim and violent. And Suge Knight was in no way spared their pervasive lesson: Everybody out here is hungry."

Suge began to dream of a better life. Compton had lost a number of businesses and many jobs. Families were poor, struggling. People began selling drugs, resorting to crime. The streets were run-down: White areas were maintained while Compton went ignored. Friends were being shot, arrested. More gangs, or "sets," appeared. Residents were frightened. The police patrolled the neighborhood just as attentively as Tree Top members, and beat just as many heads. The city of Compton crumbled, but Suge fought to stay motivated. "Mom," he kept saying, "one day I'm going to live in a house with a second floor and I'll have a lot of cars."

While Parliament-Funkadelic tapes blared from radios, his friends in the Tree Top Pirus held joints between fingers and strategized about how best to attack nearby Crips. Suge wanted to fit in, not to be seen as soft; weak people were robbed and bullied. He continued lifting weights and befriended eight or so local Bloods—who would become lifelong friends and the cause of some of his troubles. And he wanted to dress the part. "Suge always liked gold," said Maxine Knight, "and he was careful about his appearance."

While not as physically imposing as he would later become, the mere sight of Suge became enough to discourage trouble. By his senior year at Lynwood High, where he was a four-year letterman in football and track, he was tall, stocky, and affected a haircut that reached his shoulders like a lion's mane.

After graduation in 1983, Suge received a scholarship to a local community college, El Camino, where he joined the school's football team and was named defensive end of the year. After a 1984 game, a recruiter from the University of Nevada at Las Vegas invited Suge onto the school's team. "Cats from L.A. who necessarily didn't have the grades to get into USC or UCLA went to UNLV instead," said music executive Bigga B, a UNLV teammate.

Suge visited the campus, decided to enroll, and planned to move to Vegas. But other students from Los Angeles gossiped about his affiliation with the Bloods. News reached school officials, who were concerned and had second thoughts about accepting him. Suge won them over, however, and was drafted onto the team and listed as weighing 260, and not his true 245 pounds. "Back then, Suge was just a straight-up guy who worked really hard at his position and never flexed like a gangster," Bigga recalled. "He never went around fighting or trying to intimidate people."

As number 54, he brutalized anyone blocking his path to the quarterback. Coach Wayne Nunnely knew he would make it. "He always worked hard, he had good work habits, and then he also got the other guys going." Rapper RBX, who also used his athletic skills to escape from Compton, said, "Suge's style was suave. He was a fat-ass motherfucker, but he could move!"

"Most of all, he was a good player," Bigga B noted. "He was real quick off the ball and his favorite move was the head slap, even though that's illegal. But he used to always try to get away with that. The head slap and the arm over. He tried to be real physical, to intimidate guys on the field. He would do anything. He was a dirty player," Bigga fondly remembered. "He did whatever it took. And coaches loved him."

At UNLV he never missed a practice. He was named rookie of the year, was one of three player-elected defensive captains, was lettered both years, and became an all-conference player (first-team defensive lineman).

Off the playing field Suge promoted the image of a gentle giant who smiled a lot, was always eager to party, dressed casually, and told a lot of jokes. White students usually couldn't believe he hailed from South Los Angeles. The team-player attitude he promoted also impressed teammates and coaches alike. To this day Coach Nunnely says, "He wasn't a problem guy at all. You didn't really see that street roughness about him." It was common for students who were middle-class hippie wannabes to go from an initial liberation by sex and drugs to becoming disoriented, frightened, and potentially dangerous. But Suge—coming from the ghetto—impressed people with his abstinence and restraint. "I never had a problem with him bringing drugs to our house or anything of that nature," said teammate Pat Harden. "We occasionally may have had a malt liquor or two, but that was it."

Suge's path toward the music industry was begun in part by the bad reputation the UNLV team acquired in 1985, when some of his teammates were desperate for money and resorted to petty crime. "We had brothers shooting each other, a lot of gangsters on our team," said Bigga B. "The locker room was like a jailhouse. Different guys would get punked and shit taken from them. If you wouldn't stand up for your shit, you'd get run over. A lot of guys started getting in trouble during a six-month period. One guy robbed a man coming out a casino; another guy carjacked somebody. This other cat used to call the pizza man and rob him."

To protect the school's image, a member of the coaching staff began to recruit "all these sorry white cats 'cause he was trying to clean up the image," Bigga B continued. The school year ended, and instead of returning to Los Angeles, a number of students remained in Las Vegas for the summer. Though the coach tried to help all of them find summer jobs, Bigga felt the coach showed blatant favoritism toward his new white players. Whites got jobs in air-conditioned casinos while black players were expected to work construction in a one-hundred-and-twenty-degree desert climate. As an alternative, black players began hiring themselves out as bodyguards and bouncers. At the time, Vegas was a segregated place. Tourists heard only about the brightly lit strip of casinos on the white side of town, where the university campus was. "All the black people live on the west and north sides." And it was on the west side where Suge worked, bouncing for nightclubs like the Cotton Club and West Side Story. At the time he enjoyed listening to rap groups like Run-D.M.C., the Fat Boys, Big Daddy Kane, and EPMD—all of which hailed from New York.

When students returned to UNLV for the new school year in 1987, they discovered that Suge had become an intensely private person. Teammates were puzzled. "Everybody showered together," said one of them, "but he would always walk down to the next shower, to the other side of the locker room. I don't know what that was about or nothing, but when you have a hundred guys in the locker room, you don't think about shit like that."

Instead of rooming with others, as most players did, Suge somehow could afford to live alone. "He was a normal tenant," said a teammate, "no loud music or anything, but he had some guys that used to come up from Compton and they used to do some deals. I'm'a be honest with you: Suge made a lot of money before he was even fucking with the N.W.A camp. Always hustling, always making loot. And he always had a fresh ride. In college, the motherfucker had four different cars! But he wasn't the guy bragging about his business all the time. Only a few people knew about him being in the drug game. I knew because I lived right across the street from him."

Suge Knight's immersion into Los Angeles street culture had become so complete that after one important game he decided to leave UNLV with his cronies from Compton. Coach Hyde called California and asked, "What the fuck is wrong with you?! You're supposed to stay in college."

Suge replied, "Well, fuck college. I only went to play football. I'm out here now making my money."

"But he did come back," a teammate explained.

In 1987, however, in his senior year, Suge was drafted by the Los Angeles Rams as a reserve lineman and left UNLV without graduating. His childhood dream of securing an NFL contract had been realized. "But he was only there for a short period of time," said a schoolmate who followed Suge's career. "There was a strike." During the strike he played in Japan for part of a season. When the strike was resolved and players returned to work, he was let go: His performance on the field wasn't superior to the players returning to their jobs; Suge's career in professional football ended.

On top of everything else, his relationship with longtime girlfriend Sharitha Golden was souring. They had met while he was in Compton, dreaming of a career in the National Football League; she was close to his age, down to earth like his mother, Maxine, and she could be sweet and gentle, brash and assertive, nurturing or critical: overall, she truly had faith that he would succeed and give both of them a good life outside the ghetto. She was living an average life, watching TV, hanging around the neighborhood, feeling fortunate to be with him, the future football star. When he went to college in Vegas, the relationship continued through telephone calls, weekend visits, and school breaks. But he had a temper. Tired of his jealousy and the arguments they had, Sharitha thought it wise to extricate herself from the situation, but Suge wouldn't allow it. By October, a series of arguments had frightened her; she explained to her mother, sister, and aunt that she could not pacify this explosive man. With their support and encouragement, Sharitha finally got the nerve to tell Suge it was over for good.

A mama's boy, Suge suffered from separation anxiety. Sharitha Golden represented stability; she embodied his idea of the perfect woman, an example set by his fiercely independent mother. Sharitha also could adapt to Suge's own street-hardened personality—she spoke slang, resented the rich, was wary of the police, and was driven by an ambition to escape Compton's demoralizing poverty. Though she couldn't fit all the criteria in his screening process, she was close enough to Maxine to serve as a substitute. But now his plan—he'd make the money on the football field while she had the babies—was unraveling.

He begged Sharitha to reconsider. He needed her. He would change. She refused. He felt under siege, with a household of women from various generations urging her to leave him. Once stress led to paranoia, he resorted to threats, which he later recanted.

Fearing for her life, Sharitha filed for a restraining order that covered herself, her mother, her sister, and her aunt. "Once I refused to talk back to him [about reconciling]," she wrote, "he then began to threaten me and my family . . . tamper with my car. . . ."

After agreeing to pay for damage to the car, he appeared outside her home with a tow truck. When she came outside, Suge reached out, grabbed her hair, yanked her ponytail off, and fled the scene.

In Las Vegas, he saw old friends, simmered down, and tried to figure out what to do with the rest of his life. But anger got the best of him. Within two weeks he attacked a man in Las Vegas during what appeared to be a violent auto theft. For this attack Suge was arrested and charged with attempted murder, grand larceny/auto, and use of a deadly weapon to commit a crime. In court, fortune smiled: Instead of time behind bars, charges for attacking the man were reduced to two misdemeanors and a $1000 fine. Under these conditions, Suge pleaded guilty.

Free again, he came to terms with the string of bad luck and decided to return to California, where he would work as a bodyguard at local concert events. His friends Wes and Ricardo Crockett hired him to oversee security at parties they threw at the L.A. Sports Arena. On his days off from the job, Suge Knight hung around his old Compton neighborhood, working with his friends in the Tree Top Pirus to become what one reporter at the *L.A. Times* called "a distribution point for cocaine in Compton."

"And not just that," said one of his friends. "Guns. The money was so easy and such a big part of him that he never got away from that. And the whole music game was his way of legitimizing his money."

Suge found work doing security for Bobby Brown, a member of the New Edition who was tired of that group's smooth rhythm-and-blues direction and decided to try his hand at a solo career singing over hard hip-hop beats. As Brown's protector, Suge had to keep autograph seekers at a distance for fear that Brown, at that time a hard drinker, might harm them. At the time Brown was a bachelor who liked to make the scene at nightclubs; he hadn't yet met and married R&B singer Whitney Houston. With Suge in tow, well-dressed Brown made the rounds almost every evening.

Suge kept seeing the DOC (Tracy L. Curry) everywhere he went and struck up a friendship with the successful rapper. The DOC—a tall, lanky teen with a yellow complexion, a goatee, and a tentative mustache—loved to party, chase women, and crack jokes. His debut rap album *No One Can Do It Better* had just been released to critical acclaim and commercial success: His single "It's Funky Enough" was No. 5 on *Billboard*'s Top Rap Singles chart; his album was No. 41 on the year's Top Black Albums chart; the DOC himself was No. 50 on the Top Black Artists chart and No. 100 on the Top Pop Album Artists chart.

Backstage at concerts, in nightclubs, or in fancy eateries, Suge would ask the DOC about his producer, Dr. Dre, who was well known in California for his stint in the World Class Wreckin' Kru, his mixes on KDAY's afternoon *Traffic Jams* radio show, and his groundbreaking work as producer of N.W.A (Niggaz With Attitude). A flamboyant man who stood six foot one inch tall, weighed 230 pounds, kept his head clean-shaven, and wore earrings on both ears along with the baggy clothes favored by local gang members, baby-faced Dre was the most successful rap producer in the industry: Every record he released sold millions of copies and earned the DOC's label, Ruthless Records, a fortune. Though Dre played the role of gang member (firing shotguns in bank-robbery scenes in violent N.W.A music videos.) the DOC revealed that that was just an image. Dre was the nicest guy you'd ever meet.

As a bodyguard, Suge had seen the large sums of money earned by popular musicians; he knew that Dre's music helped turn gangsta rap into a multimillion-dollar business. Wanting to get his hands on some of this money, Suge began to formulate a plan: It was somewhat unrealistic, but stepping on a few toes could make it a reality. What he needed was for the DOC to introduce him to Dr. Dre. If Suge could somehow convince Dre to break his contract with Ruthless Records and join him at a new record label, they would both become very rich. Suge's money problems and days as a bodyguard would be over. He would be set for life. But he needed to persuade the DOC to arrange an introduction.

"I JUST HAPPENED TO ROLL UP AND SEE HIM AND ANOTHER GUY KNOCKING THIS GUY OUT, YOU KNOW?"

The self-appointed "World's Most Dangerous Group," N.W.A was spearheaded by producer Andre (Dr. Dre) Young, the member with the most experience in the music industry. While members of the group ran with Compton-based Crip gangs in their youth, Andre, despite residing in Compton's Crip-infested Wilmington Arms district, resisted peer pressure and focused on music. As a child he was raised—along with a sister and brother—by his young single mother, who threw parties and asked four-year-old Dre to stand by the turntable and change 45 singles. "It was like I was deejaying for the house," Dre told *Rolling Stone*, "picking out certain songs and stacking them so this song would go after that song. I would go to sleep with headphones on, listening to music."

When Dre's mother accepted a full-time day job, he was shuttled between relatives' houses. "I lived in a whole bunch of neighborhoods in Compton: Blood neighborhoods, Crip neighborhoods." He had to learn to adapt quickly to whatever environment he was in: When he stayed with his grandmother in a Blood neighborhood, he attended a Blood high school and tried not to wear too much blue clothing. When he returned to stay with his mother and was transferred to a Crip high school, he put the red clothing away and wore a neutral color like black. All the while, he looked down on gangs and the senseless violence surrounding them.

"I think my thing was: 'If you ain't gonna make no money out of it, don't do it,'" Dre told me. "I couldn't see the logic behind doing that. Gangbanging's not gonna bring in no motherfucking money: It's just gonna get you motherfucking shot at; you gonna shoot at some motherfuckers; you gonna end up in jail; dead; something like that."

Instead of gangs, he immersed himself at the age of sixteen into the emerging national hip-hop culture: hearing Grandmaster Flash and the Furious Five's socially conscious rap single "The Message" inspired Dre to become a full time DJ and slap the word "Dr." onto his name (in honor of legendary New York Knicks player Julius "Dr. J" Erving).

After buying a pair of turntables, he fell in with a crowd of mobile DJs, performed at high schools, and made a name for himself due to his versatility and willingness to cater to any crowd: He played everything—fast-paced electro-pop records by Afrika Bambaataa or Kraftwerk, rock guitars on Run-D.M.C. records, X-rated comedy albums by comedian Richard Pryor, raunchy funk by Parliament-Funkadelic, and local rap records by West Coast pioneers like Ice-T and Kid Frost.

At one performance, Dre's friend Alonzo Williams asked him to join the World Class Kru, a loose union of club DJs that regularly hosted events at Compton clubs like Eve's After Dark and the Skateland Roller Rink. "We had a little four-track studio in the back of the [Eve's After Dark] club," Dre remembered. "We'd go and make our demos during the week and play them on the weekend to see how they would do." As the Wreckin' Kru clung to the high-tempo techno-pop sound prevalent in L.A., (and a commercial love-flavored ballad or two), Dre sat and watched, hating the music, wanting to sound more like the raw New York groups he imitated on his own. But he remained in the group because it paid well; every Tuesday brought another five-thousand-dollar payment from the Wreckin' Kru's label, CBS Records. By Thursday, however, the money would be gone—spent on clothing, equipment, bills, and partying. Then Dre would hound Lonzo, the only Kru member who saved, budgeted, and invested his money into a new home, for a loan. Though Dre already owed him two to three thousand dollars, Lonz would relent and advance him the money he needed.

Then their manager, Shirley, had a brilliant idea: Why not give the crowd a complete show? The Wreckin' Kru created an image, wearing spandex jumpsuits, frilly scarves, knee-high boots, and sculpted Jheri curls. Before each show, Shirley would apply their eyeliner and mascara.

"I'll tell you what," Dre said angrily when asked about the Kru's regalia, "I never had no motherfucking lace on! That was Yella! I was motherfucking seventeen years old. I had a motherfucking 'doctor suit.' I used to put on a little get-up, do a little show. That was my little thing. I'd put on a doctor's suit, stethoscope, and get up there and mix, you know." Dre was becoming embarrased with the group.

After Alonzo Williams bought a BMW in 1986, Dre asked if he could buy his old RX7. Dre knew Lonzo didn't quite trust him—he still owed Lonz a substantial amount of money. But he also knew Lonz needed him in the group. Reluctantly, Lonz agreed, but said Dre would have to pay for the car in installments while Lonz still owned it. Dre said fine, and promised to be responsible. Soon, however, Dre got traffic "tickets up the ass, somebody breaks the back window, steals the radio, steals the car, it ends up in the pound, and I'm still paying notes," Lonzo explained.

Dre was arrested, and called Lonzo to ask for bail money. Lonzo turned him down. Dre placed a second call to Eric Wright, a drug-dealing neighbor in Compton. A short, brown-skinned youth who wore baggy, creased khakis, dark sunglasses, long button-up shirts, and an unruly puffy mass of Jheri curls under his baseball cap, Eric (also known as "Eazy-E") agreed to put up the $900 on one condition: In return, Dre would have to produce songs for a record company Eric planned to form. Seeing no other way out, Dre agreed, and upon his release accompanied Eric Wright to Lonzo's studio, which had been rented for a number of hours. In the studio Dre followed orders and, like a serf, worked off his debt. Soon, Dre realized that a partnership with Eazy could lead to more creative control of his music, something denied in the Wreckin' Kru. Already, Eazy disliked Lonzo; Eazy began to tell Dre he could do better. "That fuckin' lipstick and lace and boxer shorts shit didn't last too long."

Dre proposed the idea of starting their own record label. Eazy was open to the idea and had disposable income but wanted more information before committing to anything. Suddenly, Dre wanted out of the Wreckin' Kru. "Money wasn't right," he said. "Basic reasons. I just felt like I wanted to be in control of my shit. I was just sitting in the studio knowing what I can do. I didn't have no input on a lot of that shit that came out."

He told himself, "Yo, I'm'a find me a group to produce. I'm gonna find me a motherfucker with some money to back this."

In Orange County, a calmer suburb of Los Angeles, he met a struggling rap duo from the East Coast (the still-unknown HBO), then arranged a meeting with Eazy. Dre played the HBO demo. Overwhelmed, Eazy agreed to finance the venture. Now Dre needed suitable material for the group.

He contacted O-Shea "Ice Cube" Jackson, a rapper he had known since Cube formed his earliest group, CIA, and Dre advised them on what sort of material to write. Cube was also a member of the Stereo Kru, a group signed to the Wreckin' Kru's own label, Kru Cut Records. Asked to pen a tune for HBO, Cube said, "Bet." Studio time was booked. HBO arrived, read Cube's lyric sheets, and said, "*Yo, man, we ain't doing that song! That's a West Coast record! That's West Coast rap! We ain't doing that shit!*"

Stumped, Dre watched the duo leave. Alone in the studio with a ticking clock and Eazy paying for every second, Dre suggested that Eazy try performing the lyrics. Reluctant, Eazy yelled, "I can't do this shit!" Dre gave a pep talk: He had already programmed a beat with the Roland 808 drum machine and loaded sounds into the SP-1200 sampling computer—all the song needed was a voice. It would be a hit. Putting on his sunglasses, Eazy then read the lyric into the microphone. "The song was 'Boyz N Tha Hood,'" Dre said proudly. "He did the record, we put it out and sold it out the trunk."

To shock the media and gain the support of the thousands of Los Angeles gang members they hoped would become their core audience, Eazy and Dre decided to call their group N.W.A (Niggaz With Attitude). By fusing the blue comedy of Redd Foxx, Dolemite, and Richard Pryor to the urban grittiness of pimp-turned-paperback-writer Iceberg

Slim (Robert Beck), then injecting the social relevancy of East Coast groups like Public Enemy and Boogie Down Productions, Eazy and Dre were able to go from religiously attending concerts by visiting New York groups like Run-D.M.C. to realizing their dreams of hip-hop stardom.

When their first single sold five thousand copies, Macola Records (a do-it-yourself record-pressing plant that dealt with Mexican ranch music but was also home to artists like 2 Live Crew, Hammer, and Timex Social Club) asked to distribute the record. Once the distribution deal was secured, Dre said, *"Bam!* There it was—"

During a tour in Dallas to support their groundbreaking single, Dre saw the DOC perform with the Fila Fresh Crew, the group opening for N.W.A. After the concert Dre approached the DOC backstage and introduced himself, then said, "Your sound is tight as hell." The DOC was honored: Dre's work with N.W.A inspired music critics to label him one of hip-hop's most gifted producers. The DOC agreed with their assessment. Over drinks, Dre asked the DOC and the Fila Fresh Crew to appear on a nine-song EP he planned to produce for N.W.A. After that, Dre said, he would produce a solo album for the DOC.

Dre and the DOC instantly hit it off. Like himself, the DOC noticed, Dre liked to drink, crack jokes, and listen to East Coast rap albums. Though hip-hop was created in the South Bronx to counteract that region's gang violence, by 1986 the East Coast had created gangsta rap. That year, South Bronx rap duo Boogie Down Productions had released their debut album, *Criminal Minded*, which featured the song "My 9-mm Goes Bang," a disturbing number that found rapper KRS-One portraying a street-corner drug dealer who shoots rival dealers in the head. "He pays no price in the end," *Washington Post* reporter David Mills noted. "There's no ennobling lesson for the listener." On their album cover, BDP members Scott La Rock and KRS-One signaled the changing tide in rap music by posing with guns, bullet belts, and grenades. "This violence," KRS told *Spin* in 1988, "it's everyday to the kid in the ghetto. No big deal."

Simultaneously, Schoolly D (former shoe salesman J.B. Weaver) released a single called "PSK," which detailed the grim history of North Philadelphia's Parkside Killers street gang. "That's what I grew up around," Schoolly said of the song. "I grew up around gang wars. That's what I saw so [those are] the stories I tell."

When these records were released, California's rap scene was limited to exploitative Golan-Globus films like *Rappin'*, dance rap groups that mimicked Afrika Bambaataa's "Planet Rock" and Jheri-curled softies who wore corny fedoras and frilly scarves onstage. But California rapper Ice-T tried to change that by releasing *Rhyme Pays*, where he posed on his album cover with a fistful of dollars and a gun-shaped pendant hanging around his neck. Where Ice was once known as an East Coast–styled rapper, he now began to offer works like "6 in the Morning," where he portrayed a crack dealer victimized by the LAPD's predawn raids.

After releasing the Ice-Cube-penned "Boyz N Tha Hood" single, Dre and Eazy became even more determined to move the California rap scene past its embarrassing beginnings. Accepting Dr. Dre's invitation to appear on the *N.W.A and the Posse* compilation album, the DOC recorded three songs, left his group, and stayed in town to help create Eazy-E's solo album *Eazy-Duz-It*.

By now N.W.A's lineup was firmly established, and each member would contribute to the project: DJ Yella (Antoine Carraby) would provide drumbeats; Ice Cube would again pen Schoolly-like lyrics; new member MC Ren (former Crip Lorenzo Patterson) would perform cameos; the DOC would coach Eazy on how to recite lyrics on time, and Dr. Dre would sit behind the mixing board, engineering, creating the music, and recording the songs. After Eazy's album was completed, N.W.A got to work on their own full-length debut.

By 1988 New York rap groups had begun to actively promote their hometowns: Boogie Down Productions rapped about the South Bronx, Public Enemy represented Long Island, Run-D.M.C. promoted Queens. "The main thing was, New York had all'a the 'bomb' [powerful] groups," said N.W.A alumni MC Ren. "And all we was thinking, man—I ain't gonna lie, no matter what anybody says, I think we all was thinking about making a name for Compton and L.A. That's why our first album, *Straight Outta Compton*, that's all you'll hear about."

Throughout 1988's *Straight Outta Compton*, N.W.A described Compton as the Vietnam of the 1980s; they positioned themselves as willing participants in the gang wars erupting nightly on L.A.'s streets. They threatened to use AK-47 assault rifles on anyone who offended them. They threatened to shoot police officers and batter women, and promoted marijuana smoking and excessive drinking. To them, serving time in prison was a rite of passage; the only thing that mattered was money, and they would do whatever was necessary to obtain it. With anthems like "Fuck Tha Police," it wasn't long before the group was hailed as folk heroes by local Crips and Bloods and a fawning rap press.

But mainstream music magazines like *Rolling Stone* and *Spin* questioned their nihilistic agenda, and conservative newspapers denounced N.W.A as monsters. Black radio stations ignored the album, and MTV refused to air their video (the music channel felt it showed gratuitous violence).

While Ice Cube tried to defend the group's violent themes, saying they were merely reporting on actual events in their environment, social critic Stanley Crouch argued that gangsta rap would only erode the values of its audience. "You cannot make a powerful Afro-American culture if you're going to base it on what hustlers and pimps think about the world," Crouch felt. "Those people have a distorted, vulgar vision of life because they live in a criminal atmosphere in which they see people at their very worst. That's what street life is about—people living on a barbaric level in which almost any kind of conventional civilized morality is sneered at because it's in the way of these people achieving what they want."

As the attacks against gangsta rap continued, the artists claimed the music was another manifestation of America's longtime fascination with outlaws (dating back to Jesse James and Al Capone), that gangsta rap was a form of "letting off steam," that this was "the truth" that black inner-city youth really wanted to hear, and that their songs were no more violent than the latest Hollywood action movie. Even pioneering gangsta rapper (and N.W.A fan) Schoolly D got in on the act. "If *Rambo* can tell a story, and you go to the movies and see *Dirty Harry* and all those other flicks, why can't I tell my story?"

Despite moral panic, *Straight Outta Compton* sold over 500,000 copies within six weeks of its release; a sanitized version of their song "Express Yourself" was released as a single, and finally got N.W.A's video aired on MTV; the group increased its following through extensive touring (a fifty-city tour was set up). Then Milt Aerlich of the FBI's public relations department wrote Ruthless Records a letter that accused the group of "encouraging violence and disrespect" toward America's police officers. Sensing another publicity opportunity, Ruthless promptly made the letter public to various newspapers and music magazines. As the tour continued, police departments in different cities began using fax machines to warn one another about when N.W.A's tour was heading their way. "Inevitably," rap historian David Toop reported, "the controversy magnified sales and increased the general level of punditry over rap and violence."

Since N.W.A's anthems were detailed enough to allow whites to pretend they, too, lived in the ghetto and committed the crimes this group casually discussed on their songs, a large white audience flocked to the album and sales figures skyrocketed to two million. Suddenly the five Compton teenagers who recorded *Straight Outta Compton* were considered "crossover" superstars; their commercial success ushered in the era of the highly commercial gangsta rap genre. Rap magazines began to ignore positive acts like Public Enemy or X-Clan, and focused on violent groups like Above the Law, the Geto Boys, Compton's Most Wanted, and N.W.A. Hailed as one of the rap industry's most successful producers, Dre produced a string of million-selling albums for his label, Ruthless. But things were about to take a turn for the worse. "Looking back on it now," the DOC would later say, "if we would have stayed a unit, like it was supposed to be, man, [Ruthless] would have been the new Motown."

But he couldn't suspect what would happen next. No one could. After *No One Can Do It Better* became a huge success, the DOC no longer had to sleep on the floor in Dre's living room, where he had been staying while working on Eazy's solo album and *Straight Outta Compton*. Now that his album had sold 500,000 copies in one month, the DOC became a celebrity. He had to contend with people approaching for autographs or stepping up to test their manhood by goading him into a fight. Suge Knight decided to act as his bodyguard. At this point Suge dressed casually, appearing in clubs like Palace 90 in sweatsuits or button-up shirts with jeans. "And Suge used to come to the Palladium sometimes," said one bouncer. "He was always cool when I saw him out. He was never hoo-ridin' [starting problems] or nothin'. His head was always straight. This was when he was body-guarding for the DOC."

Since these clubs drew anywhere from 1000 to 15,000 people a night, some of them potentially dangerous, the DOC needed a bodyguard. "When there's that many people in the spot, you never know who's who," this bouncer added. "And at the time, N.W.A and the DOC were really popular. They used to get a lot of people coming up to them and stuff."

While Suge and the DOC attended parties and went to clubs, for Suge—who didn't smoke, drink, or chase women—it was business. His job was to keep the DOC safe. "I saw a couple of situations with Suge," the bouncer went on. "Like at the Palladium. I just happened to roll up and see him and another guy knocking this guy out, you know?" Bouncers arrived to break it up but feared that Suge would turn on them. As a courtesy to bouncers he knew from Compton, Suge stopped beating the guy. The bouncers were grateful. "You don't try to arrest guys like that," said one of them. "You just kinda try to escort them out of the club, you know? They roll a little too deep. You never know what they have."

In the clubs, the DOC seemed to be a magnet for weirdos. They wanted his autograph or needed help with their demos or couldn't forgive him for his success or mistook him for a rival gang member they wanted to kill. When trouble came their way, Suge was a more than adequate buffer. "I've seen Suge do some shit to some motherfuckers that's out of this world," the DOC said. "Once we were leaving a club and I was standing there, waiting for my car to come, and some nigga ran up on me like he was fixin' to hit me in my jaw. And Suge just tore his ass up—broke him down to his very components."

As the DOC partied, Suge tried to convince him that they should unite to form a record label. Suge knew there was money in this field. N.W.A's sales figures alone proved that. He also saw that most of the artists in this new gangsta rap genre, while tough onstage, were no match for his size and strength. Someone with his willingness to use violence as a means of negotiation could easily make a killing in this business.

While attending parties thrown by the DOC's label, Ruthless

Records, Suge did his best to turn the DOC against Ruthless and its head, N.W.A member Eazy-E. "He was always there and he was always cool, you know?" said one person who attended these events. In a seat on the sidelines, Suge watched people party until a fight developed. Only then would he rise, physically confront the combatants, and escort them out of the party.

By the time the DOC telephoned his old chum Mario Lavelle Johnson in Dallas and invited him to Los Angeles, *No One Can Do It Better* was an unabashed hit and Suge was taking steps to form his own record label.

Mario, a thin, clean-cut disc jockey who called himself Chocolate, had known the DOC since the DOC's earliest days in the Fila Fresh Kru. They met one afternoon in a park: Chocolate was sixteen years old and new to the Dallas area, spinning records in local nightclubs that catered to "21 and over" crowds. The afternoon they met, Chocolate was eager to show off his customized Nissan truck. He drove it to the park, hoping to impress local women and use the vehicle as a conversation piece to woo them into bed. Leaping out of the passing crowd, the DOC saw the truck's license plates, and asked, " 'You from California?' "

When Chocolate arrived in L.A. with DJ Tee-Low, another of the DOC's Texas buddies, the DOC let them stay in his apartment in the Agora Hills section of town. Chocolate and Tee-Low had hardly unpacked, when DOC encouraged them to see his new friend, Suge, about signing a recording contract. "The DOC was just like, 'Look, you got a demo that's tight . . . I know who to give it to.' And he gave our demo to Suge, who was starting a management and recording company with the DOC and a brother by the name of Tom Kline," said Chocolate.

From their conversations in nightclubs, Suge had convinced the DOC to at least say there was a chance he would help form a record company and management firm called Funky Enough Records, in honor of the DOC's hit single. Fast-talking sports agent Tom Kline was Suge's latest client: When not having to guard him in public, Suge explained the concept of Funky Enough, and the huge sums to be made by gangsta rap to Kline, who was intrigued and offered Suge the use of his Beverly Hills office as headquarters for the label. Grateful, Suge told Kline he could be part of the company.

All Funky Enough Records needed now were artists. Suge brought in his friend DJ Quik, who also lived near the Tree Top Pirus and fronted a group of gangsta rappers called the Penthouse Players; female R&B singers like Paradise and Tam Rock were also signed. Then the DOC's friends Chocolate and DJ Tee-Low arrived at the label for an audition and asked for Suge.

"That day, I remember him coming out," Chocolate recalled. "And he was big, but not as big as he is now. I was like, damn! He came out and shook our hands and was like, 'Y'all got the tape?' We were like, 'Yeah.' Went into the office, sat down, listened to the tape. Then he called a couple of other people in and was like, 'I like y'all shit. I ain't frontin' because y'all the DOC's homies. I like y'all shit. And I wanna sign y'all. Y'all need to get an attorney. If you can't afford one, I'll pay for him.' So we went out, got our attorney, shot the paperwork to him, and we signed."

Suge was generous: If DJ Tee-Low wanted to visit his home in Dallas, Suge bought a round trip airline ticket. If Chocolate needed something, he provided. If everything was all right, Suge expected both in the studio, working on tracks. "Two months after meeting him, he already had our entire album," Chocolate remembered.

As a black music executive raised in the ghetto, Suge inspired intense feelings of loyalty. Usually, artists had to deal with white execs who censored lyrics, sanitized images, forced groups to delete specific slang terms, and asked them to make their music less threatening and more "universal." The code word was "crossover," which actually means "for white audiences."

Historically, black artists were forced to tone their music down and try to appeal to whites, who devoured the sanitized product and proudly supported what they thought was "authentic black culture." Forms of black music such as rock 'n' roll, soul music, jazz, and R&B had been co-opted, overrun with whites like Elvis, Joe Cocker, Kenny G, and Michael Bolton and diluted to the point where black audiences wanted nothing to do with them and started over with new forms like rap and house music.

But in rap, despite a promising start, it was no different. In the late

1980s, after rap became a multimillion-dollar industry, record labels quickly formed subsidiaries to exploit this lucrative art form no one thought would last. And many of these so-called rap labels were controlled by white-run parent companies located in Europe, meaning no matter how "black" an art form the media considered rap to be, the truth was that white people once again dictated what images blacks could promote in the mainstream media. Some of the labels hired blacks, but only a certain type; images were softened, lyrics were excised, pop hooks were requested, and groups that started off delivering raw, uncompromising work could now be seen teaming with has-been white rock groups or singing mushy love songs.

At Funky Enough, this wouldn't happen. Suge dressed and talked like the artists; he was fiercely independent and unwilling to appease white people. His size, in fact, frightened them. Unlike other so-called black labels run behind the scenes by whites, Suge promised his artists that no matter what, Funky Enough would be a haven for black music. In a little while, he told artists, everyone would be releasing music they believed in and being paid well for their work. One afternoon he told Chocolate, "We got nothing."

"I remember this well," Chocolate said. "Me and him were riding in the car, just riding along on the 405 freeway, and he said, 'Chocolate, we don't have nothing right now but greater later. You hang in there and you will have something. Just keep writing and producing and I'll handle the business. As long as you stay down and I stay down, we'll succeed.' And then he told me, 'The reason why I always take you with me everywhere I go is because'—this is a big saying of his—'it's like I gave a big party and to this big party I invited all my close buddies, and when I invited all my close buddies, everybody came to party and drank up all the beer and tore the house up and when the party was over you were the only person who stayed to help clean the house.'"

Back then Chocolate never felt nervous around Suge. "How could I put it? When I was involved with him in the beginning, he wasn't screaming 'Blood' all the time." Though Suge knew Chocolate hailed from a Crip neighborhood, he never made it an issue. The closest he'd come to that was when he'd greet him with the derogatory term 'crab.' In response, Chocolate would say, " 'W'sup, slob.'

"We would joke and laugh." To him, Suge was not intimidating at all. "He never did that around me."

"I NEEDED TO WEAR A DIAPER THAT DAY, I WAS VERY SCARED"

In 1990, close to a year after Chocolate signed to Suge's management and his label Funky Enough Records, Vanilla Ice's debut single "Ice Ice Baby" became a huge pop hit. Immediately, Chocolate felt wronged: Two years before, he claimed, he had written and produced "Ice Ice Baby" for the bumbling white rapper. "I'm just 'startled' 'cause I ain't even thinking that the song would ever come out!" But it did. In 1990 "Ice Ice Baby" became the first rap song to top the *Billboard* Pop Chart.

Astounded, Chocolate tried to tell a nearby friend, I did this song!

"I called Suge and said, 'Suge? There's a white kid I wrote a song for in Dallas named Vanilla Ice. I'm looking at the video.' I'm leaving this on his voice mail. He called me right back."

Back in Houston, Chocolate explained, he had performed in local clubs like Monopoly's and City Lights, owned by an Asian entrepreneur named Tommy Kwon. Suge said, Uh-huh. Kwon managed a white rapper named Vanilla Ice, aka Robbie Van Winkle, who claimed to have had a shadowy past filled with gangs and guns, when really he'd been raised with an older brother and younger sister by his mother, Beth Mino, a fifty-year-old music teacher. Suge listened. This guy Kwon had been managing Vanilla Ice since he saw him break-dancing at a local mall at age sixteen, Chocolate explained. One night, after he and DJ Earthquake had finished performing, Kwon approached and asked him to write songs for Vanilla. Initially, he and Earthquake were against the idea. Kwon fumed. "Instead of being against him, why don't you help me? I'll let you guys make money. I'll pay you to do some tracks and write the songs for him." They accepted, and Chocolate began writing his songs. But at the time, he told Suge, he had nothing but a drum machine and skills. "Nobody representing me," he stressed. "No management, no nothing."

Now his work was on TV, a gigantic hit, and Vanilla would probably be trying to follow it up with an album of new songs. Suge asked a few questions, then said, Don't worry about this. I'm on it. "After I gave Suge Tommy Kwon's name and the name of the club, by eight that night, when I got home, my phone was ringing and Vanilla Ice was telling me I need to come to Texas and work on the album."

He arrived in Texas with a singer named Paradise, also signed to Suge's management and Funky Enough; Paradise drove him to the Hard Rock Cafe in Dallas, where he hand-delivered a tape of new songs to Vanilla Ice.

When Vanilla Ice's album *II the Extreme* became a major chart-topper—selling an astounding eighteen million copies—Chocolate felt he wasn't being fairly compensated. A look at the album credits made him feel worse. Though he had handed Vanilla his songs, everyone else received the lion's share of the credit and money. "Only two people worked on that album," Chocolate claimed. "Earthquake and me. I don't know why everybody else got credit. Including Vanilla. Only thing he did was learn the songs and rap. He didn't do no production. Didn't do shit."

Of twelve songs on Vanilla Ice's album, Chocolate claimed seven were his. He received songwriting credit, but wanted money. *"Vanilla was no writer or creator on the record at all! And he got paid more than anybody!"* Enraged, Chocolate called his manager.

When Chocolate called, Suge had just finished defending himself against his latest criminal charge: During a visit to Las Vegas to visit some old friends (drug dealer Ricardo Crockett and his brother Wes), Suge had an argument with a man outside of the Crockett brothers' home. The man's brother uttered a threat. Suge reacted immediately, sending his huge fist slamming into the brother's face with such force, his jaw shattered.

From the sidelines, Suge's friends, the Crocketts, egged him on. Suge walked over to his car, opened the glove compartment, loaded a round into the chamber of a handgun, and returned to the victim with the broken jaw. Apologize, he said.

Holding his shattered jaw, the man did his best to oblige. Once he finished speaking, Suge raised the pistol and slammed the thick metal barrel into this victim's already-broken jaw. This time he was charged with felony assault with a deadly weapon and eventually pleaded guilty. He received a $9000 fine, a two-year suspended sentence, and three years' probation.

This incident would be followed by his arrest for assault with a deadly weapon/great bodily force in Beverly Hills (leading to his conviction for misdemeanor battery), an arrest in Hollywood (a second misdemeanor battery conviction), his arrest in the West Covina section of Los Angeles (a conviction for a misdemeanor charge of carrying a concealed weapon), and his arrest in the Van Nuys area for disturbing the peace, for which he received five days in the L.A. County jail. Suge heard about Chocolate's problems with Vanilla Ice, then advised him not to worry. He would settle this.

"The first time I met Suge Knight was at a restaurant in L.A. called Palm," Vanilla Ice explained years later. The Palm restaurant was a hangout for Caucasian celebrities like Cindy Crawford and Alec Baldwin; it had smooth wooden booths, dim lighting, and white tablecloths. "Palm restaurant," Vanilla repeated. "And I was sitting there, eating a nice meal, and all of a sudden these huge guys—it looked like a football team—showed up." These guys were bigger than his security team. They grabbed his bodyguards, pulled them out of their seats, and sat down. Suge stared into his eyes and said, "How you doing?" Vanilla Ice was terrified.

For months Suge tried to set up a meeting. "Saw them again a few months later," Vanilla said. "Did the same thing, just kinda showed up to me, said hi, and then left. Still was thinking, 'Wow, this guy knows where I'm at at all times. How does he know where I'm at?' You know? What's going on here?"

Finally, Suge and Chocolate appeared at Palm to settle the matter. "Vanilla Ice already knew we were trying to catch up with him while he was in L.A.," Chocolate said. This time Chocolate went in alone and sat with Vanilla and his people. "I went in because we wanted conversation," Chocolate claimed: It was a ploy to throw Vanilla and his people off guard—send Chocolate in alone, have Chocolate play dumb, and see how far they thought they could go. Once they made their offer, with Chocolate feigning ignorance, Suge would then arrive to accuse them of trying to rob them, to offer open intimidation and show them what they were in fact up against. At the table Chocolate claimed they offered a settlement, then urged him not to call a lawyer or manager. "Believe us, it's fine," he quoted them as saying. He responded by saying he needed to consider the deal; he rose to his feet, left the eatery, and met Suge, who waited in their ride in the parking lot. Once Chocolate finished detailing their offer, with a baleful stare Suge threw the car door open, left the vehicle, and said, "I'm going in."

"Vanilla Ice got so afraid," contended Chocolate, "this is the God-given truth with no exaggeration, when he saw us at the restaurant doors, he jumped up and started yelling, 'the Bloods and Crips are after me!' And went running, yelling, 'Arrgghh!' Just like that. Nobody even had a chance to say anything. Security guards got him out."

That night, after taping an appearance on The Arsenio Hall Show, Vanilla returned to his suite at the Ballage Inn in Beverly Hills, presumably to relax, party, unwind, order room service, then maybe catch something good on TV late at night. "And that's when we showed up," said Chocolate. "And again, this was the incident where he said that Suge supposedly held him over the balcony and said he would throw him over."

"I had my bodyguards—they had guns—and they had their people which had guns and they had us outpowered and outnumbered," Vanilla

Ice explained. Chocolate arrived with Suge and five other men; they attacked one bodyguard then everyone in Vanilla's entourage. Suge asked the white rapper out onto the balcony for a private talk; after insulting Vanilla's retinue, he forced the white rapper to glance over the edge, a reminder that they were fifteen stories above the sidewalk. Despite claims of having run with gangs in his youth, Vanilla was horrified: Suge Knight was the sort of person Vanilla could only pretend to be in interviews. "I needed to wear a diaper on that day. I was very scared." Suge explained that he wanted Vanilla to sign publishing rights over to Chocolate. Publishing rights were one of the main ways—outside of charging club owners for live performances—that a musician could earn lucrative sums: When someone retains publishing rights to a song, particularly a hit record, every time the song is played on the radio or performed, the publisher is entitled to a payment. In addition, if another artist performs your song—a cover version, sample, or interpolation—the publisher is entitled to a payment. Knowing that a signature on these release papers would mean forfeiting three or four million dollars in future earnings for *II the Extreme,* Vanilla Ice nonetheless complied with Suge's demands. "I signed them," he said. "And walked away alive."

Chocolate dismissed Vanilla's claims as hogwash, investigated by white reporters only because Vanilla's complexion was as pale as their own. They did visit him at his room, Chocolate said, but Vanilla willingly relinquished rights to the seven songs. "Suge came there like a businessman and said, 'We could be here for ten minutes or we could be here all day.' That's exactly what he said. 'I just wanna know the truth. What contributions did you make to 'Ice Ice Baby'?" They did not, he stressed, go in there with paperwork and say, "*Here's the paperwork. You better sign this or we gon' beat you up!*" They went in to deliberate and Vanilla was receptive. On sight, he said, "*Aw man, listen to this!*" Played a few new songs. "It was not that type of atmosphere where anybody was saying, '*W'sup! Sit down!*' It was me, Suge, and Ron Brown that played for the Raiders. Us three together. *Little* Ron Brown," he said with a hint of irony. "You know how little he is, right?"

He claimed they did *not* pull guns on Vanilla's security. "I don't know who paid Vanilla Ice to say that. He acted good on TV that night. He looked like he was telling the truth, and that's the bad thing about it.

Suge came at him the right way. No arguing, nobody out of line. It was just straight, 'Look, my boy did some songs for you. I wanna know what part you took on it.' Vanilla said, 'I don't wanna talk without my attorney.'"

That night in the hotel suite in Beverly Hills, according to Chocolate, the white rapper was so racked with guilt over stealing songs that he reached into his pocket and handed over eighteen hundred dollars. "His way of saying, *'Thanks for coming down and writing and producing these songs for me. I'll pay for the flight since you're complaining.'*"

Chocolate alleged that even Vanilla's DJ Earthquake turned against the white rapper. "Earthquake didn't know that I flew in after 'Ice Ice Baby' blew up to finish the *II the Extreme* album! Earthquake produced the music and kept telling Vanilla Ice, 'We gotta go in the studio. You know you got two million back orders on the album. You gotta go in to do the lyrics so we can deliver the album!' Vanilla would say, 'I'm'a take care of it!' But didn't know I was flying in to come write them lyrics."

After receiving a demo of songs at the Hard Rock Cafe, Chocolate went on, Vanilla presented the completed lyrics as his own, prompting Earthquake to ask "How'd you get these songs so fast?"

Ice said, "I already wrote them. I already had these songs."

Chocolate maintained that once Vanilla Ice offered the eighteen hundred, Earthquake realized Vanilla was lying. "When Ice took the eighteen hundred out, that's when Earthquake said, 'Oh shit! Chocolate came to Texas and wrote these songs!'"

If anything, Chocolate claimed their meeting that night showed them they had no alternative but to hire an attorney and contest Vanilla's ownership of the songs: Suge took him to see Dick Griffey at Solar Records. In the late 1970s, Dick Griffey's SOLAR (Sound Of Los Angeles Records) had its finger on the pulse of pop radio. The label, which grew out of an association between promoter Griffey and *Soul Train* host Don Cornelius, released a string of post-disco hits that included Shalamar's "The Second Time Around" and the Whispers' "And the Beat Goes On." The Solar sound was bubbly and infectious and became hugely popular in England, where Shalamar had four top ten hits in one year.

After "music promoter" Wes Crockett hired Suge to bodyguard at some of his events in Los Angeles, Crockett introduced Suge to veteran Griffey. Griffey listened to Suge's plans for a record label and asked to be included. He could provide Suge's label with office space and recording studios.

After telling Griffey about the meeting with Vanilla Ice, Chocolate claimed Griffey said, "This is a little too big and out of my hands. I'll get you another attorney." Griffey went through friends at Sony Records, who suggested they hire New York attorney John Clark. To this day, Chocolate denies that Suge threatened Vanilla Ice, whose claims he dismisses as "bullshit." The matter of the publishing rights was settled in a courtroom, with Chocolate receiving publishing rights to the seven contested works. "That night, there wasn't any contract-signing or strongarming."

While Suge looked forward to receiving his twenty-five percent of the money generated by seven songs on Vanilla Ice's hit debut album, his plan to form his own label, Funky Enough Records, suffered a disastrous setback when a proposed partner suddenly fell out and Suge was told to vacate the Beverly Hills office.

When Funky Enough folded, Suge retained the master tapes, including one that featured a track by Chocolate that Suge really enjoyed. "And it showed up on Quik's first album *Quik Is the Name* as 'Born and Raised in Compton.' Chocolate did that at Funky Enough Records but wasn't paid for it. At the time, Quik was signed at Funky Enough as well. Shortly after Chocolate did the track, the company folded. Suge had all the reels. Next thing you know, DJ Quik has a hit song out there on his album for Profile Records. Only thing Quik did on 'Born and Raised in Compton' was put his name on it." Chocolate, however, remained loyal to Suge: That his music was used by another artist was viewed as part of the dues-paying process. Hopefully, Suge would use the song's royalty money to finance a label that would release more music—this time with Chocolate's name on it.

"DRE PICKS ME UP BY MY HAIR AND MY EAR AND STARTS SLAMMING MY FACE UP AGAINST A BRICK WALL"

Despite the seeming collapse of Funky Enough Records, Marion "Suge" Knight was more determined than ever to own a record label. As Eazy-E's success proved, there was too much money in gangsta rap to just walk away. If Vanilla Ice could earn millions, anyone could—especially when they had Vanilla's songwriters working with them. At this point Suge still had the DOC's support and a roster of acts; now all he needed was a surefire way to convince people to invest money in his label. He thought of Dr. Dre, the N.W.A producer whose every project sold in the millions. Then he thought of the Doc, who knew Dr. Dre. Then he decided to use the DOC to get to Dre. With Dre on the label still being called Funky Enough, there would be no stopping Suge.

But there were obstacles to surmount, among them the DOC's unwillingness to leave Ruthless Records, Suge's not knowing Dr. Dre, and Dre's own contract with Ruthless. Still, there were ways around it all. Suge just had to be patient, sight his opportunity, then strike without warning before anyone even knew what was happening.

For the DOC, thanks to a hit album, life in this autotopia became a nonstop party: Success had brought him fancy clothes, good friends like Suge to protect him from local gang members, the use of flashy sports cars, beautiful women throwing themselves at his feet, handfuls of money for beer and marijuana, steady work writing lyrics for the nonrhyming half of N.W.A, and critical acclaim. After "Funky Enough," his latest single "The DOC & the Doctor" reached No. 21 on the Top Rap Singles chart; his album was No. 87 on the Top Rhythm & Blues chart. He had it all. It was hard work to maintain this career but worth it. But one night all he wanted to do was get home to bed. He had spent over twenty hours working on two videos for his album, then hours partying with some of the women who appeared in the videos. Now he was on his way home to sleep it off. Tomorrow he would wake up and remind himself that everything was okay now: His recently released *No One Can Do It Better* had sold 500,000 copies. The roads were dark, so he was careful; he tried to keep the new Honda Prelude in his lane. On the freeway, however, he fell asleep at the wheel; he came out of it to discover the car veering sharply to the right. After slamming into the center median, he flew out the back window, bounced on concrete, then slammed facefirst into a tree.

He woke up in a hospital. His mother cried at his bedside, repeating that it was going to be all right. Doctors entered to report that miraculously, he hadn't suffered any broken bones. His friends Eazy-E, Dre, and Michel'lé appeared to console him: Eazy was his label president; Dre was his producer; Michel'lé Toussaint was a singer who dated Dre and sang on N.W.A songs.

The DOC's face was cut up and smashed; during the next three weeks he would undergo twenty-one hours of reconstructive surgery. "Dre told me the only way they recognized me at the hospital was because of my haircut," the DOC recalled. "I didn't like a whole lot of motherfuckers seeing me in that state." His self-esteem was gone. So was his voice.

One of the first to arrive at the hospital, Suge spent the next weeks visiting, chauffeuring the DOC's mother to and from the hospital, and acting as a steadfast family member. Since they met, Suge had been trying to convince the DOC to sign to what Suge thought would be his first label, a venture they planned to call Funky Enough. In the past, the

DOC had always been noncommittal: He still had his deal with Ruthless and his songwriting union with Dr. Dre; he was an established artist with a big future ahead of him. His next album with Dre would probably sell even more than his debut. Why start a new label?

But the accident happened and in one instant the DOC felt he had lost everything. When he was vulnerable, Suge moved in, poisoning the DOC's mind with anti-Ruthless sentiment. This time when Suge asked him to sign to Funky Enough, the DOC was more receptive to the idea. "When he had his accident and lost his voice," Suge alleged, "Ruthless Records said 'Fuck him.' I used to visit him in the hospital and give him money for his medicine." Though the DOC was still reluctant to switch labels, that didn't stop Suge from representing him unofficially. After setting up autograph signings and public appearances that got the DOC as much as a thousand dollars, he browsed through his paperwork with Ruthless and saw that publishing rights for major hits like "We Want Eazy" had been relinquished for "a watch and a chain."

"I didn't give a fuck about no publishing, no credit, none of that," The DOC would later admit. "Eric asked me one day when they were out buying their jewelry, 'If I buy you this necklace, you'll give me the publishing to those songs you wrote?' And I said, 'Hell, yeah! I'm'a write a million more songs, you can have them, no problem.' He bought me the chain and that was the end of that."

Suge felt the DOC was being shortsighted. By signing rights over, he deprived himself of profits to be reaped from radio hits. "Jerry [Heller] had the words 'watch and chain' right there in the contract," Suge claimed. (Heller denies this.) "I ain't never seen no shit like it in my life. I said, 'Don't worry, we'll deal with it.' " He told the DOC: "You still a writer, do that until you get your health together."

N.W.A, meanwhile, was racked with tension. Principal songwriter Ice Cube began to feel that Eazy-E and Ruthless Records business manager Jerry Heller were underpaying him. While Cube received a mere $32,700 for his contributions to two albums with combined sales of three million copies, he claimed Heller had pocketed almost four times that much from the $650,000 their tour earned. One day Cube asked Dre if he was happy with his salary. "Nah, man," Cube quoted him as saying, "my shit is kinda shaky too."

The situation came to a head when the group convened in Dre's home for a rehearsal one afternoon. While everyone headed to Dre's upstairs bedroom, where he kept his equipment, Cube remained on the couch. Dre said they were gonna start working. Cube said he would sit this one out, finish watching a show on television. Dre was worried. Serious about his grievance, Cube was soon telling band mates they were being robbed. MC Ren was indifferent; DJ Yella was loyal to Eazy, who owned the record company; Dre listened politely as Cube said he was quitting the group, then said, "You crazy. Don't do that."

Cube suggested they hold a group meeting. "No Jerry Heller, just us five. Let's try to get this straight." Dre got the group to agree to be at the studio the next morning. When Cube arrived, he saw that no one else showed up. Disgusted, he flew to New York and began working with Public Enemy's producers, the Bomb Squad.

By the time the DOC left the hospital, Suge Knight had found his opportunity. What he always needed most from the DOC was the connection to Dre. "After Cube left," said the DOC, "Dre was determined to prove he didn't need that cat to make hit records." As their new principal songwriter, the DOC spent a lot of time with N.W.A, helping them prepare their next EP. During studio sessions he told Dre that he also felt he might be underpaid; this was why he had his good friend Suge Knight examining his contracts. Dre was finally ready to act on suspicions he didn't want to admit he felt. He asked the DOC to set up a meeting.

"I met with Dre right around when Ice Cube quit the group and started complaining about not being properly compensated," Suge said. "Dre approached me and asked me if I would go over his contracts."

On one occasion Suge quoted Dre as saying, "While you checkin' the DOC's shit, check on my shit too."

"And that," Suge announced, "led to me looking into Michel'lé's deal too." Much as the DOC brought Suge closer to Dre, Dre brought Suge closer to Michel'lé, an R&B singer who began her career singing choruses on N.W.A songs, became Dre's girlfriend, then gave birth to his son. At the time Dre had produced her debut album, a saccharine R&B work popular with radio station DJs nationwide.

As Dr. Dre and the DOC began to distrust Ruthless, thanks to gentle prodding from Suge, Dre continued to feign loyalty to the group N.W.A, which was still his meal ticket. In response to Ice Cube's public departure and success as a solo artist, N.W.A included a skit called "Benedict Arnold" on their *100 Miles and Running* EP, which featured Dre threatening to violate Cube with a broomstick the next time he saw him.

Deniece Barnes, hostess of Fox Television's *Pump It Up*, a music video program that also featured interviews with rap groups, became a casualty in the war between them. After graduating from high school in New York, Barnes had migrated to Los Angeles and tried without much success to make it as a rapper. When she landed the hostess position at *Pump It Up*, she saw it as her big break. The show went national and Deniece became nationally known as Sista Dee.

"A year or two into the show—as things are going well—I tried to get N.W.A on," she said. In October 1990 the group rarely granted interviews, but since Barnes was an old friend of Dre's, they agreed to appear. A week after their appearance was taped, Barnes conducted an interview with a new female rapper named Yolanda (Yo-Yo) Whitaker, a former cheerleader Ice Cube was producing and managing. The interview took place on the set of John Singleton's *Boyz N the Hood*, a film starring Ice Cube, and in which she had a cameo role. In the middle of the interview Cube appeared on camera and insulted his former band mates, calling them weaklings and poseurs. After Cube's tirade, the cameraman turned his lens on Dee, who was aghast. "The cameras were still rolling, so I said 'Sista Dee always in the middle of controversy right here on *Pump It Up*. What am I gonna do?' Producer Jeff Shore said, 'Cut! That's great! I'm gonna put it on the N.W.A show!' "

Shore planned to take the footage of Ice Cube insulting N.W.A and edit it onto the end of the N.W.A interview. The "positive" N.W.A segment Dee promised would now end with the group being insulted. "And I said 'Naw, you crazy?!' Never thinking that I would be attacked. There was always gonna be beef but I didn't want it to be because of *Pump It Up*, like we instigated something." The producers ignored her protests and edited Cube's insult onto the tail end of the N.W.A segment, which aired a few days later.

When she encountered Eazy-E at a nightclub a month later, he said he was a little upset. She rushed to explain that she had nothing to do with the edit. Eazy listened calmly. She added that she would never do anything to harm N.W.A's reputation. Her explanation, she thought, had gotten her off the hook.

That December she attended a party for Def Jam recording artists No-Face and female N.W.A clones BWP (Bitches With Problems). The venue was filled with rap executives and celebrities like Digital Underground and X-Clan. But people kept warning Dee that N.W.A were upset. When she asked why, no one had an answer. Since Dre was "like a brother" to her, she decided not to worry. It was probably just gossip.

The party began to wind down. People were leaving. She stood against a wall, chatting with record promoter Doug Young and a man who worked for MTV's Ed Lover. Dr. Dre appeared suddenly, stood between them, grabbed her shirtfront. "I can't even say 'Help' 'cause I'm choking!" she said. As Doug Young tried to pry Dre's hands from her shirt, Suge Knight slammed his fist into Doug's jaw, knocking him to the ground.

"Next thing I know," Dee continued, "Dre picks me up by my hair and my ear and starts slamming my face up against a brick wall." When he released her, she crawled to a stairway. While trying to rise to her feet, Dre reappeared, grabbed her, and tried to toss her down the stairs. "I was still," she said. "Everything was muffled. I can't even remember who saw what—"

She held on for dear life as Dre grunted, stumbled, lost his balance, and continued trying to make her fall. Falling to her hands and knees, she tried to make herself harder to lift—only to feel Dre trying to kick her down the flight of stairs. Then he pushed her with his foot, she said, "because I think then somebody might have grabbed him. I think maybe he was drunk. Maybe somebody was stopping him or maybe he was high."

She made her move. "I popped up, ran into the girls' room. . . ." A woman in her path began to scream. She thought, "Why she screaming? 'Cause Dre's right behind me!" He burst into the women's rest room. The other woman escaped. Dee was alone with Dre. "By then," she said, "he grabs me by my hair again, punching me in the head, throws me to the front of the bathroom. I just duck down and just . . . take my ass-whipping, you know what I mean? There's nobody helping me and there's no way in hell I could throw a punch at him."

She felt alone. No one at this industry party tried to help. Eventually someone yanked Dre off her and helped him escape. Rising to her feet, Dee faced a mirror to assess the damage, then grew hysterical.

Dre denied her accusations. Dee Barnes was an opportunist, he calmly explained, "another one that's out to get paid. I knew she—" He paused. "She knew she fucked up, so she was saying 'It wasn't me, it wasn't me!' " He saw her at the party, then: "Damn! What happened after that? Oh! I was walking over to her and I got ready to talk to her. Somebody came, got in between us, was pushing me back. My boy that was with me hit him. Bing! 'Get your hands off him.' That kid got hit. He got his tooth broke for getting in the fucking way. I couldn't even tell who it was! I almost fucked up Ed Lover!"

After that, one of his friends rushed him out of the club. At home, he fell asleep. There had been no assault, he claimed.

The next morning, Dre continued, Dee Barnes called to denounce him. He told her he didn't know what she was talking about. Dee persisted, adding that she wouldn't press charges.

Dre asked, *You ain't gonna press no charges for what?!*

"She said she had to go to New York to film the show. She left the very next day." She called again to say she was taking him to court unless he agreed to produce three songs for her. "Something like that. I think it was three songs without putting my name on it. Then they would forget about it."

He was shocked. He didn't do anything to her. He was innocent. "But just to keep the motherfucking air clean, I'll put together some shit," he thought. "Fuck it," he told her. "Get back with me and we'll see what's up."

After negotiating with "her people," he grew weary of hearing how she could destroy him. He backed out of the deal. Then decided that he'd better listen to her people. They were right. She could fuck him up. "Fuck it," he again told her. "I'll do the song."

He claimed to have received contracts binding him to the silence-for-three-songs agreement, but before he could return them for a countersignature in June 1991, N.W.A's second album, *Niggaz4Life*, debuted at No. 2 on the *Billboard* Top Pop Albums chart. A week later, thanks to the Soundscan method of compiling sales information, *Niggaz* knocked Paula Abdul out of the No. 1 spot. "I get another call right after the record went number one," Dre claimed, "maybe two days after that." This time, he quoted Dee as saying, *"Fuck it! I don't want the songs! I want a million dollars!"*

He said, *"What?!* Fuck you. Take me to court."

"Next thing I know," Dre groaned, "the shit is in every motherfucking newspaper there is and I'm in court. I was like, 'Damn!'"

Eventually, Dre told *Rolling Stone:* "I was in the wrong, but it's not like I broke the bitch's arm."

"It was like, police, ambulance, questions, and reporters," Dee said of that brutal evening. "It was just crazy."

Her face was bruised, she said, but nowhere near as battered as her sense of self-worth. She was just happy it was over. She tried to return to work, only to discover that Dre's people were phoning in threats. Her producers were frightened; she was in a fragile emotional state and unable to deal with office politics. Dee was phased out and the show was canceled. "There's a lot of women that he beat up," Dee told me, "a lot that he smacked around. But I'm the one that fucking pressed charges. Nobody else did. Now he's got a record."

Dee filed a twenty-million-dollar lawsuit against Dr. Dre. Despite her initial fury, she agreed to drop all charges against Dre and quietly settle her lawsuit out of court. Later, they resumed their friendship and her husband, Ricky Harris, worked on various Snoop videos.

Record promoter Doug Young, who worked for Eazy at the time, claimed, "They were kinda stealing from Dre. He had just done the JJ Fad album, the DOC, N.W.A, Eazy-E, Michel'lé, Above the Law—" Most of these albums had sold over a million copies each. "And Jerry

Heller didn't have no money for Dre." Young warned Heller that Dre would leave. "I argued with Jerry back then. Telling him, 'Look! You got Magic or Michael Jordan in Dre. Take your pick. Now you gotta pay one of them.' "

Heller ignored him, he claimed, and instead, used N.W.A's royalty earnings to buy a grand piano. Then Young told Heller, who owned three cars, to cancel plans to buy a fourth and use that money as a payment for N.W.A.

As Suge continued to tell Dre and the DOC that Eazy and Jerry Heller underpaid them, and reports about the feud between Dre and Ruthless began to appear in rap fanzines, Jerry Heller denied allegations of wrongdoing: he produced Dre's 1099 tax forms for any writer interested in seeing them: In 1991 alone, the forms showed, Dr. Dre had received $690,000. "And that doesn't include performances and other appearances." Dre was also residing in a beautiful home in Calabassas, Heller noted. "We send him big royalty checks all the time."

As Dre grew resentful, Eazy-E sought out producers to fill the vacuum caused by Dre's refusal to work for Ruthless. Eazy brought in DJ Quik and the Penthouse Players and anyone with beats. This way, Ruthless would survive without Dre. "So you could see the rift starting," Doug Young explained. "Dre wasn't his 'main man' anymore. Eazy started looking for a gang of producers, being down with everybody, trying to get songs. Ruthless knew Dre wasn't happy and Suge was peepin' it. Suge whispered in Dre's ear and Dre was like, 'Fuck Jerry. Fuck motherfucking Eazy!' "

Since Dre was financially dependent on Ruthless, the label began to withhold payment, hoping this would force him to return to work. In danger of losing his home and his cars, Dre refused. "I went to a lot of record companies," Dre explained, "tried even to get a little production work to pay for rent and shoes, but nobody wanted to take a chance on me because of all that legal shit, all the cease-and-desist letters—Ruthless did anything and everything they could to fuck me up, and I have hate for everybody there."

There was a stalemate until February 1991, when Suge Knight demanded royalty payments for Dre, the DOC *and* Dre's girlfriend, platinum-selling R&B-siren Michel'lé. "We've lived in constant fear," said Heller, whose résumé listed a stint with a talent agency that booked Elton John's first American tour, and represented bands like Journey, Electric Light Orchestra, and Styx. "Suge would just walk into our office and say, 'You know who I am? I'm Dre's manager. We're taking over.'" He'd look around and tell his gangbangers to go and get guns from the car. Then Suge would bend over and there'd be a huge gun sticking out of his ass pocket."

Heller was tall and spoke with a midwestern accent. He had eyes like ball bearings and cursed as frequently as any N.W.A member. But he was old, in his fifties. His hair was gray. He was no match for Suge, who, he admitted publicly, did a good job of frightening employees at Ruthless. "There was a guy who came in one day and put his finger up to my head and said, 'I could've blown you away right now. But if you had a real bodyguard, I couldn't have come in here. . . .'"

Suge also terrorized Heller's assistant, Gary Ballen, phoning in threats, then appearing in Ballen's office one day with a phalanx of goons. In a sworn affidavit, Ballen said Suge forced him to write an apology to singer Michel'lé, whom Suge felt Ballen had been "disrespecting." That day Ballen did as ordered. Soon, however, he began carrying a stun gun and taking karate classes. And if his wife hadn't talked him out of it, he would've carried a pistol. "I still have trouble sleeping at night," Ballen stated. "And my wife and I got into arguments over the gun."

Fearing Suge would make further unexpected appearances in Ruthless's offices, Heller decided to work out of a house in Sherman Oaks. One assistant sent a letter of resignation: He couldn't work for Ruthless, he wrote, if the job meant that Suge and his men would murder his wife and child. The job wasn't worth it.

Heller was nervous. Doling out thousands of dollars hadn't pacified Suge. Like Max Cady in *Cape Fear*, he wouldn't go away. From the beginning they had all sensed that Suge had an ulterior motive. Heller realized what he wanted. It was all a matter of time. Suge would put the cards on the table, and ask Eazy to sign release forms that terminated all existing contracts between Dre, the DOC, Michel'lé, and Ruthless Records.

Trying to delay the inevitable, Heller hired a pair of armed weightlifters named Animal and Michael to serve as bodyguards. While Animal patrolled the office, never too far from the shotgun kept in a drawer at the front desk, Heller made sure that Michael was always at his side.

During one visit, Suge saw that Heller was "gone" but had "some motherfuckers up there who was supposed to stop me. I didn't hurt nobody," he explained. "Just made his boys get on they hands and knees, walk around like a dog, you know?"

When Suge finally asked Heller for the contracts. Heller refused. "But I got ahold of one on my own," Suge said. After barging into Ruthless corporate attorney Ira Selsky's office one afternoon and discovering that Selsky wasn't there, he searched until he found the document, then took it with him. "We found out that Cube was right," he said. "Ruthless was taking Dre for a ride. And not just Dre, every other artist on the roster too."

After work Heller would pull up outside his two-million-dollar Mountainview Estates mansion and wait while a bodyguard checked the house. Only after the escort searched underneath the beds and in closets, and felt certain that the house was clear, would he enter.

The home was now fortified with expensive security systems and alarms. Heller also kept canisters of pepper gas handy, and armed his girlfriend with a gun of her own and a can of Mace. "I have a minimum of two dozen guns around the house in places where I could get caught," he admitted.

The guns were placed in strategic spots: by Jacuzzis, the swimming pool, near his television set, the upstairs bathroom, his gym. "Every night that I go to sleep," he added, "I have a .380 under my pillow and I have a .25 automatic hidden nearby."

He hadn't had a decent night's rest since November 1990. He couldn't help feeling that Suge, at any minute, would finally mount his attack. "I come home a different way every day," Heller said sadly, "always looking in my rearview mirror. Every time a car drives slowly by my house, or the dogs bark, I have to get up with my gun and check it out. Every time I hear something in my attic I have to call a bodyguard to come back. My life has been absolute hell."

*   *   *

At his new headquarters in the Solar Records building, Suge planned his next move with Dick Griffey: Griffey's label, Solar Records, had a distribution deal similar to the one Ruthless reached with Sony in 1989. In the Ruthless/Sony agreement, Dre had been required to produce a set number of albums. Sony would then distribute these to stores. Solar had the same setup, but without Dre producing.

By spring 1991, however, Dick Griffey informed Sony that he could get Dre to produce albums for Solar. Dre and Ruthless were having problems, and Dre planned to leave the label, he explained: Since Dre would not be working with Ruthless anymore, if Sony wanted music by Dre, they would now have to deal with Solar. Sony expressed interest in having Dre produce the soundtrack for *Deep Cover*, a depressing attempt at an urban/espionage film starring Larry Fishburne. Griffey said that could happen, but Ruthless was putting the squeeze on Dre, withholding payments. Dre, he added, needed money or he'd lose everything he owned. A deal was arranged: Sony would buy Dre's music publishing rights for a cool million dollars. "This was before all the intimidation," Ruthless attorney Michael Borbeau explained. "They said, 'We'll give you one million dollars and you get out of the contract. We'll help you— we'll draft the releases. You just get them signed and we'll put your records out.'"

In April 1991, Eazy-E was shocked to receive a phone call from Dre, and an invitation to the Solar Records building to discuss their "differences." Once they worked things out, Dre implied, maybe he could get back to producing hit records for Ruthless. The invitation, seen by Eazy as an anodyne for a difficult year, was accepted; at the appointed time, Eazy arrived without security. He saw that the label Dre and Suge were forming comfortably occupied the entire third floor of the building. Then he noticed that Dre wasn't there. But Suge was. With two armed thugs.

Eazy was shocked as Suge calmly explained the situation. "Suge said that some of my people—Above the Law, Michel'lé, Kokane, the DOC, and Dre—wanted to leave me," Eazy explained. "I knew that they wanted me to sign releases. I was told before, if it came down to that, not to sign them. But Suge said he was holding Jerry hostage in a van. Then he told me he knew where my mother lived."

There was an element of theatricality to the meeting. Eazy sat at a table and listened; as if on cue, Suge's men entered with lead pipes in hand. Suge slid contracts across the table, in front of Eazy. "And Suge said, 'I heard you was trying to get me killed, Blood.' " With these words, Suge turned a business meeting into a gang-related confrontation. Outnumbered, facing rival Bloods, former Crip Eazy-E reviewed his options. "I figured either I'd sign the papers, get my ass kicked, or fight them." Eazy signed the papers. "They threatened my family, saying, 'We know where your mother lives, and shit.' "

Months ago, in Suge's mind, a transfer of ownership had taken place. Eazy's artists became his. That Eazy was still in possession of them outraged Suge. When he forced Eazy to sign them over, Suge didn't see it as stealing. He was reclaiming them. "I know you've heard all the stories," he later told a writer. "But you have to realize one thing: *results.*"

"It was like *The Godfather*," Ruthless attorney Michael Borbeau said later. "Sony wanted Dre, who was a very hot producer, so they had releases drafted for Knight to bring to Eric Wright. They wanted him to sign the papers. And if he didn't sign the papers, he knew the consequences."

"Next thing we know about the releases is we hear that Dre and Knight have them but they won't give them to us," said Wayne Smith, a partner at Gibson, Dunn & Crutcher, a firm retained by Sony. "They said, 'We can enter into the contracts because they have these releases.' "

According to Smith, Suge told Sony, "They were gotten legitimately, but the reason I can't give you a copy was because I promised Eazy when he signed them that I wouldn't give them to anybody without his approval."

Inevitably, Suge faxed the releases to David Glew, president of Sony subsidiary Epic Records and to Epic executive Hank Caldwell, letting both know that Dre was now available to work—once Suge and Dick

Griffey, Dre's new manager and label distributor, received a $125,000 advance, that is.

Despite warnings from Ruthless, Caldwell and Glew continued meeting with Suge to discuss Dre's contracts. "We didn't find any evidence that Knight had any criminal record whatsoever," Sony's attorney Wayne Smith claimed. If anything, they respected Suge. "What do you do with some kid who grew up in the ghetto and got in trouble and has a record and now he's gone to college and is establishing himself in the music business? Are you going to say, 'You're not good enough, you're not lily white, so we're not going to deal with you'? Should no record company release music or negotiate with Dr. Dre because his chosen manager had some altercations with the law? I don't think that's reasonable." To Sony, despite warnings from Ruthless, Suge was a soft-spoken "teddy bear."

Plans for Dre's work to appear on the soundtrack for *Deep Cover* continued. So far, Dre had been commissioned to write a song: Since Sony would not accept an instrumental, and Ice Cube and Ren were no longer around to ghostwrite lyrics, Dre asked the DOC and his newest discovery, Snoop Doggy Dogg, to come up with something.

"WE ALMOST GOT INTO A WRECK ON THE WAY TO GO SEE DRE"

Snoop Doggy Dogg, aka Calvin Broadus, was a tall, scrawny kid with a sharp chin and protruding cheekbones; sometimes he could act like a kid brother in need of guidance; other times he would squint his eyes like a villain in a Sergio Leone spaghetti western, resemble an African American Lee Van Cleef, and act like a street-hardened gang member. Snoop wore his hair in the heavy braided style favored by gang members (tied with rubber bands), smoked marijuana, spent hours listening to East Coast rap records in his home, and wore baggy blue clothing that promoted his allegiance to one Crip gang.

Born in 1972 and raised on 21st Street in Long Beach, an oceanfront city on the outskirts of Compton which was once a huge naval port, he was one of three boys his mother was raising alone after moving from Mississippi. Calvin was a collector of rap records as well as an aspiring rapper. At Long Beach's Polytechnic High School, he was the class clown. He also tried to play football and basketball and held an after-school job. When he saw that his friends on the corner earned more pay for less work, he quit his job and joined them.

For two years, as a member of the Rolling 20 Crips in Long Beach, Snoop Doggy Dogg sold drugs. "I'm a hustler now," he quipped. In his spare time he continued penning rap lyrics. By 1984, influenced by New York storyteller Slick Rick, he began making tapes for people in his neighborhood. But he wasn't ready to stop selling crack cocaine. His career choice led to a series of arrests: at age eighteen he served eight months in the county jail; a year after his release, he served six months; four months after being released, he served yet another four-month sentence.

Almost immediately after his release, he returned to selling drugs. He tried to sell to an addict and local law enforcement burst out of hiding and arrested him, earning Snoop yet another four-month sentence. This time the county jail was rocked by racial battles, Mexican gangs fighting blacks and whites. Older, educated inmates heard his lyrics and said, "Young nigga; you need to be out there rapping, getting paid."

"And it was making sense to me," Snoop recalled. "Why was I going back to the jailhouse and I wasn't making no [dollars]?"

After his release, he returned to Long Beach, reunited with his Crip friends but decided not to resume selling drugs. Instead, he recorded demo tapes and tried to find a drug dealer to invest money in his career. Unfortunately, no one seemed interested. "They don't have faith no more," Snoop remembered thinking. "So I take it here and I take it there and try to get a little known."

By 1991 Snoop hooked up with Warren G (Warren Griffin), a round-headed, disheveled, aspiring producer who drank heavily and hoped to become as famous as his stepbrother, Dr. Dre: With the local DJ, Snoop recorded a low-budget demo tape. Despite the fact that Warren's turntable had a wobbly needle, his sampling computer was an outdated model, and his tape deck produced muddy sound, they worked at refining their material. Warren hit the drums like they were an old enemy; Snoop replaced his gang-related lyrics with accessible themes and radio-ready hooks. "Not just shit that my homies were gonna like," he said. "We had to make songs that everybody was gonna get into." To make their group marketable, they enlisted Nathaniel ("Nate Dogg") Hale to sing smooth R&B hooks. A tall, potbellied Long Beach neighbor, Nate had a dull stare, a bald head, a penchant for old-fashioned derbies, and the Vandyke style of facial hair, and a past selling dope on the street. As a classmate in Polytechnic High School, Nate used to skip classes with Snoop and practice singing and rapping on a park bench. "I'd be singing Andre Crouch songs like 'Jesus Is the Answer,'" Nate recalled. "Those were the only songs I knew."

Once Nate joined the group and began to write secular lyrics, Snoop and Warren G chose a catchy name (calling themselves 213 after the local telephone area code). When they finished recording their latest batch of song ideas, Warren was sent to Dre's lavish home to play him the tape and see if Dre thought they were finally ready for a record deal. Until May 1991 Dre would hear their music, then say, "This shit is shitty." The group's future did not look bright. They didn't seem capable of pleasing him. But a month before the release of N.W.A's final album, *Niggaz4Life*, Warren passed the latest 213 tape and Dre played it repeatedly during a stag party he threw in his house. As friends urged Dre to come have a drink, Dre sat near the tape deck; Warren was ecstatic—213 had finally satisfied his finicky stepbrother. As their song played and partygoers stopped talking, Dre said he wanted to meet Snoop. "We had a little conversation," Snoop said, "and he made me do my rap all over."

When Dre needed a song to contribute to the *Deep Cover* soundtrack, Snoop was more than ready to get to work. Since a studio session was scheduled for early one morning and Snoop lived way out in Long Beach—and didn't own a car at the time—Dre had Snoop spend the night at his house. The next morning Dre's lyrics had yet to be written. "The DOC couldn't make it back to the studio," Snoop recalled.

The phone kept ringing; people kept asking about the song; instead of writing it, Dre got dressed and told Snoop he was heading to the gym for a workout. "We had like an hour and a half to do the shit," Snoop explained. "Dre told me what he wanted to start off with. 'Tonight's the night I get in some shit/*Deep cover* on the incognito tip.'"

The door slammed. Snoop spent ninety minutes with a pen and pad. When Dre returned, the song was completed—Snoop's update of an old lyric about his final arrest for selling drugs. Dre heard the lyrics and realized he had the makings of a much-needed hit record. At the recording studio, a session bassist named Colin Wolfe was waiting with his acoustic Clevinger Jr. "They just have a drum loop going," Wolfe explained to a writer, "and I'm just coming up with about fifty different bass lines, trying everything. And then we just finally come up with something. We hear something and it just clicks and we'll know that's the one." Under Dre and Snoop's vocal, Wolfe played a grave four-note bass line that would catapult "Deep Cover" to the top of the charts and inaugurate Dr. Dre's career as a major solo artist.

Once Ruthless Records accused Sony of providing Suge with the release forms Eazy had been forced to sign, Sony began to distance itself from Dre, Solar chief Dick Griffey, and Suge Knight. To save the relationship, Dre tried to defend Sony. They had nothing to do with preparing the forms, Dre said. An attorney named Michael Frisbee drafted them. In response, Ruthless characterized Frisbee as outside counsel for Sony and pointed out that the footer at the bottom of the release form was the same as the one used by Sony Music Publishing attorney Scott Aronson—a charge that would link Sony to the extortion of Eazy-E.

Accused of conspiracy to steal artists and defraud Ruthless of its assets, Sony denied everything. Sony's attorney Wayne Smith claimed Dre and Suge had been given copies of blank release forms to serve as an archetype for the one their attorney, Michael Frisbee, would draft. Frisbee was given a sample release form. "He then used those as his forms to draft the releases that freed Dre, the DOC, and Michel'lé from their obligations as recording artists and producers," Smith explained.

Despite the neat explanation, Ruthless continued to feel Sony was aware of the rift between Dre and Eazy but ignored it and proceeded with plans for the *Deep Cover* soundtrack. To Ruthless, Sony not contacting Ruthless and its lawyers confirmed this. "Where did they come off using someone like Suge to start with, knowing his reputation?" asked Ruthless Records' security specialist, Michael Klein. "Why would *any* Sony lawyer draw up releases?"

Though Suge and Dre had made Jerry Heller out to be a villain, Eazy explained to me that Heller was not a thief. He was like a father. If he wasn't, Eazy said he wouldn't have him working for Ruthless. And Jerry was only an employee, not a partner. He repeatedly stressed that he, Eric "Eazy-E" Wright, was the company's sole owner. "But everybody will come out and say 'Fuck Jerry Heller!' It's that a lot of niggas bring up the black and white thing. They don't like Jerry 'cause he's Jewish, so they'll be like 'Oh! He's gonna rob you, he's gonna steal this!' That's that black/white shit from people who don't know shit about the music business or contracts. Telling artists they should get this and that, filling heads up with bullshit.

"The people Dre's with now," Eazy continued, not daring to mention Suge by name, "they came to me, wanting me to move my company into the Solar building. Telling me the same shit. Saying 'Jerry's robbing you!' But I was too strong for that shit. So was Yella. Look who had the weakest mind and went for it. These people get mad 'cause I won't do what they want me to do. So they go around to my other artists with Dre."

They approached Above the Law and suggested that they leave Eazy and join Dre's new label, at the time being called Futureshock Records after a P-Funk song Dre loved. If they didn't sign to Futureshock, Dre explained, he wouldn't be producing their sophomore album. "They're trying to gangster me out of mine and I ain't having it," Eazy said.

Eazy filed a lawsuit accusing Sony, Suge Knight, Solar Records, and Dr. Dre of unscrupulous practices. In response, Sony attorney Wayne Smith said Ruthless was the one trying to gyp Sony. The contract between Ruthless and Sony clearly obligated Ruthless to deliver Dre-produced albums by new artists. The first batch, three albums, were delivered with credits that confirmed Dre's noninvolvement. Questioned about it, Ruthless claimed Dre did produce the albums. "And when Dre was in negotiations with us," said Sony attorney Wayne Smith, "he told us he didn't produce those albums."

Sony felt the three Ruthless albums were execrable. The first two were commercial failures, and it was obvious that the American public agreed. Sony lawyers felt the third should go unreleased, and that Ruthless Records should immediately be sued for breach of contract. "But instead," said Sony attorney Smith, "Sony came back to Ruthless with a proposal."

While the remaining album by Above the Law was hideous, it could be saved. All Ruthless had to do to avoid a lawsuit was get Above the Law to record one song with Dr. Dre. If this happened, Sony would let bygones be bygones. According to Wayne Smith, "Ruthless said, 'Great—but Dre won't work for us. Can you get him to do it for us?'" Sony contacted Suge, who got Dre into the studio with Above the Law to produce the necessary song. Once it was completed, Sony then informed Ruthless that it planned to exercise its right to "take one cut off the Above the Law album and put it on the *Deep Cover* soundtrack," Smith explained.

Ruthless tried to prove a RICO conspiracy against Sony, but Smith successfully filed a motion to dismiss. But Ruthless would not give up that easily—its attorneys worked on amending their complaint.

Technically free of Ruthless Records, "we didn't know exactly where to go," said the DOC. "To be totally honest with you, I had to talk Dre into doing his own shit. He was all we had, you know. It was either him or the fucked-up voice, and the fucked-up voice wasn't happening."

With Sony backing away from their new label, thanks to Eazy-E's accusations, money was scarce, and despite being in possession of reel tapes containing hours of new music, Suge and Dre weren't in a position to release albums. But Suge insisted that producers spend every waking moment in the recording studios at the Solar building, recording demonstration tapes of the label's prospective acts. "The label started as Futureshock and all of us were constantly working," said producer Chocolate. For producers, Suge had Dr. Dre, Chocolate, and newcomers Rhythm D and DJ Unknown; as talent, Suge was auditioning female R&B singers like Lydia Harris, whose imprisoned husband, Michael, wanted to form his own label, and Paradise, who had been involved with the label since Suge got into it with Vanilla Ice. "Then Snoop got there and started joining us in the studio," Chocolate said. "Everyone was working, so no one really had complaints."

Despite a lack of capital, Suge and Dre worked to expand their roster. Only a handful of their acts showed promise. And other groups were jumping ship. Texas gangsta rapper 3-2, whose group the Convicts imitated N.W.A's lowbrow themes and relied on prisoner costumes as a marketing gimmick, shared an apartment with their mainstay, Snoop.

But 3-2 was impatient and wanted an album in stores. When it became evident that this wouldn't be happening anytime soon, the Convicts returned to Texas and signed to an independent called Rap-A-Lot.

Then Jewell, the label's R&B siren and maiden signing, threatened to leave. Born in Chicago, Jewell was a caramel-colored woman with dark, shoulder-length hair, a ready smile, seductive eyes, and a marketable singing voice. When her family moved to California, they realized that the cost of living was higher: Instead of the middle-class lifestyle they enjoyed in Chicago, her family moved into a Compton housing project. After singing in local churches, at talent shows held in malls, and in her high school, Jewell met Dr. Dre (who was then a member of the World Class Wreckin' Kru). After Dre featured her singing on N.W.A's second album (1991's *Niggaz4Life*), she and Rage recorded a duet for the *Deep Cover* soundtrack (the forgettable "Love or Lust").

Now a solo artist, Jewell viewed her album as a means of finally attaining financial stability. She was tired of waiting for Suge and Dre to make good on their promise that she would be the label's initial release. "I signed with a manager to try to get Suge to do what I wanted," she told a fanzine, "but you can't push him to do anything because he knows what he's doing." Suge told her manager to beat it, and told Jewell she had to wait just like everybody else.

Nate Dogg, a former gospel singer who appeared on Snoop and Warren G's earliest demo tapes, went from observing recording sessions to being invited to sing on a song entitled "Deez Nutz," which would appear on Dre's solo album *The Chronic*. Once his vocal was on tape, Dre said, "Man, w'sup? Do you want a record deal? We can get a record deal hooked up.'"

Nate said, "I was like 'What?! Is you crazy? Yeah!' Back then, [the record company] was nothing but a dream. But I was a Dr. Dre fan. I believed all in that dream." Immediately, Nate moved into Dre's spacious home.

"Two or three weeks after that I hooked up with Suge. We were just sitting down talking 'cause we never had a chance to do that. 'Cause I'm new. I don't really know nobody but Dre. We were livin' at Dre's house and everything! We were doing it all in the 'broke years' as I call them.

But yeah. Suge took me to sign my contract, and from then on we were just in business."

Desperate for talent, Suge and Dre reached out to Robin Evette Allen, a 175-pound, easygoing marijuana smoker who wore her hair in huge Afro puffs, two balls of hair that protruded from her scalp like the ears on a Mouseketeer's cap. On her chest, smack-dab on the top of her breastplate, she has a tattoo of an open mouth sticking its tongue out, an image that actually resembles the Rolling Stones' logo.

As the Lady of Rage, she would be seen as the label's most complex artist—in terms of libretto, motivation, and disposition. Raised in Virginia by her grandmother, Clara, she was forbidden to be outdoors after dark, wear makeup, or invite boys anywhere near the house—a strict, repressive set of rules that evokes those Piper Laurie gave Sissy Spacek in Brian De Palma's film of Stephen King's *Carrie*.

By age six, her mental instabilities were apparent. One sunny afternoon, with her friends in the basement, she prepared soft drinks, asking them if they wanted candy in their drinks. "They said yes," she said, "so I put rat poison in our drinks. I put the most in mine."

One guest spilled it out and yelled, *"This ain't no candy! This is rat poison! Y'all are going to die!"* Her friends fled the basement, screaming. Irate parents arrived to confront her, but she had already been taken to a nearby hospital, where her stomach was pumped. "All the doctors and nurses were looking at me as if I was Satan's child," she believed. "I don't know what made me do that." A year later, she was writing poetry.

Back then, like many kids, she eagerly anticipated each Saturday morning's episode of the *Shazam!/Secrets of Isis* hour. Soon, however, the program seemed to have a sinister influence. "My grandmother had given me a necklace, a cameo," she said. "I was saying the thing that Isis says: 'O mighty winds that blow high! Lift me now so I can fly!' I turned around and around—I'm telling you, I wasn't flying with my hands out or anything, but my feet came off the ground like five or six feet! I was kinda scared because I was off the ground, and that's why I believe it."

At age twelve, living in Texas with her mother, she tried to commit suicide with Tylenol. "I told my mother but she didn't believe me." Her second attempt involved pills. The third, in Virginia, she drank Ortho weed killer, but a friend slapped it out of her hand after the first sip and called her crazy.

Back in Houston, her grandfather tried steering her into school or a job. Like Grandmaw Clara, her grandfather, whom she never named in interviews, had clear-cut morals; when he left for work in the morning, he expected the TV off and everyone dressed and ready to leave the house. Forced to enter society, Rage entered the Job Corps in San Marcus in 1985, where she took up meat cutting. "Butchery," she said. "It was fun. I stayed for two years."

She found other unemployed, music-minded people and entered a regional talent show. The appearance onstage, her very first attempt at rapping publicly, increased her interest in performing rap music. Soon after her return from the Job Corps to her grandfather's home, she had befriended a female rapper. One Saturday night, Rage suggested they journey to New York to pursue a recording contract. It was the middle of the night; the streets were empty; the tenor of the evening had changed. It was time to head home, sleep it off. She repeated the overture. Her friend was aghast. "She asked me when," Rage recalled, "and I said, 'Now.' " How? Hitchhiking. Wouldn't it be dangerous? Not if Rage sat in the backseat with a pistol. Her friend declined. Rage remained in Houston that evening. Undeterred, however, she soon moved to Arkansas: Paychecks from a job at McDonald's ultimately financed her solo trip. Her first day there, she met Beverly Goodman. Mother of Chic member Nile Rodgers, Beverly heard Rage's rap and asked her to record a rap for a public service announcement promoting AIDS awareness.

Her next appearance on a record was for the L.A. Posse, a group of producers who hailed from the West Coast and had produced the majority of L.L. Cool J's second album, *Bigger and Deffer*. After rhyming on two songs for the West Coast group, her career came to a standstill and her finances dwindled. Homeless, she spent nine months living in the Chung King recording studios, the facility in downtown Manhattan where Def Jam Records prepared Run-D.M.C. and L.L. Cool J's earliest crowning achievements. For baths she boiled water in a coffeepot, carried it into the bathroom, and washed up. She begged, borrowed, and lost sleep, skipped meals, tried to keep her clothes clean, and questioned her decision to become a rapper. One day Brooklyn rapper Big Daddy Kane appeared at the studio for a recording session. When he asked her address, she replied, "That couch you're sitting on."

When she met Chubb Rock, an artist on Select Records, who was impressed with her talent, he promised to produce her album right after he finished working with his labelmate the Real Roxanne. Despite his promise, Chubb finished with Roxanne, then had to go on tour. But he let Rage stay in his apartment until he returned to New York. For a while she was able to live like other human beings. But then Chubb's tour ended and, with it, her repose. Back on her couch at Chung King, she received the phone call that forever changed her life: A guy named Suge was on the line, explaining that the L.A. Posse had returned to California and played producer Dr. Dre their completed album. Impressed by her performances on two songs, Dre had asked the group for a contact number. The L.A. Posse said, "Call Chung King Studios. She's always there."

"Then," Rage recalled, "Dre called and was like, 'Yeah, this Dr. Dre. We getting a new record label and, um, we're interested in you and would wanna know if you down to come out here.'

"I was like, So how do I know you're Dr. Dre?

"And he was like, There's only one way to find out and they sent me a ticket."

Before boarding a flight, she told Dre she still owed her grandmother money for the phone bill. Suge sent payment to Virginia. It was a done deal, she told Chubb Rock, whom she saw before leaving. Skeptical, Chubb advised her not to go: Dr. Dre was a good producer but his success was with N.W.A. Who knew if he would make it on his own. She had to be careful, Chubb warned: Confirm what they were offering in terms of payment, when she would record, when her album would be released. Otherwise, she might just be wasting more time. Until the end of her stay in New York, Chubb Rock was supportive. "If they are not saying shit," he suggested, "then come back and *I'll* do your album."

On the plane to California, Rage befriended the Leaders of the New School, a Long Island trio who recorded lighthearted novelty raps for Elektra Records. When the plane landed, she was baffled. Crowds swarmed around her; the front of the airport was a sea of strange faces;

no one held up a sign with her name on it, a simple way of locating her in the crowd of arriving passengers. Outside the airport terminal, taxi-cabs sped past with horns blaring; passersby frowned, rushing by with their luggage. No one was waiting to meet her. Frightened, she put on a brave face. Then her new pals in the Leaders of the New School offered help. " 'Cause I was gonna stay at the airport. And they was like, 'Fuck that. You coming to the hotel with us! You can stay with us.' "

After a day in their suite, she managed to reach Suge on the tele-phone. "He was like, 'You know, you wanna stay there while they there since you know them? You wanna hang out with them? We just pay for your room and whatnot?' " Her confidence in him shaken, she said that would be fine. "So then he came and picked me up from the hotel and, um, he was cool. I never saw nothing from him like intimidation or nothing. He was cool. We almost got into a wreck on the way to go see Dre. He was talking on the phone and um—he was just cool. That was my impression." But she noticed that, even behind the wheel, he was imperious.

At the studio, Dre was mastering a project. It might have been N.W.A's final album *Niggaz4Life*, she said. Anyway, his equanimity sur-prised her, serving as a requisite inverse to Suge's impetuosity. Generally, she liked Dre; she could point to only one troubling incident. During this introductory period, she was listening to a tape by Freestyle Fellow-ship, a paradoxical West Coast group out to prove that all California rappers weren't bragging about selling drugs, running with actual gangs, or participating in drive-by shootings. To her dismay, Dre expressed in-terest in signing them. Everything she had been told, as Chubb warned, was too good to be true. "Dre was like, do I know how to get in touch with those guys," Rage said. "So it made me mad. I was like, 'How you gonna sign somebody else when you can't even take care of the artists you already got?!' "

" 'How you gonna question me on what I can take care of?'

" 'Just what I said! You can't take care of your own artists!'

" 'If you don't like it, you can leave.'

" 'Fine! Well, gimme my ticket and I'm gone.'

" '*I ain't giving you shit!*' "

The next day she met with Suge. "And he was like, 'You know, everybody's kinda under stress and, Rage, you need to trust somebody. You should stop being so—' Because I really wasn't trusting or open with everybody. I'd just stick to myself and it would just be me against them. Or me against the world. And Suge was like, 'You know, this is your family. You need to open up. Dre trippin', you trippin', and y'all will get over it and be in the studio tomorrow.' It was over just like that. It was like a brother-sister thing."

Initially optimistic, she beamed when Suge and Dre promised she would be the label's first undertaking. "Then I got out here and you know, Snoop was there." She also met an R&B singer named Jewell and Snoop's group, 213, which consisted of Dre's stepbrother, Warren G, and gospel-crooner Nate Dogg. "So it was gonna be *us*," Rage discovered. "But that's not what they told me. They were like, 'It's gonna be you.' " Her optimism continued even though "shit wasn't happening like they said it was gonna happen."

"Seven years later," she added, "I'm still waiting for that shit to happen."

But she hung in there, loyal to her benefactors, and when things weren't happening as fast as she would have liked, or as fast as Dre and Suge promised, she reminded herself that she could leave at any time. Most troubling, she admitted, was the prevailing gang culture. "You know," she said nervously, "the *gang* stuff was something, um, new to me."

Other fundamental differences between L.A. and Virginia soon disturbed her. "I couldn't just get on the train and go wherever I wanted to. You definitely had to have a car. When I first got here, I really wasn't going anywhere. I didn't know anybody. It was just to the studio and back home. I didn't hang out; I didn't do none of that. I was basically in the house. I couldn't do shit but smoke, eat, get fatter, and write rhymes."

Four months later, Chubb Rock was in town on business. "He asked me if I'd started my album, if I had this, if I had that. All of my answers were no." Chubb urged her to return to New York; she refused, wanting to give Dr. Dre's new record label (still being called Futureshock) a little more time. "After a while I couldn't get in contact with Chubb and I started to feel that [Dre and Suge] were lying to me because they kept saying we would be in the studio by a certain time and it'd never happen."

Inevitably, she made friends like Diamond, a female gang member who advised her on "what area not to go into wearing certain colors. But every time she'd introduce me to somebody it was like 'This is "O-Dog from 20s" or something like that. And I would tell her, 'You know? I don't wanna know all a' that. Just say this is 'so-and-so.' I don't need to know their history in the gang.' She's like: 'Well, it's just the *respect* thing. That's just how we do out here and it's just . . . how it is!' " Rage sighed. "I had to get used to *that*."

The rapper RBX arrived at the label. After graduating from UNLV, RBX had become a store manager. During one nighttime recording session, between takes of a song, RBX decided to amuse himself by reciting a political rap. He had been working on socially conscious lyrics since 1985, when he arrived on the campus of UNLV to play football. Once Dr. Dre heard him rap, he said, "W'sup? You wanna get down?" RBX couldn't believe Dre was offering a chance to appear on a song. But Dre was serious and the appearance led to RBX joining the label's roster. "But I wasn't 'signed' to [the label]," he stressed. "The CEO was like, 'We got these contracts I want you to sign.' He gave me a blank piece of paper." RBX was immediately suspicious. "I know from being in college that it ain't a contract if there's not a legal premise to bind it. Secondly, you have to have the litigation involved with the official 'jargon' or whatever the fuck it is to make it binding. Or it's just a paper." He signed the paper to get Suge off his back. Later, he'd want a real contract. "That was my intention," said RBX. "I figured Suge knows a *real* businessman—it's not gonna be just my name and yours on some paper. That's not how business is conducted. Turns out, they tried to take that page and say I signed a 'contract.' "

Since the age of eight, Ricardo Brown wanted to be like Rakim and Spoonie Gee, two smooth-voiced New York rappers who projected the image of sophisticated lady-killers. As Ricardo grew older in Philadelphia, he became increasingly rebellious, immersing himself completely into rap culture, calling himself Kurupt and aspiring to a career onstage. By sixteen, the rail-thin baby-faced rapper lived in a nicer suburb with his mother, but couldn't quite give up his belligerent attitude. After he stole his mother's car and wrecked it one night, he found himself being shipped to his father's home in California.

By the time Kurupt met aspiring music mogul Lamont Bloomfield, Bloomfield had moved past rough beginnings on Crenshaw and 60th Street in South Central and worked to make his tiny, impoverished record label a success, something that would require capital he didn't have. "I had a record company called Hustler for Life," Bloomfield recalled, "and I was sitting in my car one day, playing a tape. And this guy walking down the street heard the tape and said, 'Man, I got a friend who will serve [upstage] that rapper.'

"I thought this tape was pretty good, so I was like, 'Whatever. Come over here. Listen to this next song.' After hearing that one, this guy said the same thing: The rapper he knew was much better than the tape. So I was like, 'Where's he at? How old is he?' And he was like, 'Man, he's sixteen.' And I laughed. I was like, 'Yeah right.' "

The passerby led Lamont to Kurupt, recently arrived from Philadelphia and living with his father. "He came outside and ripped my rapper to pieces. He was free-styling, pointing to things and rapping about them without no rehearsal; you knew he was making it up as he went along—something I never saw before, totally remarkable. I couldn't believe it. I was like, 'Damn, this little skinny guy just slayed my top rapper.' So I kinda asked him if he had tracks, if he was hooked up with anybody. He said he had never been in the studio before. So I felt like I had something."

Two days later, he had Kurupt in the studio. "We had a battle song called 'Lyrics of Destruction,' " Lamont said, "and I suggested he call one 'World of Kuruption,' after his name. I did a few songs with him. One called 'That's What Love Is,' and a smooth little track called 'Dark and Lovely.' I was just trying to round it off so I'd have a better chance of giving him a deal." But finding a commercial image for the nondescript rapper was difficult. "I tried to find his image and what he'd look best in. I tried him in different kinds of clothing, suits. I even took some pictures of him in a junkyard, dressed like a 'hard guy.' " This ploy didn't work. "When you look at his face, he looks so innocent. You could look at the picture now and say, 'This guy wasn't hard.' "

Sometimes Lamont would even ask Kurupt to rap gospel lyrics, anything for an image to market. "I did a variety: three songs hard, three songs like church music, three songs R&B music. 'Cause right then, I didn't know where rap was going and I wanted to make sure I had three of whatever I could send somebody. If they wanted 'hard,' I'd give them hard. If they wanted 'smooth,' I'd give them smooth."

In 1991, Kurupt was a nice kid, Lamont remembered. "He was the perfect artist. He used to listen. He didn't talk to nobody. If someone handed him a business card, instead of going behind my back and dealing with them, he would give it to me. He was perfect." But Kurupt was anxious. "He got at that desperate stage 'cause it didn't happen for him overnight, and people were telling him how good he was. So he wanted to take the first deal I hooked up. I actually got him work on the S.O.S. Band. People don't even know his first project was on their album *One of Many Nights*. If you look on the cover, you'll see my credit. It was in 1991, and he was signed to me, and that was the first work he ever really did to get released commercially. If people go get this album, they'll hear Kurupt talking some 'party' stuff, 'That's what love was about . . .' They'll see he does have 'another side' to him."

A tape reached Dr. Dre. "And Dr. Dre told me he loved Kurupt," Lamont explained. "So I thought everything I was doing was starting to pay off, you know. Once this guy named Suge Knight came into the picture, it became a horror story. Suge was telling me things while he was telling Kurupt things behind my back, turning us against each other."

Lamont's first meeting with Suge Knight was a positive one. Suge agreed to everything Lamont proposed. "Everything was all good. 'Yeah, yeah, yeah.' I should've known when a person says 'yeah' too much, that must mean 'no' and 'yeah, right.' But Suge was so cool with everything I asked about. We were going to do a joint venture and he told me I was going to produce Kurupt's record. I mean, he told me everything I wanted to hear."

But then things changed. According to Lamont, Suge told Kurupt his deal with Futureshock Records was being held up because Lamont was being finicky. Lamont, meanwhile, said he was just trying to protect Kurupt's interests. Then David E. Kenner—a short, stocky white man with a black Reagan-like pompadour, a slicked-back ponytail, an unyielding stare, and a no-nonsense demeanor—began to sit in on their meetings. From the beginning, Lamont distrusted Kenner, a family man and USC law graduate who had defended Mafia-linked scam artist Barry Minkow in 1988, then became the lawyer of choice for some of the country's most infamous drug lords. The fifty-five-year-old Brooklyn-born attorney lived in an Encino mansion surrounded by high gates and surveillance cameras. He was said to keep a fully loaded Uzi on the desk in his home office and was good friends with Tony Brooklier, a respected criminal lawyer who was also the son of Dominic Brooklier, one-time boss of La Cosa Nostra.

"Kenner would just sit back and try to tell me why it was good that Kurupt signed with [the label]," Lamont Bloomfield remembered. "He was just some little gangsterlike attorney, like he should be working for the mob or something. Like Bugsy Siegel or somebody, that's who he reminded me of. I knew he was up to no good then. But I kept going on what Suge was telling me 'cause I knew Suge hired him. So Suge would tell him to pay me and I would get my money. But he was telling Suge how to run his record company and, at the same time, how to take everybody's money. That's why they're all caught up in this mess right now."

By then, Kurupt was recording vocals on tape and Lamont was concerned about publishing rights and whether Dre and Suge would be releasing a Kurupt solo album. Then Lamont wanted to ensure that Kurupt and the label signed a contract for any work Kurupt did on Dre's solo album, scheduled to be the label's first release. Unfortunately, no paperwork was ever prepared, Lamont claimed, and any work Kurupt had done on Dre's multiplatinum *The Chronic* would be for free. "I was trying to handle his business," Lamont added, "and it was very difficult when Suge was constantly trying to steal him from me all along. I was thinking, Maybe I'm doing something wrong. So I hired an attorney by the name of John Smith and he was dealing with him. And Suge stopped calling him back. David Kenner stopped calling him back. By then they already had Kurupt on the *Chronic* album."

The more Lamont complained, the more Kenner restated anything Suge said. "Yes, yes, okay," he said. "Everything will be fine! Tell your attorney to call me." After leaving countless messages and mailing a slew of letters, Lamont's lawyer realized Futureshock Records (later Death Row) had no intention of honoring the terms of their deal in reference to Kurupt—that Kurupt would appear on the label's albums and Lamont would be paid a portion of the profits.

But Suge was so persuasive, Lamont actually began to aggressively promote the label himself. "Suge had my guards down," he admitted. "He's a very good talker. He's smooth."

Originally from Long Beach, Delmar "Daz" Arnaud was living in his mother's home in Tulsa, Oklahoma. His mother was attending college there, and wanted him away from the gangs and drug wars in Crip-infested Long Beach, California. When Daz's cousin Snoop called to report that he was now working with world-famous Dr. Dre on a solo album for a new label, Daz immediately wanted to be involved with the project. A moon-faced rapper with thick eyebrows and a short, nappy Afro, Daz had no real experience with hip-hop. His rhymes were substandard and filled with clichés; his keyboard riffs were atonal; he did not know how to DJ. But he could laugh at other people's jokes when he needed to; he could play the role of eager apprentice; he could convincingly play the role of good friend to anyone in a position to help him rise above the mediocrity that characterized his life. Hearing of Snoop's opportunity, Daz immediately returned to California, haunted the recording studio at the Solar building, instantly befriended Dre, and kept suggesting ideas for his album until Dre relented and finally used one or two minor ones on the album. Then Daz and Kurupt became good friends and the two money-hungry rappers decided to work together.

Then Suge Knight turned his sights on artists at other labels, said a writer from *Vibe* magazine. "It was 1991 and my girlfriend was working for Dallas Austin. Dallas Austin used to have this group called Illegal. Dallas had signed these kids. They had made this record. Somehow these kids met Suge and Snoop and Suge decided that he wanted to take Illegal from Rowdy and put out their records. So they had a meeting.

'Cause Dallas didn't want to give up the group, of course—he had in-vested all of his money and time. And at the time, Left Eye of TLC was managing these kids. But Dallas had signed them. So Dallas decided to meet with Suge, right? He went to a meeting. When he walked in, they patted him down to make sure he wasn't strapped. Dallas wasn't, so they let him into the room and he sat down. Before the meeting started, everybody from [the label] who was at the meeting pulled their guns out and put them on the table—pointing toward Dallas but still on the table. And this, of course, scared the shit out of Dallas. He didn't give up the group, but it wasn't pleasant."

At this point, however, Suge and Dre's artists were starving. Literally. "It's a reality," said Chocolate, who was staying with the DOC. "But I was fortunate to have known the DOC before I met Suge. When I came back to Cali and stayed with the DOC, I had it a lot easier. I didn't have to rely on living somewhere and Suge paying my rent or bringing me food. But some artists hadn't eaten. Or the rent hadn't been paid and they were sitting up in their apartment, starving."

Suge had begun to resemble Cliff Bernstein's description of the typi-cal inept manager. "Okay," said Bernstein, manager of Metallica and Def Leppard. "First he sells himself to his acts as God's gift. He says, 'I'm gonna make it happen for you.' Then he's helping the band in the stu-dio. Before you know it, he's co-producing or executive-producing the albums. This is the kind of manager who tells the band how to write songs, how to record them.

"When the band is out at the bar and going after chicks, this guy is going after chicks at the *same* rate. And whatever the musicians are doing, he's got to have it *better*. He's convinced himself he's part of the band. And at the same time, he's always telling them, 'You'd be nowhere without me.' He tries to become indispensable to them—by being there all the time, making all the decisions, and not letting anyone else know what's going on."

When new artists arrived at the Solar building with malnutrition-distended stomachs, Chocolate would stop working on music, buy them a fried chicken meal at Popeye's, and listen to their woes.

Doug Young, who wanted to work for the label, remembered these hungry days. "They were begging for weed," he said.

"I'VE NEVER MET SUCH A LOVELY GROUP OF MEN"

During the summer of 1991, defense attorney David E. Kenner started coming around the label's temporary headquarters. He would pull his gleaming black Mercedes into the parking lot at the Solar studios on Cahuenga Boulevard, go upstairs, and call Suge aside to talk privately. Kenner was around so much, everyone assumed he was an established industry figure.

From the beginning, Suge Knight wanted his record company to be seen as the Motown of the '90s. He wanted to be like athlete-turned-record-mogul Berry Gordy and emulated Gordy's business practices. He learned the basics of the industry, maneuvered himself into the right circles, and remained observant of the industry climate. Once he understood how the record business worked, he began to build relationships. At this point most people saw him as someone with a logical plan.

Like Gordy, he surrounded himself with shrewd people he could control and motivate. Most of the artists were entering their twenties, coming from broken homes, so the concept of a family appealed to them. Through pep talks, Suge led people to believe that the label's success would mean theirs as well. This was why artists happily recorded for free and subsisted on Popeye's chicken. Instead of a corporation, they believed they were contributing to a family.

According to Suge, loyalty was key. Everyone would watch each other's back. But slowly, said one label insider, a despotic side appeared. "I never knew why, but that's what Suge wanted to be. As far as with power and the business? He wanted to be another Eazy."

With Kenner's help, Suge signed his artists to deals that also made the label their manager. But as David Geffen once said to William Knoedelseder, "You cannot be in the record business and manage artists on your own label—it's a conflict of interest. How can a manager get the best deal for his client if the manager also works for the record company? It's very disturbing. If it's legal, it shouldn't be."

Suge tried to defend this unscrupulous practice. "I don't take a management fee. I'm the record company." And as the record company, he did what was best for his artists, saving them the twenty percent commission most managers charged. Artists, he added, were welcome to seek outside management but "the truth is, no one can get anything from me like my artists. We family."

In addition to being their record label and manager, as he had done for his artists since his days at ill-fated Funky Enough Records, Suge planned to serve as "executive producer" of every release and receive the lion's share of publishing rights. "And everyone knows that along with songwriting fees, publishing rights are where artists can make the most money," music executive Martin Moor explained. "That's why record labels and producers are always eager to take the publishing from artists."

While Suge had Dre and the DOC ready to help with his newest label, a stable of artists eager to record and contracts ready to be signed, various other legal situations continued to hold them up. Though Suge felt Solar chief Dick Griffey had botched the Sony deal, a written agreement gave Griffey the lion's share of the company. Suge would have to deal with that matter soon. For now, however, he had to deal with

Eazy-E making life difficult by telling anyone who'd listen that Suge had stolen his artists—assertions he also made in a lawsuit filed on August 23, 1991. Dre was the best producer in the business, but no one would work with him. Eazy-E kept warning record labels that Ruthless Records would sue anyone dealing with artists he considered in breach of contract. Then the $500,000 Sony gave Suge, Dre, and Dick Griffey in April—for publishing rights to Dre's work as a producer—was gone, swallowed up by recording *The Chronic*, an album Dre still had not completed. They were strapped for cash.

David Kenner had a client who, like Suge, had an interest in music and forming a record company. Unlike Suge, this client had millions of dollars to invest. Even behind bars, Michael Harris, a Blood member known throughout Los Angeles as Harry-O, was a force to be reckoned with. Standing six feet five inches tall, Harris was a local legend: He could associate with drug-dealing gang members in black neighborhoods from Compton to Watts or make an entrance at film premieres or parties in Beverly Hills, Hollywood, or any other affluent white part of town. Unlike other dealers, who squandered their earnings on cars, homes, and the latest fashions, Harris invested in a number of legitimate businesses: Kartier [sic] Limousines, a deli, a Beverly Hills hair salon, Beverly Hills Auto Leasing.

Arrested for trying to kill a criminal associate in 1987, Harris had become a favorite target for politicians and the local media, including the L.A. *Times*—which called his arrest the "most dramatic move yet against major suppliers of cocaine in the South Central area"—and L.A.'s Channel 2, which labeled him the "gang godfather." Harris was so public a figure that the mayor at the time, Tom Bradley, announced that Harris's holdings had been seized, including three opulent homes in the Valley, five expensive cars, and a speedboat authorities planned to pull out of Long Beach harbor, where it lay since an accident that killed Harris's brother.

Though imprisoned, Harris was no less ambitious than he had been in the real world. With telephone calls and during visits with close friends, relatives, and his wife, Lydia, the R&B singer, he had been able to continue to run a production company called Y-Not, and finance a Broadway play called *Checkmates*, for which he personally cast then-struggling Denzel Washington.

While Suge and Dre sought out acts for their Futureshock Records, Harris urged his wife to find acts for their own record company, Death Row Records. At the time, music executive Soup Henderson was a young aspiring rapper whose group the Rebels of Rhythm haunted local talent contests. "And they had this little cable access show out here called *Slam It or Jam It*, where you could say your rhymes," Soup explained.

When his group arrived on the set for an audition, a promoter told them, "Yo, we know this sister who's about to start this label called Death Row."

Michael Harris's wife invited Soup's group to her home. They auditioned. She liked what she heard and expressed interest in signing them. "So I'm thinking, cool," Soup said. At this point, however, Dr. Dre wasn't part of the deal, Soup explained. "She told us, 'We're *tryin'* to get Dre down with it.' That's what it was. To see if he *wanted* to. Not that he was or nothing. And Suge came out of nowhere. I don't know how he got involved."

When Soup placed a routine call to her to see how plans for Michael and Lydia Harris's label, Death Row Records, were proceeding, he reached an answering machine that said the number had been disconnected. "I never heard anything from them again, so I thought the Death Row situation was shot."

For Kenner's client, Michael Harris, it wasn't. He had just altered his plans to include new partners. According to Harris, his attorney, David Kenner, set up the initial meeting with Suge Knight in September, which established the terms of their agreement and expectations each had of the other. Each party, it was decided, would hold fifty percent of a joint venture. David Kenner would form the corporation and help run its parent company, Harris's corporate entity, Godfather Entertainment. The label would still be named what Lydia and Michael Harris had been calling it: Death Row Records.

They met again that October, Harris claimed, inside the Metropolitan

Detention Center. During this jailhouse visit, Kenner produced paperwork binding them all to the deal. They would be equal partners in GFE (Godfather Entertainment), which would be parent company to a smaller division called Death Row Records: Suge Knight would actually run the business. Michael Harris would provide $1.5 million in start-up money and the label's "overall philosophy and direction." Kenner, Harris claimed, would handle the paperwork and work at creating more new businesses.

On November 27, Woodland Hills attorney Sheldon Ellis, a friend of Kenner's, filed articles of incorporation for GFP Inc. with the California secretary of state. GFE and GFP Inc. were the same company with different names.

By year's end, however, Dre gave Harris an idea of what to expect from the people he thought were his newest business partners. Dre credited Suge Knight with coming up with the idea for Death Row Records and asserted that they and they alone were equal partners. "We like brothers and shit," said Dre.

About the label changing its name from Futureshock to Death Row, the label's R&B siren Jewell now claimed, "This guy named DJ Unknown came up with the name Def Road. Dre asked me what I thought about the name. I was like, 'Naw, Death Row, nigga, if anything, 'cause all of us got [court] cases."

Michael Harris was slowly being edged out of the picture.

The new year, 1992, began with David Kenner getting paperwork together for the deal Michael Harris claimed they reached in his jail cell. After filing articles of incorporation for GFP Inc. with the California secretary of state, Sheldon Ellis did his friend David Kenner a second favor. On January 24, 1992, he incorporated a second company, GF Music, but didn't file a statement of officers.

Within a month Norman Winter, once CBS Records head Walter Yetnikoff's West Coast publicist, was hired to serve as the label's spokesperson. On February 23, 1992, Winter told the *Hollywood Reporter* about the formation of a new label, Death Row Records, which was "under the umbrella of a new, diversified media company, GF Entertainment." Suge Knight was listed as CEO of Death Row. David Kenner was listed as chairman.

Within forty-eight hours Death Row and GF Entertainment would be publicly unveiled to six hundred guests at a party held at Chasen's restaurant in Beverly Hills. The party's invitation was designed to resemble a court summons.

Among the guests that night was Bryan Turner, chief of Priority Records. Suge presided over the event. Many of the label's new acts performed live. "The whole spread—seafood platters and Chasen's chili," *L.A. Weekly* reported, "cost more than $35,000." By night's end, Chasen's maître d' said, "I've never met such a lovely group of men."

Days later, a *Hollywood Reporter* item on the bash noted that Death Row Records was associated with GF Entertainment, the company Lydia Harris and David Kenner controlled. The *Reporter* also mentioned GF Music and GF Prods, planned film and television arms as divisions of GF Entertainment. Norman Winter said the label had fifteen acts signed and ready to go. What was unsaid was that Death Row needed cash.

On March 2, 1992, a statement of officers was filed, and named Kenner and Michael Harris's wife, Lydia, as sole directors of the corporation. This time Kenner put his law office address down as GFP's place of business. Within two weeks the company registered "Death Row Records" as the business name with the county recorder. Again David Kenner was identified as "Chairman, Board of Directors" of GF Music Inc.

By May 1, 1992, GF Entertainment—another name for GFP—was registered at the L.A. county clerk's office. A second filing, in Sacramento, listed Kenner and Lydia as directors of GFP. Two weeks later GFP registered to do business as GF Entertainment. By month's end, however, the name GF Music Inc.—or anything having to do with Harris—would no longer appear on paperwork having to do with Death Row Records.

Accountant Ronald Chodorow, a friend of David Kenner's listed as chief financial officer for GF Entertainment's parent, admitted the corporations were little more than shells. Chodorow would not elaborate further, but his mention of "shells" is damning enough. Suge and Kenner had no intention of ever including Michael Harris in owning and operating Death Row. Kenner, Chodorow explained, asked him to set up accounts for the GF companies. Asked whether business was transacted through the companies, or why they were formed, he gave no answer.

"NIGGAS WERE STILL CLEANING UP THE BLOOD, THEN NEXT THING YOU KNOW, THE FBI AND ALL THAT SHIT CAME"

By May 1992, the *Deep Cover* soundtrack was in stores, and the Dre-produced material was copyrighted to Sony and Solar. Ruthless Records had their attorneys mail letters that said Dre was signed to Ruthless, and Sony's deal with Dre was interfering with that. The letters also described the violent means by which the releases were obtained, and asked if Sony didn't think it strange that Eazy received nothing in return for releasing his artists.

"We told them that the releases were invalid," said Michael Klein, a security specialist hired by Jerry Heller. "But they then drew up a *Deep Cover* contract. We told Sony, 'Don't put it out,' but they did anyway. The whole goal was to raid Ruthless's assets. And while this may go on in the music business all the time, it doesn't make it lawful."

Dre insisted that Eazy signed the release papers because it was the right thing to do. "I'm not a gangster," he said.

Ruthless Records included him in the RICO claim it hoped to file against Suge, Solar, and Sony Music.

Through Wayne Smith, a partner at Gibson, Dunn & Crutcher, Sony expressed their position: Dre was having a problem with Eazy-E and Ruthless Records. Sony was interested in signing Dre as a songwriter, producer, and artist. But Sony didn't sign anything but a publishing deal because they felt Dre wasn't free to enter any other agreement. Sony's position was that they entered into deals with Dre believing that Dre was not prohibited from selling publishing rights to his work as a freelance producer due to any preexisting contract with Ruthless Records.

"If he was not free to do it, *Ruthless and Dre* have a breach of contract," said Smith. "If it turns out Dre did not have the right to sell us what he sold us, then Ruthless has a breach of contract against *Dre*, and *Sony* has a breach of warranty against *Dre*. But that's not a RICO suit or a conspiracy."

After filing motions to dismiss and getting Ruthless's case thrown out twice, Smith predicted that Ruthless would be unable to file a complaint that could withstand a motion. "And for all their wild ranting and raving," he added, "they haven't gotten past the simple litmus test of the judge saying, 'You've actually stated a legal claim here.' "

According to Smith, Ruthless's attorneys said the label's relationship with Dre was dead as of December 1991. The judge asked, "Well, if it was dead in December 1991, why are you complaining about anything Sony did in 1992?" They would reply, "Holy cow, we just realized Sony entered into a conspiracy in December 1991!" This would be inserted into their latest complaint. Since judges in California felt too many people invoked RICO statutes, the odds were clearly against Ruthless.

But Ruthless was not about to back down. The label's attorney, Michael Borbeau, prepared a third amended complaint. "They never thought we were going to sue," said Ruthless security specialist Michael Klein. "They thought they'd be able to work something out, pay peanuts for what happened, and they'd have Dre. Dre was going to go with Sony. They had it all planned out. They had this new album scheduled to be released. *The Chronic* was going to be a Sony release, but not until we sued did they take it off the release schedule. Then [Sony] said, 'This is too deep for us, and we're going to have problems if we go ahead.' "

At this point Sony backed out of the deal. "And after Dick Griffey at Solar Records lost that deal with Sony," said Doug Young, "it wasn't the same. Yeah, they would go up there and go through the motions—like everything was cool and he was down—but it wasn't really crackin' no more. That's when they lost faith in Griffey. Trust me. I remember this part."

In losing the deal, Griffey gave Suge the ammunition he needed for a takeover. Until then, *The Chronic* was going to be a Death Row/Solar release, distributed by Sony. The connection between the labels was so tight, " '187' was on that version of the album," said *L.A. Times* reporter Cheo Coker. When Suge decided that Griffey had to go, they yanked the song and replaced it with a new number called "Bitches Ain't Shit."

That the deal fell through wasn't Griffey's fault, Young pointed out. Suge expected him to sell the label on the strength of "Deep Cover," during one of rap's worst censorship periods. After Ice-T's heavy metal group Body Count released "Cop Killer," politicians began to attack rap. "And all the labels got scared and started dropping motherfuckers left and right," Young said. "After that 'Cop Killer' shit, Sony dropped [Death Row] 'cause they had a 'Deep Cover' song talking about killing an undercover cop. Although this was to a movie called *Deep Cover.*"

With Griffey on the way out, Suge began to rely on attorney David Kenner. Artists like the DOC and RBX realized that the balance of power was shifting. Dre was reduced to dealing strictly with the music. "They peeped it early in the game," Young explained. "Death Row was supposed to be Dre and the DOC's label, but they saw that it was about to be all about Suge. More and more, Suge was becoming 'the man.' "

While attending the Black Radio Exclusive convention in New Orleans, a peaceful annual event that allowed black label executives to meet record store owners and radio DJs, Dre and four other men were arrested. The DOC and Suge were among those placed in handcuffs. "The Death Row people had this big-ass fight in the lobby of the hotel and the fuckin' New Orleans Police Department—being that they're also a little psycho—rode their horses into the lobby of the hotel," said a writer from *Vibe* who attended the convention.

A fifteen-year-old fan was stabbed, four police officers were injured, and the New Orleans district attorney's office was deciding if charges of criminal damage, resisting arrest, battery of officers, and inciting a riot would be pressed. "The New Orleans thing?" Dre said. "That shit got pumped so out of hand!" Sighing heavily, he described how he, Suge, and the DOC were in a hotel lobby, minding their own business and discussing a scene in Eddie Murphy's *Harlem Nights* film: Midway through the film, a prizefighter approaches gambler Eddie Murphy at a restaurant table and reassures Eddie that it's safe to bet on him.

"You know the part where the kid stutters?" Dre asked. "It's like 'Come Friday night, I'm knocking somebody the fuck out!' These kids overheard us saying that shit, right? So they walk up to us, just out of nowhere, and say 'Yo, I bet you can't knock my homeboy out right here.' They were talking to Suge, who said, 'Go on with that shit. Get out of here!'

"So the kid walked up on him and my boy pushed him back. He walked up again so my boy hit him. *Bam!* And all this shit broke out. They start coming at us. *Boom!* We got in a little tussle and uh—I start heading for the front door! Police grabbed me. *Boom! Boom! Boom!* Throwing me in there. I'm like, well, 'Yo, what y'all grabbing me for? Heh-heh.' "

Mysterious other people were responsible for hitting those police officers, Dre said. While he cooled his heels in a jail cell, the real criminals were running loose. "They saying I beat up seven police and I incited a riot and some other shit. I was like, 'Damn, that ain't saying much for your motherfucking police force if I beat up seven police.' "

At the time, Dre said he had evidence to contradict the district attorney's claim that he was involved in the stabbing of a fifteen-year-old. "I ain't even know nothing about that shit," he claimed. "I didn't see nothing like that. Matter of fact, we got the shit on videotape. This kid from New Orleans sent us a video of the whole episode. It has me on videotape. It doesn't have how it started, but it has me going to the door, *then* you hear a big ruckus. Yo, man, *I didn't do jack!*"

To Eazy, it seemed that Suge was leading Dre to ruin. "He had that Dee Barnes thing, breaking that kid's jaw, driving his car off the cliff, getting shot, New Orleans." Eazy groaned again. "None of that shit ever happened to him when he was down with us. Dre's into something he can't get out of! Musically and personally. In every way. He's got people who don't know shit about the music business filling his head with bullshit, telling him he could be this and that, get 'this and that'—fuck that! I'll show his contract in public and compare it to those of other producers. Nobody was ever robbing him!"

But Dre believed Eazy did underpay him, so he remained with Suge and worked to finish his album. One evening in July 1992, at the Solar building, artists were gathered in a studio completing a song for Dre. Until then, Suge made sure the office and studio sessions were free of violence. "It wasn't like you came up to Solar, to the record company, and saw blue or red rags," said Chocolate. "It wasn't that type of atmosphere. Suge was never saying 'Blood' and all that."

"People were in there smoking a lot of weed and just having a good time," Lamont Bloomfield recalled. "It was like a party, actually. That's probably why the music came out so good."

Suge, however, ruined it by making his Blood-affiliated friends a permanent fixture in the recording studio. That night in July, Suge was in a blissful mood—rushing around the Solar building, taking phone calls, dropping into various studios for progress reports on how songs were coming along, greeting guests and overseeing the partying—until he saw Lynwood Stanley on his phone. Lynwood was one of the many aspiring artists surrounding Dre, an acquaintance who hoped Dre would finally make good on his word to produce his music and make him a star. At this point Dre was surrounded with this type of friend. They all wanted to be as famous as Dre's old group N.W.A, or his more recent discovery, Snoop Doggy Dogg. So they would hang around and do anything Dre asked, waiting for the day Dre finally said, "Why don't you go in the recording booth and deliver a vocal."

When Suge saw Lynwood on the phone, he told Lynwood to hang up. He needed to use the phone. Lynwood did as told and returned to the studio. Then his beeper went off and he rushed back to the phone. By now Suge felt dissed and stepped over to Lynwood. The DOC quoted Suge as saying, "Say, Blood, don't be on the phone."

Lynwood said, "Don't be coming at me with all that gangbang shit. I'm not from L.A." Suge exploded. The ensuing argument brought Lynwood Stanley's brother George, another aspiring rapper and friend of Dre's, into the room. Suge told them to stay off the phone, then left the area. Thinking the argument over, George led his brother to the company cafeteria, where he could use the pay phone in peace.

While Lynwood was on the phone, Suge marched down the third-floor hallway with a loaded semiautomatic pistol in hand. Entering the lunchroom, he aimed the gun at Lynwood and told him to hang up. Lynwood refused. Suge pushed the receiver down and aimed the gun at Lynwood's head. "W'sup?" Suge asked.

Then, according to the DOC, Suge "beat their asses! Just knocked the fuck out of them all the way back to the recording studio."

Snoop, Dre, Kurupt, and the DOC were among those who witnessed this. Once the brothers were in a room, Suge addressed the crowd. " 'Get out. Close the door. Go upstairs.' "

Lamont Bloomfield said, "We knew he was fittin'a do something scandalous, and whoever was in there was scared shitless. It was like: You're in the space in the back fucking room, fittin' to be just locked up—you can't get out this motherfucker, you don't know if you fittin'a die! It had to be a horrible feeling. I felt sorry for them."

Back in the studio, Suge punched the brothers around, then ordered them to their knees. While George obeyed, Lynwood again refused. So Suge fired a shot, then slapped Lynwood on the side of the head with the gun. If they didn't listen, he warned, he would kill them both.

"He just made them, you know, take their clothes off," said Doug Young, present that night. "He wanted to see one nigga's butt and the other butt."

When both Stanley brothers were half nude and lying facedown on the floor, Suge said he would release them. Then, in a move inspired by the film *GoodFellas*, he removed a wallet from Lynwood's trousers and rummaged through it until he found an identification card that bore their address. Just as actor Robert De Niro did in the Martin Scorsese movie, Suge said he would hold on to the card so he would know where to find them if they decided to go to the police. That his retaining the ID card wouldn't keep them from relocating, then going to the police, didn't cross his mind. The brothers were vulnerable and at Suge's mercy, and now seemed as good a time as any to determine if lines from the gangster movies he devoured at home would play well in the gang-infested Los Angeles music scene.

With Suge's permission, the Stanley brothers dressed quickly and fled the building. Suge returned to the studio and his work.

On a higher floor the artists Suge had ordered out of the studio finished smoking marijuana. "We were upstairs for about two or three minutes," said Lamont. "After one person started going back down there, it
was like follow the leader. You figured it was cool to go back down."

Downstairs, they saw blood on the studio floor. "And I was like,
'Damn, that's fucked up!'" Lamont said. Whoever had been beaten was
helpless, "with a whole building of motherfuckers against them!" He
watched as a goon began to clean up the mess and thought, "Damn,
what happened in this motherfucker? What just happened?"

The excitement eventually died down, and everyone got back to work.
A half-completed track was playing, when the phone rang. "Niggas were
still cleaning up the blood, then next thing you know, the FBI and all
that shit came. And everybody went crazy. 'The cops are coming! The
cops are coming!' Motherfuckers just ran! Like they were trying to get
out a rock house knowing cops was on the way. People were screaming,
leaving out the back, yelling, 'They coming up the elevator!'

"Others yelled, 'Take all the weapons out!' They were locking themselves in rooms—all kinds of shit. It was just a big ol' mess. Next thing
you know, the police were rushing up in that motherfucker looking for
people. I doubt it was about somebody using the telephone. I thought
that cat was in there asking somebody for chips."

Police officers entered with the Stanley brothers. "We had to wait as
they brought them back in, to point out the people who did it. The
police kinda like blocked the whole building down, and they were 'looking for Mr. Knight.'"

The Stanley brothers pointed Suge out. According to an insider,
"Suge said, 'Naw, I didn't do that.' But they got him anyway." After
visiting the studio where the attack occurred, officers dug a bullet out of
the wall. "That's how they got the police to believe Suge did it. 'Cause of
that bullet."

At first Suge planned to fight the case. The police tried to subpoena
employees like Doug Young. "I heard they were looking for me," he said.
"'Cause my coworker DJ Black told me that. And he asked me, 'Have
they talked to you yet?' I told him no. He said, 'Well, you know they
looking for you.' And I was like, 'Well, they could just keep looking.'"
Death Row had a code that forbade cooperating with police.

As the summer of 1992 was winding down, Dre was accused of attacking aspiring record producer Damon Thomas outside Thomas's home. Asked about the incident, Dre widened his eyes and arrested another grin. "Busted him up with my hands? I'm'a tell you what happened in that episode . . ." It was a sunny afternoon and Dre was with a woman in her home—leaving actually—when the woman saw this guy she thought had slept with her fourteen-year-old niece. "Something like that." He was entering his car to leave as this creep pulled up. *"She hit the mother-fucker! She hit this kid!"* The victim sustained broken ribs and a shattered jaw.

"Next thing I know this kid's saying I hit him, broke his jaw and all this kinda shit!" Nineteen ninety-two just wasn't his year. "I figure as hard as a motherfucker works to make his money, there's always somebody out there working just as hard to take that shit away. Always!" He sighed wearily. "Damn. Everybody's trying to get paid. All this shit was falling right at the same time too."

In a Van Nuys courtroom on June 2, 1992, Dre would ultimately plead guilty to a count of misdemeanor assault, pay a $10,000 fine, and be shackled with a tracking device and sentenced to ninety days electronic house arrest.

To unwind, artists and producers dropped by to lounge by Dre's swimming pool. "Snoop would kick his feet up against a wall and make a beat and rap for an hour," said Chocolate. Artists from the label brought friends from their neighborhood to drink beer, smoke marijuana, and party with Dr. Dre, Suge, a gaggle of local strippers, and eager female groupies.

Dre's parties were raucous—wilder than any thrown by Ruthless Records—and attended by the sort of gang members Dre tried to avoid during his adolescence. As Crips and Bloods drank beer and smoked weed, Dre felt a little uncomfortable. At any moment, tensions could flare. But Suge was there to protect him, to ensure that no harm came to the label's greatest asset. Troublemakers knew Suge would give them the beating of their life. "He was the man," said one frequent guest. "He had Dr. Dre. I'm sure he felt like King Tut when he walked in. Everybody went up to ask him questions but he kept to his little self. He didn't really party too much. He was trying to keep that 'Alphonso Caponey' image: Come in the room, have everybody staring in awe, go upstairs; next thing you know, he's leaving and everybody's watching him again. Suge played his role perfectly."

Despite Suge's formidable presence, the gang members reverted to type; they turned one of Dre's sociable get-togethers into an unbridled free-for-all. "Actually, after the swimming party was over," said this frequent guest, "some niggas got into it and turned the inside of Dre's house into a little boxing match." One fighter was knocking a taller opponent around Dre's extravagant living room. "And when the little dude was getting the best out of the homie, Suge and them went over there and bum-rushed the little dude. Knocked him out. But it was weak, 'cause this little nigga was hanging and whipping somebody's ass. But Suge went over and knocked the nigga out for no reason. 'Cause I guess this little dude was getting the best of Suge's friend."

The guest continued. "I saw it and couldn't believe it. If people can turn on you like that—from being so cool and partying to knocking you out—then that ain't no cool shit. I felt uncomfortable. I knew what kind of people they were right then and there. 'Cause everything was going smooth, then they got into an argument and started clearing out the way to fight. And I'm thinking, Man, everybody standing around them should be breaking that shit up. Fighting in a million-dollar Calabassas house! They shoulda been breaking it up instead of promoting it."

On another occasion, the younger brother of Dre's lumbering body-guard, B.J., got into it with Dre's hard-drinking stepbrother, producer Warren G. Once they started arguing, B.J. intervened. "Then Warren and B.J., who was Dre's right-hand man, got into it," said this frequent guest. Everyone was eager to see a fight. Warren tried to stand up for himself. B.J. was enraged. Why was Warren beefing with his brother? The brother himself was preparing for yet another fistfight in Dre's mil-lion-dollar home. The crowd began moving chairs out of the way, to give them room; some partygoers got into the fight themselves, slinging in-sults and threats at rival gangs they were forced to tolerate while working in the label's office. All hell was about to break loose. They were arguing, Suge noticed, but might soon be fighting with the hands and guns.

"Everybody was tryin'a make it a Crips and Bloods type thing," said one Death Row employee present that afternoon. "But it turned out that it wasn't. Evidently Suge got mad and slapped Warren G." The party continued. "Suge squashed their problem. Warren G and the dude—I think they made up."

One afternoon Dre invited his new friends from the label over for a barbecue. Ruthless business manager Jerry Heller, who lived a few doors away from Dre, remembered driving home and seeing flames rise from a neighbor's place. At first Heller and his girlfriend didn't think it could be anyone they knew. Until Heller saw a visibly intoxicated Dre standing by his burning home, "laughing with some of his friends."

Dre's affluent white neighbors were shocked. This sort of thing—loud music, incessant fighting, and excessive drinking—didn't happen in their quiet neighborhood. The tranquillity had been shattered; these elements, the worse the city offered, which they desperately tried to escape had taken root next door. The fire raged on as the sunny afternoon continued. Sirens blared as huge fire trucks arrived. Trying to control the flames, two firefighters were injured. The house was ruined; Dre's friends left and Dre salvaged what he could and moved into a small apartment on Venice Boulevard. When asked if the fire was caused by a "drunken barbecue," Dre laughed and said, "Oh shit. I'm'a tell you what happened with that incident. I don't know how the fire started. This is what the fireman's saying: Some motherfucking electrical problems with the air-conditioning."

There was a barbecue behind the house, he admitted. But the fire started out *front*. "One of the neighbors came over and said, 'Yo, the side of your house is on fire!' We went over there and put it out. Next thing I know, it was on the roof!" While he had to live at home again—another setback in his war with Ruthless, which was withholding payments until Dre returned to work for them—he wasn't worried. He expected to have it repaired within a year. "I'm insured," he added. "It was like $250,000 damage."

By October, Dre had most of his upcoming solo album completed. His life was a simple one. He was either at home or in the recording studio. With each passing day, however, his year was getting worse. Just as the single "Deep Cover" finally entered the *Billboard* charts, Dre had been kicked out of his apartment on Venice Boulevard. "These guys were eating chicken wings and McDonald's," one record executive told *L.A. Weekly*.

Since Dre was now living with his mother, after having been evicted from his apartment on Venice Boulevard, Suge and the Death Row entourage held their industry parties at the Solar building. The typical industry party usually features an open bar, a performance or two by upcoming bands, executives networking and passing business cards to each other, and overcaffeinated publicists trying to convince journalists to write about whatever these publicists were promoting. "It was supposed to have been a pajama party, but when I got off the elevator, I saw that everybody in there had on red outfits," said one artist who attended this Death Row event. "Except for me and my buddy, everybody wore red." This guest squeezed past a throng of slit-eyed thugs; he finally spotted the DOC sitting in the center of a horde of rowdy Bloods, his facial expression saying "Help! I didn't mean to get off the elevator either!" Even the label's artists were frightened. And for good reason. Within minutes one gang member's actions led to a fight. The Bloods charged onto the elevator and rushed down to La Cienega Boulevard. "Next thing you know," said this artist, "the guy got kinda worked over. I eased in quick and I eased *out* right quick."

The mood at the Solar building "was pretty intense," said author Brian Cross, who visited Solar to conduct an interview with Dre for his tome *It's Not About a Salary*, a study of the West Coast gangsta rap scene. "I went up there wearing a T-shirt that was red. Not even tripping. I didn't associate Dre with any of that type stuff or whatever, but Dat Nigga Daz sort of stepped to me a little bit when I came in. When I got off the elevator, he came up like admiring my shirt, but then he was on some shit: 'Why you coming up in here wearing that color?' Whatever. But Dre told him to shut up and sit down."

Snoop's cousin, the rapper RBX, couldn't understand what was happening. Death Row was supposed to be a business. Not a battlefield. Rap music was a way out of the ghetto. Suge, however, kept bringing the ghetto into their business. "My family and Suge's family just happened to have ties in the past. They used to beef or something, acting stupid." Suge's family were Bloods while RBX's were Crips. "And that just happened." RBX shrugged, willing to forget the past despite Suge always trying to goad him into a fight. "Suge would be saying '*I remember!*' " It didn't seem to matter that RBX was now an artist on the label; Suge wanted to show RBX that the Bloods were stronger. "I used to try reasoning with him. 'Aw, what can I do?' I mean—how can I be faulted for some shit my *uncle* did to your *cousin* back in 1962?! When I got to Death Row, I told Suge and everybody else, '*Man, just squash that dumb shit and start making those records!*' "

Songs were recorded but Suge didn't stop bringing his childhood friends to the office. Now that he was about to earn some serious money, he wanted to share the wealth with the Tree Top Piru members he had known since childhood. In return, they would offer loyalty and protection. "You can now say, 'When I go places, I want forty gang members with me,' " Chocolate felt. "I think that's what that was—even though Suge probably wasn't a hard-core gang member."

Despite this, Suge had a reputation for having forced Eazy-E into signing release forms for his artists. And the reputation, added to Dre's after battering Dee Barnes, made it hard for Death Row Records to secure a distribution deal. Dre's résumé listed seven platinum albums, but the violence surrounding the label frightened industry executives who otherwise wouldn't have thought twice about dealing with the company. "People didn't want to take a chance on us, and it pissed me off," said Dre. "I mean, I had talent—talent that had already been proven with huge record sales from N.W.A. So you had to wonder what the fuck the problem was."

"I ALWAYS KNEW SUGE WAS A REAL GANGSTER"

In November 1992, Suge and Dr. Dre had entered into serious talks with Interscope Records, a two-year-old label run by Jimmy Iovine, the son of a Brooklyn longshoreman who had grown up around noisome Italian and Latin hoodlums before pursuing a career in the music business. After working to become a well-respected engineer, Iovine moved into production, working with artists like Bruce Springsteen, Tom Petty, U2 *(Rattle and Hum),* and John Lennon.

As his career slowed down, Iovine married an attorney (and former *Playboy* centerfold), had kids, and moved into a beautiful oceanfront mini-mansion in Malibu. When Marshall Field retailing scion Ted Field called in 1990 to offer a job, Iovine asked for more details. Field explained that the new label was a $30-million joint venture with Warner Bros. and could easily keep up with the other labels sprouting up, among them, Giant, Hollywood, Morgan Creek, Imago, and Zoo. Iovine listened but considered Field's reputation: After growing up rich in Chicago and Alaska—attending college and racing cars—Field moved to sunny Los

Angeles and immediately became immersed in the Hollywood lifestyle. In the early '80s Field was known as a hedonist who chased blondes but wanted to make films; he started a film company and produced commercial successes like *The Hand That Rocks the Cradle, Three Men and a Baby,* and *Outrageous Fortune.* Suddenly people took Ted Field, a white millionaire who sported a graying ponytail, seriously.

Then Field wanted to form a record label called Interscope: His first move was to recruit Tom Whalley. As head of the A&R (artist and repertoire) department at Capitol, Whalley signed the group Crowded House and worked with Bonnie Raitt. At first Whalley was reluctant to meet with Field: He felt Field might be just another trust-fund kid trying to suddenly become a music mogul. "I said, 'No thanks,' " Whalley said. "Then people told me, 'Everything Ted does, he does very well." Whalley joined Interscope. Then Ted Field called Jimmy Iovine.

"Some said Jimmy was not a guy who could run a record company," Field told *Rolling Stone.* "Tom had been at Capitol. We were kind of a ragamuffin band of guys starting a record company." As Field explained the label to him, Iovine knew the odds would be against Interscope. But at his first meeting with Field, he instantly liked him. Iovine came on board.

Now Suge Knight and Dr. Dre appeared in Interscope's offices, asking Iovine to be involved with their new label, Death Row. Iovine had heard all the rumors about Suge. "But I just knew they had great music and that they were a bunch of guys who wanted to make it out of the ghetto. That's something I can understand."

Ted Field was equally vocal in his support. "Dre—it's no accident that everything he touches turns to gold. He's a musical genius."

Despite their adulation, Suge said Interscope was initially cool toward Dre's album. "They didn't get it. They was sitting around the room, looking at each other, trying to figure it out." Suge tried to convince them that Dre's mellow duet with Snoop, "Nuthin' but a 'G' Thang," would be the song of the decade. Iovine and Field didn't agree. "So we said, 'Fuck it.' I snatched the tape up and we left the meeting. When we came back, we had the entire album completed—artwork, video treatment, marketing plan, everything."

Suge continued. "The guys in the corporate suites have so little respect for rap, they actually told me that Dre did not deserve to get the same amount of royalties they pay pop acts. I remember sitting there, trying to explain to those guys that Dre was a genius and that we were about to create this hugely successful record label, but they would just look at me like I was fucking crazy."

By November, after Dre posed on the cover of *The Source* pointing a .44 Smith & Wesson handgun to his own temple, Iovine had changed his opinion. Now he felt Dre was a genius and wanted to sign him and his label to a deal. During negotiations between Death Row and Interscope, Dre's former label, Ruthless, filed a multimillion-dollar lawsuit against Death Row, Sony, Solar Records and its head, Dick Griffey. Dre's work on the *Deep Cover* soundtrack, Eazy-E felt, constituted a flagrant "breach of contract." "It's like being married to one person then marrying two others: being married to three people."

While Suge feared that the Death Row/Interscope deal would crumble, Iovine worked even harder to make it happen. He knew Eazy was reluctant to free Dre from his contract—and that Dre refused to honor the terms of his deal with Ruthless. The only way to settle this, Iovine knew, was to pay Ruthless and Death Row and get both to agree that Interscope should distribute Dre's newest album. In a deal finalized on December 3, Interscope signed an agreement with Ruthless that recognized Dre's contracts with Ruthless. As part of the agreement, Ruthless assigned its rights to Dre as an exclusive producer and artist to Interscope. For this Interscope would pay Ruthless a percentage of royalties from anything Dre produced for Interscope. "If Dre leaves Interscope," Ruthless attorney Michael Borbeau reported, "all rights to him as a producer and artist revert back to Ruthless."

While the Interscope deal called for Eazy never to disclose the amount he made from each Dre production, he did say, "I probably make more off of Dre's albums than he does. He should have stayed with me and done his solo stuff. He'd be a lot better off."

Jerry Heller said, "We licensed *The Chronic* just to mitigate our damages. That record would've been ours if it hadn't been stolen."

Now that Interscope would distribute *The Chronic*, Iovine became one of Suge's most vocal supporters. While everyone else dealt with the violent Suge, Iovine got a chance to see Suge as CEO: choosing artwork and promotional materials, picking out singles and B sides, casting directors and female extras for videos, deciding where parties would be held, composing guest lists, and telling his artists what to wear. Thanks to Suge's ability to shape street culture for mass consumption, Death Row became the first rap label to get their videos in regular rotation on MTV. "They told us there was no way in hell that we were going to end up owning our own masters," Suge said years later. "They laughed at us when we said we were going to get a gangsta rap single on mainstream radio. Ain't nobody out there laughing now, are they?"

Following the deal, Suge reinvented himself: From silent behind-the-scenes enforcer, he took to promoting himself as a great businessman. He told anyone who would listen that he would be the next Berry Gordy, and that Death Row would be the Motown of the '90s. Despite Interscope promising to return Dre to Ruthless if Dre ever left Interscope, Suge told a reporter, "If we leave Interscope, we take Snoop, *The Chronic*, everything. That's ownership. That's independence."

In the studio, Dre was putting the finishing touches on *The Chronic*, a solo album that sounded more like a commercial for Death Row, or one long endorsement for NORML (National Organization for the Reform of Marijuana Laws). On every song, strange new artists like Rage, RBX, or Tha Dogg Pound would say rhymes seemingly built around the label's name or smoking pot. For music, Dre abandoned the old dusty records he used for N.W.A albums and enlisted live musicians to produce drowsy cover versions of songs by Parliament-Funkadelic ("Chocolate City"), Tom Browne ("Funkin' for Jamaica"), Marvin Gaye ("Inner City Blues"), and others.

"But Dre's work, even judged purely as pop artifice, was dreadful," wrote author Jory Farr. "Though he was touted as a 'genius' by many critics, his music was a throwback to a soulless period in black culture. Instead of ingenious sampling fused to a ferocious live performance, Dre served up lame raps over monotonous bass and drums. In seven years, gangsta rap had gone nowhere and Dre was the embodiment of that stagnation."

Lyrically, Dre spent much of *The Chronic* discussing his hatred for Eazy-E, his contempt for the police, his love of old funk music, and his recently acquired marijuana habit. In 1988, on N.W.A's song "Express Yourself," Dre had rapped, "I don't smoke weed or sinse [a Jamaican strain of marijuana]/ 'cause it only gives a brother brain damage/ and brain damage on the mike don't manage." By 1991, however, the South-gate Los Angeles rap group Cypress Hill had released their eponymously titled debut album—celebrating incessant marijuana use on songs like "Stoned Is the Way of the Walk." After Cypress Hill sold a million albums, and appeared on a best-selling cover of *High Times* magazine, rappers who once derided drug use finally admitted to being heavy smokers. On *The Chronic*, Dre sang: "Make my bud the chronic. I want to get fucked up."

As Dre was finishing the album, videographer Matt McDaniel dropped by the Solar building to say hello. A friend from the days when Dre played records for local radio station KDAY, McDaniel also interviewed Dre's group, N.W.A, for various magazines. Like other Los Angelenos, McDaniel heard stories about Suge and Eazy-E. "Basically, I heard that Suge went and pulled a gun on Eazy and got him to release Dre. I didn't really believe any of that. But it actually turned out to be, you know, kinda true."

Dre was working on a song about the Los Angeles riots. He was especially proud of the sound bite of dialogue that prefaced the song. "He used audio from some old blaxploitation movie." The song, titled "Mr. Officer," was a verbal attack on specific LAPD officers. For the chorus, Dre got most of the label's roster to join him in "We-Are-the-World" fashion, chanting, "Mr. Officer, Mr. Officer, I wanna see you laying in a coffin, sir." At song's end, McDaniel remembered that Dre looked glum. Dre said Death Row's new distributor, Interscope, was forcing him to remove the song from the album. In light of the uproar caused by rapper Ice-T's song "Cop Killer," which stirred politicians to clamor for scrutiny of the rap music industry, "Mr. Officer's" themes were too controversial. Though concerned with Dre's subject matter, Interscope's official reason for pulling the song from the album had to do with the audio dialogue Dre used for its intro. The owners of the old film wouldn't grant Dre the right to use the audio, he was told. And the song wouldn't work as well without it.

"Dre couldn't get the movie clips cleared and they were just gonna take it off," McDaniel said. "So I started explaining to him about some of the audio from my video." He gave Dre a copy of his latest documentary, *Birth of a Nation 4-29-1992*, which detailed the Rodney King riots.

Dre was excited about the documentary and promised to pay for use of McDaniel's audio material. But the filmmaker never received a penny. "We never really got to work out a dollar amount," he admitted. When he alluded to being paid, Dre would become visibly agitated. Fearing he'd lose the opportunity to have his work seen by a worldwide audience, McDaniel decided to forego payment. "Look," he told Dre, "whatever we do, the most important thing to me is credit. And get me a framed disc if it goes platinum."

Eventually, McDaniel formally introduced himself to Suge Knight. "I'll never forget it," Matt McDaniel said.

McDaniel was in a recording studio at the Solar building, watching Dre coach performers on how to deliver their lyrics, when a huge, muscular black man entered and everyone grew still and silent. Suge took a seat and started talking about Eazy; McDaniel was in awe and said, "Oh, you're Suge?" Suge's eyes met his, searching for signs of hostility. Unnerved by the stare, McDaniel quickly added, "Yeah, I heard a lot of stories about you."

Deciding that McDaniel posed no threat, Suge chuckled at the fear he had inspired. "I kinda understood from the way people reacted to him that he was 'the man,'" McDaniel added. "He was serious. Everyone gave big respect when they dealt with him. He wasn't just 'another homie.'"

On the streets, McDaniel explained, Suge Knight was already a legend. "At the time, Eazy-E was the perceived bad guy. People used to tell me, at their meetings with Jerry Heller at Ruthless, Jerry would have one of his bodyguards sitting up there, showing a weapon in his side holster and reading gun magazines, basically trying to intimidate people. As if to say, 'Don't start no shit, won't be no shit.' When Suge came on the scene, it was like—all of these people who were supposed to be the shit? Suge was just taking them out!"

With news of Dre's new label came interest from national music magazines. But Suge had no desire to be in the limelight. While magazines like *Rolling Stone, Spin,* and *The Source* asked about his involvement in the Vanilla Ice and Eazy-E incidents, Suge would discuss only Death Row's formation, early meetings with Jimmy Iovine, and Interscope's misgivings about Dre recording a solo album. "He told me they put *The Chronic* together, then presented it as a completed package," said *Source* writer Dream Hampton. "Then I asked about the thing with Eric, about him pulling a bat. Suge was a big guy and he said, 'That's some Hollywood shit. I ain't gotta pull no gun on Eric. Motherfuckers who can't make hit records need to make up stories. Do I look like I need to pull a gun or a bat on Eric?'" With that, he ended this five-minute conversation.

At the label's first show, held at the small downtown nightclub the Casa, Matt McDaniel learned how secretive Suge could be. The event was supposed to be nothing but an intimate test run for the lighting and sound effects the label hoped to bring to stadium arenas. The show, however, drew a standing-room-only crowd. Matt McDaniel filmed the concert from the audience. Onstage, Dre and Snoop held microphones and performed "Deep Cover" in unison. The crowd was ecstatic; while singing along, they waved their arms from side to side. McDaniel filmed the arms swaying, and behind them Dre and Snoop holding microphones and pacing around the rainbow-lit stage. When McDaniel noticed Suge nodding his head to Dre's compelling instrumental, he tried to include Suge in the scene, aiming the camera lens in Suge's direction, only to see Suge immediately leap out of the way. "I always knew Suge was a real gangster," McDaniel said. "I knew that vibe. I always knew that real gangsters would not want to be taped. Not to mention the countless 'I got beat up by Suge' stories," McDaniel quipped.

Despite the fear Suge inspired, people still wanted to work with the label: Dre's reputation was just as tarnished, but that wouldn't stop his albums from continuing to sell millions of copies. By then, in fact, hip-hop was becoming a grim art form. In the past, Dre's attacking Dee Barnes would have led to his album being boycotted and his being black-listed from appearing in reputable music magazines or television shows. But the attack seemed to impress segments of his multicultural audience, the beating serving as proof that Dre really was the gangster he portrayed on N.W.A records.

Like everyone else who would work at Death Row, promoter Doug Young was ambitious. He wanted a job but didn't dare approach Suge. Instead, he asked Dre, whom he had known since his days at Ruthless. Dre was easier to deal with and—despite the one or two fights he got into while drunk—only pretended to be a merciless gangster.

Young admitted that he used Dre's October 1990 attack on Dee Barnes as leverage. Interscope was preparing to release *The Chronic* (in conjunction with Death Row and Priority Records, both listed as co-distributors on the album sleeve). But Dre was facing serious consequences for battering Barnes. Aware of this, Doug Young offered a trade. "I'm about to tell you the truth and you can put it down the way you want to. I knew I had that on them, and they needed my, either testimony, or saying I ain't testifying when the D.A. called me." By taking Dre's side, Young knew he would hurt Dee Barnes's case. But the job at Death Row was a once-in-a-lifetime opportunity. It seemed that every album Dre produced was a major chart-topping success, and here was a chance to get in on the ground floor of his newest venture. "After Dre whupped her ass, I was there," Young explained. "So I told him, 'Look, I won't say nothing if you can guarantee me the job at Death Row.' It was kinda slimy, but I had to do it."

Impressed by how Doug promoted N.W.A's albums, Dre gave him a job in the promotion department, where Doug would have to convince program directors at radio stations nationwide to begin playing the album—a job accomplished by lengthy phone calls, visits, free tickets to concerts, free promotional T-shirts, copies of upcoming albums months before their actual release date, and incessant adulation. At Death Row, Doug worked alongside Kim, the office manager; Roy Tesfay, the receptionist at the time and later "a big partner"; Kevin "DJ Black" Connell, whom Suge hired after hearing him spin records at a Los Angeles nightclub; Sharitha Knight (nee Golden, who had reconciled with Suge after he threatened her family, tampered with her car, and hacked off her ponytail—marrying him and giving birth to his daughter), and, of course, Marion "Suge" Knight, the CEO responsible for breaking Doug's tooth that night Dre attacked Dee.

A month later, *The Chronic* was released. That same day, articles of incorporation were filed for Death Row Records listing Suge Knight and Dre as the company's sole directors. GF Entertainment had been moved out of the picture, and with it, by Michael Harris's account, his hold on Death Row's profits. Even though, on the album's liner notes, Dre acknowledged Harris with a heading that reads: "Special thanks to Harry-O."

Seeing the album in stores, Matt McDaniel finally felt that his decision to forego payment had been a wise one. He loved how Dre had used his audio material and said, "People reacted to me immediately." True to his word, Dre had given him a credit on the album—"Live L.A. riot scenes on 'The Day the Niggaz Took Over' & 'Lil Ghetto Boy' Provided by Matt McDaniel." Immediately, McDaniel's work offers doubled.

The Chronic became the highest-selling hard-core rap album of all time. It remained in *Billboard*'s Top 10 for eight months. At Ruthless Records, Jerry Heller and Eazy-E kept calculating how many millions of dollars Ruthless could've earned. In addition to selling three million albums, *The Chronic* also changed the direction of rap music: Artists now rushed to deliver lyrics about smoking pot over keyboards riffs as heavy as those Dre had used.

Death Row Records moved into 10900 Wilshire Boulevard, near Westwood. The door to its suite of offices led to Interscope as well. "It was just a little ragtag, piece-of-ass beige office that was really ugly," said Doug Young. At first Doug spent his time creating proposals, dealing with product allotments, and conducting daily business with Interscope. He shared an office with promoter Kevin ("DJ Black") Connell, a former

New York City DJ who relocated to Los Angeles in 1986 and met Suge while spinning records in a club one night.

Soon Suge began to hire ex-convicts like Lip Dogg to keep watch over the office, said a label insider. "Lip spent more than half his life in prison. He was a very mean and intimidating guy, about six feet three, like Suge, just as big too. Big scars all over his head. All kinds of knife wounds from getting shanked in jail. Bullet wounds. A big motherfucker. He used to sit there and smoke Camels with no butt. Now, can you imagine that dude?"

The Death Row office was soon overrun with Bloods. "The gang shit was something I had to deal with," said Doug. "The left side of the room was all Bloods; the right side would be all Crips. You had to understand: That office was so fucked up when you first went up there. I don't think it was intentionally divided—Bloods or Crips. That's just the way it was."

These gang members sat on stools, chain-smoking Newports and Kools and telling each other stories about gang wars or bloody prison fights. "Telling crazy stories," Young sighed. "And when you looked down at their shoes, they had guns tucked in them." The office had the feel of a prison cellblock. The towering convicts would loom over weaker employees, then relieve them of their "lunch money." Suge's henchmen were indirect about it, asking, "You gon' buy us a pizza today, uh? How much you got on our pizza? Whatchu got on that pizza?"

People who tried to chat with them were attacked. "You'd be thinking you're just gonna hang out, then these motherfuckers would pull a Dr. Jekyl and Sister Hyde on you."

People who came to the office uninformed met these ex-convict gang members under less than ideal circumstances. Messengers and business associates had their pockets patted down and money taken. "And Suge just covered up for their group."

Eventually Doug kept himself going by telling himself that working for the label was similar to pledging in a fraternity. "There were just certain things people knew they were gonna go through," he explained. "You were either down with it or you weren't."

He tried to stay on their good side but knew why they were in the office. Suge wasn't the type to take someone to court; he had no patience for extensive proceedings. Why pay an arm and a leg in legal costs when situations could be handled directly in minutes?

If Suge felt someone was trying to cheat him, the offender would be dragged into a storeroom by his goons and pounded to a bloody pulp. Death Row employees went about their filing and faxing as blood-curdling shrieks filled the office. They saw the doorknob jerking, knowing that people were desperately trying to escape a beating, thinking, *I'm trying to get out this motherfucking room that they done locked this door on!* Even young black women were dragged into the room: While being battered, these women screamed, *"Roy! Roy!"* They hoped Suge's assistant, Roy Tesfay, would call these psychopaths off.

"There'd be two motherfuckers beating a woman up for doing something that was 'wrong,'" said an insider. "They'd beat the bitch *down!*" The insider sat forward in a seat. "Niggas done beat the bitch *down!*" He rose to his feet and swung both fists, imitating moves and attitudes. "Beat the bitch down! You understand what I'm saying? And wouldn't hesitate! 'Cause these are some messed-out-the-ass motherfuckers! The mentality is prison."

"I just know it was fucked up," said one Death Row artist. "It shouldn't have gone down that way. I don't think there's nothing that can't be handled by two people sitting down and talking. Nobody should put no hands on nobody."

To distract himself from the screams, Doug Young made phone calls. "It was a non-reaction after a while." He would tell himself, "Wasn't none of your business." As long as it wasn't happening to him, he wasn't worried. "And no," he remembered thinking, "I'm not going out there to look. So that way I ain't gotta be no witness."

At night Doug would reflect on the day's events. Working at Death Row was the most stressful experience he ever had in this industry. But he always looked on the bright side. It wasn't happening to him. "I'd smoke a joint, drink a beer, and take my ass to sleep," he said. "Be in a deep coma."

During the day, however, he eagerly grabbed any opportunity to leave the office. He would make deliveries to the studio. He would grab the phone and dive into conversations. He would rush to arrange flight times with travel agents, and book hotel rooms in other cities. "And that's just how I rolled," he explained. "Got up there, got all the T-shirts and hats and posters and whatever we were gonna need to take on the road with us."

With his coworker DJ Black, he would leave the office on Wednesday and return to California on Sunday—on the road, he gladhanded radio station program directors, arranged meetings between touring acts and local journalists, handed out free T-shirts emblazoned with logos promoting the label's acts, and generally made sure everyone was thinking positive thoughts about the company. Monday morning he would return to the office and immediately plan for their next trip. By Tuesday he knew what city he would visit next. "We didn't have to be up there every day," Doug said with gratitude.

Eventually, employees banded together and calmly expressed their fears to Suge. "After a while he cut that down. He did. People brought it to his attention, but somehow it always filtered back to that."

When Suge ordered his friends to leave the office, they moved their get-togethers to Can-Am Studios, an unmarked one-story recording facility in the suburb of Tarzana that Death Row was now using for every release. If anyone saw Dr. Dre, it was in this studio. He didn't want anything to do with Suge's barbaric friends. "Dre's office was the studio," said one Death Row rapper. "Suge's office was the office. When I was present, they never crossed paths too much at all. Unless it was in the studio. They were homies, but even homies get into shit."

Soon, artists and label employees working out of Can-Am complained about Suge's friends: These Bloods were arguing with rival gang members, artists, and employees; they were trying to extort anyone they considered weak; they distracted people from their work; they were drinking heavily and trying to goad people into fights; they scared everyone with tales of murder, robbery, and vicious assaults; they threatened to rape males who offended them.

Once more Suge acted, telling his henchmen to clear out of the studio. "Everybody filtered back," Doug Young lamented. One by one the Bloods returned to their stools in Death Row's office. Employees were aghast. "They'd cool out for a week, then filter back! It was a constant rotation of this: from the office to the studio, then back again."

Finally, Suge began to ignore his employees' complaints. These purported "criminals" were his childhood friends. If Death Row employees couldn't cope with having them around, then maybe these employees needed to find work elsewhere. "A lot of niggas were getting fucked up," one Death Row artist, also a Crip, remembered. One of his friends, a producer, had been slapped. "He got into some shit in the studio with [a Blood] and next thing you know, he offended Suge. He said Suge slapped the shit out of him. I said, 'Wow.' He said, 'Dog, that nigga straight slapped me!' And I took it like, 'What? And you didn't do shit?' He didn't 'cause there were too many niggas around and he didn't want eight or nine of them to trip on him."

As Death Row's staff of ten tried to promote the label's releases, members of various Blood gangs continued to police the office, carry out Suge's orders, and use the storeroom as a makeshift torture chamber. "There'd always be a gang of them in there," Doug Young groaned. "On one side of the room, four or five of them Bloods walking around, telling employees, 'I heard you was pissed, Blood! And you stopped the meeting!' Then you go over to this side of the room, and Crips were saying: 'Cuz this, cuz and cuz!' You understand what I'm saying? This was every day at work. Every day! They were all on you until you felt, 'I can't wait to go out of town!' "

A flower child at heart, Doug nonetheless considered bringing a handgun to work. Crip members who worked for the label were also cautious; they banded together, kept to their side of the room, and tried not to notice that some of their coworkers were members of gangs that on the streets normally killed each other on sight.

Though Suge was always on his best behavior around Interscope's Jimmy Iovine and Ted Field, word of these intraoffice atrocities spread throughout the recording industry. Still, the Interscope staff was always treated cordially. "And that was one of the things that was very, very strange," said Young. "As ghetto as the mentality was at Death Row, none of the drama ever crossed over to Interscope's side of the building. It was always just peace."

Asked if Interscope knew of the beatings, Doug almost yelled, "Of course they did!"

"EVEN AFTER 'THE CHRONIC' CAME OUT, I WAS BROKE AND STARVING"

In Pennsylvania, Sam "Sneed" Anderson went from loving Sugar Hill rap records to promoting local shows and creating beats. After booking New York rapper Kevin "K-Solo" Madison and playing him a demo, Sam was invited to New York to work on Solo's second album for Atlantic, 1992's *Time's Up*. There he met his idols, EPMD (an acronym for Erick and Parrish Making Dollars). But the Long Island–based rap duo was breaking up. Before finally splitting, however, the duo dragged their Hit Squad of artists on the road for one last tour.

"Even before the tour, I always had plans of hooking up with Dre," said Sam. "I thought Dre was the illest producer and pooled my resources to try to find people who knew him." When the tour hit Sacramento, Sam was partying with female groupies. "And one of them said that she used to baby-sit for Michel'lé, you know, Dre's son. She said, 'I got his phone number,' and I ain't believe her but stayed in contact until she gave it to me."

At first he was reluctant to call. "Then one day I came to my grand-mother's house and she said, 'Some guy from California called you.' But it wasn't Dre that called. It was another guy who was trying to hook me up with Dre."

When Sam finally got Dre on the phone, he was shocked to discover that Dre already knew who he was. Still, Sam was nervous. "I asked if he was interested in a project I was trying to put in effect: a guy named Black Caesar, who was also from Pittsburgh. And Dre was saying they just started with the label and had too many artists. But he was still interested in what the guy sounded like. So one day I had the guy on the phone so Dre could hear him, and Dre was just stunned. He said, 'Man, y'all need to come down here.'"

Sam and Black Caesar accepted the invitation and flew to California at their own expense. "He showed mad love, put us up in the place he was staying at, and it was on."

Dre lived in an enormous French colonial house in West Valley, near doctors, lawyers, and businessmen with seven-figure annual salaries. When Dre looked out the window, instead of Crips and Bloods, he saw miniature golf courses, fake French châteaus, and locations for old west-ern films. After a day of work he would park his Ferrari in the garage, hang up his jacket, and settle in a patio chair by the pool with a glass of white wine.

The label's other artists, meanwhile, were still going through hard times. "Even after *The Chronic* came out, I was broke and starving," said Nate Dogg. "I used to sell dope to get gas money to go to Solar Records to do *The Chronic* and *DoggyStyle*. Wasn't nobody making money right then." Nate hoped to follow up his critically acclaimed appearances on Dre's album with an album of his own: Unlike countless aspiring rap artists, Nate didn't view the music as a forum for political discussion. For him, and Death Row, the music was a way to get paid. As Nate wrote lyrics and thought up melodies for a rap/R&B fusion album he felt would sell millions of copies, Suge kept stepping in: Once Suge heard Nate's song 'Ain't No Fun,' he ordered that it appear on Snoop's album. At the time, Warren G was working on his own album, having finally accepted that he, Snoop, and Nate would no longer be the group 213. Another of

Nate's songs, a collaboration with Warren titled "Regulate," was placed on Warren's album.

After claiming this was fine, Nate admitted, "Actually, I used to be mad about it, thinking, 'Damn, what's my album gonna sound like if I keep giving songs away?'" To calm himself, he remembered that no matter what, he was making music and receiving token payments from Suge. Things, he knew, could be a lot worse. He could still be in Long Beach, hating his life and worrying about his future. "All of a sudden I had hope. I dealt with not having money for a long, long time. Actually all the way up till whenever my album comes out. That's how long. Since back then."

Snoop was installed in another apartment close to the Solar building. His roommates were his cousin Daz of Tha Dogg Pound and Lil' Malik of Illegal. After a tense meeting with Suge Knight in 1991, Rowdy Records owner Dallas Austin reluctantly allowed Malik to appear on albums by rival label Death Row. When Malik arrived in California, he appeared on Snoop's "Pump Pump" and seemed to have been inducted into the Death Row family. "But he was just a little kid," said *Source* magazine writer Dream Hampton. "He just really seemed to look up to Snoop. Before that, Lil' Malik used to be around Treach, and that's actually where I first met him." Anthony "Treach" Criss was the front man for New Jersey rap group Naughty by Nature, which produced commercial hits like "O.P.P." and "Hip-Hop Hooray" for their label Tommy Boy Records. "He was a little quieter when he was with Treach," Dream recalled. "Snoop acted like a little boy with Malik, while Treach was like a man, saying, 'This is my son.'"

"When Snoop was living in that apartment, he didn't have any furniture," said author Brian Cross. "He had a car and an apartment with no furniture."

Poverty and the lengthy process of recording his album took its toll: At times Snoop's spirits flagged. Seated at the mixing board, Dr. Dre reassured him that his music would pay off. Though Snoop might not have been able to see beyond his immediate troubles, Dre urged him to be patient. "You're going to be the biggest thing to black people since the straightening comb," Dre said.

*   *   *

Now that Death Row was successful, the label's inner circle had expanded. Along with Nate Dogg, Kurupt, Daz, Rage, Warren G, Snoop, and the DOC—artists who partied with him while recording *The Chronic*, Dre also hobnobbed with newcomers to the label like Hugg, D-Ruff (son of late Temptations member David Ruffin), D-Ruff's bassist, Tony Green, volatile guitarist Ricky Rouse, and Snoop's short, muscle-bound bodyguard McKinley "Malik" Lee. Though new arrival Sam Sneed was eager to work—having waited years to finally have a chance to work with esteemed instrumentalist Dre—Sam's first few days in Dre's home were spent "just hanging out," Sam Sneed recalled. "We weren't even working on nothing at the time. We were really just getting familiar with each other, you know what I'm sayin'? I let him hear a few things I had on tape and that was basically it." Throughout the partying, Sam came to realize that next on Dre's list of priorities was an album for Snoop Doggy Dogg, which would also be filled with cameos by many of the artists partying in Dre's home.

When the label's artists visited, Dre sat and joined them in talking tough, drinking hard liquor, and smoking marijuana. The latter was a habit picked up after leaving his old group, N.W.A; smoking pot had become such an obsession, Dre had devoted most of *The Chronic* (a California slang term for marijuana) to discussing its virtues, and planned to do the same for Snoop's debut. At the time, Dre believed that marijuana was a healthier, safer habit than drinking alcohol. He didn't know that despite the claims of other potheads, smoking marijuana could become a psychological addiction. With all his friends over, he turned the stereo volume to its highest setting and blasted a mixture of demo tapes and current rap and R&B hits. His guests filled the air with loud curses, insults, threats, and dreams of success. Sam Sneed, who also partied with them, noticed how tight knit the Death Row records camp was: It was a change from the tense silences he encountered in the EPMD camp right before EPMD disbanded. The artists at Death Row were committed to working hard to make the label a success. Sam came to see these artists, and Dre, as hardworking young black people. He was grateful that the others accepted him into what he realized was a sort of family. "I mean, everybody showed me love, man. Everybody."

Numb from heavy drinking and smoking weed, Dre didn't realize how loud his parties actually were. When his wealthy neighbors voiced complaints, he was shocked. While they protested, he listened politely. His new friends, just as high as he was, stood in the background, ready to pounce on anyone they felt insulted their gracious host and artistic benefactor. Dre waited until the neighbors seemed to be finished talking, then slammed the door in their faces. "I paid a mil-plus for this house," he reasoned, "so I figure I can do whatever the fuck I want to do in it. As far as I'm concerned, this house right here is the only house on the block."

At the time, Dre was under house arrest: After breaking the jaw of aspiring record producer Damon Thomas—after Thomas caught Dre cheating with his girlfriend—Dre was convicted (for misdemeanor assault), shackled with an electronic monitoring anklet, and sentenced to remain in his home. If he wasn't home when police officers called, Dre would be violating the terms of his sentence, an arrest warrant would be issued, and Dre would be imprisoned. When producer Sam Sneed arrived, Dre was bored with being indoors; his parties were a way to ease his tension.

Dre was able to use his position at Death Row to bend a few rules. Under the pretense of conducting important music-related business, "we did a lot of clubbing then," Sam admitted. "Every week we were just chillin'. Out having fun." The get-togethers at Dre's house also continued.

One night the authorities allowed Dre to attend a business meeting at a nearby restaurant. Dre took Sam Sneed along and introduced the new producer to Suge Knight, but without noting that Suge was CEO of the label. Initially Sam thought slang-talking, casually attired Suge was just another of Dre's distant party-buddies. "I was ignorant at that time. I thought Dre was the one running everything. Suge was pretty down-low about it. I didn't know he was the man really running and controlling the label."

That night Suge wouldn't speak with Sam; he shook Sam's hand, then turned to Dre to get down to discussing important business. Sam slumped in his chair, ate quietly, and tried to stay out of their way. "Man, I was just playing my part," Sam said, "trying to create music. We would spend time in the studio. We would go in there all the time, working on Snoop's album. That was all it was with Dre: from the studio to the crib. 'Cause Dre was still on house arrest all that time, so he had to be at the crib right after the studio."

Much as he did with *The Chronic*, Dre was assembling Snoop's *Doggy-Style* one component at a time—recording a batch of songs and choosing the most powerful moments. After spending hours on a song, Dre would shake his head, turn away from the Akai MPC60 sampler, and toss the reel tape into a growing pile against a wall. "There's thirty-five or thirty-six reels of Snoop in there," Dre said. "Each reel holds three songs. So far, I have five that I like. That's just a small example of how . . . how deep I'm going into this album. I feel that the tracks that I'm doing for him right now are the future of the funk. I've never heard of the perfect hip-hop album, but I'd like to make one."

Thanks to the entourage—artists like Snoop, Tha Dogg Pound, the DOC, and a few of their hard-drinking gang-affiliated buddies—Dre and Snoop were ejected from nine studios (including the Village Recorder, the Complex, TRAX, Larrabee North, Larrabee West, and the Enterprise). As pressure to finish the album mounted, Dre began to ask newcomer Sam Sneed for help: Sneed provided "verbal ideas," including Snoop's "Intro," based on the hot-tub scene from Gordon Parks's film *Superfly*. Suge offered unsolicited opinions.

"I remember one time Suge was mad!" said a label employee. "Them fools were in there doing their verses and making Snoop's album." Enraged, Suge arrived at the recording studio and confronted Snoop, Tha Dogg Pound, and Warren G, who were recording "Ain't No Fun." "Suge said, 'Man, every time I come in here, y'all talking that Crip Crip shit!'" Suge wanted his Crip-associated artists to also promote the Bloods gang in their songs. After all, Suge implied, it was *his* record label and he clearly favored the Bloods. Snoop and other artists ignored Suge's mandate; but Warren G, who had been slapped in the face by Suge at a party held near Dre's swimming party, was terrified. "That's when Warren G said, '6-4 Chevy, *red* to be exact,'" a label employee said. "For Suge. 'Cause Suge was getting mad in the studio."

Snoop grew resentful. Despite their friendship, Dr. Dre represented the record company, and record executives would say anything to get an artist to do their bidding. In addition, Dre had shoved Nate Dogg and Warren G aside and seemed to be taking all the credit for the work the entire roster was responsible for. In interviews, Snoop tried to promote his former band mate Warren. "Look out for my DJ Warren G, the one who plugged me up with Dre, to produce some tracks," Snoop told a reporter. "He's the bomb-ass nigga! And I'm gonna let my cousin Daz get down too."

Despite these claims, Snoop realized that in the studio Dre would continue to be in charge. As Dre suggested ideas for songs, Snoop began to see Dre as a control freak who could always be counted on to shoot down Snoop's best ideas. "Dre was more or less a visionist [sic]," Snoop told me later. "He'd say, 'I wanna do the whole album! I got a vision of this album! You just rap on this song about this! Do this or go in there and freestyle on this and I'm'a put it all together!'"

At the time, Tha Dogg Pound—Snoop's cousin Daz and rapper Kurupt—were also getting tired of Dre's overbearing studio manner. A newcomer to creating music, Daz nonetheless felt jealous that Dre was singled out for praise in every article written about the label; rapper Kurupt wanted to finally be allowed to record a solo album featuring the sort of sophisticated East Coast rhymes he truly enjoyed. The Lady of Rage was upset that her own album, despite a promise from Suge and Dre, would not be Death Row's premiere release. Now she was reduced to guest-starring on albums for misogynist rappers whose large white audiences devoured every lyric about sex, violence, and the Los Angeles gang subculture that annually claimed the lives of hundreds of young black and Latino men. Warren G was tired of playing second fiddle to Dr. Dre: Warren tried to create beats and win his stepbrother's respect, but Dre wasn't interested in promoting him as an artist: To Warren, it became obvious that Death Row claimed they wanted 213, but needed only his vocalist, Snoop.

Despite their resentments, which were well hidden, videographer Matt McDaniel said the artists still respected Dre. "When the artists would just be chillin'—smoking blunts, freestyling, playing around, doing whatever they doing—if the phone rang and it was Dre? Everyone would get quiet. They would hang on every word he was saying."

Snoop, however, wanted to exert a little control over his own career. When it came time to design the cover for *DoggyStyle*, Snoop put his foot down: No matter what anyone said, he wanted another of his cousins, recently released from the penitentiary, to provide the cover illustration. Suge and Dre agreed: The album cover hit stores and led to its creator being commissioned to design the Snoop-themed promotional posters requested by the makers of St. Ides malt liquor. "Now *he's* getting paid," said Nate.

"SUGE PULLED OUT A GUN, GAVE IT TO HIS HOMIE, AND WAS LIKE, 'HOLD THIS'"

When **The Chronic** sold a million units, Dre sent Matt McDaniel the framed platinum disc he promised and an invitation to a party. McDaniel hadn't received one penny for the use of his audio material, but the album had brought him more work on film sets. Even though he would have preferred cash, McDaniel decided to forget about it and move on. He decided to attend the Death Row party.

By now Suge had Bloods present in Death Row's office and studio sessions. " 'Cause that's where Suge was from and those were his people," said a label employee. "That's who he was employing and taking care of."

"When he first started Death Row," said a Rolling 60s Crip, "he may have had two or three people with him—little bitty dudes. But he got that loot, so you started seeing all these penitentiary guys around. My cousin's a Blood and he told me Suge came and got a few people out of his neighborhood and flew them to Vegas just to hang with him. The word on the streets was he was buying people. When he started rolling with his entourage, it looked like he had about fifty or sixty niggas with him. But he was paying for it. They didn't care about him. They were just caring about the money he paid. Who wouldn't wanna be around that life?"

According to this Crip, Suge had an agenda. "He told me what he was gonna do. He said he was gonna put it down. He told me, 'All these niggas in the record business is bitches!' He named Russell Simmons, James Smith at Rap-A-Lot, Jermaine Dupri—all of them—and said, 'They some little bitches! They some punks!' That's when he went on his little putting-it-down spree. Right after *The Chronic*. He said, 'We fittin'a blow up and all these other little punk-ass niggas ain't shit.' "

Everywhere Suge went, his men bashed people. "That's why I got tired of hanging with them," this Rolling 60 Crip sighed. "I swear! They'd jump on people every time, and I thought, 'These niggas are cowards, man!' It would take a whole room of niggas to jump on two or three people, and they didn't care who it was.' "

People who attended Dre's platinum birthday party were unprepared for what happened next, said Matt McDaniel. "It was in March or April, held at the Strip Club at Century City. It was cool—Dre had invited people he knew, and a lot of industry people. They had that little strip bar, and a big giant *Chronic* cake." The cake featured a huge marijuana leaf drawn in icing. Strippers sat at tables. The *Chronic* album—including McDaniel's audio contributions—played at full volume. Everyone had positive things to say about the album, Dre's new label, and this party. As usual, Dre had provided enough booze, marijuana, and good music. And, of course, more than enough strippers had been invited.

"But then Suge was kinda walking around the party with a big platter full of money," said McDaniel. "Five-dollar bills, dollar bills, and ten-dollar bills. He was basically asking for 'donations' for Dre's birthday." The guests, however, saw a frightening subtext to Suge's request. There was an unspoken message in his vocal tone. He wasn't so much asking as demanding. And by now, thanks to gossip and allusions to Eazy and Vanilla Ice, which were included in various articles about Death Row Records and Dre, people understood what could happen to anyone who denied Suge.

"Supposed gangsters" turned pale with fright when confronted by

Knight and his tray. " 'C'mon, you got some money!' Knight barked. 'Put some in!' And they were doing it." To McDaniel, Suge looked not like the CEO of an up-and-coming record label so much as a common street thug. Many of the partygoers, in fact, left the party feeling the same way: They came to celebrate with Dre, drink prodigiously, and ogle strippers, but ended up being extorted by Knight and his red-clad buddies.

By the time Dre directed the video for "Let Me Ride," a year after the "Deep Cover" single, his album *The Chronic* had spent eight months in the *Billboard* Top 10 and sold over two million copies. *Rolling Stone* loved the album and printed a huge feature on Dre. "Who came up with that term 'gangsta rap' anyway?" Dre asked a writer.

"Dre. You did."

"Oh, maybe so. Never mind, then."

Despite the fact that he and Suge co-owned Death Row, Dre tried his best to avoid having to visit the label's office on Wilshire Boulevard. Suge had decided to run the office as he saw fit and, in one of his more controversial decisions, decided to hire Daryl Henley as general manager. Henley, a former teammate during Suge's brief stint with the Los Angeles Rams, was enthusiastic about the position even though he didn't know the first thing about the entertainment industry or overseeing day-to-day operations at a multimillion-dollar record company. In fact, Suge hired Henley, a violent man who trafficked in drugs as a sideline career, only as a favor.

"Henley's employment was basically a front to show his probation officer that he was doin' something," said Doug Young. " 'Cause he wasn't playing for the Rams." Suspended from the Rams due to an arrest in connection with the drug ring he helped run, he needed a steady salary. At Death Row, as per Suge's orders, he demanded that employees present written reports summarizing what they had accomplished during each workday. "I didn't know why," Doug said, " 'cause I would *tell* him everything in the goddamned report anyway!" By then Death Row had a staff of ten people and others willing to work for free as interns. Many employees found Henley to be a nice guy, but were ultimately confused by his presence in the office. Though Henley did try his best to justify his employment, following Suge's orders and spying on employees, Henley's stay at the label would not be a long one. The cocaine trafficking ring he ran after hours would lead to Henley and four others being arrested, convicted, and imprisoned.

Dre decided that the best thing to do was ignore Suge's eccentric little decisions and focus on the label's creative output: Suge was becoming difficult to deal with, but Dre couldn't worry about that just then. The video for "Let Me Ride" was only half finished; he had to get it done, then find some time to work on the second half of Snoop's album, which Interscope was demanding. Then Dre had to prepare for the following month, when *The Chronic* tour with Onyx and Run-D.M.C. would get under way.

Filming in Leimert Park, an area described by *Rolling Stone* as "the intellectual center of African American life in Los Angeles," Dr. Dre wore a black Ben Davis shirt, baggy pants, and a black baseball hat with a marijuana leaf on it, a *Chronic* promotional item.

He stood near a camera and arced his eyes over the motley crew of characters his video shoot attracted: Muslims in suits and bow ties stood on corners, trying to sell copies of *The Final Call*, their newspaper; white rap fans wearing baseball caps with the brim facing backward swayed to reggae music blaring from a nearby record store; hordes of real gang members smoked marijuana, drank forty-ounce bottles of beer, and scowled at each other. "I don't know," Dre told the crowd. "I guess everybody should do their own thing and shit." This was his directorial technique.

As the music started, Dre took his place in front of the camera and mouthed lyrics. Behind him, Snoop Doggy Dogg bobbed his head in support; low rider cars bounced; a sea of background extras waved arms in the air, passed forty bottles around, and pretended to be involved in heated dice games. Without warning the music stopped and an assistant director grabbed a megaphone. "Hey, hey! I've just been told that nothing we shot is usable, because y'all were throwing gang signs." Some extras chose this occasion to curl their fingers so that they formed letters of the alphabet, letters that represented the gangs they were in and challenged rival gang members forming different letters on their own fingers. "MTV won't play anything with gang signs," the assistant director stressed. "And if y'all want to throw them, you'll have to go home." The crowd was tense until the music resumed.

Steely-eyed Interscope chief Jimmy Iovine watched Dre direct from the sidelines. To white reporters he tried to present Dr. Dre as a rarity in the rap music industry: Dre, he told white reporters like Jonathan Gold, could rap, produce music, and direct a video with humorous themes. "Do you know how hard that is?" Iovine gushed to a nearby reporter from *Rolling Stone*. "Famous movie directors can't do that!"

Pointing a finger, Iovine added, "See that kid over there? That's my twelve-year-old nephew from Staten Island. You couldn't get more white and suburban than him. But Dre's record is all the kid listens to. When you sell this many albums, they are not all going to the South Bronx."

RBX grew unhappy with the label's direction. As CEO, Marion "Suge" Knight had surrounded himself with vicious Blood members, and RBX was one of the few people who noticed a subtle change in Suge's personality. "When we were in hotels and little gang members would bang into him—trying to start shit—he wouldn't even look back," said a Crip who worked with him and also noted the change. "And niggas were calling him Slob and all that, but he would just keep walking." *Slob* was a derogatory way of addressing a member of the Bloods. "He wasn't all that violent until he got around his people. That's when he pulled the cape out from behind his suit and turned into Superman! These ol' penitentiary niggas he brought in were the ones I feared more than anybody. I knew they'd jump in front of a bullet for this man—'cause they never had nothing."

With them around, Suge continued to get into fights. On the night of May 25, 1993, he had taken business manager Steven Cantrock and a few henchmen to Prince's Glam Slam, a club in Los Angeles. Before night's end, Suge got into an argument with security guard Roderick Lockett and pounded him, Lockett's lawyer explained, until Lockett sustained injuries to the spleen that required multiple surgeries. Another night, one person close to Suge said, "He got into a shootout at Prince's club. Somebody tried to peel his cap coming out of Glam Slam. He was coming out and somebody took a few shots at him."

Backstage at their concerts, the Death Row entourage got into a number of close calls, said Doug Young. "Many times. I'll give you one which was no big deal. Just a backstage fight. That was with [reggae musician] Shabba Ranks and them. That's when Dre's *The Chronic* was out and we were on the road with them fools. DJ Black got into it with one of them bodyguards backstage. There was a scuffle and a push. One of the by-laws of this is that Suge would rather bail you out of jail than for you to punk out. So we got our hands up with them fools and Suge came to the rescue. He started pulling niggas off Black. It was the type of shit where you better jump into the pile or you were gonna get 'got' at the hotel." It was no wonder that the *Chronic* tour—due to violence and "creative differences"—was canceled after a mere six performances.

On the road in Chicago, before the remaining dates were called off, RBX thought about how, under Suge, Death Row had gone from business enterprise to marauding gang. "He's smart," Kurupt's former manager, Lamont Bloomfield, said of RBX. "He went to college. He ain't no fool. That's why he bailed out from Death Row first. He saw where it was going and knew he wasn't gonna get paid after he did the work. He spoke up about his money, and that's what really caused the problem. 'Cause he was the only one asking about his money. Since he was asking for what was rightfully his, I guess everybody else too scared to do this viewed him as a problem person. I mean, his cousin Snoop got into it with him because Snoop was telling him he wouldn't be shit without Dre and all these people helping him. But it didn't matter. 'Cause they wouldn't have been shit if RBX and Kurupt and Snoop didn't rap on Dre's songs. The label didn't know that they needed each other. Just like they need each other now."

"RBX had a beef with Suge," said Dr. Dre. "We were performing at the New Regal Theater on the south side of Chicago, and he got into a fight."

"It was over some bullshit," RBX sighed. "There were eight people performing that night—Snoop, myself, and Tha Dogg Pound. And we came into the dressing room after the show and saw eight things of chicken. So whatchu think? My mind? I didn't even think about it. I just went and grabbed some chicken and started eating it. And everyone followed and started eating too. I didn't think 'Whose chicken is that? I ain't touching it.'

"Turns out that Suge had invited some of his homeboys up there and ordered the chicken for them. For us, for him and them, or whatever. And he came up there: 'Who eatin—?! Aw, you motherfuckers eatin' my chicken?!' I didn't wanna be fucked with. 'Cause I just ate. I was tired from eatin' and said, 'Man, why you beefin' over fuckin' chicken!' That's what it was. Motherfuckers took that shit and blew it up."

One of RBX's Crip friends said, "Suge pulled out a gun, gave it to his homie, and was like, 'Hold this.' Acting like he wanted to scrap but someone had a gun in their hand. And RBX said, 'I was fittin'a fight you and whup your ass. But your homeboy has a gun. If I win, this nigga's liable to shoot me.' And Snoop told Suge, 'That's my cousin, just let him pass.' Suge was fittin'a put it down on him. But RBX ain't no punk nigga. It's true that he backed down, but only 'cause the odds were against him. The nigga ain't stupid! Whatever Suge did to him, if he didn't do nothing back, I understood why. He probably didn't wanna get shot.

"I'm sure all the artists woke up after that. They gotta know what situation they in now. RBX was helping Suge sell millions of records and Suge's gonna get mad over a piece of chicken?! That should've let everybody know how much they were worth to him. If they didn't, and they continued rapping and all that, and having to worry about food—and if they should get a cheeseburger off the table—then that's on them."

Back in Los Angeles, RBX told Dr. Dre he was leaving the label. Dre was saddened by the fact that Suge had alienated one of Death Row's most original talents. But the fight wasn't the only reason for his departure. RBX explained: "You think I would leave billions of dollars over some chicken? It was a little deeper than that. That's why we fell out on that end, but it was one of the many straws that broke the camel's back."

Another was his publishing deal. "Nothing serious," he quipped. "I gotta know what it entails. I was like: 'Well, before I sign anything like this, I have to go do research to find out what's going down.' They were like: 'Aw, do it now!' I said: 'No, no, no. I'm not gonna do it now.' They said, 'Well, we *gotta* do this now. We have a deadline.' I said: 'Well, okay. I guess I won't meet your deadline, then. 'Cause I ain't gonna sign this.'

"All day them motherfuckers would say, 'I ain't in it for the money!' 'You ain't in it for the money?! Well, then—why you always talkin' 'bout you want the flyest Benz?! Just stop that, fool! 'Cause you in it for the money.' "

Proof of this was Snoop's decision to begin writing glam-raps like "Murder Was the Case," a dismal number where he portrays a young father who is murdered, makes a deal with Satan, and returns to Earth. Asked to supply vocals for the song's "devil" character, RBX refused. This abomination, he told Dre and Snoop, went against all his spiritual beliefs. "I told them: 'No, I'm not doing it! Y'all are entering some shit! You don't even know what you're getting into! And I want no part of this! And don't be trying to take my voice and do some shit with it on them computers, to put me on there doing that. 'Cause if you do, I'm coming at you—straight up," said RBX, who stands over six feet four inches tall. "It was just disagreements," he said while exhaling smoke from a Newport cigarette. "Before it got to a boiling point, I defused it and left."

After his departure, an industry executive brought him to Disney-owned Hollywood Basic, then the label sent faxes to music magazines announcing that he had signed with them. Asked about RBX's deal, Suge claimed it wasn't true. Dre, meanwhile, skirted the issue. "I don't know," he told *The Source*. "He been having those motherfuckers running up in his ear. See, it's like this: When RBX came down—" Dre didn't even have the energy to finish the lie. "That's Snoop's cousin, you know."

Trying to protect the label's image, he composed himself and said that contractually, RBX was still bound to him. "I'm just gonna wait to see what happens. Soon as he blew up, soon as my record came out, you got a gang of motherfuckers talking about what they should be doing, where they should be, what they should have—motherfuckers that didn't give a fuck about him before the record came out."

In interviews, Dre couldn't escape the fact that RBX's departure mirrored Dre's own defection from Ruthless. But RBX's situation was different, he stressed. "My business *was* fucked up. I'm not fucking over my people." He wanted his artists to be happy, he explained. Snoop wasn't a commodity. He was like a younger brother. "I'm just watching everybody's back," Dre added.

Snoop watched his cousin RBX leave Hollywood Basic and sign a deal with Irving Azoff's Giant Records. There, RBX recorded an album that was critical of Death Row, and most especially Dre. Snoop heard the album and stopped talking to RBX. "We were close until he made that record *AWOL: Escape from Death Row.* I didn't take offense. Suge didn't. Nobody from Tha Dogg Pound."

The next artist to leave was the DOC. But the DOC didn't say he was leaving. All he was doing, he explained, was traveling to Atlanta, Georgia, to help a rapper named MC Breed create an album. Responsible for the groundbreaking funk-rap "Ain't No Future in Yo' Frontin'," Breed was present during sessions for *The Chronic* and now wanted his own *Chronic*-styled sales breakthrough. Along with Dre's bassist, Colin Wolfe, and stepbrother, Warren G, Breed invited the DOC to Atlanta. Away from California, the DOC decided to leave Death Row. "Atlanta was one of the easiest places to work, 'cause I couldn't go back home, because I would have to deal with too much shit interfering with trying to come up with some dope shit. I couldn't do it in L.A., there was too much drama out there."

Despite two artists leaving, and Suge's growing reputation for violence, more artists were eager to join Death Row's roster and social circle. The public image continued to be that the label was a family. "See, this is a family thang on Death Row," Snoop said, "and Dre is the godfather."

Publicly, Snoop credited Dre with helping the label's stars realize their full potential. "He's been doing this shit for the longest and you can't mess with that nigga, dawg!" Dre gave good advice; he never asked his artists to appear on horrible songs; if he disagreed with their tastes, he was honest and said so. This was why Snoop foresaw that Death Row's releases would continue to be successful. "Believe us," Snoop added, "we wrote some wack shit. Y'all just didn't hear it!"

When Suge and a few artists and employees from Death Row flew to the Jack the Rapper music convention in Miami, they were entering Luke's territory. Luke, a Miami native born Luther Campbell, made a name for himself with 2 Live Crew, a group whose albums fused energetic dance beats to X-rated lyrics and produced hits like "Me So Horny." His concerts usually featured an array of half-nude strippers dragging audience members onstage, then sitting on their faces. A favorite target of right-wing conservatives and sheriffs in nearby Dade County, he owned and operated Luke Records and released music by rap bands like the Poison Clan, who recorded a song insulting Dre after the attack on Dee Barnes. When Snoop Doggy Dogg heard the song, he urged Dre to insert a number of insults against Luke, the group's label owner, on *The Chronic*. Once Luke heard Dre accuse him of being a homosexual, Luke, who stands six feet four inches tall and is constantly surrounded by friends and former Florida gang members, was enraged. A feud between Death Row and Luke Records had been developing ever since *The Chronic*'s release: In response to Dre's insults, Luke released a song called "Cowards in Compton." His video for the song featured a Dre impersonator wearing tight spandex and mascara and bending over.

In the hotel lobby at the convention, camps from Death Row and Luke Records met and kept circling each other "like they were in a mall," said one convention attendee. "They'd start with stare-downs but pretty soon it was escalating. One person would bump into another and they would have a confrontation. Then break up and go their own ways."

Unhindered, the camps kept meeting up, bickering, then coming to blows: The brawls and overt hostility soured the mood of the yearly event. Industry executives feared being caught in the midst of the next skirmish. "These two camps kept meeting up, and when they did, you knew something was gonna happen."

Rumors began to attach themselves to Suge's name like lint on a cheap suit. One executive recounted how he saw Suge holding a gun and charging down the street. "They're runnin' around like common thugs," the executive whined. "But they're making money! It just doesn't add up. It's pretty hard to see them being around after a while."

Back in Los Angeles, work on Snoop's album continued, but Dre became preoccupied by the fact that his relationship with Michel'lé—mother of his three-year-old son, Marcel—had cooled. He planned to produce her second album right after completing *DoggyStyle*—and was ready to marry her—but she kept refusing his marriage proposals. "She says she won't marry me until I stop being Dr. Dre."

Interscope was pressing for the album: They wanted it completed by

Thanksgiving, so they could rush it into stores and give the millions of *Chronic* buyers something new to own. Under house arrest, Dre had a lot of time to reflect on his situation with Death Row. In doing so, he realized that deep down he was tired of being connected to Suge, who alienated the DOC and RBX to the point where both were no longer present during studio sessions. Though he started the *DoggyStyle* project with high hopes, wanting to produce a classic album, Dre suddenly gave in to pressure from Snoop, Interscope, and Suge. If Snoop wanted his inexperienced cousin Daz or novice Warren G producing songs, Dre felt, fine. Do what you want. "The whole second side of Snoop's album was done in two days," Dre revealed. "We went through about nine fifths of Hennessy. We was up for like two days. I was under house arrest at the time, and I couldn't leave the studio anyway."

After the liquor wore off, Dre had second thoughts about the Snoop album. Ultimately, Dre was a perfectionist. This trait was the secret of his success. Despite having sold millions of albums in the past, Dre still harbored an irrational fear that his audience might hear his latest work, dislike it, and spread the word that Dre's reign at the top of the charts was over. He listened to the songs they had created for Snoop's album while intoxicated and realized they needed work. Like producer Phil Spector, Dre continued going to studios to fine-tune the album until he felt it was perfect.

Snoop, meanwhile, felt as if he would finally be a star. Interscope and Death Row were planning to film a series of videos to promote his songs; everyone in America would know his face; he would finally be a household name. He failed to realize that due to his past with the Rolling 20 Long Beach Crips, his career would also make him an easy target for old enemies.

When it was time to film "What's My Name," a clip with special effects that transformed Snoop into a Doberman pinscher, the video shoot became a riot. "For the most part, when we're working on videos," said film crew member Johnny Simmons, "all those guys are trying to do is get it done." What happened that day was typical: Film crews entering different communities encountered gangs who made them feel unwelcome.

"We started off at eight in the morning, shooting at the VIP record store." The store was located in Snoop's hometown, Long Beach. The shot called for Snoop to stand on the record store's roof. Once they had footage of him rhyming, the producer planned to film the remainder of the video—an idyllic picnic scene—in a park four blocks away.

"Maybe it looked good on paper, but in reality it was a bad idea. 'Cause at eight-thirty in the morning we must have had about a thousand people: friends and enemies of Snoop Dogg standing out there in the crowd; people sucking on forty-ounce beers at the crack of dawn that morning. And tensions were really high. They were all going crazy. But that always happens on videos. You can't imagine how many times I've had to jump underneath a truck because someone rolled by and started popping off some shots. Usually it's a no-name video some drug dealer's paying for out of his pocket, a group that never gets on TV and is never heard from again."

But this time was unlike anything Simmons had ever experienced. The crowd truly wanted to get their hands on Snoop. After his performance, Snoop left the roof and rejoined Tha Dogg Pound and Lil' Malik. They entered minivans and drove away without incident. The film crew quickly packed everything and drove to the park.

The next step would be to film a picnic scene that gets overrun by a pack of Doberman pinschers. "Man, we got there and those thousand people were already there," Simmons remembered. *"I'm talking about all hell broke loose!* Snoop had his bodyguard [McKinley Lee] there." A member of the audience stood in Snoop's face and uttered threats. "This guy must have had some kind of beef with Snoop. He started a fight out there."

Soon, police helicopters arrived. "Flying so low, you could see the screws on the bottom of the helicopter! It was a mess, man. And I remember that was the first time I met Suge Knight. All the police in the world were there and it wasn't just Snoop and Malik that were fighting! There was a gang of people out there throwing shit at the police. The dogs were barking. It was your basic little riot in the park." Things escalated. The LAPD brought out riot gear, plastic shields, and heavy nightsticks. They were marching across the field, driving people back, containing the crowd, and restoring order, Simmons recalled. "It's wild in the park! Then all of a sudden this little fly Mercedes comes driving through the crowd. The police tried to stop it."

The car swerved around them, kept rolling, pulled to a stop on the field. "Suge drives up, throws Dre and Snoop in the car. For one moment, everything stopped. The police stopped, the fighting stopped. Everything stopped. The car pulls in, picks up Snoop and Dre, throws them in the car, then splits. I said, 'Who in the hell is that?!' They said, Suge Knight, owner of Death Row Records. Even the police respected him." Simmons watched the car leave, saying, "They bad. Damn."

During the filming of another Snoop video, for "Gin & Juice," Doug Young said, "They were in a Crip 'hood, you know, with Suge and them bein' Bloods. And the Crip gang in that neighborhood rolled up on the film crew and were about to start takin' cameras. They were tellin' Snoop to get his ass out here right now! Just mashed on the whole shoot when they found out it was Death Row. It was like a hoo-ride. So Snoop came out and calmed the little ringleader down and it was all good. But Suge and them heard about it and were on their way. About to bug. And that's when some shit almost jumped off." Suge and his Blood friends cornered the Crips and began to shove them around. During the fight that followed, a gun dropped to the floor. "But it got squashed in the end," Doug recalled.

Then Snoop and Tha Dogg Pound went to film a video in one of Compton's Blood neighborhoods. "I show up to this motherfucker in *all* blue," Snoop lamented. "I'm standing outside with a blue comb in my hair, blue khakis, blue sneakers, blue motherfucking shoelaces! So I'm in the trailer, niggas roll up. They're Bloods. They're strapped. They got bats and they're like, 'W'sup, Blood? Y'all gotta leave!'"

Luckily, Topcat was with them. Owner of T&D's, a local record store, Topcat was a Blood member who was friendly with Tha Dogg Pound. "So Topcat came in and asked me, 'W'sup, dawg. You wanna handle this?' I was like, 'Yeah, we all black and shit.' They was basically mad I had on blue. I went outside and hollered at 'em though. Everything was cool. I wasn't there for banging. I was there to make money. They saw I wasn't no punk-ass nigga. It was cool."

Still, Snoop began to worry. Days later, while riding toward a photo shoot in a three-car caravan, he entered "the jungle," a part of town run by the Black P. Stone Bloods. At a red light, Snoop stared into the eyes of a black teen waiting at a bus stop. Recognition flashed in the teen's eyes, but Snoop was unsure of whether the teen was seeing a former Crip or famous rap star. When the teen wrapped a red bandanna around his face and pulled a .22-caliber pistol, Snoop had his answer. As the teen raised his gun, Snoop told the chauffeur, "Just keep on driving." But this time Snoop was prepared. Until the car left the armed Blood behind, Snoop held on to his pair of .380 handguns, ready to open fire through the window if necessary.

"At the time, Snoop was all about work," said videographer Matt McDaniel. "He was excited that him, Dre, and Cube had just had a meeting and were supposed to do something together." He would see Snoop on a daily basis. "Actually, I was going to buy Bud from Snoop at the time and Snoop's father was out here." He was doing security. "But at that time, the fame was all brand new for him. 'Nuthin' but a "G" Thang' was out and he lived in this apartment that faced the street, one of them deals where you pull in the driveway and right above the car, on the second story, would be Snoop's apartment. With the bathroom window facing the street and two bedroom windows on both sides. So if someone was coming by and throwing up their set, you're in a vulnerable position."

In August 1993 Snoop continued giving interviews to promote the upcoming album. Though Snoop told West Coast rap fanzine *Rappages* that he wanted to be the "hip-hop Al Capone," *Source* writer Dream Hampton said, "I remember Snoop being kind of shy, like a gentle spirit. My time with him was spent in a car and I remember him playing a wide pantheon of black music—from the Dramatics to Too $hort to Onyx. He really loved music."

"Snoop was not out spending his time gangbanging," Matt McDaniel stressed. "For one, he was making videos, making appearances, doing shows, writing treatments for himself, and like I said, meeting with Cube and them."

On August 25 Snoop's friend Sean Abrams stood in front of the apartment building Snoop lived in while recording *DoggyStyle*. The building was located in the multicultural, working-class Palms district of L.A.

Upstairs, in his second-story apartment, Snoop was gossiping with his bodyguard McKinley "Big Malik" Lee about events about the label. At the time, twenty-one-year-old Snoop was out on bail for a concealed-weapons charge.

Twenty-year-old Philip Woldemariam, a neighbor, drove by the building. When Abrams saw Woldemariam and two friends in their car, he thought they were rival gang members and curled his fingers to form symbols that represented his own gang. The car stopped and Woldemariam argued with Abrams.

The neighborhood was basically a quiet one, so the sounds of the argument filtered in through Snoop's windows. The brawny McKinley Lee heard the bickering and rushed downstairs to break it up.

At the sight of Snoop and McKinley rushing to join the fray, Woldemariam ran back to the car he was riding in. One of Wolde-mariam's two companions stepped on the gas pedal, and the trio escaped the area. Sean Abrams, McKinley Lee, and Snoop mulled over what just happened: Snoop was tired of being harassed by local gang members; they heard Snoop rapping about his old gang the Long Beach Crips, and seemed to want to prove that they were tougher; ever since he moved into this neighborhood, this guy Philip Woldemariam had been trying to goad him into a fight. If Woldemariam wasn't driving past and glaring at Snoop, he was confronting him whenever they happened to run into each other. Recently, Woldemariam—then on probation for a weapons violation—had approached Snoop at a nearby gas station and aimed a gun at Snoop's head. By then Snoop was tired of the feud with Woldemariam. He and his friends decided to confront Woldemariam and settle the problem once and for all: with a fistfight or a handshake.

Within minutes Snoop, Abrams, and Lee entered a Jeep: Snoop be-hind the wheel, the burly Lee in the passenger seat, the hostile Abrams in the rear. They chased Woldemariam's car for a few blocks, then turned onto a side street. Woldemariam and his two companions, Duchaum Lee Joseph and Jason London, believed the incident was over. They drove to a Mexican restaurant, ordered takeout, and planned to eat outdoors in nearby Woodbine Park. As soon as they sat to eat their food, however, Snoop's Jeep appeared.

Woldemariam set his food aside. What happened next depends on whom you believe: Snoop, McKinley Lee, and Sean Abrams claimed that Woldemariam reached for the .380 handgun he pointed at Snoop on two prior occasions. In self-defense, bodyguard McKinley Lee drew his own gun and blasted Woldemariam. Woldemariam fell to the ground, mortally wounded. Snoop, Lee, and Abrams fled. Initially, Woldemariam's two companions, Duchaum Lee Joseph and Jason London, said Woldemariam had been unarmed. Snoop maintained otherwise. "The danger came to us," he said. "We perceived it as a threat. That's the reason why Malik acted the way he acted in the situation. You know, I look at it like this. If Malik would have waited another second, I might not be here doing an interview with you right now. If he would have waited another half a second, I might have a hole in my head."

A week later, in early September, the many interviews Snoop had given during the year suddenly appeared on newsstands. Accused of first degree murder, Snoop graced the covers of *Rolling Stone*, *Vibe*, and *The Source*. Though *DoggyStyle* was the most anticipated album of the year, two weeks before its release Dre still refused to let Interscope's Jimmy Iovine hear more than two songs outside the studio. Dre was paranoid that Compton bootleggers would obtain a copy, create duplicates, then sell them to a legion of fans who already knew Snoop's song titles by heart. Despite Snoop's current troubles, Dre felt the show had to go on.

Snoop appeared at the MTV Music Awards to promote the album. During his performance he seemed nervous. By the time he was expected to present the award for best rhythm and blues video, he had calmed down. Unknown to the audience, detectives waited backstage, ready to arrest him on charges of first degree murder. After his participation in the awards event, Snoop managed to avoid arrest by sneaking out of the building, but hours later wisely decided to turn himself in. Death Row attorney David Kenner began the chore of defending him. "[Broadus is remorseful] that this happened," Kenner told *Newsweek*. "But he also feels that but for the bodyguard, we'd be reading about *his* death." Snoop's bail was set at one million dollars; his arraignment was scheduled for October 1. It would be years before he was brought to trial.

*   *   *

Right before *DoggyStyle*'s release, Fabian "Fade" Duvernay was running Interscope's rap promotion department. In addition to working Dre's *The Chronic*, he made sure radio stations were playing an album by a Queens New York rapper named Akinyele. On the side, Duvernay managed a West Coast rap group called Tha Alkaholiks, who were signed to Loud/RCA Records. One night Suge invited Fade to party with him at Prince's club Glam Slam, where seven months earlier he had argued with a security guard named Roderick Lockett. "This was from Fade's mouth," said a former coworker at Interscope. "Him and Suge were walking into the Glam Slam club and this DJ named Mark Love was spinning. Mark Love happened to see him and yelled, 'Yo, Fade! What's going on, man? Where's my Snoop?' He had been asking Fade for an advance copy of *DoggyStyle*. Fade said, 'Nigga, shut the fuck up! Hold up, homie, hold up!' But Mark kept saying, 'You didn't hear me? I just played Tha Alkaholiks!' Suge was sitting right there and Fade said, 'Boy, would you just shut up!' "

That evening Suge didn't comment on the remark about Snoop and Tha Alkaholiks. Fade spent the weekend relaxing, then returned to work. That Monday morning a staff meeting was scheduled to be held in the conference room. Fade attended and Interscope discussed its release schedules, which albums would be released on what date. Midway through the meeting the doors flew open. "Suge just came in yelling," said Trevor Trev, who worked at Loud Records. "He was yelling, 'I don't like to get fucked around!'

"Suge was yelling, '*You my ho!*' "

Fearing they'd be attacked, some Interscope executives sank low into their seats and remained silent, said a former Interscope employee. "Suge was telling Fade Duvernay, '*Are you trying to fuck me?! You tryin'a get Tha Alkaholiks hot on Snoop? Snoop is hot! Are you trying to have them on Snoop's coattails? If I hook you up with an advance Snoop, you gonna play it! You trying to blow Tha Alkaholiks up off 'a Snoop?!*' That's how Suge took what he heard Mark Love tell Fade that night at Glam Slam. And Suge gave Fade an ultimatum: You either leave Interscope right now or get your ass rolled up."

With an annual salary in the six-figure range, Fade Duvernay told Suge he would not quit. "Then Suge was like, 'Well nigga come and get this ass-whupping!' " In front of Interscope's highest-ranking executives, Suge's men reached out, yanked Duvernay out of his chair, and began shoving him toward the conference room door. "And they were gonna rough him up some more until one white guy asked everybody, 'Are you just gonna let them do this to him?!' They were pushing him around, giving him a couple of hits and body blows."

Dwarfed by Suge's two helpers, Fade was forced into the next room. Suge followed, closing the door behind them. Inside, Fade was terrified. Suge grabbed his throat and said, "Nigga, how you gonna try to fuck me?!"

"They threw him up against the wall," said an editor at *Rappages*. "Suge was choking him with one hand and lifting his ass off the floor while his two big-ass bodyguards started beating him. Then people from Interscope opened the door and saw that shit."

The white Interscope employee entered just as they began to beat Duvernay. "Naw, it can't go down like this!" the employee protested. "Let's sit down and talk about it. We can't have you beating him! There must be another way to solve the problem.' "

"Then Suge told the white kid, 'Okay let's do that.' But Fade said he was heated! That white kid coming in was the only thing that saved Fade. The only thing."

"It was horrible," said Trevor Trev, one of Duvernay's friends. "I knew Fade before and after that incident. Before that, he didn't really care for guns. He became a gun advocate. He also stopped working with Tha Alkaholiks."

Beatings from Suge's henchmen weren't reserved for people in the recording industry, said one frightened Death Row employee. "Once they went out to the Vegas fights. Suge had given Tommy Hearns's brother a certain amount of money to lease hotel rooms for Tha Dogg Pound, Snoop, and everybody. They cut him a check, then came to learn that he paid for the rooms with stolen credit cards. They got that nigga's ass up there in Suge's office, then here come those doors getting locked on his ass." Hearns was given a beating to rival those his famous brother gave opponents in the ring. He emerged from the room bruised and battered. "They would famously lock the doors on you," said the Death Row employee.

"THEN SUGE'S NIGGAS CAME FROM NOWHERE AND STARTED JUST BEATING THEM UP!"

Released on November 23, 1993, *DoggyStyle* sold 800,000 copies in its first week and entered the *Billboard* charts at No. 1. "I didn't make a lot of money doing this Dre shit," said promoter Doug Young, who worked at Death Row. "But the Snoop shit? Everything came home. Oh, heck, yeah! I made a gang of money! Spent it all, but made a gang of it. Definitely when this Snoop thing hit! Whoo! Jesus! That was raining Xmas. All good for everybody."

"Death Row knew they were hot," said Soup Henderson, who worked at Interscope. "It wasn't no, 'I think we're gonna blow up.' Everything they released was doing high numbers. So their attitude was: 'Don't even ask. It's gonna sell.'"

"I ran into Suge at a jewelry store in Beverly Hills," said Johnny Simmons, who worked on various Snoop videos. "When I got off the elevator, all these people were crowded around this big dude who looked like a football player. I couldn't really see who it was. All of a sudden, the dude said, 'Johnny Simmons!' Called me over there. 'Man, we made a million dollars off that "What's My Name" video! That video was slamming! Anything you want, man, just gimme a call!' Then Suge left and I had the red carpet treatment in the jewelry store. I musta had every salesman in the world hanging on me, thinking I was getting ready to get up there and spend paper like Suge."

Though Death Row generated more than $60 million in sales on records and merchandise, and received millions of dollars in financing from Sony, Time-Warner, and Interscope, the label was short on cash. With the success of *The Chronic* and *DoggyStyle*, Suge began to buy luxury cars, expensive Rolex watches, yachts, and jewelry. On the road, Suge demanded that accountant Steven Cantrock have stretch limousines lined up outside their five-star luxury hotels twenty-four hours a day.

Cantrock was a junior partner at Gelfand, Rennert & Feldman, an informal fourteen-partner accounting agency with clients like Michael Jackson, Bob Dylan, and Whoopi Goldberg. After Gelfand founder Irwin Rennert was introduced to Marion "Suge" Knight in November 1992, and Suge told him that Death Row needed someone to manage the financial end of Death Row Records, Rennert passed the account over to Cantrock. With his staff, Cantrock was responsible for paying the label's bills, haggling with suppliers, handling their income taxes, and advising them on investments.

As Death Row's de facto controller, Cantrock had sole authority to write checks for the company. He managed Suge's personal finances as well as those of his artists. "Until Mr. Cantrock got on the case," *The Wall Street Journal* explained, "Mr. Knight had never owned a credit card; Snoop Doggy Dogg had never written a check."

Against his better judgment, Cantrock signed off on Suge's extravagant purchases and watched as Death Row's name kept appearing on overdraft reports. As the overdraft reports circulated among Cantrock's partners at the Gelfand firm, Cantrock tried to keep Death Row's checks from bouncing. Since Gelfand had a good professional relationship with City National Bank in Beverly Hills, Cantrock persuaded the bank to allow Death Row to be overdrawn within certain limits. By now Interscope began to question the label's finances. Cantrock was at a loss for words. Then he explained that Suge got upset when people told him no.

The invitation to Snoop's album release party featured a drawing of the red and yellow doghouse that was on the back of his album cover. The party was being held on a boat, docked at Marina del Rey. In the parking lot, a Death Row employee distributed posters of Snoop standing by a "1-8-7 Street" sign. To board the vessel, partygoers passed through a gate, then walked down a ramp. Men from the Nation of Islam handled security. "But they weren't letting people onto the boat fast enough," this label employee said. "They let the shit get crowded."

Since the narrow gangway leading to the boat could accommodate only one person at a time, the Nation of Islam guards separated people. "They had girls entering, then guys," said Matt McDaniel. "If you came with somebody, she might've gotten on the boat first."

This policy soon irritated people, McDaniel said. "They were yelling, 'Look! Let us in!' They were taking a long time, then the captain basically panicked and said, 'Okay, nobody else on the boat.' That got people waiting outside and on the boat pissed off."

"Then they had a lot of balloons out there," said a label employee. "So every now and then balloons would pop and people would think it was gunfire. Then the owner of the boat's dumb-ass got to talking shit to people. The captain. And that was some of the wrong people to be talkin' shit to, you know? They were ready to throw his ass into the water too!"

On the boat, everyone was having a good time. The DJ played Snoop's long-awaited new album in its entirety. Warren G had arrived with friends from the gang in his Long Beach neighborhood: These gang members were feeling good and singing along to the music. But a voice in the label employee's head said, *"Just get off that fucking boat and leave!"*

"I swear," said another guest, "Suge's people whupped on Warren G's people and threw them off the boat—beat Warren's whole neighborhood up! That's when Suge put the fear into Long Beach niggas. But none of them did anything. They were just up there, chanting 'Long Beach!' And throwing up their little gang set. Then Suge's niggas came from nowhere and started just beating them up! People were running off the boat; people getting carried off the boat and I was like, My goodness. And the party went on. Then Warren G came with one of his people and said, [sad voice]: 'That's messed up, Suge. Why you do to that to the homies?' And I was like, 'Damn, these niggas are getting beat up by their own record company.' It was so funny."

The beating ushered in a new era. In the beginning, Crips and Bloods from different neighborhoods worked together in peace. Upon the release of *DoggyStyle*, Suge became a tyrant.

Outside, the crowd waiting to board the vessel was uncontrollable. There was yelling and cursing and it scared the captain. Someone called the police: Within minutes, police helicopters and twenty sheriffs' vehicles pulled up. What happened next was described in local newscasts as a "rap riot," Matt McDaniel sighed. "It wasn't really a problem until the police came and ruined the party. 'Cause the boat was circling in the harbor and they had three helicopters: one police helicopter and two from the media. And the police helicopter was shining lights on the boat. Then you had the loud helicopter sound. So you're trying to chill at a party, but you got helicopters drowning everything out."

After the party ended, Suge went over the details in his mind and began to feel he'd been wronged by the man who leased the boat and arranged the party. Two days passed, then Suge invited this black promoter up to Death Row's office to discuss more business. The man arrived, eager for another opportunity to book a party for the world's leading rap label. Instead of business, Suge's men locked the office door and administered a severe beating. Some Death Row employees couldn't help but wonder, "When will these motherfuckers lock some doors on my ass?"

The fiasco on the boat proved to be the last straw for Dre's stepbrother, Warren G. In addition to having Snoop plucked from his group, his music ignored, his face slapped at pool parties, and his songs altered to include pro-Blood lyrics, he now had to watch Suge's Bloods pound his oldest friends to a pulp. "When Suge left Warren G on the shelf," artist manager Lamont Bloomfield said, "Warren woke up, signed to Def Jam, and 'blew up.' Then he came back and told me and Kurupt, 'I got a deal for you at Def Jam. W'sup?' And Kurupt just turned him down, saying, 'I'm rolling with the Row.' Well, roll with the Row and don't get your money! 'Cause Warren G had more money than all of them. But Suge was mad 'cause Warren G woke up, left Death Row, and sold four million copies. Even though Suge would've never spotlighted Warren G like [Def Jam mogul] Russell Simmons did."

By now Suge had another artist to replace Warren. Interscope head Jimmy Iovine was asking Suge to accept Tupac Shakur onto Death Row. At first Suge wasn't a Tupac fan. He looked like any other wanna-be gangsta rapper glutting the market. But Tupac started getting into brawls, shooting off-duty cops, and facing accusations that he was a rapist. Sensing the potential for sales of albums built around Tupac's new outlaw image, Suge's opinion changed. Tupac's legal troubles would make him more appealing to Death Row Records' core audience, the suburban white kids who went from listening to heavy metal acts like Slayer and Danzig to buying millions of copies of gangsta rap albums. Suge told Iovine he wanted to sign Tupac as soon as possible.

"Y'ALL SHOULD BE APPLAUDING ME! I MADE IT THROUGH THE GHETTO"

Tupac Shakur grew up around nothing but self-delusion. His mother, Alice Faye Williams, thought she was a "revolutionary." She called herself "Afeni Shakur" and associated with members of the ill-fated Black Panther Party, a movement that wanted to feed school kids breakfast and earn civil rights for African Americans.

During her youth she dropped out of high school, partied with North Carolina gang members, then moved to Brooklyn: After an affair with one of Malcolm X's bodyguards, she became political. When the mostly white United Federation of Teachers went on strike in 1968, she crossed the picket line and taught the children herself. After this she joined a New York chapter of the Black Panther Party and fell in with an organizer named Lumumba.

She took to ranting about killing "the pigs" and overthrowing the government, which eventually led to her arrest and that of twenty comrades for conspiring to set off a race war. Pregnant, she made bail and told her husband, Lumumba, it wasn't his child. Behind his back she had been carrying on with Legs (a small-time associate of Harlem drug baron Nicky Barnes) and Billy Garland (a member of the Party). Lumumba immediately divorced her.

Things went downhill for Afeni: Bail revoked, she was imprisoned in the Women's House of Detention in Greenwich Village. In her cell she patted her belly and said, "This is my prince. He is going to save the black nation."

By the time Tupac was born on June 16, 1971, Afeni had already defended herself in court and been acquitted on 156 counts. Living in the Bronx, she found steady work as a paralegal and tried to raise her son to respect the value of an education. From childhood, everyone called him the "Black Prince." For misbehaving, he had to read an entire edition of *The New York Times*. But she had no answer when he asked about his daddy. "She just told me, 'I don't know who your daddy is.' It wasn't like she was a slut or nothin'. It was just some rough times." When he was two, his sister, Sekyiwa, was born. This child's father, Mutulu, was a Black Panther who, a few months before her birth, had been sentenced to sixty years for a fatal armored car robbery.

With Mutulu away, the family experienced hard times. No matter where they moved—the Bronx, Harlem, homeless shelters—Tupac was distressed. "I remember crying all the time. My major thing growing up was I couldn't fit in. Because I was from everywhere, I didn't have no buddies that I grew up with."

As time passed, the issue of his father tormented him. He felt "unmanly," he said. Then his cousins started saying he had an effeminate face. "I don't know. I just didn't *feel* hard. I could cook, I could do clothes, I could sew, clean up the house. I could do all the things my mother could give me, but she couldn't give me nothing else."

The loneliness began to wear on him. He retreated into writing love songs and poetry. "I remember I had a book like a diary. And in that book I said I was going to be famous." He wanted to be an actor. Acting was an escape from his dismal life. He was good at it, eager to leave his crummy family behind. "The reason why I could get into acting was because it takes nothin' to get out of who I am and go into somebody else."

His mother enrolled him in the 127th Street Ensemble, a theater group in the impoverished Harlem section of Manhattan, where he landed his first role at age twelve, that of Travis in A *Raisin in the Sun.* "I lay on a couch and played sleep for the first scene. Then I woke up and I was the only person onstage. I can remember thinking, 'This is the best shit in the world!' That got me real high. I was gettin' a secret: This is what my cousins can't do."

Afeni, meanwhile, hooked up with Legs again and began hitting the crack pipe. "That was our way of socializing," she admitted. "He would come home late at night and stick a pipe in my mouth."

When Legs was arrested for credit card fraud, Afeni moved the family to Baltimore. She called New York to let Legs know, and learned that a crack-induced heart attack killed him. "That hurt Tupac," Afeni said. "It fucked him up. It was three months before he cried. After he did, he told me, 'I miss my daddy.' "

Since Tupac didn't know who his pop was, Legs's death was a big issue. "It made me bitter seeing all these other niggas with fathers gettin' answers to questions that I have. Even now I still don't get 'em."

In Baltimore, at age fifteen, he fell into rap; he started writing lyrics, walking with a swagger, and milking his background in New York for all it was worth. People in small towns feared the Big Apple's reputation; he called himself MC New York and made people think he was a tough guy.

That September he enrolled in the illustrious Baltimore School for the Arts, where he studied acting and ballet with white kids and finally felt "in touch" with himself. "Them white kids had things we never seen," he said. "That was the first time I saw there was white people who you could get along with. Before that, I just believed what everyone else said: They was devils. But I loved it. I loved going to school. It taught me a lot. I was starting to feel like I really wanted to be an artist. I was fucking white girls."

Head of the school's theater department, Donald Hickens, thought Tupac was extremely gifted; he had confidence and took risks; he was serious in the studio. "For Tupac, it was a new situation to be around white people who really cared about him and really wanted to help him," Hickens explained. "I think that shocked his expectations."

Tupac adopted Hickens as a father figure: "I could feel him trying to bring me up. He couldn't do it though. I was a little black kid from the ghetto and it was too much. I could see it in his face, he was trying to help me but it was a problem beyond him."

In the throes of a learned self-pity, Tupac attended the school until June 1988, after his junior year. When a neighborhood boy was killed by a gang, Afeni feared her gentle son might be next: She sent Tupac and his sister, Sekyiwa, to spend the summer at a friend's house in suburban Marin County, across the Golden Gate Bridge from San Francisco. "Leaving that school affected me so much," Tupac said. "Even now I see that as the point where I got off track."

Within weeks the friend called Afeni and admitted to being a drunk. The next day the friend would be enrolling in a detox, so Afeni had better get her ass over there and get her kids. Afeni's arrival in Marin County shattered her vision of it as a safe, green-lawn suburb. Labeled "the jungle" by local police, Marin County was a ghetto surrounded by hills and expensive condos. The county had one main street, one liquor store, one housing project, one school, and one bad reputation. But Tupac liked it there; at seventeen he reinvented himself, fooling everyone into thinking he was MC New York.

After arguing with his mother, he moved in with a group of kids who lived in an abandoned building. With them he sold drugs and soon tried to join a local gang. But these gangbangers saw right through him. "All through my time there they used to dis me. I got love but the kind of love you'd give a dog or a neighborhood crack fiend."

Soon Tupac met Leila Steinberg, a young white single mother of three. They met in a park one afternoon. Steinberg sat on a bench reading a copy of Winnie Mandela's *A Part of My Soul Went with Him.* Tupac said, "That's a good one. It really moves well."

"I turn around," Steinberg said, "and see this stunning young man."

She asked if he really read the book. He recited lines from memory. She offered him a room in her home and became his manager. Tupac suggested she tell labels he'd be the highest-selling rap artist ever; she called Atron Gregory, manager of Digital Underground and owner of TNT Records and repeated Tupac's claim. "The most ever, huh?" Gregory asked. "Okay, I'll give him a chance." As a dancer in Digital Underground's show.

Onstage, as Digital Underground performed their 1990 hit "The

Humpty Dance," Tupac humped a rubber blow-up doll and demonstrated how Digital Underground leader Shock G's dance step should be performed. It was his very first show, so far so good. Then the sound system malfunctioned; Tupac tossed the blow-up doll aside and started ranting. His band members knew real tough guys don't talk. They remain quiet until it becomes evident that the only way to solve a problem is to hit it. Tupac swaggered around the stage, waving his arms and yelling that he wanted to batter the harmless soundman. Shock G shook his head. "We said, 'Okay, we can't use you.' Two hours later, Tupac's back like nothin' happened. It was like that all the time. He'd flip on you, then the incident didn't exist."

He was like one of those punks who fights with siblings: He knows his family members won't hit back. But they would never try that on the street, where people don't have family ties or conscience. "The only way you couldn't depend on 'Pac was to keep his cool," rapper Money B learned.

During the tour, Tupac learned his mother was a crack addict. He began taking his problems out on the world, representing the group Digital Underground as if it were a territorial street gang. By January 3, 1991, visionary Shock G allowed 'Pac to appear on the group's *This Is an EP Release.*

"I knew him when he was in Digital with his first manager, Atron Gregory," said promoter Doug Young. "When he was just a dancer for Digital Underground. In the beginning he was not as nearly as, I guess you could say, angry. Matter of fact, we did a show with them in San Francisco when I managed that group KMC on Priority Records. It was a Gavin Convention, in the early days before Gavin moved out of San Francisco, and we were all gettin' drunk with forties of Olde English and St. Ides backstage. Tupac was up there and he was the coolest cat, man. I used to see him periodically with Atron, who was the first person to tell me how dope he was and how he was in the theater and arts."

After finishing his tour with Digital Underground in 1991, Tupac Shakur sought a recording contract of his own. He had enough songs for an album and tried to send Monica Lynch a demo. Lynch, president of Digital's label Tommy Boy, said, "He was funny, adorable, a real flirt. But as an artist he wasn't there yet."

Interscope A&R person Tom Whalley, recently hired by Ted Field, obtained a copy of the tape and disagreed. Whalley passed the tape to his boss, Field, who then passed it to his white teenage daughter. While awaiting word from Interscope, Tupac's bandmate Money B announced that he was going to audition for a movie. At the audition, Tupac watched Money test for the role of a character named Bishop. In the film, producers explained, Bishop would undergo a transformation. In the first reel he would be loyal to his friends. By the finale he would own a gun and murder his friends to conceal his crimes. Money couldn't quite get into character, so Tupac grabbed the script and said, "I can do this shit."

Producer Neil Moritz said, "All right. Do it."

Tupac read for the part. Moritz cast him on the spot. Ernest Dickerson, until then known as Spike Lee's cinematographer, directed the film in Harlem. It would be called *Juice*.

Money never said how he felt about having his so-called friend rob him of his opportunity.

In Los Angeles, Tupac's manager, Atron Gregory, finalized a deal with Interscope. Since his white teenage daughter loved Tupac's demo, Ted Field felt confident about signing Tupac. In the office, A&R person Whalley kept raving about Tupac's "presence." He told an assistant, "Have you ever seen eyes like that?"

Once Tupac was signed, Whalley raved, "Right away you could tell that this guy was different from the rest of the world. I couldn't slow him down. I never worked with anyone who could write so many great songs so quickly."

The release of Tupac's first album, 1991's *2Pacalypse Now*, coincided with the release of *Juice*. The album sold 500,000 copies and persuaded Time Warner to increase its stake in Interscope. "Atron gave me his first album," said record promoter Doug Young. "I always call it the 'Brenda Got a Baby' album. I told them that song was blowin' up in the 'hoods and they needed to do something about it."

Offstage, Tupac began having trouble with the law. In Oakland he mouthed off after being ticketed for jaywalking. The cops took him into custody and beat him bloody. He filed a $10-million lawsuit, charging the Oakland police with brutality during the arrest.

In 1992 Tupac Shakur moved to Los Angeles and became fascinated with its gang culture. "Each gang element wanted to claim him," his stepbrother "Mopreme" told a magazine. "The cover of *Strictly 4 My N.I.G.G.A.Z.* was red, so everybody thought at first he was a Blood." He remained neutral, associating with members of Blood and Crip gangs and soaking up their bloody tales about gang warfare. Like a method actor, he inserted these details into his songs. His fans came to view him as an authentic street gangster. His own road manager, Charles "Man-Man" Fuller, admitted that Tupac was like a sponge. "He could be with this poet, this pimp, this thug—he could suck everything from each of them and that would be part of him."

Despite his approach to the rough genre, no one believed Tupac was a gangster. His soft features inspired people to call him a sucker. In response, like the character he played in *Juice*, Tupac sought power from a gun. He began practicing with his new gun at firing ranges. Then, to more closely resemble the gangsters he associated with, he covered his torso with ganglike tattoos and began lifting weights. But no matter what he did, no nonwhite person took him seriously. People called him a softie. In private he would yell at his stepbrother. "I'm from the dirt," he claimed. "Y'all should be applauding me! I made it through the ghetto. I made it through school with no lights. I'm real."

On April 11, 1992, a nineteen-year-old black male murdered a Texas trooper. His attorney claimed 'Pac's "Trapped," a number on *2Pacalypse Now* found in the teen's cassette deck, made him do it.

When Tupac tried to visit Marin County on August 22, 1992—for a celebration of Marin County's fiftieth anniversary—he got into an argument with his former neighbors. Guns were fired and a six-year-old boy was shot in the head. Tupac denied involvement, and his half brother, Maurice Harding, was arrested but ultimately released due to lack of evidence. On September 22, 1992, Vice President Dan Quayle denounced him, saying *2Pacalypse Now* had "no place in our society."

But there was another side to him, said rapper Son Doobie of the group FunkDoobiest, who met Tupac at a club in New York. "He only had 'Brenda Had a Baby,' and he was real warmhearted, real cool. No ego included. He was telling me, 'God bless you, much success.' 'Cause we just got a record deal."

In 1993 Tupac Shakur kept at his desperate attempt to get respect from real gangsters without record deals. By March, Tupac's critically acclaimed second album *Strictly 4 My N.I.G.G.A.Z.* was in stores. While going to the Fox lot in Hollywood to tape a segment for *In Living Color*, Tupac was involved in yet another fight. A limousine driver said all he did was accuse Tupac and his friends of using drugs in his car. Tupac claimed the driver yelled at them and rushed to get a weapon from his trunk. Ultimately, the limo driver was beaten and Tupac was arrested. Later, all charges were dropped.

After the beating of the limo driver, Tupac flew to Lansing, Michigan, and performed at a concert. Midway through the show, he got carried away and challenged the audience to produce a rapper who could defeat him in lyrical battle. A local rapper accepted the challenge, mounted the stage, and upstaged Tupac. In response, Tupac lifted a bat and tried to beat the rapper. The audience jeered and Tupac was arrested. He was convicted and sentenced to ten days in jail. By then his friend Charles "Man-Man" Fuller was tired of hearing Tupac's shtick about being "hard," and would accurately note, "Most gangsters are people who wish they didn't have to be hard."

Fearing he would never receive the respect he craved—a respect that comes not from merely living in the ghetto but actually being out there and throwing joints—Tupac tried to hide behind politics. He told friends to join him in getting tattoos that said "50 NIGGAZ," a term that meant a union of blacks in fifty states. Then he told reporters that NIGGA was an acronym for Never Ignorant Getting Goals Accomplished.

"What it really stood for," said former *Source* writer Clarence Mohammed, "is Non-Intelligent Gun-Grabbing Asshole."

But Tupac continued with his scheme to gain respect, and announced his next move—he would form a group called Thug Life. He had the phrase tattooed onto his torso and dreamed of a future where each Thug Life compilation would feature a new cast of actual gangbangers rapping. Tupac's label, Interscope, was unenthusiastic about the project: Executives heard songs from the first album and promptly rejected them. But this didn't deter him. He kept his new gangbanger buddies close and sucked their histories out of them. Even Syke, one of the rappers who appeared on the album, eventually realized that Tupac was a leech. On one song, Tupac said, "Remember Kato."

"Big Kato was like my brother," Syke explained. "He got killed for my car. It had Dayton rims—they cost twenty-five hundred dollars. They killed him for it."

Tupac's friends warned him about the consequences of posing as a gang member onstage. Real gangsters would confront him, especially if he kept wearing those bandannas tied around his head. "He started wearing red around Crips and blue around Bloods, so that when he was around Crips, Bloods wouldn't think he was a Crip, and Crips wouldn't think he was a Blood."

That summer Tupac was cast as a postal worker opposite Janet Jackson in director John Singleton's *Poetic Justice*. Singleton hoped the role would calm Tupac down. Before they filmed any kissing scenes, however, Janet Jackson insisted that Tupac be tested for HIV.

By fall, like the DOC, Tupac Shakur had relocated to Atlanta, Georgia. His manager had purchased a home in the area in hopes that Tupac would finally settle down. Within weeks, reports came in that Tupac was getting smashed in strip clubs with Oakland's Too $hort and causing scenes that got both of them ejected. That Halloween, after midnight, he left a concert at Atlanta University, entered his Benz, and led two carloads of friends back to his hotel. At Piedmont and Spring streets, two blocks from their destination, he stopped for a red light. In the vehicle ahead of him, he noticed a quarrel. Two white men reached into that car's window. Certain that the lone driver was black, Tupac left his car and demanded an explanation. The white men released the car; it sped away. Enraged, the Caucasians—brothers Mark and Scott Whitwell— turned to vent their anger on Tupac, only to see three carloads of people behind him. Hoping to frighten them away, Mark Whitwell pulled a gun. "Run!" he yelled as if it were a track meet.

Instead, Tupac reached into his car, pulled his own gun, leaned over the hood of the Benz, and started shooting. A frequent visitor to firing ranges as well as a cinéaste who favored shoot-'em-up gangster films, he hit Mark Whitwell in the abdomen and his brother, Scott, in the ass.

An hour later, wrathful police officers rushed the Sheraton and arrested him: His targets, he discovered, were off-duty police officers.

Charged with two counts of aggravated assault, he was released on $55,000 bail. To the national media the shootings were considered a municipal outrage, civic perfidy—he was branded a societal menace. The negative coverage persisted long after it was revealed that the gun Mark Whitwell brandished had been swiped from the precinct's evidence room, that both brothers were drunk, that on the day of Tupac's hearing one of the officers was charged with aggravated assault and both with writing a report that claimed, '[n-words] came by and did a drive-by shooting.' "

Though the rap press lauded Tupac as a revolutionary hero who did more than sing about shooting police officers, white-run newspapers nationwide denounced him.

In November 1993 Tupac Shakur was in New York, filming *Above the Rim* and trying to escape the negative publicity generated by shooting the two white off-duty officers in Atlanta. "The Tupac I met in New York had calmed down a lot," said video production assistant Johnny Simmons. "I mean, homeboy had been trying to play that character from *Juice*. But by late 1993 he had been in a bit of trouble; he was paying a lot of money for lawyers; he kept going in and out of the joint. All of that made the brother more mature. He wasn't that same crazy cat looking for trouble." During meetings to discuss a music video, Tupac kept saying, "I have to change my life. You know how much money I'm spending on lawyers?!"

"He told me how much money," Simmons continued, "then said, 'I have this case here, that case there. Man, I have to stay out of trouble.' That's how he was. But after that, we once again started hearing stories about how Tupac was acting."

Suge Knight sensed the time was right to lure Shakur to Death Row. He offered Tupac a whopping $200,000 for one song. Tupac was confounded but enthusiastic; with court cases piling up, he needed money to pay the fleet of defense attorneys he had retained. Happily accepting the offer, Tupac—under the name Thug Life—recorded "Pour Out a Little Liquor," a downcast ode to friends killed on the streets.

When the song was finished, Suge offered a contract with Death Row. To his surprise, Tupac rejected the offer. By then Tupac had been introduced to Haitian-born music promoter Jacques Agnant and his circle of friends. "I'm going to look after you," Agnant said upon meeting him. "You don't need to get in no more trouble."

"I got close to them," Tupac said. "I used to dress in baggies and sneakers. They took me shopping, that's when I bought my first Rolex and all my jewels. They made me mature. They introduced me to all these gangsters in Brooklyn. I met [Jacques's] family, went to his kid's birthday party—I trusted him, you know what I'm saying? I even tried to get [Jacques] in the movie, but he didn't want to be on film. That bothered me. I don't know any nigga that didn't want to be in the movies."

On November 14, 1993, his new friend, Agnant, took him to Nell's, a racially mixed downtown Manhattan venue that instantly impressed him. Instead of a crowded space brimming with hostility, what he was used to seeing in California, Nell's was an atmospheric spot filled with wanton groupies, easygoing dancers, and venerable admirers. Bartenders kept the drinks flowing; the DJ alternated between playing voluble reggae, scabrous house, and topical hip-hop; well-dressed scenesters lounged on battered sofas with anorexic aspiring models. Minor celebrities greeted each other in the dim basement area; athletes mingled with outer-borough fashion-plates. Ronnie Lott of the New York Jets and Derrick Coleman from the Nets approached to commend him, and Tupac said. "I felt above and beyond, like I was glowing."

Someone introduced her. One of his friends said, "This girl wants to do more than just meet you." He walked away, danced by himself to Jamaican music. Then the young hen appeared waving her buttocks and sizable mounds, Tupac claimed. "She's touching my dick. She's touching my balls, she opened my zipper, she put her hands on me." She led him to a dark corner, lifted his shirt. "She starts kissing my stomach, kissing my chest, licking me, and shit. She's going down and I'm like, Oh, shit. She pulled my dick out, she started sucking my dick on the dance floor."

"When I first met Tupac, he kissed me on my cheek and made small talk with me," wrote Ayanna Jackson, the woman Tupac claimed chased him around Nell's. "After a while I excused myself and started to walk to the dance floor. When I felt someone slide their hands into the back pockets of my jeans, I turned around, assuming it was my friend, but was shocked when I discovered it was Tupac. We danced for a while, and he touched my face and his body brushed mine.

"Due to the small dance floor and the large number of people, we were shoved into a dark corner. Tupac pulled up his shirt, took my hand, traced it down his chest and sat it on top of his erect penis. He then kissed me and pushed my head down on his penis and in a brief three-second encounter, my lips touched the head of his penis. This happened so suddenly that once I realized what he was trying to do, I swiftly brought my head up. I must reiterate that I did not suck his penis on the dance floor."

"That shit turned me on," said Tupac Shakur. "I wasn't thinking, like, 'This is going to be a rape case.' I'm thinking, 'This is going to be a good night.' You know what I'm saying?" Once he was erect, they left the dance floor. "I've got to get out of here," Tupac told his friend Jacques. "I'm about to take her to the hotel. I'll see you later."

At the hotel they coupled. "As soon as I came, that was it. I was tired. I was drunk. I knew I had to get up early in the morning. So I was like, 'What are you going to do? You can spend the night or you can leave.' " She passed her phone number, then left. Tupac walked over to where his pal Jacques was sleeping. At the time, Jacques usually spent the night in his room. He told Jacques about Ayanna fellating him on the dance floor. His friends Jacques and Trevor were visibly agitated. "Trevor is a big freak," Tupac explained. "He was going crazy. All he kept asking me was, 'D-d-did you fuck her in the ass?' He was listening to every single detail. I thought, 'This is just some guy shit, it's all good.' "

Four days later, Tupac was in his suite, drinking to kill time before that night's performance at the Club 88, a violence-plagued dive in New Jersey. Jacques, he said, asked, "Why don't you give her a call?" Tupac wasn't interested. Jacques persisted: "I called her. I mean, she called me and she's on her way." The telephone rang. The front desk announced her arrival. Jacques gave Tupac's manager, Charles "Man-Man" Fuller, money to cover cab fare. "Let that bitch pay for her own cab," Tupac protested.

Ayanna Jackson claimed Tupac called her: During their conversation the night before, he gave her his pager number and said he wanted to see her. The next day she paged him. Charles "Man-Man" Fuller returned the call and said, Yes, Tupac did want to see her, but he had to do a show at Club 88. Why didn't she just take a cab to the Parker-Meridien? They would pay for the ride. "Once I got to the hotel," Ayanna wrote, "I met Charles Fuller for the first time; he paid for the cab and led me upstairs. Inside the suite, Tupac, [Jacques], and Trevor were seated in the living room, smoking weed and drinking Absolut. Tupac told me to come in and pointed to the arm of the sofa near him and I sat down."

Tupac said she was dressed provocatively. Her presence made him uncomfortable. Instead of sitting with Jacques and Trevor, she decided to perch on the arm of his chair. "And [Jacques] and Trevor are looking at her like a chicken, like she's food. It's a real uncomfortable situation. So I'm thinking, 'Okay, I'm going to take her to the room and get a massage.'"

In the bedroom, she massaged his back. When he turned around, her fingers kneaded his chest. "This lasted for about a half an hour," Tupac recalled. "In between, we would stop and kiss each other. I'm thinking she's about to give me another blowjob. But before she could do that, some niggas came in and I froze up more than she did!"

But she didn't object to their presence, he claimed.

"They came and they started touching her ass. They going, 'Oooohhh, she got a nice ass.' [Jacques] isn't touching her but I can hear his voice leading it, like, 'Put her panties down, put her pantyhose down.' I just got up and walked out the room."

"Just as we began kissing," Ayanna wrote, "the door opened and I heard people entering. As I started to turn to see who it was, Tupac grabbed my head and told me, 'Don't move.' I looked down at him and he said, 'Don't worry, baby. These are my brothers and they ain't going to hurt you. We do everything together.' I started to shake my head. 'No. No, 'Pac. I came here to be with you. I came here to see you. I don't want to do this.'" As she rose from the bed, Tupac slammed her head down. Her lips collided with his penis. He squeezed the back of her neck until she gagged. With Jacques, Tupac restrained her. Freaky Trevor forced his member into her mouth. Ayanna realized she was being raped.

"I felt hands tearing my shoes off," she wrote, "ripping my stockings and panties off. I couldn't move. I felt paralyzed, trapped, and I started to black out. They leered at my body. 'This bitch got a fat ass!' She's fine!"

They would not allow her to leave, she said. They alternated between joking with each other and trying to assuage her. She reached the elevator car, studied its mirrored walls. "Once I caught sight of myself, I sank down on the floor and started to cry. They came out, picked me up, and brought me back into the suite."

Tupac claimed he woke up and saw Jacques standing over him. Jacques was saying, " 'Pac, 'Pac." The suite was brightly lit. The mood had changed. Tupac felt drugged. How much time had passed? "You're going to the police," Jacques yelled. "You're going to the police!" Confused, Tupac watched Jacques bring Ayanna into the room. He claimed she was fully dressed in undamaged clothing.

She stood before the couch. "In my mind," she wrote, "I'm thinking, 'This motherfucker just raped me and he's lying up here like a king, acting as if nothing happened.' " She cried hysterically. "How could you do this to me?! I came here to see you. *I can't believe you did this to me!*"

"I don't have time for this shit," Tupac said incongruously. "Get this bitch out of here."

Tupac quoted her as saying, "This not the last time you're going to hear from me!" She left, door slamming behind her. Jacques said, "Don't worry about it, 'Pac. Don't worry. I'll handle it. She just tripping." Tupac asked, What happened? Jacques quipped, "Too many niggas."

By chance, immediately after Ayanna was assaulted, rapper Biggie Smalls arrived to hang out.

Tupac reportedly met Biggie in 1993, on the set of John Singleton's *Poetic Justice*: As soon as he heard Biggie's debut single, the dour "Party and Bullshit," he became a fan. During breaks from filming, Tupac incessantly played the single on a radio. In town on business, Biggie stopped by the set, met Tupac, then visited his home, where they smoked marijuana and bonded. "I always thought it was like a Gemini thing," Biggie said. "We just clicked off the top and were cool ever since."

When Biggie stopped in at the Parker-Meridien on November 18, 1993, Tupac's friends immediately said they were going downstairs. Then Tupac explained what happened, repeating Ayanna Jackson's words, said one law enforcement source. Nervous, Biggie prepared to leave. Then they heard sirens outside, raced to the window, and saw a host of red lights approaching. Biggie rushed to the door; Tupac numbly dropped onto the couch with a lit joint. Smoke hung in the air like a bitter accusation. The telephone rang. Tupac's publicist, Talibah, was in the lobby. "The police are down here," she said.

In the lobby, uniformed police officers called Tupac over. Ayanna stepped forward, identifying him and Charles Fuller. Officers released Biggie from handcuffs, allowed him to leave. Tupac was cuffed and led past reporters. Chest puffed out, he said: "I'm young, black . . . I'm making money and they can't stop me. They can't find a way to make me dirty and I'm clean."

As negative publicity in the mainstream media increased, and more editorials denouncing Tupac appeared in print, Interscope chief Jimmy Iovine worried that Tupac would damage Interscope's relationship with Time Warner, which started in late 1990, when Interscope was formed as a $30-million joint venture with Time Warner's Atlantic Group.

By 1993 Interscope was grossing as estimated $88 million and expanding, thanks to Death Row's success, into other genres: Iovine signed Trent Reznor's volatile Nine Inch Nails, low-fi "alternative" bands such as Bush, Tom ("What's New Pussycat?") Jones, and Cheap Trick's Robin Zander. Interscope would soon be expanding into R&B as well.

But Time Warner had come under attack from right-wing politicians; the conglomerate was accused of peddling obscenity for profit's sake. Critics stressed that rapper Ice-T's side project *Body Count* (a heavy metal album that featured the incendiary "Cop Killer" song) had no socially redeeming value. Though the song was a heavy metal number, the fact that Ice-T was African American led to renewed attacks against rap and hip-hop. Soon politicians went from attacking rap music to leveling charges that Time Warner was advocating the murder of police officers. Bowing to pressure from the media, politicians, and shareholders, Time Warner dumped Ice-T.

Iovine needed to distance himself from Tupac, so he asked Suge Knight to accept him on Death Row. Since December 1992, Iovine and

Suge had had a close relationship. Suge allowed Iovine to take a hands-on approach to helping run Death Row: Iovine appointed Interscope employees to handle marketing and promotion for Death Row albums; Iovine's employees paid video companies and independent promoters; Iovine was able to disagree with Suge and walk away unharmed. Iovine was the man with the checkbook.

Iovine told Suge, "Take this kid. Take him *please*. He's out of control. *Take* him." Suge was enthusiastic about signing Tupac. A meeting was scheduled between Iovine, Suge, Tupac, and his manager, Watani Tychimba. At the meeting Iovine said it would be better for everyone if Tupac went to Death Row. Tupac asked, Why? Iovine sugar-coated the reason. Tupac, he said, would be able to work with Dr. Dre. His albums would sell millions. He would be rich. He would be with a label that supported his sort of music. Tupac said he liked his relationship with Interscope. Being with Death Row, Iovine stressed, wouldn't necessarily mean leaving Interscope. The two labels had a "unique relationship." Again Tupac refused to leave Interscope.

"THEY WENT AND HAD HIS MEETING IN THE BATHROOM, WHICH, TO ME, IS SOMETHING FROM AN OLD MAFIA MOVIE"

Suge's truck-driving father liked to come home after a long, hard day of work and listen to some relaxing rhythm and blues music. Like his pop, Suge also enjoyed the smooth sounds of R&B. In the early 1970s, groups such as the Chi-Lites, the Delfonics, and Blue Magic, and the performers Curtis Mayfield, Isaac Hayes, and Marvin Gaye were using R&B as a means to promote political change and social consciousness. The emotional music, pleasing to the ear, was also a comfort to a community that had just lost Martin Luther King Jr., Malcolm X, the Black Panthers, and other inspirational leaders.

At Death Row Records, gangsta rap may have paid the bills and pleased the kiddies, but Suge felt there was room for some sophisticated R&B as well. When Tupac refused to sign to the label, Suge decided to search for some rhythm and blues singers.

At the time, R&B was undergoing a transformation. Gone were the days of dapper quintets wearing suits, performing choreographed dance steps, and serenading the ladies. As hip-hop began to sell more, R&B

producers pressured their artists to wear baggy, rap-style clothing, boots, gaudy jewelry, and gold teeth; instead of champagne, modern R&B singers tried to woo the ladies with tall bottles of cheap malt liquor; smooth, gentle music was replaced by clunky beats, mechanical noises, and vulgar slang. These singers frowned, grabbed their crotches, and seemed to be trying to intimidate the ladies into loving them, or else.

The group Jodeci was one of the first to nationalize this modern "R&B" philosophy: Jodeci began when sixteen-year-old Donald "Devante Swing" DeGrate ran away from home, traveled to Minneapolis, and tried to land a job with Prince's label, Paisley Park. "K-Ci and Jo-Jo and them was like, 'If you make it with Prince, don't forget about us.' "

In Minneapolis, Prince's employees wouldn't even listen to his demo. "The receptionist kept saying she couldn't help me. I wasn't gonna leave until they put me on. But then I started realizing that Prince was the only one making real money in his camp. So I took my ass right back to Charlotte, North Carolina."

During a telephone conversation back home, he played his friend K-Ci a new love song he had written, and said he was thinking of visiting New York City. Devante, his brother, Dalvin, and his friends, Jo-Jo and K-Ci, traveled to New York together and rented rooms at a hotel in Queens. Then they went to Uptown Entertainment's Midtown Manhattan office: Since they were new to the big city, and got lost a few times, the trip took these hicks five hours. "We got to New York with twenty-nine songs on three tapes," Devante said. "And at first they was not trying to hear us." A&R people felt their demos lacked energy, but rapper Heavy D arranged a live audition for Uptown's president and CEO Andre Harrell.

At the time, Sean "Puffy" Combs—a flamboyant man with a childlike build, a neatly trimmed fade haircut, mild overbite, a taste for European designer clothing, and huge thick-framed eyeglasses—worked as an intern at Uptown. "I was bugging that they were my age and able to sing like that. K-Ci was smaller than he is now. I couldn't believe all that came out of him."

The group signed a deal and Puffy helped find them quarters in a Bronx housing project. In the studio, Puffy helped shape their sound, injecting the hip-hop flavor dominating the sales charts. By the time *Forever My Lady* was completed, Puffy had been promoted from intern to head of artist development. Puffy realized that the group needed a marketable image. "Their style was country, not nationwide 'hot' or East Coast refined." It was Puffy who noticed that Jodeci members always seemed to be carrying rap cassettes. Pressed to design an image for them, he suggested they wear baggy hip-hop-style gear. The audience reacted immediately. *Forever My Lady* sold three million copies, yielded a gold single ("Come & Talk to Me"), and soared to No. 1 on the R&B albums chart.

By the time Jodeci finished recording their follow-up album, *Diary of a Mad Band*, Suge Knight entered the picture. "When I interviewed K-Ci and Jo-Jo, they were saying a lot of stuff was happening at Uptown," said writer Michael Gonzalez. "The rivalry between Andre and Puffy was going strong."

With the success of albums by Jodeci and R&B singer Mary J. Blige, Sean "Puffy" Combs was suddenly a feature of articles in rap magazines. Envious, Harrell began to remind Puffy that there could be only one lion in the jungle.

At this point Devante met Suge Knight. He introduced Suge to his bandmates in Jodeci, who respected Suge's plans for the future and tried to break their management contract with their record company, Uptown, so as to sign with Suge's independent Death Row Management.

Then Jodeci member K-Ci introduced Suge to his girlfriend, Mary J. Blige, a troubled R&B singer signed to Puffy's Bad Boy production company. "[Mary] conducted interviews where she did as much drinking as talking and looked like a zombie on national television," *Vibe* reported. "Then there was the concert in London where she was so out of it the crowd booed her off the stage." Unhappy with her career, Mary blamed it all on her manager, Puffy. "Nothing was right," she said. "Everything was wrong with my management company." Like Jodeci, she asked Suge to serve as her manager.

Until matters were settled, Jodeci played hardball with Uptown, a record label the group felt wasn't showing them the respect due a band whose debut sold three million copies. Jodeci refused to participate in any videos, a decision that may have led to their follow-up *Diary* selling a mere one million copies. Faced with decreased sales, Jodeci accused Uptown of penalizing them by underpromoting their album. This was when Suge Knight stepped in.

"Andre Harrell was scared to death of Suge to the point where he had bodyguards," said one *Vibe* writer. "Suge and Andre were going to have some meeting but Suge wouldn't have it in Andre's office. He wanted to meet inside the bathroom. Because he thought the office was bugged and Andre would try to get some shit on him. They went and had this meeting in the bathroom, which, to me, is like something from an old Mafia movie."

Suge was said to have threatened to violate Harrell if he wouldn't sign papers. "I heard it was some crazy shit where he had homeboy's pants down and was like, 'Sign this or you're gonna be shitting blood for a minute,'" said one magazine photographer. "They said he'd be violated if he didn't sign something. Far as I know, Suge had some of his goons with him and it was some ol' jailhouse shit." In this version, Suge also held Harrell's head over a toilet bowl and threatened to shove it in. "I guess that was part of their repertoire."

A New York record executive heard another version: Suge aimed a gun at Harrell's head and said, "Sign this or else."

No one quite knows what, if anything, happened. After the meeting, however, everything changed. Suddenly Uptown agreed to upgrade Jodeci's contracts and grant them greater creative control. In addition to a substantial retroactive back payment, the group's royalty rate doubled from nine to eighteen percent, industry standard for platinum-selling artists. Then Suge bought Devante Swing a $250,000 white Lamborghini Diablo sports car.

Now it was time for Suge to help Mary J. Blige. "She was signed to a little production company which went through Uptown and then to MCA," Suge told a reporter. "By the time the money got to Mary, it wasn't shit. I met with the guy who ran the production company right here in this room, him and his people and just me and Mary. I don't need to run in no packs."

The meeting with Bad Boy representatives occurred in a suite at New York's Four Seasons hotel. "I told Mary to speak her mind, that she didn't have nothing to worry about, and then I told them they was lettin' Mary out of that fucked-up deal. And they did."

Newsweek reported on Suge's subsequent West Coast management contracts with the group Jodeci, their producer, Devante Swing, and singer Mary J. Blige. "There is speculation about how he got involved with those acts and how he renegotiated their contracts with Uptown Records. One rumor has it that Knight and his associates paid an unfriendly visit to Uptown CEO Andre Harrell. Both Knight and Harrell deny the story, but the latter has since hired the Nation of Islam's security arm, the Fruit of Islam, for protection. These days, they go where he goes."

Vibe reported, "There were rumors that Knight threatened Harrell. But both deny the story."

Spin magazine wrote: "Rumors abound in the music industry about how coercion might have played a factor in the coup—an allegation Knight denies."

Devante Swing insisted that Uptown simply took Suge's energy out of context and warned the group that his presence might endanger its relationship with the label. "But the negative vibe they expected never came across." Rumors about Suge, he felt, were spread by envious business rivals. Suge was nothing but an honest businessman who protected his artists. "And a lot of people really resent that."

Originally, Mary J. Blige agreed. She, too, had been taken advantage of by mendacious industry executives, she said. But it was comforting to finally have someone on her side. "Suge's like that guy in the movies who goes around getting the bad people: Charles Bronson, right?"

Interrogated by a *Vibe* reporter about the meeting with Harrell, Suge said people had this business mixed up. Reporters eagerly attacked someone trying to help black artists, and willfully ignored thieves who robbed talented groups of their rightful earnings. "When you stand up for right, people should tip they hat to you and keep movin' and mind they own business."

As more stories about Suge and Harrell appeared, both sides denied everything and continued expressing respect for each other, one *L.A. Times* reporter chuckled. "Something *definitely* happened. You'll hear different versions, but ultimately Suge at one point threatened Andre over Jodeci and Mary J. and got both. And at one point he threatened Russell Simmons of Def Jam, but nothing worked out because Russell had heavy hitters on his team that weren't gonna stand for that.

"There was a profile of Mary J. Blige in *Request* magazine around the time her album *My Life* came out. It's funny because all these Uptown staffers were saying, 'Oh, yeah, Suge is a really great guy! He's real cool.' But it also alluded to the fact that Andre had twenty-four-hour surveillance, security guards, and all these different locks to his office. Then again, this is the same Andre who was dealing with [singers] coming up and trashing the office all the time. But it's basically an open secret that Suge threatened Andre."

In print interviews, Suge said he did not regard himself to be a violent individual. If someone wanted to sit and discuss positive things, he could do that all day long. "But even the nicest person in the world is not going to let somebody just walk right up and do harm to his family," he warned. "When a man is threatened, he's got to defend himself and stand up for what's right. I mean, that's just common sense."

The attacks on his character, he felt, seemed to be racially motivated. "I know there are still individuals in this society who can't stand the thought of a young black person with a gang of money in the bank."

Soon, Mary J. Blige decided that maybe Suge wasn't such a hero. Her label president, Andre Harrell, told *Vibe* that Puffy and Steve Lucas were once again her managers. "I think she decided not to work with [Suge]. On the album credits it says Sean 'Puffy' Combs and Steve Lucas. That's who I call."

The matter ended with Puffy continuing to deny that Suge forced Harrell to free Blige and Jodeci from their management contracts. "There were no problems or anything like that. He was like, 'Yo, Puff brother, if you need me, it's all good.' But no, he's not her manager."

Instead, Suge called himself Blige's "consultant," and featured members of Jodeci singing on albums by Death Row.

"NIGGA, YOU WASN'T SAYING THAT SHIT WHEN I WAS WHOOPIN' YO LITTLE ASS ALL UP AND DOWN THE SET OF YOUR VIDEO!"

Whether he was in his home in Anaheim Hills, his residence in Westwood, or his abode in the Valley, Suge Knight's day began with an arduous workout. In his mirrored gym, as a stereo blared soul music by artists like Al Green or Marvin Gaye, Suge bench-pressed heavy weights. His cellular phone never stopped ringing; his beeper kept sounding; running Death Row was a twenty-four-hour occupation. But Suge focused on thrusting the barbell into the air. After admiring himself in the mirror, taking a quick shower, then slipping into casual clothing, he got in his customized Mercedes convertible and began making his rounds.

His first stop was Let Me Ride, the label's nonentertainment venture, a custom hydraulic shop located near stores with small barred windows and security gates. "A company can't just barge into the 'hood trying to provide some fake charity bullshit," Suge once said. "You got to deliver something real or it just won't work."

Over the door Suge had hung a painting of the customized Chevy Low Rider Dre used in the "Nuthin' but a 'G' Thang" video. Suge's employees—ex-convict buddies or friends from the Bloods—would join him in idle talk about cars, neighborhood beefs, upcoming artists, or old friends who needed jobs. At the sight of Suge, homeless people stepped forward, knowing he could always be counted on to hand over a dollar bill. Police cars slowed at the sight of his clique. "Sometimes it's as if the police are just out looking for trouble," Suge told a reporter. "It don't bother me none though. That's the way it's been as long as I can remember. I'm used to it."

When his cell phone rang, he ended conversations, leaped into his luxury car, and sped over to the label's Westwood office. At the time, Suge was overseeing the production of the *Above the Rim* soundtrack. He was working with Dre; MC Hammer's brother, Louis Burrell; and executives from New Line Cinema, the company releasing the film. In addition to his stable of Death Row acts, the album would include all-new music by female R&B trio SWV (Sisters With Voices), Luke's R&B group H-town, and New York crooner Al B Sure. Since the film starred Tupac Shakur, Suge viewed the soundtrack as another opportunity to try to get Shakur on the label.

Suge knew twenty-two-year-old Tupac was going through a rough period. On February 1, Tupac appeared in Los Angeles municipal court to face charges filed against him by film director Allen Hughes. After Allen and Albert Hughes directed a number of his music videos, Tupac landed the starring role in *Juice*. The Hughes brothers then asked if they could use Tupac's name to secure a movie deal: They were working on their debut, *Menace II Society*. Tupac agreed, then worked with John Singleton on the film *Poetic Justice*. When Tupac told the Hughes brothers he wanted only a small part in *Menace*, they said they had the perfect role. After reading the script, Tupac felt they had offered "a sucker role."

"They was trippin'," he said, " 'cause they got this thing with John Singleton. They feel like they competing with him." While watching MTV one evening, a segment on the Hughes brothers, the directors said they dropped Tupac from the film. Tupac was enraged that he had to learn this while watching television.

He and his friends visited the Hughes brothers on the set of the video for Spice One's "Trigger Got No Heart," *Menace II Society*'s theme music. Instantly, Tupac slugged Allen Hughes; his friends leaped on Allen and tried to grab his brother Albert, who wisely fled the scene. "If I have to go to jail," Tupac said, "I don't even want to be living. I just want to cease to exist for however long they have me there, and then when I come out, I'll be reborn, you know what I'm saying?"

In court, the Hughes brothers arrived with a security team. "Aw, you lil' bitch!" said Allen Hughes upon seeing Tupac alone.

"Lil' bitch?" Tupac tossed his Walkman to a friend. "Nigga, you wasn't saying that shit when I was whoopin' yo little ass all up and down the set of your video!"

"You and twelve of your niggas!"

While restraining the Hughes brothers, one of their bodyguards accidentally shoved Tupac, who began to rant and rave until white sheriffs arrived. *"Officers,"* Tupac said then in as docile a tone as he could muster, "I'm so glad you arrived! These men were trying to attack me! Can you *believe* that? They tried to attack *me* with the Nation of Islam. Those are Farrakhan's boys, you know."

On March 9, a day before his sentencing hearing, Tupac left his room at the Montrose Hotel, where he lived while in town. He steered his rented Lexus LS 300 coupe to a Shell station on Sunset, parked, entered the convenience store, and searched for magazines and snack foods. Five Crips appeared, one of them asking, Where you from?

All over, Tupac replied.

"No you ain't," said the Crip. "You from Baltimore. But you don't never claim it. I know 'cause my homeboy used to take care of you."

Tupac said, Your homeboy lied. No one took care of me in Baltimore.

Just then, white teenagers stepped up to ask for an autograph. Tupac turned to sign one. Infuriated, the Crip yelled, *"I'm finst to jack this nigga!"*

Sensing danger, Tupac quickly reached over to a display case filled with scissors and grabbed a pair. But it was too late. The wily Crip slammed a ham-like fist into Tupac's eye, then left the store with his four friends. Holding the pair of scissors like a dagger, Tupac burst onto Sunset Boulevard and saw the Crip enter a car and take off.

The next day, local and national television stations (including MTV) had film crews stationed outside the L.A. County Courthouse. Inside, the prosecution claimed Tupac could not control his anger. When clos-

ing arguments ended, the judge pronounced sentence: For striking director Allen Hughes, Tupac would have to serve fifteen days in a Los Angeles jail.

After his release, Tupac flew to New York, fell in with new friends and
bodyguards, and partied with them on the set of *Above the Rim*. On April
2, he dropped by NBC studios to watch his friend Snoop Doggy Dogg
record an appearance for *Saturday Night Live*. Suge Knight reminded
Shakur that he could still sign with Death Row: The label would support
him and provide lawyers; they would pair him with hip-hop's most commercial producer; they would buy him cars, install him in a fancy house,
and pay well—all he had to do was say the word and sign the contract.
Thankful for the $200,000 Suge had paid him for one song, Tupac none-
theless refused Suge's offer: He still didn't feel comfortable with the idea
of leaving Interscope Records or his own management.

Three weeks later, in early May, the lights dimmed at New York's
Paramount Theater and the very first Source Awards ceremony began.
The Source started as a pamphlet thrown together by students at Harvard
University; three years later, in 1991, it was the top-selling, most-imi-
tated hip-hop magazine in North America. At their very first awards
ceremony, a hip-hop version of the annual Grammy Awards, the guest
list included Long Island's De La Soul, Tupac Shakur, New Jersey's
Queen Latifah and Treach (of Naughty by Nature), Queens, New York's,
A Tribe Called Quest and Run-D.M.C., Mount Vernon's Pete Rock &
CL Smooth, Staten Island's Wu-Tang Clan, *Menace II Society* star
Larenz Tate, Brooklyn's Masta Ace and DJ Premier, Harlem's Doug E.
Fresh, South Bronx rapper KRS-One, Luther Campbell from Miami, the
R&B group SWV and Death Row artists such as the Lady of Rage.

That evening, Suge felt on top of the world. Death Row's *The Chronic*
and *DoggyStyle* had sold a combined total of more than seven million
copies: For eight months in 1993, *The Chronic* remained on *Billboard's*
Top 10 list; five months after its release, Snoop's *DoggyStyle* was still in
the Top 20.

While this may have gratified most executives, Suge Knight vowed to
make Death Row the most successful company of the decade. In addition to monopolizing R&B and rap, he talked of creating a union for
rappers; forming an organization that would help veteran soul singers get

back on their feet; hosting a Mother's Day celebration at a Beverly Hills hotel for fifty single mothers; buying a stable of horses in the country (he had recently taken up horseback riding and figured his artists would have an escape from their troubles); sponsoring toy giveaways at churches and hospitals as they did last Christmas; establishing an antigang foundation in Compton; opening businesses that would provide young black men with jobs; helping to underwrite U.S. House of Representatives member Maxine Waters's youth program—a decision that moved Waters to tell reporters, "The only thing Suge is threatening is the status quo."

Despite his magnanimous intentions, Suge couldn't help but note that music executives at the Source Awards were frightened of him. But he knew that these same executives had to regard him: Thanks to Death Row, California rap groups now outsold their resentful East Coast counterparts.

"It was the first annual Source Awards and the shit was mad disorganized," said a *Vibe* writer. "A Tribe Called Quest had come onstage to accept the award, then all of a sudden Tupac came out onstage and started 'rapping.' He stopped and went backstage. He always said it was the fault of stage managers because they told him to come out there at that minute. In the audience, when he came out, it looked like an immediate dis to the East right off. I thought, '*Who the fuck does this nigga think he is coming out onstage when A Tribe Called Quest, who ain't never did nothing to nobody, are trying to accept the award?!*' Nigga just pissed me off and shit!"

The Source admitted, "This sparked some ill feeling as far as the crowd was concerned, and the mood degenerated into the old East vs. West conflict."

The incident only increased Suge's desire to sign Tupac to the label, which, by night's end, won awards for Solo Artist of the Year (Dre's *The Chronic*), Producer of the Year (Dre); New Solo Artist of the Year (Snoop), Lyricist of the Year (Snoop), and Album of the Year (*The Chronic*).

"THEY'D BEAT THE BITCH DOWN!"

In California, people were literally gunning for Suge. But Suge rose to the occasion. "He became Suge Knight, the don," said someone close to him at the time. As word of his violent nature spread, Suge took to wearing expensive suits and ostentatious jewelry.

In an average week he would be involved in three major problems. "Then that week's gone and it's a new week with more drama! He would have one or two problems that week. It was consistent. He would say, 'I done beat up Tommy Hearns's brother this week for cheating me on the hotel rooms I was tellin' you about.' 'I beat that motherfucker on the boat.' 'Beat the motherfucker who gave the party on the boat, Snoop's album release party, for cheating me outta such-and-such money.' " Most of the attacks were for trivial reasons, the insider said. "But to some motherfuckers, these things are a big deal."

"Suge didn't stay the nice guy he was when I knew him," said a former schoolmate. "I think the money and the power got to him. 'Cause he got into a lot of shit. I heard he used to make people kiss his ring and that his whole office was painted red. He kinda went off a little. I always thought that. And not only that, but there were several attempts on his life."

Though enemies were hunting him, Suge returned to partying in flashy nightspots. One evening, at Larry Parker's restaurant, Suge was said to have argued with another patron over a table. Legend had it that out front they had a gunfight and Suge wounded four people (no one knows if this ever happened). Another time Suge was leaving the Roxbury Club with a friend, when rival gang members appeared. "Someone shot at him," said a friend of his, "and he threw his homeboy in the way." His homeboy was a promoter named Phillipe. "And his homeboy got shot in the ass just for standing next to him."

On another occasion Suge was riding in a woman's car. People had warned this woman that she should not associate with him. " 'Cause people were trying to kill him at that time," said a friend of Suge's. As she was driving, another car pulled up on the passenger side. People in the other vehicle spotted Suge and gave chase. The other car caught up and a passenger aimed a gun at Suge. The woman stepped on the gas and left them behind. "And he told her to pull over," said Suge's friend. "She kept driving. Suge said, 'Pull over, let me drive.' She knew he was serious 'cause he screamed at her. He wasn't playing. She stopped the car. Suge jumped out and pulled a gun from under his seat. The other car sped off, then Suge started chasing them! That kinda cooled their relationship off."

On another afternoon Suge took Madeline Woods to lunch at Lawry's. Woods, a voluptuous former anchorwoman for the Black Entertainment Television cable network, was Suge's "personal assistant". At a nearby table, one of Suge's enemies sat with killers from his Crip gang, watching Suge enter. The enemy, a revered Crip, couldn't believe his eyes. Recently, he and Suge had had a falling out over $50,000. To collect on the debt, Suge had sent Blood members to the Crip's apartment, where they surrounded his roommate, demanding to know where he was, ripped phone wires out of the wall, and blocked the doors and windows. One of Suge's men, pulled out a cellular, called Suge, and handed the phone to the Crip's terrified roommate. "Where's your business partner?" Suge asked that day.

The roommate, a music producer, told Suge he didn't know.

Suge said, "Well, man, he owe some money. That nigga's just trying to run from me. Tell that nigga I'm trying to catch up with him. Give him my pager number."

For collateral on the $50,000 debt, Suge's men took musical equipment the Crip and his roommate kept scattered around their apartment. The Crip kept calling Suge, reaching his voice mail. Finally, he left a message: "I done paged you like four times. You ain't return my call. Since you ain't callin' me back, I take it you're looking for me. Since you're lookin' for me, I'll be looking for you. And you better have your 9mm, nigga, 'cause I got mine." He slammed the phone down.

Now Suge was entering Lawry's restaurant. "Suge didn't see him," the roommate explained, "so [the Crip] put his mobile phone on the table and snuck out of there." In his car in the parking lot, the Crip used his car phone to call the mobile he left on the table inside. One of his fellow gangsters answered the phone. "Ay!" the Crip said. "Suge is in there! I wanna get him! He know me but he don't know you!"

After ending the call, the Crip's friends quietly left Lawry's. In their own cars they loaded guns and waited. When Suge appeared with his assistant, Madeline Woods, the friends began their drive-by shooting. Just as they were about to open fire, a black and white LAPD squad car appeared. The Crip's men hid their guns and drove past Suge. Within the hour, he called his roommate to yell, "Ay! *We had him! We had Suge's life! Coulda had him right there!*" Suge never knew how close he had come to being murdered.

"HE WAS CARRYING GUNS, MAN. 'CAUSE OF THAT INTERVIEW WITH THE SOURCE"

When Suge learned of Warren G's comments in *The Source*'s May 1994 edition, he was enraged. After leaving Death Row, Warren G had produced the song "Indo Smoke" for the *Poetic Justice* soundtrack, signed to Def Jam Records, and released his *Chronic*-like debut *The G-Funk Era*. Warren also ran G-Funk Productions with Snoop, a company that signed Lil' Malik and newcomers like Lady Levi and the Twins to deals.

When *The Source* asked why his solo album had been released on Def Jam as opposed to Death Row, Warren said, "When I first hooked up with Death Row, it was like I was getting dissed. Even though I brought Snoop there. A lot of personal shit. But you know: I ain't with all that old bullshit. You know that shit how motherfuckers be trying to punk motherfuckers and shit? I ain't with all that."

Though he went unnamed, Suge felt Warren was insulting him. "On my album," Warren continued, "I have that song with Nate [Dogg] singing on it. And the only way I could use [the hit single "Regulate"] is that I do it on this *Above the Rim* soundtrack. I thought that was quite fucked up, 'cause I made Death Row, if you ask me—and I'll tell 'em straight up, 'Nigga, I made y'all!' I made the motherfucking company and they can't tell me shit. Please quote me on that one, *they can't tell me shit.*

"'Cause I made that motherfucker . . ."

Days after the courageous interview, Warren phoned *The Source.* "I heard that Warren G didn't want some shit printed," said a source close to Death Row. "He wanted some shit off the record."

Warren tried to recant his comment about having "made" Death Row: He was drinking; a little upset; it's not how he really felt. *The Source* understood, but it was too late. Warren offered his publishing rights. Just pull the issue. It had nothing to do with payment. *The Source* would do it for free, but the issue was already on newsstands.

"I don't know if he had a meeting with Suge or something, but Warren was carrying two 9mms at one time," said Soup Henderson, who worked for Interscope. "This is some true shit. This ain't no, 'I heard' or 'I read off the back of a Cracker Jack box.' This is some true shit! He was carrying guns, man. 'Cause of that interview with *The Source.* When they got ahold of him saying he 'made' Death Row, motherfuckers didn't like that. They, uh—some niggas broke in his house and woke his ass up with guns in his motherfucking face. They kinda put it on him a little bit: *'Nigga don't you ever come out your face saying some shit you know ain't true!'*

"And Warren was like, *'Man, I never even said that shit!'*

"They smacked this nigga up a little bit. That's why later he was strapped. I'm pretty sure he didn't want that *Source* interview to come out."

"It was just the fact that Warren wanted that rep like that," said a source close to Death Row. "I guess he wanted to be known as an intimidating motherfucker. This is off the record 'cause I don't wanna get fucked up my damn self."

When Suge saw the article, "I think that hit home," this source confided. "When you're dealing with someone who drives off one hundred percent ego, that shit will offend them." The only way Suge could save face "was to do what he did, which was bum-rush Warren G at his house and give him that warning: an ass-kicking and a warning at the same time."

This late-night meeting changed Warren's official reason for leaving Death Row. "There are so many groups signed to the label," he said in an interview after Suge's men confronted him, "my record couldn't come out till 1998 or something like that. Don't believe none of that bullshit in the paper. It's about love."

As 1994 continued, the label continued to recruit new artists. One of them, a rapper named CPO, ran into Dr. Dre at Gladstone's, an ocean-side seafood restaurant in Malibu. Dre knew CPO since the N.W.A days, when CPO, real name Vince, was a socially conscious karate teacher and best friend to Clarence "Train" Lars, a local DJ who provided scratches for N.W.A albums. The last time Dre saw CPO was in 1992, when *The Chronic* was nearing completion and former N.W.A member MC Ren brought CPO to Galaxy Studios.

As Dre took a break from recording a song, CPO mentioned that he was unhappy with his deal at Capitol. When his Ren-produced album *To Hell and Black* flopped, CPO blamed the major label. "And Dre said, 'It's like this: If you're gonna leave Capitol, come sign to Death Row. It'll be like leaving one job and coming to another. I'll hook you up.' " CPO couldn't quite extricate himself from his contract that quickly.

CPO had gone from burly political artist to towering gangster rapper. This time in Gladstone's, Dre said, "I got the *Above the Rim* soundtrack coming up. You wanna get on it, come to the studio tomorrow. We'll hook up."

Released from Capitol, CPO appeared at Galaxy Studios. "Then Suge walked in. I didn't even know who he was. He was trying to do a few things, then said, 'W'sup.' It's weird, dog. A nigga don't really remember meeting Suge. You just know him."

CPO began to appear at all Dre's studio sessions. When Dre moved to Larrabee's North in North Hollywood, CPO followed. Then Suge called him aside one evening, saying, "I heard you were signed."

" 'Naw, dog," CPO replied, "I'm not signed to nobody."

"Well, look: If you ain't signed, come and hook up with the Row."

CPO arrived for an appointment at the label's office. An hour late, Suge immediately asked, "Whatchu want?"

"What do I want?" CPO lifted a magazine from a table. "I want the cover."

Suge sighed. "Well, nigga, you ain't said nothing. Turn it over."

CPO said, "It was a *Vibe* magazine with a big-ass picture of Snoop. I said, Yeah, that's what I'm talkin' about."

Attorney David E. Kenner drafted CPO's contract; CPO signed it; he didn't quite know that signing to Suge Publishing gave Suge *all* the publishing earnings. He thought they would share them. Suge handed him six thousand dollars and said he would receive a monthly payment of one thousand dollars. "Before signing," CPO admitted, "I was on general relief." General relief was what Californians called welfare. "And G.R. was giving like two hundred and twenty dollars a month. So a thousand dollars a month for me was *great!*"

But the gang in his Compton neighborhood, the Neighborhood Crips, were apprehensive about his signing to the label. "They started asking, 'Why you wanna hook up with them Bloods? Why you wanna hook up with "that side?" ' " Because the label employed Crips and Bloods, all of whom were being paid well. "But they were like, 'Well, why didn't you hook up with Def Jam?'

"Because," CPO sighed, "Def Jam was an East Coast company. I ain't got nothing against the East . . . but I can't handle my business in the *West* while dealing with an East Coast company! I mean—I *knew* Suge and Dre and Snoop. Why wouldn't I wanna be with people I know?"

He didn't mind not being paid for "Jus So Ya Know," his Snoop-like contribution to the *Above the Rim* soundtrack; he saw it as doing a "favor." Without his deal, he knew he would have be back in professional oblivion, with nothing but his measly "general relief" check. "I was thinking, '*Shit, I'm fittin'a get my album out! This is Death Row! It's liable to sell about platinum! I'm not fittin'a trip. I'm fittin'a get on here and get heard!*' "

"It was still hectic when *DoggyStyle* came out because the label was still somewhat in debt to Interscope," said promoter Doug Young. "But a month after it came out, everything was cracking. Then *Above the Rim* came out and the label was just at its peak, man. They went up a scale, to the top of the pile, another income bracket."

During Dre and Snoop's concerts, the lights would dim. After the opening notes of the theme from the *Scooby-Doo* cartoon slipped out of huge speakers, concertgoers heard a sound bite from a KRS-One album: "How many real hip-hoppers in the place tonight?" Clad entirely in black, Dre would enter from the left side of the stage; from the right, in a long Pendleton shirt, khakis, and watch cap, Snoop would shamble into view. "Tonight's the night I get in some shit," Dre would yell, "Deep Cover" music joining in. At song's end, Snoop would yell, "Yo sound man! Turn my motherfucking mic up!"

Dre and Snoop were like Abbott and Costello. "Yo, Snoop," Dre would say. "What will we do if that sound man don't fix the shit?"

On cue, Snoop would croon, "Never hesitate to put a nigga on his back," lapsing into *The Chronic*'s "Rat-Tat-Tat-Tat." Crowds usually went crazy. Then Snoop would perform his cover of Slick Rick's "La-Di-Da-Di" over an instrumental by Brooklyn rap group Black Moon. Then the Lady of Rage would appear to recite her lyrics from Dre's "Lyrical Gangbang," his "Stranded on Death Row," and her own *Above the Rim* single, "Afro Puffs." By now Rage was tired of waiting for her own album, tentatively titled *Eargasms,* to hit stores; she was tired of the gang members hanging around the studio and the label's by-now dated gangsta rap sound. While describing her album for *The Source*, her feelings became evident. "Well, I have two songs with [N.Y. producer] Premier that I like," she said of *Eargasms.* "They have that hip-hop flavor. I don't want the G-Funk era. I'm not a G child. That's not really my taste, but I can flow to it. I'm down with Death Row, and Death Row is the West Coast, but you can't take the East out of me. That's where I'm from."

Onstage during Dre's concerts, she managed to play her part. After her medley, Dre and Snoop would perform *DoggyStyle*'s "Gin & Juice," *The Chronic*'s "Dre Day," *DoggyStyle*'s "What's My Name," and *The Chronic*'s crossover hit, "Nuthin' but a 'G' Thang."

"Their show was tight," said former writer Louis Romain, who attended the label's Hawaii concert. "But Rage told me they weren't getting too many shows. This was about a year after *The Chronic* tour got canceled. And even though they had the hottest records out, Rage said no one wanted to book them. They had only about six shows."

One of them was in London, where Lee Pinkerton of *HHC* magazine wrote, "Confusion reigned as to whether the media-shy Dr. Dre would appear or not." Overseas, the Death Row crew stayed at the Metropole Hotel, and were scheduled to perform at the Brixton Academy. By now Suge's wife, Sharitha, was representing herself as Snoop's manager. "She's nice but she's scandalous," said one artist manager. "And she ain't no manager. Suge would call Sharitha and say, 'I'll hook up a movie soundtrack for this group. Go tell 'em.' For relaying that message, she'd get twenty percent of their money. That's all it was."

"I dealt with her when we were shooting the Rage cover for *Rappages*," said photographer Brian Cross. "I don't remember the name of the publishing company or whatever—Knight, something-Knight—but I remember thinking it all seemed kinda funky. I ran into Sharitha over there and I saw that it was some all-in-the-family shit. There was no independent aspect to where artists were involved, or made their own decisions. And that was a little shady. It didn't seem like good business."

When reporters in London wanted to speak with Snoop, his manager, Sharitha Knight, told them to wait in the lobby. About an hour later she reappeared with an explanation: Snoop wasn't answering knocks on his door. He was watching television.

The English journalists settled for an interview with Rage, who sanitized her life story, saying she *worked* at Chung King Studios as a receptionist instead of telling the truth, that she lived on their couch for months and showered with a coffeepot. Her relationship with Dre was wonderful, she told English writers. "He was gonna tell everyone that I was his little sister because people said we looked alike! He's always been cool with me! Even in the studio!" Overseas, Death Row could escape its horrific reputation and act like traditional pop stars: They could shack up in hotel rooms with groupies, wave to the kiddies outside their window, sign autographs in record stores, keep reporters waiting, insult the local talent, then see their names in print.

*   *   *

In America, holding the cover of the *Above the Rim* CD and staring at the words, rapper CPO was at a loss for words. How many times had he told the label's employees, from now on I wanna be known as 'Boz Hogg.' He even signed his contract, 'CPO aka Boz Hogg.' But there it was: The credits for his song "Jus So Ya No" listed him as "CPO Boss Hogg." He shook his head and hoped the label would get it right next time. Then CPO realized he should have been paid for his publishing rights: "I looked up and saw niggaz riding around in Lexuses and Grand Cherokees and all that but didn't trip 'cause I said, 'Well, they were on *The Chronic.*' They got a gang of shit cause they *did* a gang of shit.' "

"SUGE CAUGHT HIS 'DADDY' THAT HE USED TO BRAG ON ALL THE TIME AND WENT AND SLAPPED HIM UP!"

"After the *Above the Rim* album," a former Death Row employee said, "Suge was trying to step to the Wu-Tang Clan, who had that really big hit, 'Anything,' with SWV. And Suge knew they were on Loud Records."

After wooing Jodeci and Mary J. Blige from Uptown Records, Suge became known for approaching record label moguls and telling them he wanted certain groups. "He tried to usurp all the artists he could get," said *L.A. Times* reporter Cheo Coker, "Be it Wu-Tang or Biggie, who I know for a fact he wanted on Death Row at one point."

"Suge wanted any wild act that sold a certain amount of records," said a label insider. "If he'd been more businesslike and calmed down, he could've had anyone he wanted."

The rumor that the Wu-Tang Clan had signed to Death Row circulated through the Los Angeles music industry. "A couple of people like DJ Black said they wanted Wu-Tang," Loud's Trevor Trev recalled. "And I heard rumors that *Suge* wanted the group. But that's all it evolved into. Bottom line: They were on contract. What was he gonna do?"

According to a Death Row employee, Suge and Loud Records owner Steve Rifkind met at a party. "It got into some 'disrespect' thing between those two. I couldn't really pinpoint for sure what happened, but I remember when you would even mention Suge Knight's name to Steve Rifkind, he would just shake and shiver and want to stay clear of him."

Matt McDaniel recalled hearing that Suge encountered Rifkind's father in a restaurant. "Suge caught his 'daddy' that he used to brag on all the time and went and slapped him up! *Slapped Jules Rifkind up!*"

Trevor Trev doubted that McDaniel's story was true. "Whether you know it or not, Steve is tied in with Interscope. He's tied in with a lot of these motherfuckers." If anything, Steve Rifkind joked about the situation with Loud employees. "He was like, 'Somebody told me that Suge Knight wants to sign Wu-Tang. Well, if Suge wants them, he has to pay me.' Because the bottom line is: How are you gonna get out the contracts?

"Steve knows a lot of people because of his father, who has been in the business so long," Trev added. "And it's so easy to 'blacklist' somebody, regardless of whether they have the dopest product. It's so easy. And Steve's tied in with Interscope real well," Trev reminded me. " 'Cause Loud Records had been doing promotional accounts with Interscope since *2Pacalypse Now*. And if Suge is as smart a businessman as he is intimidating, he knows that. I'm not saying Steve has mad-mad-pull, but Steve ain't dumb."

Steve Rifkind, meanwhile, denied ever meeting Suge Knight. "No, I have not," he said one morning. He claimed that he had no idea why people would involve him in the Death Row story. "I really don't," he said. "I swear on my son's life. Actually, on my life, that I never met Suge." He claimed that he never heard anything about Death Row wanting the Wu-Tang Clan. "Naw," he said. "There were . . . wherever that came from—ah, I don't know what 'former employees' or whatever . . . You were the first person that ever told me that they were interested in Wu-Tang Clan."

Asked if he walked around the office saying his father was a mobster, Rifkind replied, "That I would walk around the office? Wherever you're getting . . . These are all . . . I don't know whose . . . what ex-employees or whatever but . . ." He exhaled heavily. "I would walk around saying my father was a mobster?! Never in a million years." He began to stammer. "You're—you're the first person that I ever called—I consult Interscope Records. I'm up there every single day for the past two years." Asked if he could discuss Interscope, Steve Rifkind said, "Yeah. What do you want to know?"

How he got there.

"I'm—I've had a relationship with Interscope for the past five years."

Asked for a final comment, he said, "I don't know. I mean, I'm . . . I'm laughing right this second. Everything, whatever you heard, it's either somebody just talking shit or trying to stir something up. But . . . Would it . . . If my father was a . . . a gangster, would I—None of this makes sense."

Eventually, videographer Matt McDaniel was once again on speaking terms with Rifkind. "I was gonna do a project for Steve and I remember when he found out I was dealing with Death Row. His whole vibe changed up." At the time, McDaniel didn't know about Suge feuding with Rifkind. "He got tense. I never knew what that was about until later." Ultimately, the Wu-Tang Clan did not sign with Death Row. But group member Ol' Dirty Bastard told a journalist: "It's about the motherfuckin' money. Suge Knight gets mad love."

"YEAH, SUGE WAS ON QUIK'S SIDE BECAUSE QUIK WAS A BLOOD! AND SUGE WAS A BLOOD TOO!"

Death Row's next release would be *Murder Was the Case*, a soundtrack to the eighteen-minute Snoop video Dr. Dre was directing. Originally a song on Snoop's *DoggyStyle*, *Murder Was the Case* was now a bloated eighteen-minute "minimovie" complete with its own fifteen-cut soundtrack. Since *Above the Rim* had sold well, Suge confused a movie soundtrack, the ultimate one-shot, with the beginnings of a hit career.

Suge asked DJ Quik—a frail Compton rapper who talked tough in interviews but wore his hair in an overblown perm—to record a song. A DJ since 1981, Quik didn't actually start rhyming until after *Straight Outta Compton* sold millions of copies without radio play and opened the floodgates for gangsta rap. Then he signed with Suge's Funky Enough Records. When that company folded due to the imprisonment of Suge's partner, sports agent Tom Kline, Quik signed to Run-D.M.C.'s label, New-York-based Profile Records.

During his career, David "DJ Quik" Blake had taken to promoting the Tree Top Pirus on his albums. After he named his production company

TTP—in honor of the gang around Suge's neighborhood, one of L.A.'s oldest Blood groups—rival Crips began crossing Quik's face out of posters advertising his albums and replacing it with the names of their Crip neighborhoods. As more and more Crips decided that Quik was an enemy, Quik began to deny any affiliation with the Bloods. After stressing that he never wore the red rags, red shoes, or red shoestrings other Bloods used to promote their gangs, Quik added, "I'm about hard work and I'm not going to let a bunch of gangbangers ruin what I've built up and accomplished."

Despite these denials, Quik had spent the years 1991 to 1994 insulting a Crip rapper named MC Eiht. Quik felt that Eiht had dissed him on a song; Eiht denied it. It was all a big misunderstanding, he said. But Quik wouldn't listen. He kept recording songs that threatened Eiht's life. "He used to make tapes for his 'hood," Eiht recalled, "but within the tapes he talked about how he was gonna blast up my group, Compton's Most Wanted."

By September 1994, DJ Quik had signed to Suge's management firm and been asked to record a song for *Murder Was the Case*. "And he dissed a motherfucking Crip, which was MC Eiht," said Doug Young. "Yeah, that was a turning point. Yeah, Suge was on Quik's side because Quik was a Blood! And Suge was a Blood too!"

On his song "Dollars & Sense," DJ Quik complimented the Tree Top Pirus, spelled his name without a 'C' (to antagonize Crips), and belittled MC Eiht for trying to talk peace. During a meeting at a local airport, Quik rapped, he and some of his Blood friends had confronted Eiht. Though Eiht was visibly nervous, fearing that Quik's companions would assault him, Quik rapped that the meeting had ended amicably, with Eiht handing his pager number over and saying, Keep in touch.

When Quik did call, his rap continued, he discovered that Eiht had changed his number. This meant war. According to Quik's chilling lyric, MC Eiht was driving his Camry, when a brown car pulled alongside him. Bloods pointed .357 handguns at Eiht's chest. Eiht held up his hands and asked for mercy. The Bloods let him go, but Quik ended his record by warning Eiht to watch his step. " 'Cause this game you think is funny is some real shit," Quik rapped. "So you need to be more careful who you fuckin' with."

Quik's contribution angered many local Crips and led to a renewed relationship with Suge Knight. When journalist Cheo Coker had to write a feature for *Vibe* on Quik, he was told to drop by Can-Am, a studio located in a tiny industrial park in the middle of nowhere that served as Death Row's headquarters. "That was the first thing that was kinda weird," Coker said. "After entering the front door, there was a very small lobby." The lobby walls were covered with giant reproductions of magazine covers, framed platinum discs, and an enormous Death Row Records logo. Armed security guards stepped forward and frisked him. They searched through his bag and made him sign a guest register. Coker thought, "Damn, what is going on?"

In the studio, now the label's Blood-infested garrison, Coker watched Quik finish recording a new song. A tall, muscular black man with a goatee loomed over him, saying he worked with Quik. "He was like, 'Yo, you the cat from *Vibe*? You got any problems, man, just let me handle it. They call me Jake. Jake the expediter.' "

Though Coker knew Suge now had an office at Can-Am, he was still shocked to see the CEO enter the studio. "He walked in while Quik was working on a Jewell track, and I thought, 'Oh, my God! That's the legend!' He walks in and he's talking to Quik, pats him on the back, listens to his tracks, then walks out."

CPO was eager to appear on the soundtrack. "Them motherfuckers was fittin'a come up with another fucking soundtrack! Thanks to Dre and my manager, Michelle Hunt, I was s'posed to get on that. But I think Suge had beef with one'a them niggaz who did my track, so for some reason, my beat—my song wasn't gonna be on there.

"I said, 'Fuck that!' Michelle went and talked to Dre and Dre said, 'Yeah, we gonna put it on there.' And at that point in time, shit was all cool." This time, however, Suge didn't offer CPO anything to sign. "And I didn't see no money as a result of that! Nor did I see no money as a result of what I did on 'Pac's thing! The only reason I didn't trip was because I was thinking, 'Maybe they gotta go through a period of time when *they* collect and *then* they pay off to us.' "

Kurupt brought his friend Slip Capone's demo tape to the label. "Slip did a few songs and Suge or CPO decided to use one," said artist manager Lamont Bloomfield, who represented Kurupt and Slip. "But we didn't know Capone was on there until two days before the fucking album came out! Suge pretty much kept us in the dark. We didn't even know until we saw the credits in the office; we didn't even celebrate until we found out. That's how they were doing their business over there, keeping people in the blind. That's part of why I'm suing—to get me some of my money. 'Cause they never did any paperwork and took the song from us! We didn't know they were gonna use it.

"The way Suge does it," Bloomfield added, "he goes into the studio he owns. He has everybody coming in there: Whoever wants to can come in and record. That's how Death Row gets the hit songs. Everybody in there collaborating on shit. But they can't take one master out the studio. Suge has so much shit with different people on it, he can probably sit back and listen to what he wants and put the shit out without any paperwork.

"When a person does a song, Suge has them thinking he doesn't know if he'll use it or not. People were hoping they'd get used. And if he never said anything, they never said anything. Next thing you know, the song is out. Of course there's no paperwork on it. Whoever was asking for paperwork thought that would bring attention on them and they wouldn't be on the record. So they wouldn't ask for paperwork. That's how Suge had them niggas: scared to ask him for paperwork, fearing they'd get beat up or perhaps he wouldn't even use their song. So niggas were just trying to get on a song. The God honest truth. I remember telling the artists, 'Y'all ain't gonna ask for y'all money?' They always said, 'Man, naw, I'm just trying to get on.' "

At age twenty-nine, Dre was no stranger to courtrooms. In October 1992 he pleaded guilty to battery of a police officer during the brawl in New Orleans and served thirty days under house arrest; in 1993 he settled out of court with former *Pump It Up* hostess Deniece Barnes, then pleaded no contest to breaking a rap producer's jaw (receiving yet another house arrest sentence). What Dre wanted to do in 1994 was focus on creating music. But he also carried a gun. "It's defense," he told a reporter. "If everybody on the street has one and you don't, you automatically lose the chess match. Checkmate."

Dre realized he was tired of the label's direction. But his work with Death Row paid the bills. He now lived in a French Colonial home with his girlfriend Michel'lé and their three-year-old son, Marcel, surrounded by gates, in an exclusive community in the San Fernando Valley. He owned this home, a swimming pool, and a car collection that included a convertible 325ic BMW, a white Chevy Blazer, a Nissan Pathfinder, and two 1964 Impalas. He also had gold chains and bracelets, a Rolex, and an $11,000 ring with sixty-eight diamonds in it. "With so many diamonds I've lost count," he told *People*.

But Dre was understandably nervous. Suge seemed to be taking over. After *DoggyStyle*, Dre thought Death Row would release albums by the Lady of Rage and his girlfriend, Michel'lé. After that they would work on music for Tupac (whom Suge still hadn't signed), Sam Sneed's former vocalist K-Solo, and R&B singer D-Ruff, whose dad, the late David Ruffin, had fronted the legendary Motown group the Temptations. But Suge went out and arranged the *Above the Rim* deal, an R&B soundtrack for a lousy film about basketball and drug dealers.

The rift between them, and creative differences, began to develop. Suge wanted R&B stars like Mary J. Blige, Jodeci, and Devante Swing on Death Row and albums by Nate Dogg, Jewell, and Tha Dogg Pound in stores. Dre, meanwhile, really wanted to finish recording *Helter Skelter*, his album-length reunion with N.W.A songwriter Ice Cube, which he hoped to have in stores by fall.

But Suge put his foot down: *Helter Skelter* would have to wait; *Murder Was the Case* would be Death Row's next release, with Suge hoping to have it on sale during the lucrative holiday shopping season, when consumers generally spent more on CDs and cassettes.

On the set of Snoop's *Murder Was the Case* video, Dre met young Nasir Jones, a gifted Queensbridge rapper who was in town to promote his Sony Music debut album. As "Nas," the young drug-dealer-turned-Islamic-scholar had created *Illmatic*, an alternative to the gangsta rap sound dominating the sales charts. The intricate work that redefined rap music was labeled a classic upon its release. "It was like, five in the morning," Dre recalled, "and we kicked it around for a minute." A fan of

N.W.A's, Nas asked Dre to consider producing a song on his sophomore album *It Is Written*. "Everybody felt *The Chronic* and all that," Nas explained, "so everybody know Dre's one of the illest niggas. I always wanted to hear an East Coast nigga rhyme to one of his beats."

For now, Nas and Ice Cube would have to wait. Dre had to devote himself to *Murder Was the Case*. "Dre's a very smart, creative person," artist manager Lamont Bloomfield conceded. "He's a good orchestral conductor—the best at that—but he's not a real producer. He's best at taking different people's thoughts and putting them together to form something extraordinary. As for playing instruments and everything people are hearing [on his records]? It's everyone else, but Dre gets the credit for it. Why do you think he liked Sam Sneed so much? He was using Sam for his beats and bass lines."

So far Dre had had a phenomenal year. In March 1994 he won a Grammy Award for best rap solo performance; at the Source Awards he won for producer, solo artist, and album of the year; in May, *Newsweek* was calling him "the Phil Spector of rap." But his remix for Snoop's "Murder Was the Case" confirmed that he definitely needed a talented cowriter: the remix's torpid drumbeat, drab heavy metal bass lines, and fatuous pop keyboards were dreadful.

Ambitious producer Sam Sneed was staying in Dre's colossal home. "I was taking advantage of the [free] studio and trying to come up with stuff. And it wasn't until they started doing the *Murder Was the Case* soundtrack that the stuff I was creating was in effect."

"I met Sam at a party," Lamont recalled. "He always reminded me of the DOC. He was a nice guy. See, Dre knows how to manipulate 'nice guys.' Sam Sneed was no gangster rapper. He was a nice guy who had talent as a producer. And Dre needed that talent, so he scooped him in. Dre was gonna hook Sam up, but I'm sure Dre was gonna benefit a lot more than he was."

Sam's musical productions were originally intended for his own Death Row debut album. He had already recorded a demo version of a song called "Recognize," which ridiculed the gang subculture his label mates relied on as their sales gimmick. After playing the song for Dre, Sam began writing his album in earnest. "It was on some ol' player shit, you know? That was the thing at the time. As a lyricist, I wasn't so 'positive.'

Because I was blind. Not really peer pressure. I was just on that 'player pimp' stuff. But I woke up and smelled the coffee.

"When I let Dre hear a coupla things," Sam continued, "he was asking, 'Whatchu gonna do with them?'

" 'Whatever you wanna do.'

" 'Man we need to put that on the soundtrack.'

"Originally," Sam explained, "the 'Natural Born Killaz' track featured me and Dre rapping on it and Ice Cube providing the *chorus*. But Death Row was so excited about Dre and Cube on one song again, they took me off and let them do the song together. You know what I'm sayin'? They took me off. I wasn't trying to hear that. I was excited about that song."

Dre tried to pacify Sam, reminding him that "Recognize" would appear on the soundtrack. "But I wasn't crazy about that song," Sam admitted. "I didn't like the way I sounded on it. I liked the way I sounded on 'Natural Born Killaz.' " Dre and Cube ignored him; they appeared on the song, which featured the following credits: "Performed by Dr. Dre & Ice Cube. Produced by Dr. Dre. Coproduced by Sam Sneed. Written by Dr. Dre & Ice Cube."

Dr. Dre was unhappy with Death Row. "I found out by accident," said promoter Doug Young: R&B singer El DeBarge wanted Dre to produce a few songs for him. At the time, El was trying to leave Warner Bros. He asked Doug to set up a meeting. "So I called Dre and said, 'Man, El is really interested in you maybe doing something on him.' "

The meeting happened at Larrabee's Sounds, a recording studio in Hollywood. "At that time Dre was putting the final mix on that 'Helter Skelter' song he did with Ice Cube." The song was titled "You Can't See Me" and featured a special appearance by Dre's primary influence, funk musician George Clinton. "Dre took a little time out, took us upstairs by where the pool tables were, and basically ran it down to us that, yeah, he'd like to do something with El. Then I said, 'Well, do I need to talk to Suge?' Dre was like, 'Naw, naw, man. Lemme just talk to [office manager] Kimmy. You don't wanna do that.' "

Doug had known Dre since his days in the World Class Wreckin' Kru;

he worked with Dre during his stint with N.W.A, then followed him to Death Row. Dre's reaction aroused Doug's suspicion. "You don't gotta say too much for me to go 'Hmm,' " Young explained.

Another business trip was done. While attending the Freaknik in Atlanta, an annual weekend party that drew thousands of black college students to the region, Death Row promoters Doug Young and DJ Black had stayed in five-star hotels, used laptop computers, and driven two rental cars around town. On the return flight from Atlanta, Doug reflected on his experience with the label. To date, he had earned about $125,000, paid directly by Interscope. The pay would continue to be good. But there had been problems at the Freaknik. "It really wasn't anything different from any of the other times," Young pointed out. "Go out someplace, get into a fight at a club again— At that point in time, I had had it. I wasn't with it anymore. I didn't come into danger. It was just that something hit me. I said to myself, 'Man, they're gonna have to go through this shit every fucking place we go. We got this motherfucking Jesse James mentality.' After a while everybody's gonna wanna be a faster shooter than Jesse James." Every American city had ghetto areas, and each of these areas had someone who felt they were tougher than the next man. If he stayed with Death Row, Doug thought on the return flight, he would continue seeing the label's entourage get into brawls.

Turning to DJ Black in the next seat, Doug said, "Man, I'm quitting." Black couldn't believe it. Doug meant what he said. He stopped going to the office. "That's when dude from New York came to work there, Hank Caldwell from Atlantic. He came up there to be in charge of daily operations. Basically the president of Death Row while Suge was still CEO."

Black called Doug at home. "Well, man, you coming in today?"

"No, man. I told you I quit."

"You ain't gonna tell nobody you quit?"

" 'Nope. I'll just quit and go away.' "

Since he had finished promoting *Above the Rim*, the label wouldn't need him. Other people would leap at the chance to work for Suge and love the job. "They ain't gonna miss me," he told Black.

"THEM NIGGAS GET TO TRIPPIN', THEY COULD START BUSTIN' SHOTS!"

One morning at 10900 Wilshire Boulevard, the Beverly Hills business tower that housed offices for Interscope and Death Row Records, some of Suge's henchmen entered the empty office of Fade Duvernay, head of Interscope's rap promotion department.

Promoters Soup Henderson and Michael "Emz" Green arrived at the label that morning. Soup, a former rapper whose group the Rebels of Rhythm almost signed to the earliest incarnation of Death Row Records, entered his cubicle and began planning his day: He was working in the label's promotion department. His coworker, Emz, a New Yorker who relocated to California to find a record label job, shared an office with their superior, Fade Duvernay. Soup watched him enter the room. "Next thing I know," Soup said, "I saw furniture that was in their office coming out! Being moved by Jake Robles and some other people."

Jake "the Violator" Robles was Suge's right-hand man, a powerfully developed gang member who followed orders. When Soup asked Emz, the liaison between Death Row and Interscope, to explain what was happening, Jake Robles answered. "Don't start no problems," he growled, "and there won't be none."

Dumbfounded, Soup retreated a step. Emz silently watched Robles and his men scatter their office furniture around Interscope's reception area. Soup later discovered that Death Row wanted their employee Kevin "DJ Black" Connell to have Duvernay's office. "It's not that they *wanted* to give it to him. They gave it to him. And motherfuckers weren't saying nothing."

Emz broke his disapproving silence. "Man, fuck it. I'm gone. Man, I can't take it."

"Actually, I left too," Soup mentioned. "I was thinking, 'You know what? I'm a little "traumatized" myself. Time for a free day, nigga! I need to get my ass off.' But that was some funny shit. Because you didn't know why they were just putting their shit in the lobby."

Due to its affiliation with Death Row, Interscope had "gangbangers walking all through the offices," said one source who regularly visited Interscope's offices. "That's just the way shit went down. But I don't think it's any different than any other labels. It's just that, this time, you had a black motherfucker doing it instead of a little, short Jewish guy. You had a motherfucker who didn't really need to hire thugs, who could handle it himself."

As noted earlier, Suge didn't consider his people thugs: "At Death Row," he said publicly, "we ain't out to impress nobody. Nobody here has any desire to get all caught up in that old Hollywood game. We're just a bunch of regular people trying to run a business. And we haven't forgotten where we came from."

This was part of the problem: Many of his associates brought the gangbanger mentality into tranquil professional settings. "No matter how much money's being made," Soup felt, "street niggas are gonna be street niggas! And people get upset, but that's true."

Another afternoon, a fight next door exploded into Interscope's office. "I didn't see them," said a former Interscope employee, "but you could hear them. They were arguing, louder than a motherfucker! Going at it. And the door that leads to Death Row opened, so I was like, 'Man, what the fuck's going on in there?!' Then you heard a gang of ramming, like these kids were throwing blows, and this one kid comes in. He didn't run, but he was 'walking fast' to get his ass over to Interscope's section. So I asked, 'Man, what the fuck is going over there?!' He said, 'Look, man! I'm coming over here.' " The employee repeated the question. "He said, 'Man, I don't know.' 'Nigga you don't know?! You must know! *You running over here!* Don't run over here 'cause you "don't know" what they doin' over there!'

"Them niggas get to trippin'," this former employee sighed, "they could start bustin' shots! Doin' anything! This kid wouldn't say what it was but ran his ass over to our office! That's the thing: Niggas in Death Row weren't talking. They're still like this. They tell you they don't know? Leave it at that."

Interscope's unwritten policy regarding Death Row became "handle your business." "If it's Death Row business, nigga handle that business *quickly.* Not only because 'something might happen,' but also because you gotta keep your moneymaker happy, you know?"

In late 1994, Death Row Records was paranoid about songs from *Murder Was the Case* being leaked to radio. Earlier that year, a remix for SWV's "Anything," an *Above the Rim* number that now featured raps by the Wu-Tang Clan, had appeared on radio before the single was in stores. "It fucked everybody up saleswise," said one of Emz's friends. "That song was the hottest shit out and everybody wanted it but it wasn't ready yet." Unable to find the single in stores, fans simply taped the song off the radio. Upon its release, the single sat in stores; Death Row (which released the single and counted on the Wu-Tang's appearance increasing sales) lost money. Everyone, it seemed, had taped the song off the radio.

By now the Death Row crew had unveiled *Murder Was the Case,* Snoop's new eighteen-minute music video, a short film similar to the bloated extravaganzas Michael Jackson filmed during his *Thriller* heyday. At the Jack the Rapper radio convention held in Orlando, Florida, three hundred reporters in a hotel conference room fought for chairs. Onstage, Snoop tried to introduce the video. But no one listened until Suge stepped up to the microphone and said, "Y'all shut the fuck up so we can watch the motherfucking movie or get the fuck out."

Before the *Murder Was the Case* album's release, Interscope promoter

Michael "Emz" Green decided to give loyal Death Row supporters a treat: one underground radio DJ would be allowed to air Snoop's new song "21 Jumpstreet." By previewing the album, Emz hoped to secure a large audience in advance. Emz delivered a cassette of the song to Mike Nardone, host of KBBT's late night rap show, *The Joint*. If Nardone played the new song on his after-midnight show on Friday, it would constitute a leak—but one Death Row wouldn't be aware of since Nardone's show aired after office hours.

Emz gave Mike Nardone a cassette of the song. Nardone took it to radio station KBBT (92.3 "The Beat," one of the city's most popular rap stations). As Nardone was preparing to edit profanities out of the song, another DJ, Theo, became jealous that Nardone would feature the very latest Death Row release on his program. Behind Nardone's back, Theo grabbed the cassette and returned to the airwaves, telling his audience he would be playing the newest Snoop song immediately.

If twenty-one-year-old Japanese-American Theo Mizuhara played the song during his popular daytime program, Death Row and Interscope would know the song had been leaked. Since KBBT played many Death Row releases, Interscope and Death Row kept radios in the office tuned to the station.

On the air, Theo said he would play the new song. Emz rushed to a telephone and called the station. "Look, man," he said. "Do not play it." Theo was recording their conversation.

"Look," Emz continued, "you do not know the situation that you will put me in. Please do not play that, you gonna get me fucked up, you gonna get me fired. Do not play it."

"Yo, man," Theo replied. "Why can't I play it? You gonna get in trouble?"

Emz pleaded. "Come on, man. *Don't do that shit!*"

Theo hung up, played the new Snoop song, then aired portions of the conversation with Emz.

A coworker recalled Emz saying, "Oh, man, I'm'a get fucked up! I'm'a get fired! Man, I'm gonna get my ass kicked!'

"He was in some deep shit," the coworker said. "I told him, 'Man, them cats prob'ly weren't even listening to it.' My dumb ass." That

Friday afternoon, nothing happened. Monday arrived. At noon a friend of his arrived at Interscope to take him to lunch. Frazzled, Emz declined the invitation, escorted his friend to the building lobby, then said, "Look, man, I think some shit might go down because that song leaked. Hopefully, I'll just get fired."

His friend said, "Who you need to knock out is that punk-ass Theo! Because he knows how Death Row thinks! Even if I hadda go down there on the bus and bomb on a motherfucker, he wouldn't have played that shit!"

On Wednesday, Suge Knight arrived at Interscope with one of his tall, bodybuilding henchmen. "I thought, 'Aw man!' " said Emz's coworker. With his burly associate, Suge entered Emz's office. At a desk nearby, Emz's coworker eavesdropped. "Suge said, 'How in the fuck did they get that?' He wasn't loud 'cause they closed the door. But I wasn't gonna go in there anyway! Anything could pop and I'm not fittin'a be no 'nosy-nigga' getting my head split open."

"Why'd you leak the tape?" he heard Suge ask. "Why'd you leak the song?! You know you fucked me right?! I *should* have one of my boys straight-out-the-pen just straight-fuck you to let you know how it feels! But this shit ain't gonna happen again, right?!"

Emz said weakly, "I'm just gonna do my job."

Then Suge delivered his trademark ultimatum. Emz could quit Interscope and leave unharmed, or submit to a beating and remain at the job. Emz was wary: If he quit, Suge might keep his word and let him leave untouched. But he might also accept the resignation, then attack him on the spot. Or he might decide to let him leave untouched for now, catch him later, and beat him then.

Having gone through a similar situation with Suge—he himself had been yanked out of a meeting, dragged into an adjoining office, and choked—Fade Duvernay entered the office and fired Emz. "He was like, 'Emz, you gotta go,' to save his ass. 'Cause Emz was fittin'a catch a beat down." Appeased, Suge and his henchman left. Emz packed his things into a box; his coworker said he looked as if he had been "pushed around." Before entering the elevator, Emz said, "It was nice working with you."

"It could have been worse," the coworker sighed. "He got his ass saved. It's just by the grace of God that he didn't get beat the fuck up. Because he was as close to catching it as you are to that tape recorder."

Interscope rehired Emz and placed him in their New York office, where he recently said, "I don't want to be interviewed. Definitely not. Not even as a 'label rep.' *Don't you know Suge is gonna get out?!*"

According to a number of young black males who dealt with the label, Interscope Records decided to turn a blind eye to the violence. Iovine, they felt, knew Suge and his men had dragged Fade Duvernay out of a meeting and choked him in an adjacent office. "If Jimmy wasn't at the meeting that day, he heard about it," said Soup Henderson. "Mother-fuckers who didn't even work at Interscope heard about it. You know how many times people asked, 'Aw, man, is it true?' It's some ol' *classic* shit. Niggas working at other labels, DJs from fucking New Hampshire—all wanting to know if it really took place."

Many people connected to Interscope felt, since Death Row was earn-ing the label millions of dollars, Interscope could not afford to risk dam-aging the relationship because a few black employees were being threat-ened or slapped around. "Suge ain't never struck me as being no 'Yessir' or 'No sir' type'a nigga," one Interscope employee explained. "But I never heard of no white boys getting whupped on."

In interviews, Jimmy Iovine continued showering Suge and Death Row with compliments. "I think that what scares people is that Dre and Suge are opening the nation's consciousness to a revolutionary new art form," Iovine believed. "What you're up against here is two young black guys from Compton who are turning the entire music industry on its ear."

The label's next video, *Natural Born Killers* was a big-budget master-piece that received special mention in an MTV special entitled *The World's Most Expensive Videos*. "I was the still photographer on that," said Brian Cross. "It was shot in San Pedro. The biggest video I ever worked on. A monster production by F. Gary Gray. Two units of 35mm.

People shooting continuously. That video could've been a movie by it-self."

The video featured Dre and Cube sitting on thrones perched atop mounds of rotting flesh, killing a Nicole Brown Simpson look-alike and a white male, then doing in an older couple; rapping to the camera with quick edits transforming their scowling faces into an old man, a child, then a skull; fleeing from an army of police officers in a gleaming con-vertible; cornered in a towering inferno with armed SWAT officers (in-cluding guest-star Tupac Shakur) aiming rifles and waiting.

After footage of Dre and Cube firing shotguns at the camera, some-one leaps off the roof of a burning building. Then a lustrous convertible bursts through a fiery wall, soars through the air, and splashes into dark water.

During filming, Suge wore a baseball jacket and jeans. Between takes he marched over to the crowded catering area and ordered everyone away from the table. Then he demanded that free food and beverages not be distributed. The video's expenses may have had him worried.

Death Row paid $6,000 for a location fee, rented a fire truck for a thousand a day, bought SWAT uniforms for $140 each, rented a low-rider car for $3,000 a day, paid two hundred extras $100 apiece, rented a police boat for $3,500 a day, paid stunt personnel $12,000, rented a smoke machine for $220, rented a skull for seventy-five dollars, paid a thousand to rent a house, paid close to $4,000 for a strobe light, bought meat hooks for twenty-five dollars each, invested $18,000 in pyrotech-nics, got a camera crane for $685, spent $17,000 on a rotating set, $120 for each fireman's uniform, and $3,500 for the helicopter camera mount.

In addition, they spent $600 to rent an airplane hangar, $750 to hire a dog and trainer, $190 to rent a four-wheel-drive vehicle, $200 to hire a child and an old man, $1,200 on "throne construction," $140 for each rented gun, and $6,750 for each leap performed by stunt people.

"I had to get clearance from Suge for photos," said Brian Cross. "That was the first time I met him. I went to meet him on the set. Death Row had their own photographer, but I was shooting for the label. I was being paid by Death Row and I was shooting for a story the L.A. *Times* was doing. 'Cause Chuck Philips at the *Times* found out that the O.J. and Menendez brothers murders were gonna be in the video. The journalist was there, writing his story, and I was shooting photos for the story. But the way they had it worked out, the photos had to be approved by the label. So the first night I shot a lot of stuff on the set, where Dre and Cube were spinning on this electric chair back to back on top of this set that smelled so bad. They had so many dead cow parts, all kinds of shit built into the set. And that shit was just reeking. But we stood there until six in the morning.

"Then, two days later," Cross added, "they shot at a house in Hancock Park. The 'Menendez' part of it. I got some cool photos of Dre and Cube facing the camera with sawed-off shotguns in their hands, firing them, just blasting. I remember I was really proud of these shots, but the woman at the label said, 'Naw, this isn't the type of shit we want going into the L.A. Times.'"

Though the set was filled with rough characters, when Suge appeared, everyone adopted their most docile expressions. "A bunch of hard motherfuckers were laughing like women in his presence," Cross remembered. "If he said something, everyone would giggle like he was the man. I'm talking about complete hard rock type of kids that always got a frown on. There was no question in anyone's mind who he was. Suge Knight was powerful."

"During The Chronic," said artist manager Lamont Bloomfield, "Kurupt told me, 'Just let Suge have all the money on this first record and we'll make it on the second one.' Which was DoggyStyle. But the same shit happened again. That's why I couldn't take it no more. Because he did all these little soundtracks in between and Suge paid him $10,000—when I'm sure Suge was making $60,000 or more off of him." Despite this, Kurupt insisted Lamont not stir up any trouble.

In December, when Death Row received royalty payments for The Chronic, DoggyStyle, and Above the Rim, Suge went on a shopping spree: In one night he bought a 400 Lexus coupe for Nate Dogg, a Land Cruiser for Rage, and separate four-door Lexus sedans for Daz and Kurupt. "That's my dream," Suge explained, "to make Dre and Snoop and every artist on this label a multimillionaire. If that makes me a bad guy, then I guess I'm a bad guy."

Even business manager Steve Cantrock received a brand-new green Jeep Cherokee, which prompted him to retire his aging Porsche and make the scene in his new gift. Coopers & Lybrand (parent company to Cantrock's firm) didn't know about the gift. Cantrock didn't tell them. "As a matter of business practice," *The Wall Street Journal* explained, "Gelfand accountants weren't supposed to accept gifts from clients because of potential conflicts of interest."

Suddenly the label's image changed. Artists began to show off. Happy with his new 400 Lexus Coupe, singer Nate Dogg said, "I ain't even gonna talk about Snoop! He got like six cars and a house. Daz got a house and two new cars. Kurupt has a house and a new car, and I got a house and a '95 Lexus that's paid for. I don't even have an album out."

Sam Sneed shook his head. "Because I was a hustler before," he explained. "I had already owned a lot of flashy things. Getting with them, I did see larger and greater things, but I still wasn't fascinated. They weren't showing me nothing new."

Artists like CPO were downright upset. "All I know is I didn't get paid. That was all that mattered to me. I wasn't making any money. I always thought you got paid for doing shit."

After the car-buying spree, Kurupt entered a penthouse apartment on Wilshire Boulevard in Beverly Hills that the label provided for his use and which he shared with Lamont. "Come outside," Kurupt told Lamont.

Lamont Bloomfield, who still felt he was Kurupt's manager, followed Kurupt out to the street, saw the Lexis, and asked, "Where's mine?"

Kurupt said, "This is what Suge just gave me for Snoop Dogg's album."

"*What?! You accepted a car?!*" This was the oldest trick in the book: Instead of paying Kurupt what he was owed for contributions to an album that sold three or four million copies, Suge bought a car worth less than half of what Kurupt was due. "I knew something was wrong right then and there," Bloomfield said. " 'Cause that's all Kurupt cared about. So I had to take a different route to get my share of the pie."

During a meeting at Death Row's office, Lamont reminded Suge that Kurupt was still his artist. "Kurupt was out of the room. Suge was blaming everything on him, calling Kurupt a 'little ho'—saying, 'I knew he was sneaky.' He was on my side but still trying to con me out my artist. Then when Kurupt walked in, Suge changed his whole act: Now he was taking Kurupt's side, saying, 'That's my little homie! I gotta stay down with my artists!' "

Lamont compared the situation to pimps fighting over a curbside hooker. "This ho chose him. That's the situation I was in. I mean, I ain't gonna have myself killed or try to kill this man over something my artist did, you know? I just faded away. I knew what I had to do: Prepare me a lawsuit and hit these motherfuckers with it. It was kinda like I was 'plotting,' but I didn't need Suge to find out and try to have me beat up or sign papers."

As of this writing, no lawsuit has been filed.

"WHAT'S ALL THAT COUGHING? YOU GOT AIDS OR SOMETHING?"

Fifty-six-year-old Los Angeles district attorney Lawrence M. Longo had wanted, for a long time, to put Suge behind bars. "He is a thug," Longo told *Newsweek*, "and he gets the charges pushed back because he has money."

The son of a wealthy investor and developer, Longo graduated from Laverne Law School in 1969. A year later he became a district attorney and acquired a reputation for being a tenacious courtroom battler. The subject of Lawrence Taylor's *The D.A.*, a book detailing a year in the life of the district attorney's office, Longo had already been tough with Suge. By autumn 1993, Suge had pleaded guilty to eight separate charges: Seven of them were misdemeanors, the eighth was a felony weapons charge. When Suge failed to appear for a September 1993 court date, his attorney, David Kenner, explained that he was keeping a bedside vigil for his sick girlfriend, who had been injured in a car accident. Instead of sympathy, D.A. Longo offered the following: "The defendant has no justifiable reason for not being here today."

In October, Longo wrote a confidential memo detailing the strengths of his case against Suge. The memo, read and initialed by his immediate supervisor, Richard Sullivan, and higher-ups Marcia Clark and Bill Hodgman, raised two red flags: that famous rappers would make it a high-profile case, and that Johnnie Cochran had signed on to spearhead the defense team.

Despite plans to finally enter a courtroom, legal gridlock and shuffling defense attorneys kept the case from going to trial. As Longo waited, his case disintegrated. "What's the deal?" Cochran asked during a phone call.

Longo said, "Two counts of assault with a deadly weapon. Admit the use of a gun."

"Larry, I don't think I can plead my man to that. Do you mind if I go over your head?"

Longo said, "You know how the office works."

In February 1994, Suge's lawyer, Johnnie Cochran, met with Bill Hodgman, head of central operations at the D.A.'s office. Though Cochran wanted closure, he said, "We did not work it out before I had to leave for Simpson. But that's what we were trying to do."

By now, once-cooperative witnesses refused to talk. "They said, 'You've got no case against Knight.'" Then the victims (George and Lynwood Stanley) filed a civil action against Suge and stopped cooperating with the criminal case. To get their testimony, Longo had to obtain their civil suit depositions, which found the Stanleys offering an account of the attack that differed from those of other witnesses. Then Longo worried about Jerry Heller being his main source of information. Though Heller was technically a business competitor, Longo decided he would put him in front of a jury. "I thought that was my ace in the hole," Longo recalled. "Supposedly Knight came in one time with some bad guys and threatened to hurt people if Ruthless Records didn't sign over some [artists]."

Then Longo considered the physical evidence: Police reports and victims' statements identified Suge's weapon that July 1992 evening as a 9mm semiautomatic. During the assault, Suge had fired a shot into the wall. Investigators found the slug, pried it from the wall, and sent it to the ballistics lab. Longo was confident, until results from the ballistics lab showed that the slug was a .45 caliber. Then, through attorneys, the Stanley brothers said they were reluctant to testify: Their civil action against Death Row had been settled for a $1-million recording contract—the brothers received an advance of $350,000 and recorded an album.

By February 1995, when the Stanley brothers' case reached a courtroom, Johnnie Cochran had been replaced by defense attorney Howard Price, and a deal had been reached. But Larry Longo had nothing to do with it, Cochran stressed. "When I was on the case, it was Bill's [Hodgman's] call. There was another deputy D.A. there, too, in the early meetings when I was on the case. Norm Shapiro. He was between Larry and Hodgman in the pecking order. Larry was like the low man on the totem pole on this one."

Three years after the Stanley brothers were assaulted and forced to remove their trousers, District Attorney Larry Longo sat and watched Frank Sunstedt speak for the prosecution. A probation report on Marion Hugh Knight had been favorable. Its authors noted that since the attack, Suge had been a productive citizen. "Now the head of one of the foremost record companies," they wrote, "he employs numerous people."

Suge pleaded no contest. Longo settled the case with a plea bargain: Instead of nine years in state prison, Knight would receive five years of formal probation, report regularly for drug tests, and be expected to notify authorities before he left the country.

The judge handling the case, John Ouderkirk, felt it was a rather "unusual and somewhat complicated grant of probation." Longo explained that it was a no-risk deal: If Suge so much as smoked a marijuana cigarette or got into a fight during the next five years, he faced nine years in the state penitentiary. A successful businessman, Suge had a lot to lose, Longo explained. Reluctantly, Judge Ouderkirk agreed to the deal, and Suge returned to work.

In March 1995, Dre and Snoop Doggy Dogg were shocked to hear that their old nemesis Eric "Eazy-E" Wright was dying. Since January, Eazy had been hosting the *Ruthless Radio Show* on KBBT (92.3 "The Beat") and expressing a more positive attitude toward Death Row. "My show's more of a street type thing," Eazy explained. "I play everything: East Coast, West Coast, Dre, Snoop's stuff, Rage, Tha Dogg Pound, Death Row—whatever sounds good."

After Suge forced him to sign over Dre, the DOC, and Michel'lé, Eazy had seethed with rage. Former N.W.A band mate MC Ren remembered visiting Eazy in October 1993. What he saw wasn't pleasant. Around his old friend, Ren saw a Roman circus of hangers-on, ass-kissers, gangsters-turned-rappers, and yes-men. Like Caligula, Eazy sat at the center of the debauchery and listened to Dre's *The Chronic.* "Aw, it ain't all that!" he roared. "Ain't all that!"

Ren disagreed: To him, Dre's album was a contemporary masterpiece. Eazy's clique of gang-affiliated songwriters turned on him. "Hey don't do that!" they warned. Ren sighed wearily. "If you would've been there, you'd see everybody taking Eric's side."

The subject of Dre's album, and solo success, inspired more heated disputes between Ren and Eazy. Without Dre, Ren said, N.W.A was finished. Why promise *Rolling Stone* the group would have a new album in stores by March 1994? "How could you have N.W.A without Dre? *How?!*"

Eazy was obdurate. "*We're gonna do it anyway! You gonna do it, be down or what?!*"

An N.W.A album without Dre, he knew, would sound lousy. "Man, I can't do no shit!" Ren said miserably. "It ain't gonna come out right."

That Eazy publicly attacked Dre was appalling. If anything, Dre had been directly responsible for Eazy's success. And these sycophants Eazy had in the studio? "They were probably saying 'Fuck Dre' and all-this-and-that about me, but they weren't there in the beginning."

By shielding Dre, Ren injured his friendship with Eazy. "The only relationship I have with Eazy is that I'm under contract to Ruthless Records," he numbly reported in 1993. "That's it. It ain't like we all 'homies' and shit because I just ain't got time. I don't want to get all deep into it because I'd rather, like, tell him the shit I got to say to his face. All people have to do is look at the stats: Look at Cube. He left. Dre left. Now look at how me and Eric's relationship is. Evidently some-thing's wrong."

Next, Dre belittled Eazy on Snoop's *DoggyStyle.* Over a funk-styled

N.W.A. at the 1991
MTV Music Awards:
Yella, Ren, Dre, Eazy-E

© BOB V. NOBLE, FOTOS
INTERNATIONAL/ARCHIVE PHOTOS

Eazy-E and Dre, 1991

© SUE KWON, OUTLINE

Snoop Doggy Dogg in court in Los Angeles on March 11, 1994, with Johnnie Cochran et al. for a hearing in which he pleaded not guilty of involvement in the drive-by shooting of Philip Woldemariam

© JOHN BARR, GAMMA LIAISON

Snoop is embraced by his former bodyguard, McKinley Lee, after they are acquitted of first and second-degree murder charges on 20 Feb 1996

© REUTERS/POOL/ARCHIVE PHOTOS

Notorious B.I.G. (aka Biggie Smalls)
at Bobby Brown's party, 1996

© ERNEST PANICCIOLI, CORBIS-BETTMANN

Suge with Daz,
1996

© L. GREENFIELD, SYGMA

Biggie's wife Faith Evans – who Tupac claimed to have bedded – with son Christopher at the 1997 MTV Music Awards

Sean "Puffy" Combs at
the 1997 MTV Music
Awards

© GREGORY PACE, SYGMA

Suge with Danny Boy,
January 1996

© L. GREENFIELD, SYGMA

Dre with date Nicole at the 1996 MTV Music Awards

Tupac and Suge caught on video, 7 September 1996

© JAQUES M. CHENET, GAMMA LIAISON

In October 1996, Marion "Suge" Knight appeared in Los Angeles superior court with his lawyer following hearings on the murder of Tupac Shakur

© L. GREENFIELD, SYGMA

Marion "Suge" Knight
© TED SOQUI, SYGMA

drumbeat on selection No. 6, Dre and Snoop's cousin Daz simulated playing a raucous game of dominoes. "Where'd Snoop go?" Daz asked. Dre said Snoop was upstairs with a "big booty" groupie. "Ayo," Daz continued. "What's up with them niggas that was on the TV dissing you?"

"Man, fuck them niggas," Dre replied. "Man, I ain't thinking 'bout that ol' shit, man."

Daz started ranting. "Them busta-ass-HIV-and-pussy-havin' mother-fuckers—"

"Yo, yo, yo, Daz," Dre cut in. "*Eazy* come, Eazy—" Dre was inter-rupted by the sound of a gunshot.

"Eazy was sad," said Doug Young, who returned to Ruthless Records after quitting Death Row in 1994 and receiving a lump sum payment from Interscope. "And he was upset. We had been together since Macola. We went from there to Priority to his own thing with his own offices." During their first conversation, Doug remembered telling Eazy, "Look, you were wrong. You should have paid Dr. Dre. Maybe you paid him what you were supposed to, but Dre became the Michael Jordan of production."

One night in 1994, Eazy was working on a biographical fact sheet at his publicist Phyllis Pollack's home. The fact sheet and his new album would be mailed to reporters, so as to influence them to write about the artist and the product. But Eazy wouldn't stop coughing, Doug Young recalled. "It sounded like something was stuck in his chest. So I asked, 'Man what's wrong with you, nigga? What's all that coughing? You got AIDS or something?'"

At the Audio Achievements studio, a facility he used since his earliest days with the group Niggaz With Attitude, Eazy-E worked on a new solo project. "His spirit was broken," said Doug Young. "He became a broken man after Dre left. And it was sad to see 'cause I knew what Eazy had really done for them guys in N.W.A. You have to remember: When Eazy lost Dre, he also lost the DOC and Michel'lé. Then he had the group Above the Law grumbling at him. His self-esteem was falling apart.

"Since I was seeing everything fall down around him," Doug added, "I was giving him pep talks on the business tip." One night Doug was moved to call Eazy at home. "I was kinda buzzin'. I had drank a few beers, smoked a joint, and told him, 'Man, you better get them fools back! What are you doing?! 'Cause rap is a contact sport. You can't sit around saying, It's cool, it's cool . . . 'Cause it *ain't* cool. They'll start making you look bad with your public!'

"This was when Death Row was trashing his ass on wax. I'm the one who gave Eazy the idea for his song: 'Motherfuck Dre, motherfuck Snoop—' And all that 'Dre day is my payday' shit? I stuck that in his head. I mean, it was just all in good fun, youkno'msayin'?!"

In a studio at Audio Achievements, BG Knoccout and Gangsta Drester, who had recently been shot in the Nickerson Gardens housing project, were writing Eazy's lyrics: They soon began filling his songs with insults against Dre, Snoop, Tha Dogg Pound, and anyone else connected to Death Row. For music, Eazy recruited Rhythm D, one of the stable of producers present during Death Row's earliest period. Behind the mixing board, Rhythm created Drelike beats. Eazy promised *The Source*, "There's gonna be like forty to sixty songs on the album. Titled *Str.8 Off the Streets of Muthaphukkin' Compton*, *Volumes 1 and 2*, it would feature production by N.W.A band mate DJ Yella, Above the Law member Cold 187um, Rhythm D, and Eazy himself. It would be the longest new hip-hop album ever.

"Pulling out a box of tapes," *The Source*'s Carter Harris wrote, "he plays me numerous samples, which range from a low-ridin' War-type cut with a singsongy chorus and scattered scratches, to a hardcore street funker, punctuated by synth blasts and gunshots, to a straight heavy metal number courtesy of Guns N' Roses."

But Eazy seemed most excited about a skit which dissed Dre. On tape, a goofy Dre clone yelled, "Remember me, the doctor? We should get back together again." Eazy replied, "Man, get this motherfucker outta here."

"I don't give a fuck about the money," Eazy said publicly. "I give a fuck about being real. Dre comes out on his record tellin' me where I ain't from or what I am. Don't talk about me and where I'm from if you ain't never been there. I'm from the streets of Compton with an ID that says so. Dre's claimin' he's from a place he ain't really from, a place he packed his bags and left. He ain't never gangbanged or sold dope. Never, never in his life."

During interviews, Eazy pulled out enlarged photos of Dre during his stint in the World Class Wreckin' Kru, when Dre wore a sequined bodysuit and eyeliner. "This," Eazy intoned, "is what Dre is about."

Though Eazy and his group of Compton vocalists released bitter attacks against Dre, Snoop, and Tha Dogg Pound, Eazy's heart wasn't in it. Doug Young said, "You can tell Eazy had reached a point where he burned out, you know? But it's how you recover from being burnt out that'll determine if you last in this business or not."

In the summer of 1994, while discussing *Helter Skelter* with a reporter, Dre and Ice Cube said there would be an N.W.A reunion. This time, they joked, the group would be called NWE: Niggaz Without Eazy. Later, Dre admitted that they were joking. He and Cube were working together "but there was never any reunion planned or nothing like that. We're gonna try to get Ren on a couple of songs, but there was never any talk of an N.W.A reunion."

By late 1994, however, Eazy and Dre were on speaking terms again. Ice Cube said, "We'll never do business but we talk. They paid me my money and that was my whole beef from the beginning." After spending years attacking Eazy, Cube now said he didn't hold any grudges.

"They were gonna resolve things," said Doug Young. " 'Cause Dre and Cube said he had to get rid of Jerry Heller if they wanted to do anything." Eazy was ecstatic. " 'Cause they were really gonna reunite. At that time, we found out Eazy was obviously getting rid of Jerry. That was one of the stipulations: 'You get rid of that motherfucker, we'll get back together.' "

At the office, Eazy became secretive. "You couldn't really tell what was going on with him." Even when people knew he had to be depressed, Eazy stuck to his happy-go-lucky facade. During stressful marketing meetings at Priority Records, he would blow spitballs. "He was like a child," said Doug. "He had the personality of the little boy he looked like. Always laughing and smiling and giggling."

By January 1995 he was hosting a weekly radio program on KBBT-FM. "I figured I wasn't getting no love from radio anyway, so either I'd get my own show or I'd buy my own station somewhere." He approached the station with a proposal; The Beat gave him a shot; Jesse Collins was hired to engineer and Greg Mack (of the bygone twenty-four-hour rap station KDAY) was presented as his first guest. The pilot led to a regular time slot; each episode improved on the last. He played any record that sounded good, he explained. "But I don't play my own records. I'm not on my own dick like that. I don't give a fuck about my shit when I'm doing the show."

His program reunited some of the KDAY mixmasters, put DJ Yella back in the public eye, and brought listeners freestyles from New York rappers like Redman and Method Man. The show became the center of his life. "I got my kid's birthday coming up, so that's gonna be busy. But the show's a priority. I do what I got to do."

He had also finalized a deal with Aura systems. "They make these interactive vests where kids could hit each other in the arms and chest and noise comes out." Aura would produce Eazy-E's Ruthless Bass-Shaker stereo speakers. Then there was his appearance in a new Rap Jams video game. "They got a bunch of rappers playing basketball against each other on different courts. I also got my own Super Nintendo game coming out, but I'll tell you about that at a later time."

Most important, *Str.8 off the Muthafukkin' Streets of Compton, Volume 1 and 2*, his long-awaited solo album said to contain sixty to eighty songs, would be released in April, to coincide with his latest *Source* cover. "But I'm'a still keep doing the show. Hell yeah! So to any artists that's coming through town, everybody's invited to come on, West Coast or East Coast! Just call my office, speak to Keisha, and she'll hook it up."

Shortly thereafter, his bodyguards noticed that his persistent cough and cold symptoms were worsening. Originally, they thought he had a cold, said Mark ("Big Man") Rucker, who had known Eazy since their childhood in Compton. "He'd had bronchitis off and on since he was a kid, so it wasn't completely new." On Thursday, February 16, Eazy's bodyguards took him to see a doctor at Norwalk Community Hospital's emergency room. "He sounded worse than I'd ever heard him," said Rucker, "but he wouldn't have gone if it were up to him. We practically had to force him to go." Norwalk Community Hospital admitted him for a breathing problem, then released him three days later.

For five days Eazy rested at his home in Topanga Canyon, trying to get over what everyone assumed was asthma. "That Thursday, we slept over at his house," said a bodyguard. "Eazy was still wheezing and short of breath."

On February 27, Eazy went to a doctor's appointment and was admitted to Cedars-Sinai under the alias Eric Lollis. In Room 5105, he was given antibiotics for a lung infection. "He was smaller because his appetite had decreased," said Charis Henry, Eazy's former personal assistant and longtime friend. "But there were no lesions or dementia. None of the other things you associate with AIDS."

His work shirts, khakis, and wool caps had been replaced with a hospital gown and black Calvin Klein long underwear. Instead of the adventures he described on his records, Eazy lay in bed, listening to the radio, watching TV, and trying to finish the home cooking and fresh fruit his mother brought during visits. His friends tried to get him to sit up and move around, but his breathing made it difficult. "His spirits went up, then down, and we'd try to cheer him up," said Charis Henry. When R&B singer Montel Jordan's radio hit "This Is How We Do It" played, Charis did the "Running Man" dance and Eazy managed a weak smile.

By March 1, Eazy had been diagnosed with AIDS, and told his friends he didn't want to die. Charis Henry remembered: "He said he wouldn't care if he didn't have a dime. He said he wouldn't care what anybody said, if he could just drop the top on his car and ride up the coast one more time—"

Eazy's latest girlfriend, Tomika Woods, kept a bedside vigil. His bodyguards appeared, and Eazy asked, "She told you right?" The next day he was scheduled for surgery. Doctors hoped to drain excess fluid from his lungs. Fearing death, he decided to marry Tomika. At nine-thirty P.M., his parents, Kathie and Richard Wright, and his siblings, Kenneth and Patricia, watched Eazy recite his wedding vows. "He was unable to stand," writer Carter Harris reported. Once the ring was on her finger, Eazy signed a will naming Tomika and his attorney, Ron Sweeney, co-trustees of his estate.

The next morning he didn't go into surgery. At dawn he was transferred to the intensive care unit and hooked up to life support. He began fighting for his life. Almost two weeks later he was still in critical condition. Heavily sedated, he needed a respirator tube in his mouth to help him breathe. His new wife and a pair of huge Samoan bodyguards remained at his bedside. One guard had been with Eazy the last few days, hoping he would finally speak. "Then we said, 'If you can hear us, just squeeze our hand.'" Eazy responded. Then a friend slid a gold ring on Eazy's index finger—a ring this friend's wife had given him on their tenth anniversary. The friend told Eazy, "I want you to give this back to me when you get out of here."

The next day, Eazy's attorney, Ron Sweeney, read a statement outside of the Motown building in Hollywood. Fans, friends, and journalists wept openly. "I would like to turn my own problem into something good that will reach out to all my homeboys," the statement said. "I want to save their asses before it's too late. I'm not looking to blame anyone except myself." The statement implied that Eazy felt he had contracted the virus through unprotected sex with different women. "I have seven children by six different mothers," he said in his statement. "Maybe success was too good to me."

Moved, Snoop called radio station KBBT and went on air to say he was praying for his former nemesis. On March 17, Ice Cube called the station and also went on air. "Me and Eric worked out our differences," he revealed. "I had just seen him in New York and we talked for a long time. We was laughin' and kickin' it about how N.W.A should get back together. I'm just waiting for a call that says he's cool enough for me to go to the hospital and check him out—and let him know that he's still the homie, when it comes to me."

Later that afternoon, Dr. Dre arrived at Cedars-Sinai, went upstairs, and visited his old friend. Seeing a weakened Eazy in bed, Dre regretted feuding with him during the last three years. "I didn't believe it until I went to the hospital. He looked normal. That's what makes the shit so fuckin' scary, man. But he was unconscious, so he didn't even know I was there."

At a panel discussion in Virginia, Suge's old friend DJ Quik told an audience Eazy knew he had AIDS two years ago and vowed to spread it. On KBBT, Eazy's radio co-host Keisha Anderson said, "Eazy was tested eighteen months ago, and it was negative."

On March 24, Charis Henry visited an unconscious Eazy. "I was talking to him, but he didn't respond. It looked as if he was asleep. It was the first time he looked comfortable in a while. He looked peaceful." Within forty-eight hours the infection in his lungs put him into a coma. At six thirty-five P.M. on March 26, 1995, AIDS-related pneumonia killed Eric Wright.

His obituary was surprisingly neat. He was thirty-one. Born Eric Wright. With N.W.A, he "brought the rawness of the inner city to the suburbs." Despite Quik's claims, he didn't know he had AIDS until a few weeks before. Doctors informed him he was in the late stages of the disease. He had no idea how he contracted it. He issued a warning to "all my homeboys and their kin. I've learned in the last week that this thing is real and it doesn't discriminate. It affects everyone."

The short obituary in the *Daily News* mentioned that Eazy was a "former drug dealer who claimed to have fathered seven children by six mothers . . ." His contributions—good and bad—were summed up in three sentences: "N.W.A scored a hit in 1988 with *Straight Outta Compton*. The album's hard-core themes sold more than two million copies. The group's second album was the first hard-core rap album to top the rap charts."

Dre felt horrible. As people battled for ownership of Ruthless Records, Dre thought about Eazy's seven children. "That's who's really going to suffer for this," he said. "We were talking about doing an N.W.A album and giving Eazy's share to his kids."

"SHE DIDN'T KNOW HE DIED. THEY BROKE HIS SPINE"

Marion Knight is one of the few guys I have ever prosecuted who I actually believe can turn his life around and really change the community from where he came," District Attorney Lawrence M. Longo said a month after Suge received a suspended sentence for his attack on the Stanley brothers. "I have never seen a guy transform as much as this guy has since he was first booked. It's remarkable."

"That's when everything was getting wild," Lamont Bloomfield felt. "That's when Suge brought the whole little gang into it. If you weren't from his gang, you'd feel uncomfortable being around them. 'Cause it would be the littlest guy in there starting some mess with you. Next thing you know they'd all be jumping on you and beating you up."

A few weeks before the 1995 Soul Train Awards, Death Row threw an industry party that attracted celebrities and high-ranking industry executives like Mary J. Blige, Sylvia Rhone of East/West Records, and Jodeci. "What really surprised me was walking in and seeing Dee Barnes there," said videographer Matt McDaniel. Despite Dre beating her to a bloody pulp, Barnes was at the party with her husband, Ricky Harris, another of Snoop's cousins, who now worked with Death Row and most recently contributed ideas to the *Murder Was the Case* video.

"Other than that, the party was cool," McDaniel explained. "Death Row was on top of the world at that moment. There were over seventeen hundred people there—all chilling and havin' a ball. It was really off the hook."

That night McDaniel noticed the big change in Suge Knight. "That was the first time I saw him in a three-piece suit. Looking more large, more businesslike." Unfortunately, the festivities ended with police officers outside the building. "They basically tried to shut it down 'cause there were so many people. But there weren't a lot of problems. It's just that Death Row was running things at that time. They were the hottest thing in L.A. and everybody in the industry was trying to get into that party."

At the time, Death Row claimed its roster consisted of Dr. Dre, Snoop Doggy Dogg, Tha Dogg Pound, Nate Dogg, Rage, Jewell, Hug, B-Rezeel, K-Solo, Operation from the Bottom, CPO, YSG, Lil' Bow Wow, Sam Sneed, and David Blake (who, as DJ Quik, was actually signed to New-York-based Profile Records).

The label's public image was at its peak: Its artists drove around town in the newest, most expensive sports cars; they wore the flashiest jewelry; they dressed in the latest fashions; lived in the most-exclusive areas; and drank the finest champagnes.

In addition to overseeing a multimillion-dollar company, CEO Suge Knight was also consulting for Jodeci, Mary J. Blige, Devante Swing, DJ Quik, and 2nd II None. Suge was about to release Tha Dogg Pound's debut *Dogg Food* ("the most anticipated, talked-about rap release of all time," originally titled *After All This, What Do You Have*) and distribute Snoop's new *DoggyStyle*, which had signed talented newcomers like the L.B.C. Crew, Tracy Dee, Lowlife, and the G-Funkers.

In addition, Suge planned to begin producing his own rap magazine (*Death Row Uncut*), and a number of action movies (through his Death Row Films division). As Death Row began to resemble the Motown of the 1990s, everyone suddenly wanted to be affiliated with the record label.

After the 1995 Soul Train Music Awards, where Death Row Records brought a bouncing 6-4 Impala onstage—celebrities and industry executives headed for the afterparty the label held at the El Rey Theater on Wilshire Boulevard. According to promoter Doug Young, David "DJ Quik" Blake, then twenty-four years old, arrived with some friends and was standing in front of the theater, when a member of the Rolling 60s Crip gang approached. "This guy fucking punked Quik! Quik's friends just ratpacked that fool and beat the shit out of him. Right down there in the lobby area, before you enter the door."

Despite the fight out front, the party was incredible, said CPO, then a Death Row artist. "You walked in, they had Death Row ice sculptures. The logo was a big-ass ice sculpture. It was really nice, man. It wasn't 'street.' It was *classy*. People from all walks—from your average homeboy to Mr. 'Who's Who'—were in there enjoying themselves. Outside, hundreds of people were trying to get in. It was maxed out. The music was cool. Everybody mingling, things were beautiful."

One *L.A. Times* reporter agreed. "It *was* a peaceful event. They had Bloods and Crips in there, and strippers up there performing. Everybody was cool. Then you had Suge walking around, looking more 'excited' than the rest: coming up to women, rubbing his body on them, grabbing their asses. And he had this wild, excited look in his eyes. One of my homies that kick it with Tha Dogg Pound said he was tweaked out [high on cocaine]. I guess I could see it then."

The party also attracted gang members, said one Neighborhood Crip. "It's too easy to see. I mean, colors say everything. If someone walks in just draped in all blue, he's definitely Crippin'. If someone's coming in draped in red, hell, that speaks for itself. 'Cause red is the most 'attractive' color you can think of! If someone's coming in with white tennis shoes and red shoestrings, what does that tell you? But it ain't like brothers can't hook up and be cool. Usually at functions like that, they can. But at some point someone's gonna say the wrong thing."

DJ Quik did not suspect that the fight out front would continue. A music producer who worked with Death Row explained why Rolling 60s Crip member Kelly Jamerson was upset. "During the Soul Train Awards," the producer began, "they showed a picture when Snoop won: the picture of Snoop's profile with that rag on his head." The photo was prominently featured in *Vibe*. "And that rag Snoop wore was *blue*. But when they showed the picture at the awards . . . you know how they can colorize stuff? Well, they colorized the picture and the rag looked kind of reddish. So Kelly Jamerson came up to them at the party and was saying, 'Man, you trying to confuse this?' Pow! It started right there. And Quik's guys were like, 'What? What? We'll talk that "Blood" talk.' "

During the argument, "a gun accidentally dropped out of someone's hand and sparked," said Doug Young. "*Pow!* Went off when it hit the ground." Onstage at the party, Snoop and the R&B group BLACKstreet began their performance. "But Suge got on the mic saying some shit and uh, [Jamerson] got killed by Quik's boys."

Jamerson had approached Quik inside the party and called him a "slob," which is a disrespectful way of saying "Blood." Quik's friends were furious and began to surround Jamerson, who continued yelling, "Aw, man, you a slob, Quik! You a punk!" Finally, Quik's friends exploded. They began to beat Jamerson; they knocked him to the ground and lashed out with their feet; people who were standing nearby scattered; the savage beating continued as more of Quik's friends rushed across the club and joined in; soon a large mob was stomping on Jamerson, who was a member of the Rolling 60s Crip gang. Jamerson wasn't moving, but Quik's friends continued stomping. One or two people even lifted chairs and beer bottles, which they smashed on Jamerson's head.

A woman standing right next to the attack called a friend to report what happened. "She has no reason to lie to me," this friend emphasized. "She was standing right there when it happened. She said, 'Them motherfuckers from Death Row is crazy! Some dude got beat up.' She didn't know he died. They broke his spine."

Lamont Bloomfield said his friend Kelly Jamerson was a good person. He had a few kids and a day job. "He wasn't no punk," Lamont clarified. "If somebody came over and sweated him, he would have stood up for his, not caring what was in there. But four niggas jumped on him like that. Everybody stomped on him and hit him in the head with bottles and chairs. That wasn't cool 'cause the guy was little. But that's all Death Row would do. Jump on somebody. That's how it was. The odds were against you, whoever you were."

The LAPD arrived in full riot gear. Jamerson was airlifted to Cedars-

Sinai Medical Center and died from his injuries the next day. Police interviewed hundreds of partygoers, all of whom claimed to have seen nothing. Despite this, said a reporter at L.A. *Weekly*, a police document listed seven suspects for the Jamerson murder: Two of them were DJ Quik and Suge's right-hand man Jake "the Violator" Robles. "But Quik's involvement has always been rumored," said Cheo Coker of the *L.A. Times*. "No one's really ever been able to confirm whether or not he was actually a part of those people that stomped Jamerson down."

Most people felt Quik's entourage were responsible. "It's never the artists themselves," said a Neighborhood Crip who attended the party. "It's the people they kick it with. 'Cause they're not artists. They're just niggaz in the street, and niggaz usually have beef with each other."

After Jamerson's murder, the Rolling 60s received reports suggesting that DJ Quik and Suge were to blame. "I think [Kelly] said something to Quik and Quik went back over there and told Suge," claimed one Rolling 60s Crip. "This is the story I'm getting. He said something to Quik 'cause everybody knows DJ Quik is a Blood. Kelly probably said a personal comment or cuzzed him and Quik went and told Suge. That's when the bum rush came. Quik feels responsible for that shit. I'm sure he do. Especially if he hit [Kelly] in the head with a chair, which I heard he did. I mean, he's gonna have to answer to that one day. I really hate to say it, but they gonna get [Quik] one day. I'm saying this because I know how it felt when people said he had something to do with it. People were calling me saying, 'Man, where that nigga stay at?' Niggas were *serious*. I said, 'Man, I don't know nothing about that nigga, you know?' And left it at that. But Quik got himself into a serious situation." This Crip is not alone in his views, but no one knows how such rumors start.

Allegedly, a contingent of furious Rolling 60s appeared at Death Row's office and demanded to see Suge. When Suge appeared, he was understandably nervous: The third-largest Crip gang in Los Angeles's south central area, the Rolling 60s were known for raiding army surpluses, stealing hundreds of semiautomatic rifles and handguns, and using them in bloody wars against gangs like the Eight Trey Gangsta Crips. When a member was killed, the 60s would recruit two new members to replace him.

At Death Row, the gang demanded an explanation: Why was Kelly murdered at a party thrown by a record label? Suge was diplomatic. "He was trying to say he didn't have nothing to do with it," this Rolling 60 Crip claimed. Despite his explanation, the gang was upset with him. They vowed to avenge Jamerson's death. "He knows they're mad. 'Cause he's a Blood and Kelly was a Crip. They don't like each other anyway."

To date, no one has been apprehended for the murder, said Cheo Coker. "But some people say that was one of the reasons Suge had five 'hits' out on him."

"WHY TIME WARNER ALLOWED ITSELF TO BE INTIMIDATED BY ANYBODY AS IDIOTIC AS BILL BENNETT IS BEYOND MY UNDERSTANDING"

In the early 1990s, Harlem reverend Calvin Butts revived the movement to have gangsta rap banned: He organized a protest march in front of Sony's corporate headquarters in midtown Manhattan. As news cameras rolled, the lanky reverend dumped compact discs and cassettes by various gangsta rap artists onto the road; he got behind the wheel of a bulldozer, crushed the albums, then delivered a speech accusing corporate hydras of profiting from music that celebrated black-on-black crime.

When Butts changed his mind about the music—deciding that artists were only trying to draw attention to social ills plaguing inner city areas—Dr. C. Delores Tucker stepped up to replace him.

A Philadelphia minister's daughter, Tucker was a tiny, gray-haired sixty-something woman who wore turbans and called herself "Dr." despite the fact that she never received a college degree. In 1971 she became the highest-ranking black woman in state government when she was appointed Pennsylvania's commonwealth secretary, the equivalent to secretary of state, a position she held for six years. "But during her

tenure," *Vibe* reported, "she was criticized for spending more time raising her political profile than working at her desk."

In 1973 Tucker and her husband owed almost $25,000 in real estate
taxes on twelve run-down rental properties they owned in North Philadelphia. A former Democratic politician in Philadelphia said, "We were
always concerned that the Tuckers' personal financial dealings would
prove to be an embarrassment to the [party]." By 1975 Tucker had been
publicly admonished by Governor Milton Shapp for accepting thousands
of dollars in unreported honoraria. Despite this, Tucker was appointed
for a second term.

Within a year, however, she was criticized by a state senator for using
her title and office to solicit funds for Bella Abzug's New York congressional campaign. Though she denied the accusation, within a year
Tucker was fired by Governor Shapp—who felt "she was running a private, profitable business at state expense." At the time, Tucker was on
President Carter's list for both U.S. treasurer and director of the U.S.
Mint. But Governor Shapp said a three-month investigation proved she
had used state employees to write speeches for which she received
$66,931.

After an unsuccessful primary bid for a U.S. Senate seat in 1980,
Tucker realized she had lost her political clout. But then Dionne Warwick and Melba Moore approached her at the 1993 annual brunch held
during the Congressional Black Caucus weekend: Dionne had gone from
pop music success to promoting psychic hotlines. Melba Moore was a
has-been who appeared in *The New York Times* when it was revealed that
the R&B singer was on welfare, complaining about how public assistance
really needed to send her more food stamps and cash benefits. Tucker
said, "Those young women said they were tired of being disrespected
and insulted."

Prior to the conversation, Tucker didn't know a thing about rap. But a
nephew she was raising listened to the music. "He told me it was a nice
kind of music, like we used to hear. He would let me listen to some of it,
but I didn't really know the lyrics."

After hearing a few albums, Tucker founded the National Political
Congress of Black Women, a nonprofit, nonpartisan crew devoted to
"the political and economic empowerment of African American women

and their families." She set up shop in the new Kennedy Center in Washington, D.C., and decorated her office with a watercolor of Rosa Parks, a photo of Tucker and Martin Luther King Jr. marching arm in arm, an iron sculpture of Sojourner Truth, and a coffee table covered with copies of *Jet* magazine.

With Warwick and Moore as cochairs of the entertainment commission, Dr. Tucker led the academics who joined her organization into battle, igniting the debate over gangsta rap and denouncing Dr. Dre and Snoop during every interview she gave. While leading her group in protest marches, Tucker got herself arrested and used the publicity surrounding the arrest to publicize her crusade against Dr. Dre, Snoop, and Death Row: After a slew of print interviews, she was booked on *Rivera Live*, where she exposed her ignorance of rap culture by telling innocuous (and highly successful) MTV comedian Ed Lover she didn't want children to end up like him.

Despite her ignorance of rap culture, the mainstream media, black churches nationwide, the NAACP, the United States Congress, and other groups supported her cause. Then she convinced Senator Carol Moseley-Braun to hold a congressional hearing on the matter and literally put rap (in its entirety) on trial. "I didn't call the Senate hearings for [gangster rappers]," Tucker claimed. "I called for these hearings against racism and greed, pure and simple. [The music industry] can't stop it. They don't do it to their own. They won't let it be sold to Jews. They won't let it be sold to white kids, only to black kids."

Though segments of the black community distrusted the government, Tucker proudly dragged the issue of gangsta rap in front of a predominantly white Congress. "They did act in our best interest when Rosa Parks sat in the back of the bus," Tucker claimed. "We don't have to sit there anymore. How do you think we came to where we are if they didn't ever do anything?"

During the early 1994 Senate hearings, Congresswoman Maxine Waters sat at a desk with a microphone stand in front of her and stared white congressmen in their eyes. Waters was still trying to create LA 17 to 30, an organization that would help young people develop job skills and reenter the mainstream; she still needed $17 million to put this positive program into effect and hoped the entertainment industry would help. "These are my children," Waters told Congress. "I do not intend to marginalize them or demean them. Rather, I take responsibility for trying to understand what they are saying. I want to embrace them and transform them. I don't encourage the use of obscenities. I just think we should stop pretending we are hearing them for the first time. . . . Let's not lose sight of what the real problem is. It is not the words being used. It is the reality they are rapping about. For decades, many of us have talked about the lives and the hopes of our people—the pain and the hopelessness, the deprivation and destruction. Rap music is communicating that reality in a way we never have."

By 1995, C. Delores Tucker had the support of former Bush-administration drug czar William J. Bennett, his Empower America movement, and sixty black organizations; her letters were printed on the *New York Times* op-ed page. She was rising to power. "I had to take Ben Chavis on at the NAACP—you know I'm on the board of trustees—'cause they wanted to give Tupac Shakur the 1994 Image Award. I said, 'Not in this life, you won't.' The Image Award is given to those who promote the best images for our children, not Tupac."

Asked to define gangsta rap in 1995, Tucker said, "I looked in the dictionary. Gangsta rap is criminal activity. A gangster is a criminal, and to teach children to become criminals is a sin."

To her, the sensitive love story *Poetic Justice* was dangerous—even though she admitted she never saw it. "I hear there was a lot of profanity in it." She claimed that gangsta rap originated in Compton—and not, more accurately, in the South Bronx. "It's pornographic smut." She didn't even know Snoop and Tupac had legal troubles. *"There's a trial going on?"*

But the uninformed public was eager to believe anything she said. With its support, she grew overconfident. "I don't blame the Tupac Shakurs and Snoop Doggy Doggs. I took my fight to where it belongs: in the boardroom."

Time Warner had invested over $40 million in Interscope. By 1994 the parent company had earned a $50-million profit. This was why Warner Music Group's Doug Morris extended Time Warner's deal with Interscope on April 12, 1995. Morris was one of Jimmy Iovine's biggest supporters at Time Warner; he enjoyed the music and realized that investing another $80 million—would raise Time Warner's ownership to fifty percent and yield greater profits.

Tucker decided to change strategy. Instead of attacking gangsta rap artists, she would target the labels. If anyone could step in and prevent Interscope and Death Row from releasing Tha Dogg Pound's *Dogg Food* album—expected to shoot to No. 1 and sell as many copies as Snoop's 1993 *DoggyStyle* (4.5 million)—Tucker felt it was Time Warner. "I bought stock [in Time Warner] so I could tell the chairman of the board and the board of directors to stop pimping pornography on our black youth," she said.

At the Time Warner shareholder meeting, 2500 people sat through her seventeen-minute tirade. "I asked the [CEO] of Time Warner, 'Do you know what you're doing to our black boys?' I looked him dead in the eye and said, 'You are destroying not just a generation, but a race of people. That's what your music is doing.' He didn't say a word." White corporate types saw Tucker in her turban and polyester suits and feared this clueless know-nothing. "And I'm gonna tell you something," she boasted in print: "They gonna *drop* Interscope. You hear me?"

In addition to Tucker, Death Row, Interscope, and Time Warner had to contend with Senate Majority Leader Bob Dole (who delivered a speech about "nightmares of depravity" in popular culture) and William J. Bennett, who continued to criticize Time Warner board members for releasing rap albums.

Time Warner chiefs decided to fire executive Doug Morris, who had recently invested another $50 million into controversial Interscope. Then Time Warner chiefs asked Suge to delay *Dogg Food*'s release.

C. Delores Tucker claimed victory, telling reporters that her actions forced Time Warner to hold the group's album. Death Row publicist George Pryce denied this. "She is lying through her teeth," he said. "It's business as usual around here." Despite Time Warner's request, Death Row continued with plans to release the album; the label rented a $4-million mini-mansion to serve as a location for Tha Pound's *Let's Play House (Runnin' fo' the Fence)* video. "There is a lot of crazy stuff going on right now," Suge said, "but my focus is on Daz and Kurupt getting their due."

Due to pressure from C. Delores Tucker, Time Warner now wanted nothing to do with *Dogg Food.* Time Warner also wondered whether it should end its relationship with Death Row. During the summer, the head of the Time Warner music division, Michael Fuchs, tried to arrange a prison meeting with Michael Harris, the drug dealer who claimed to have provided Suge and David Kenner with $1.5 million in seed money for Death Row. "He was trying to decide whether the company should yield to the political pressure about gangsta rap and sell its interest in Interscope," *The New Yorker* reported, "and he believed that it might well be Harris, not Knight, who could speak with authority about the future direction of Death Row."

Time Warner executives urged Fuchs not to bother. It seemed they had already reached a decision. But on August 7, Michael Fuchs flew from New York to Los Angeles. The newly installed chairman of Time Warner's music division planned to meet with Suge and Tucker at Dionne Warwick's home in Beverly Hills. Warwick, a member of Tucker's National Political Congress of Black Women, and Fuchs waited for Knight to arrive. After five hours passed and he never appeared, they gave up on him.

Bowing to pressure, Time Warner decided to discuss an amicable part-ing of the ways with Interscope: Ted Field would be allowed to buy back Time Warner's fifty-percent share in Interscope for a low price. Inter-scope accepted the deal, bought its shares back, and negotiated a deal with their old friend Doug Morris, who landed at MCA after leaving Time Warner. At the time, MCA had just been acquired by Edgar Bronfman Jr., the CEO of Seagram. "The decision to dump Interscope was a gigantic error for Time Warner and a great opportunity for Edgar Bronfman," David Geffen told *Rolling Stone.* "Why Time Warner al-lowed itself to be intimidated by anybody as idiotic as Bill Bennett is beyond my understanding."

On the sidelines, Suge Knight seethed with rage. C. Delores Tucker's yapping had forced Interscope—and, by extension, Death Row—to be dumped. In retaliation, Suge stepped forward and claimed that he had met with Tucker briefly while both were in Seattle. There, he claimed, she asked him to leave Interscope and work for her new Time Warner–distributed label. This whole beef with Death Row, Suge inferred, had less to do with gangsta rap and more to do with the demos Tucker kept in her office. She wanted Death Row dropped, Suge went on, so that she could sell Time Warner her own cheerful groups. In Seattle, Suge said she promised $80 million and two state-of-the-art recording studios—but only if he censored Death Row's lyrics to meet her undefined standards.

Three days after Suge kept Michael Fuchs and Dionne Warwick waiting, Interscope's Ted Field and Jimmy Iovine stopped negotiations with Time Warner. They said they heard about the wooing of Knight and promptly filed suit seeking unspecified damages against Tucker—for interfering with contractual relationships. A week later, Death Row Records filed its own suit against C. Delores Tucker, Time Warner's new music division chairman Michael Fuchs, Time Warner chairman Gerald Levin, Warner Music Group, and Time Warner.

These individuals and organizations, Suge's suit claimed, were guilty of contractual interference, extortion, and violating the RICO statute. "Tucker certainly has had her own agenda with this thing," attorney David E. Kenner said. "Our lawsuit is basically a way for us to show that we won't allow this unethical act to go unnoticed."

Tucker was now forced to defend herself. While admitting that she discussed a deal with Suge, she maintained that money was never mentioned. Due to Suge turning the tables, Time Warner began to distance itself from Tucker. "Any efforts undertaken by Ms. Tucker with Death Row Records were undertaken by her acting as a well-intentioned volunteer," said a Time Warner spokesperson, "without any authorization from Time Warner, Warner Music Group, Gerald Levin, or Michael Fuchs."

Death Row continued its counterstrike: Their two-page ad in the October 1995 issue of *The Source* featured a list of "Freedom Fighters." Under Martin Luther King Jr., Nelson Mandela, Malcolm X, Frederick Douglass, Marcus Garvey, and Harriet Tubman, readers saw, ". . . and ~~C. Delores Tucker~~." In typical gang fashion, her name had been crossed out with a red line. On the streets, a crossed-out name usually meant someone was going to die. For Suge, it was show business, part of the image, an inside joke for his Blood buddies.

On Halloween, Tha Dogg Pound's *Dogg Food* hit stores and Suge slighted Tucker again by taking credit for the delay. "It was supposed to come out earlier," a reporter wrote, "but Suge thought, They're all so scared of it, I'll release it on the scariest night of the year."

Suge explained that *Dogg Food* had *not* led to the end of Death Row's association with Time Warner: Even as C. Delores Tucker, Bob Dole, and William J. Bennett foamed at the mouth and attacked gangsta rap, Les Bider, who ran Time Warner's publishing division (Warner Chappell), renewed Death Row's publishing deal—advancing the label a cool $4 million. "The Warner Bros. thing was frustrating to me," Suge explained, "because I knew whatever's gonna happen is gonna happen. Period. Can't nobody stop that. I knew I had to do one thing. I had to make sure we released our records." Distributed by Priority Records, *Dogg Food* went to No. 1 on the sales charts. "Tha Dogg Pound record is in the stores," Suge added, "so what did Delores Tucker accomplish?"

"What she really wanted was to buy the company," said David Kenner.

"YOU GOT YOUR FUCKING GUN?! YOU GOT YOUR FUCKING GUN?"

Promoter Soup Henderson left Interscope and arrived at Solar Records just as Solar chief Dick Griffey took steps to file a $125-million lawsuit against Suge Knight and Death Row Records. During Soup's final days at Interscope, employees were encouraged to ignore rumors about Death Row: Imprisoned drug lord Michael Harris had written a letter to Interscope head, Jimmy Iovine, to inform him of his intention to sue for his share of profits earned by a label he claimed to have financed with drug money.

"I heard stuff about [Suge] beating kids, killing them," Soup remembered. "Real stupid shit. The type of shit you wouldn't believe. He was at this club and these kids started acting wild, then they got in a shootout and supposedly Suge killed two of them. But I thought, 'Suge ain't gonna be out there killing nobody. If anything, the man has enough money to have someone do it for him—if that's what he wanted to do. But for him to actually be somewhere pulling out a gun and shooting three or four niggas down? I thought, 'Naw.'"

When a business competitor named Happy Walters vanished, however, Soup began to wonder about Suge.

Everyone knew Happy Walters, who worked at Buzztone Management with West Coast rap groups like Cypress Hill, FunkDoobiest and House of Pain. "At one point," said reporter Cheo Coker, "Happy was a very hot rap manager."

Author Brian Cross had known Happy for years. "He always struck me as a guy who didn't know a whole lot about hip-hop," said Brian. "I don't know if he came from loot but he had a sense of how to make money. He's like six foot one inches tall. Not built or anything. Plays a little bit of hoop, had a hoop team. Used to play softball and had Cypress Hill and all them kids on his team. He's in his early thirties and managed Erick Sermon, RZA, [Wu-Tang Clan's], Supercat, Redman, Cypress Hill, House of Pain, FunkDoobiest."

During the summer, Happy was said to have had a shouting match with Suge. "Over some soundtrack," Cross explained. "He said some shit to Suge, and not too long after that he ended up missing for a few days."

During an afternoon visit to an ATM machine, Walters vanished. To this day, most people believe he was kidnapped by Suge's men. "Held and the whole nine," said Soup Henderson. "How they do it on TV. That ol' Mafia shit. How they did it in Spike Lee's *The Drop Squad*. Made him start thinking about some shit, I guess. My wife and I thought he was dead. When he came up missing like that—and Happy ain't no broke brother—I thought they were gonna find his body somewhere."

During the three days Walters was absent, people in the music industry were terrified. "There's this kid, Bigga B, who works at Soul Assassins now," said former Loud Records employee Trevor Trev. "Bigga's like six three and played football with Suge at UNLV." Every morning for close to two weeks, Bigga had to appear at Loud owner Steve Rifkind's home at a certain hour. Only when Bigga arrived would Rifkind dare to leave for the office. "And Steve stays right up the block from the damn office," Trevor explained. "Every time Bigga came over, Steve would ask, 'You got your fucking gun?! You got your fucking gun?' That was the only time I really saw Steve nervous about some shit."

Though Rifkind denies this—"That's not true either"—Bigga B said he didn't know much about any abduction. "All I know is that Steve was scared. He wouldn't even go take a piss by himself. I hadda follow him around a lot, so I guess I *was* playing bodyguard at that time. We just didn't know the full situation or who was next."

While Los Angeles rap music executives had always known the business could be dangerous, Walters's rumored abduction forced them to acknowledge how dangerous the business had become. "People were losing their lives, getting smacked up and beat, hung out of windows for certain things," Bigga explained. "So a lot of people were afraid."

When Happy Walters showed up a few days later, on the streets of Long Beach, Cheo Coker said, "He was incoherent, shaved, and naked. Walking through the streets. He basically got choked up and kidnapped for a space of three days and never talked about what happened during the time he was missing. Everyone was saying, 'He got mugged.' "

Brian Cross said, "I heard he had cigar burns on him too."

In the hospital, however, Happy said he had amnesia. No one abducted him.

"He wouldn't say Suge's name," said Coker.

"They said he, uh, got amnesia but I think he was roughed up," said Soup Henderson. "That's the only time niggas come up missing. You don't just 'go to the bar, have two Budweiser beers, get in your car, and then lose all thought of who you are.' I think somebody grabbed him and punched him around. Because the minute he resurfaced, he dropped all his groups."

The disappearance of Happy Walters, and why it occurred, remains a mystery. "Nobody really knows except for Happy," a music industry insider explained. "Because he was the only one there." But Happy refuses to discuss it, said Sam Anson of *L.A. Weekly*.

Instead, Happy worked to detach himself from hip-hop management, said Brian Cross. "He let RZA go. And anybody who's anybody knows, at that moment in time, if you were trying to make money in music, RZA was your top guy. There were a lot of gold records out there with his name on them but Happy let RZA go. I guess he didn't wanna manage him anymore." At this time, Cross mentioned, Death Row was said to have wanted to sign RZA's group, the Wu-Tang Clan. "It was around that time. When I saw Happy, he seemed shook. He showed up in a hotel in *Long Beach*. It could've been anywhere. Why the fuck did it have to be Long Beach?"

Despite the gossip about Suge, Soup Henderson said, "You weren't gonna be at Interscope, investigating shit. You heard things, but you weren't even allowed to talk about them. Even the true shit. You couldn't because people would say, 'Man, watch what you say 'cause the phones could be tapped! I remember brothers saying that all the time." As to who would have tapped the phones, Soup said, "No telling. Interscope . . . You know what I'm saying? It could'a been the feds . . . I know people used to say that."

Ultimately, working at Interscope proved too disquieting. "I fucked around and nearly had a miniature stroke," Soup reported. "I got this thing called Bell's palsy, when your face just stops working, your arms stop working. It was, like, the nerves had just shut down. Man, you be so stressed out, your shit shuts down." His eyes and nose began to twitch involuntarily. "I couldn't move the left side of my face, man—the whole left side. I couldn't whistle. I could barely talk. I couldn't form a sentence anyone could understand."

When he arrived at Solar Records, the label's albums—Top Authority's *Somethin' to Blaze To*, Johnny J's *I Gotta Be Me*, Bossman & Bandit's *16 Keys*, and Chocolate's *Life-N-A-Day*—weren't selling as well as Dick Griffey hoped they would. "So Solar was closing its doors," Soup explained, and Griffey was focusing on his lawsuit, which, for years, had been a running joke in the music industry.

Everyone knew Griffey for being what Rob Kenner at *Vibe* called "Yoda to Suge's Luke." After meeting convicted drug dealer Ricardo Crockett in 1990, Suge Knight worked security at Crockett's hip-hop events in Los Angeles and was soon introduced to Griffey, a veteran music executive who taught Suge about the music industry and provided professional advice when Suge and Dre were speaking with record labels. But now, like imprisoned drug dealer Michael Harris, Griffey believed that Suge had robbed him of his rightful share of Death Row's earnings.

Though Griffey vowed to unleash a multimillion-dollar lawsuit, he also remained loyal to Suge. When a magazine writer arrived in Los

Angeles to write a profile on Death Row for *The New Yorker*, it was Dick Griffey who offered to drive the writer to Can-Am Studios. "[The writer] was in Suge's office and he asked Suge a question," said a Los Angeles reporter. "He didn't like Suge's answer, so he said, 'Come on, man, that's bullshit.' Suge got out of his chair, grabbed him by the shirt, lifted him out of his chair, and dragged him over to this fish tank he keeps in his office. And in that he has these piranha, fighting fish. He told the writer, 'What if my fish eat your fucking face?!' Suge held his face near the tank, then threw him back into his chair. Then he pointed at the writer's recorder and said, 'Rewind your tape and ask me the questions again.' This time Suge gave better answers. But, yeah, Griffey drove him over there."

"At first the label was supposed to be Death Row/Solar," Soup Henderson said. "But Interscope came at Suge and Dre with some money, so they bounced. Then Dick Griffey was like, 'Okay. That's fucked up, but all right.' He waited until Death Row made millions and the DOC had a falling-out with them, then made his move."

But everyone knew the dangers inherent in preparing the lawsuit. "DOC was in Atlanta," Soup remembered. "Griffey flew him into Los Angeles and wouldn't tell anyone where he was staying. They were hiding him so that no one could get to him and make him alter his story. It was some ol' top secret shit. Then after he got the DOC on his side, he got RBX. Now Griffey could finally bring the lawsuit out."

The $125 million lawsuit would claim damages for breach of contract: Griffey and the DOC said they were original partners in Death Row but forced out of the company by Interscope, Suge Knight, and Dr. Dre after Solar released the *Deep Cover* soundtrack.

Soup, meanwhile, continued hearing stories about Suge's violent temper. "Suge and this guy were in the studio and Suge mistook this cat for some dude who was supposedly talking shit to the the DOC. Suge slapped the shit out this nigga! Just slapped him. Didn't give him no fair warning. Just said, 'Ay homie! C'mere real quick.' "

The guy walked over. "Yeah, what's going on?"

"POW!" Soup shouted. "Homie was like, 'What the hell just happened?' Suge slapped him one time, then called the DOC on the pay phone. 'Yo, man, remember that nigga you said was talking shit to you? I just slapped that nigga like a bitch!' Come to find out that it wasn't even the right nigga. That shit was funny, but sad. He had just slapped this man for no apparent reason, and the only thing Suge told him was, 'Oh, I'm sorry.' "

"HOW YOU LET A MOTHERFUCKER IN A WHEELCHAIR WHUP YO ASS?"

During the second annual Source Awards, held on August 3, 1995, long-simmering tensions between the rap communities of the East and West coasts flared. While *Above the Rim* won Motion Picture Sound-track of the Year, Dr. Dre won Producer of the Year and F. Gary Gray's clip for *Natural Born Killers* won for Video of the Year, Dat Nigga Daz of Tha Dogg Pound felt that the East Coast maligned the West Coast at every opportunity. He said, "They was trippin' in there talkin' 'bout, 'Is the East Coast in the house'? Shit! We know they in the house. We in *New York City.*"

During the televised event, Suge Knight marched to the stage with the label's newest act, R&B singer Danny Boy from Chicago, trailing like a hound. "Danny was basically adopted by Suge," *L.A. Times* reporter Cheo Coker explained. " 'Cause Danny came from a very poor home and Suge believed in his music and went to his dying grandmother and said, 'Look. This kid has a chance and I'd like to take care of him. I'd like to look out for him. And I'll treat him like he's my own.' Suge basically saved him from a bad spot, you know? Just had him around."

While climbing the stairs leading to the stage, Danny threw his thin arms up and flashed Blood and Crip gang signs. He looked like a scarecrow in baggy jeans. The Death Row entourage occupied two to three entire rows: At the sight of the gang sign, they leaped to their feet. At the podium, Suge pulled the mic closer. Facing the audience with a steely glare, he said, "If you don't want the owner of your label on your album or in your video or on your tour, come to Death Row." People in the audience were shocked. Suge didn't mention any names, but everyone knew he was speaking about Sean "Puffy" Combs, the Bad Boy Records executive who made cameos on almost every record and video he was involved in creating.

Cheering, the Death Row entourage swung fists at the air. Tense New York executives and artists eyed them warily. Suge pushed the mic away. Danny Boy had his arms up in a victorious gesture. Suge turned to leave the stage and Danny's elbow collided with the side of his face. Conscious of his image, Suge pretended to ignore it and shoulder to shoulder the couple left the stage.

As Suge dissed him onstage, Sean "Puffy" Combs couldn't believe his ears. "I thought we was boys," he said. By now, the twenty-four-year old Combs had helped oversee the production of two platinum albums (Jodeci's *Forever My Lady* and Mary J. Blige's *What's the 411*); he inked a multimillion-dollar distribution deal with Arista Records (for his own Bad Boy Records label); he signed rap artists Biggie Smalls and Craig Mack; he produced sophomore albums for Mary J. Blige and Jodeci, remixed singles for Supercat, Caron Wheeler, and Keith Sweat. "But he wasn't satisfied with just music, he had to make [sic] the next logical step in his quest for total control," *The Source*'s new editor, Adario Strange, crowed in print. "He added a new title to his jack-of-all-trades reputation, as *auteur*, producing and codirecting videos for B.I.G., Mary J., Outkast, Usher Raymond, and others. Are you a control freak? Puffy responds, 'Naw. I just want our shit to be *right!*'"

Though David Mays's "new" *Source* promoted Combs as an overnight sensation, it had been a long road to success. "Bad Boy Records began as an idea, then a marketing swell," said former *Source* writer Dream Hampton. "Before Puffy even had product, he made sure he was getting the name Bad Boy out there. So the company would have an identity. Then he went through different stages of struggling, in terms of finding a home for his label. Then, of course, the arduous process of recording Biggie's album."

Christopher "Biggie Smalls" Wallace, aka the Notorious B.I.G., had once sold $3 vials of crack cocaine in front of a Chinese restaurant on Brooklyn's Flatbush Avenue. He was six foot three, weighed close to three hundred pounds, and had an unfocused left eye that always seemed to be facing something in his periphery (no matter what direction he faced). While selling drugs on the street, he could be seen in terry-cloth headbands, year-round Timberland boots, fashionable Karl Kani jeans, and colorful hockey jerseys. Being mistreated by classmates in the past (for having attended school in ragged outfits) had made new clothing one of Biggie's main obsessions. Another was rap music, which earned some rappers quick fortunes and allowed them to move out of the ghetto.

When a demo tape Biggie had recorded reached Big Daddy Kane's DJ Mister Cee, Cee told Biggie to deliver a copy to Matt Capuluongo, a white original editor at *The Source* who oversaw the magazine's "Unsigned Hype" column. A talented A&R person who went on to work for Steve Rifkind at Loud Records, Capuluongo loved the tape. "He played it for Puffy," Biggie recalled. "Puff told me, 'It sounds like you could rhyme forever. I want to sign you.' "

An R&B man at heart, Puffy was drawn to Biggie's melodic delivery. "It was like he was rapping, but it was so catchy! It was almost like he was singing. And he was such a clever poet, the way he put words together, the way he saw things." Head of artist development at Uptown Records, Puffy signed Biggie to the label and oversaw the recording of his debut single, the dour "Party and Bullshit" hyped by *The Source* in every issue. Away from Puffy and Uptown Records, Biggie continued to sell drugs. "I'm fucked up," he told anyone who would listen.

But Puffy was optimistic; he believed that the right song and look would turn this overweight Brooklyn crack dealer into a major star. However, one night in 1993, his boss, Andre Harrell, barged into his office and said there could be only one lion in the jungle. Harrell fired Puffy. When Biggie heard about it, he grew depressed and drank an entire gallon of Hennessy. He also slipped into smoking marijuana to escape the many problems in his life: His girlfriend was pregnant; his best friend, Damion, was in jail again; his mother had been diagnosed with breast cancer; everyone in his neighborhood felt his career was over.

To keep Biggie from dealing drugs, Puffy had him appear on remixes for other artists. But Biggie quickly spent the money these projects earned him. Puffy was in a bind. His plans for his own label hinged on Biggie. "Once, when we were having dinner at the Shark Bar with Puff," former *Source* writer Dream Hampton wrote, "I made a mistake and mentioned a trip Big was making out of town. Big tried to dead me with one of his looks before I got it all out, but Puff had heard and put it together."

Puffy said, "I swear to God, Big, if you're going out of town to do one illegal thing, if you run a red light in North Carolina, I'm never fucking with you again."

Outside the restaurant Puffy handed Biggie cab fare, then left. "This nigga," Biggie told Hampton. "He stay sweatin' me. He's from fucking *Westchester*—he ain't never been broke in his life. Man, if this shit don't happen soon . . . If this shit don't happen by the end of summer, which it's not, I'm taking this train right uptown and buying some fucking weight. Fuck Puff."

Despite Puffy's protests, Biggie returned to North Carolina and moved in with a drug connection he didn't know or trust. Then Puffy called from New York with good news. "Puffy called me on a Monday and told me that the contracts would be ready on Tuesday," Biggie remembered. "He said, 'Come on up, and I'll have the check waiting for you.' I was gonna stay till Tuesday because it was near the first of the month and we were gonna get those crackheads' welfare checks."

He left that night. As his train headed toward New York, police in North Carolina busted down the apartment door and barged in with drawn guns. "It turns out the nigga that we didn't know had been on the run for over seven years and the other two niggas that was with him got conspiracy charges."

Now that Puffy had a deal for Bad Boy, and Biggie was returning to the city, he could begin to assemble the label. He offered Biggie a contract and a modest advance (under $20,000). Biggie, however, was unhappy. "When I stopped hustling and started making songs, it was the worst." His advance was "petty money," nothing compared to what he earned selling drugs on Flatbush Avenue. But Biggie signed the deal.

In the studio they bickered over what to record. Puffy, who worked with Jodeci and Mary J. Blige, wanted to cling to his proven, innocuous R&B sound; he wanted to record a nonthreatening blue-collar version of Dre's concept album *The Chronic.* Biggie preferred unyielding numbers like "Machine Gun Funk," which he hoped would be his first single, or his duets with underground artists Ol' Dirty Bastard (Wu-Tang Clan), Brand Nubian's Sadat X ("Come On"), and Tupac Shakur.

"When we were in our beginning stages," Puffy told *Rolling Stone,* "Death Row was established. Bad Boy was kinda modeled after Death Row because Death Row had become a movement. We wanted to model ourselves behind the record companies that were movements, like Motown, Def Jam, Death Row. These were record companies that were the sound of the culture, and we wanted to become another sound of the culture."

A perfectionist, Puffy spent eighteen months preparing Biggie's debut, *Ready to Die:* He pointed out that popular songs of the time all featured catchy choruses; though Biggie was satisfied with the album as it stood, Puffy called him back into the studio and stressed that the album needed its marketable moments. Biggie reluctantly recorded vocals for two new commercial songs ("Juicy" and "Big Poppa"). Then Puffy informed him that "Machine Gun Funk" would not be the album's first single. "Puffy was on some: 'Yo, let's get rich. If we drop "Juicy," you'll have a gold single.' "

Money kept them together, said former *Source* writer Dream Hampton. "Whenever you have a partnership where you built something together, there's a bond there. Puff might have been making ten million and Big might be making two, but they were both becoming millionaires because of one another. There's certainly people that Biggie was closer to, but no one shared what they had. No one Big ever hustled with on the streets made him a millionaire. He never made anyone else a millionaire."

"Whenever Suge would come to town," Puffy said of this halcyon period, "he would come by the office. Whenever I was in town, he would come pick me up and we'd hang out. There were maybe two times I went over to Snoop's house. It was all cool. No way in the world I could foresee any problems."

But that night at the August 3, 1995, Source Awards ceremony, Suge had made it a point to insult Puffy. Though Puffy considered Suge a friend and influence, Suge viewed Puffy as an arrogant little upstart. When they met, Suge said, Puffy was having a dispute with Mike Concepcion, a wheelchair-bound but very intimidating former member of the original Los Angeles Crips gang. "The little nigga come cryin' to me," Suge said. "How you let a motherfucker in a wheelchair whup yo ass?"

After his insult, the audience was astonished. The air filled with resentment. After years of seeing West Coast acts outsell New York rap groups, Puffy Combs and Biggie Smalls had finally produced *Ready to Die,* an album that looked to end the East Coast sales slump and sell as many copies as the average Death Row release. Why was Suge Knight, CEO of Death Row, insulting the creative force behind it?

"White people have been in the record business for years," a *Vibe* writer pointed out. "You know, Tommy Mottola and Clive Davis, from what I understand, cannot stand each other. They cannot stand each other from way back in the fucking day. But you don't see them trying to fucking shoot each other! You don't see fucking Clive trying to steal Mariah Carey from Sony. He says, 'Fuck you, I'll get my own Mariah Carey.' So he got Toni Braxton.

"I understand Puffy is flamboyant and wanted to be seen in the videos, but I have to give credit where it's due: I may not know the whole thing behind the Death Row family, but Puffy taught his groups how to dress and perform in videos. He was a perfectionist. I don't know what

Suge did. Besides intimidate motherfuckers and give them a whole lot of weed so they'd be so blunted, they wouldn't realize how much money was being stolen from them."

As the event continued, Puffy was called upon to hand Snoop Doggy Dogg his award for Artist of the Year (Solo). Distressed by Suge's reproach, Puffy made it a point to hug Snoop and warmly congratulate him. Then he stepped behind a microphone and implored the East and West coasts to remain united. Later in the show, Daz of Tha Dogg Pound stepped onstage and ruined everything. As usual, there was arrogance on his face, as if he didn't approve of the world around him. "Yo, from the bottom of my heart," he told the audience, "y'all can eat this dick."

Suge's next step was to open Club 662 in Las Vegas. The building had a history: Its first owner was a Studio City entrepreneur whose stint as owner ended in 1982, when he was indicted on racketeering charges and convicted for mail fraud. He was accused of being involved in an arson-for-profit scheme in Vegas and Los Angeles. The building then began to house a series of night spots. The first, Suge remembered from his days at UNLV, was called Botany's and owned by Carl Thomas, a man who had been convicted in the early 1980s for helping Chicago-based mob figures skim money from the Stardust Hotel. When accountant Steve Cantrock and Suge's lawyer, David Kenner, decided to help Suge realize his dream of owning a club, they negotiated with Thomas's wife, Helen, who held a long-term lease on the space.

Cantrock introduced Suge to Robert Amira, a Las Vegas businessman who had also experienced trouble with the law: In 1982, due to his penchant for associating with organized crime figures, Amira was indicted with New York Mafia figures Joseph Colombo Jr. and Alphonse "the Whale" Merolla: Though the trio was accused of bilking the Dunes Hotel-Casino in an airline junket ticket scam, the case was dismissed. The judge saw the prosecutor and jury foreman communicating in a manner he felt was improper. With Robert Amira's assistance, after Cantrock brought him in, Suge was able to finally open his club.

Suge Knight remembered the place from his days at UNLV, when he would drive past and watch affluent whites enter through its well-guarded threshold. Now he could reopen it for black students who liked hip-hop and would pay steep prices for the privilege of seeing his Death Row acts perform.

"It's a cool little spot," said former UNLV teammate Bigga B. "It's not that big. Capacity's around eight or nine hundred. It was real plush though. He remodeled it. Made it even nicer than it used to be."

The stage wall had been painted black: The word "club" (in large red letters) was near a crude rendering of three playing cards—a red six of diamonds, a black six of clubs, and a red two of hearts. On each side of the stage he had erected a tall column of speakers. He added well-stocked bars and a few tables, then opened his doors.

"There were a lot more black people there," Bigga B recalled. "Back when it was Botany's, it was mostly Italians, mostly white people used to go in there. It was a real upscale, dress-up spot. Not too many black folks. When Suge took it over, it was predominantly black. There were so many after-the-fight celebrities in there. Suge was charging eighty dollars a head and getting it.

"After the first Tyson fight, with Peter McNealy on August 19, I went to Suge's afterparty and saw him regulating the door. I was like, 'Man, this dude has millions of dollars and he's doing the security at his own fucking club?' That shit was bugging me out. I was with RZA and Wu-Tang Management. Suge let us in, no problem; showed us a lot of love. But he was throwing a couple of cats out." Suge did not want two rowdy individuals in his club. After flinging a drink on them, he grabbed them and threw them out. "Then somebody got shot out front and it got kinda ugly in there. I don't really know what happened but, uh, someone got shot out front after he threw someone out. It might have been related to the guys he threw out. And they stopped serving alcohol. But the thing is, Suge didn't have to do security. He had fifteen security guards there, all being paid to work. But on top of that, *he* was doing security. I was laughing, thinking, 'What is he doing?' "

On September 24, 1995, Suge Knight flew to Atlanta to attend Kriss Kross producer Jermaine Dupri's birthday party: Among those who received invites to the affair were Biggie Smalls; his supporting act, Junior M.A.F.I.A.; Sean "Puffy" Combs; and the Death Row contingent. After the actual cake-cutting ceremony, an afterparty was held at another venue. Puffy attended the party without bodyguards since "there wasn't really no drama," he said.

Throughout the evening, he claimed he didn't see Suge. "He gets into a beef in the club with some niggas," said Puffy. "I don't know who he got into the beef with, what it was over, or nothing like that." Puffy left the club and chatted with women until his limousine arrived. He entered the limo just as screaming partygoers began fleeing the party. Suge Knight appeared in front of the club. Puffy left the limo, he claimed, to ask Suge, "What's up, you all right?"

"I'm trying to see if I can help," Puffy explained.

As he continued questioning Suge, gunshots rang out. Both label heads turned in time to see someone standing directly behind Puffy. Jake Robles, Suge's popular friend, had been wounded. When Robles fell to the pavement, Suge immediately turned to Puffy and yelled, "*I think you had something to do with this!*"

"*What are you talking about?*" Puffy replied. "*I was standing right here with you!*"

A week later, Jake "the Violator" Robles died from his injuries. A local newspaper fingered one of Puffy's cousins, a member of his entourage present that night, as the trigger man. Puffy denied everything. "Why would I set a nigga up to get shot?" he asked *Vibe* magazine. "If I'm'a set a nigga up, which I would never do, I'm'a be in Bolivia somewhere."

"I heard there was a contract out on my life," he added. "Why do they have so much hatred for me? I ask myself that question every day. I'm ready for them to leave me alone, man."

With Robles's murder, the feud turned deadly. Robles had been a soldier for Suge, said record promoter Doug Young. "Actually, a lot of Bloods were mad at Suge for Jake getting killed like that. They're saying Jake took the bullet for Suge. Jake covered him up out in Atlanta. Everybody said Jake was the coolest guy you'd ever wanna meet. And a lot of them Bloods were mad. That's why you hear rumors saying they're gonna get Suge when he gets in jail."

Though the rap press wanted Suge and Puffy to reconcile, Suge was intent on avenging his old friend's death. Reporters asked Suge, If Puffy called, would you speak to him? Suge answered, "He done that shit a hundred times. What the muthafucka need to do is stop lyin' in magazines! Sayin' shit didn't happen!" In Suge's opinion, Puffy had orchestrated the murder attempt on his life—his friend Jake died while trying to prevent what Puffy had planned for Suge.

Suge accused Puffy of hiding at the Soul Train Awards, paying "Muslims money for protection" and buying "niggas to hang wit' him." But this "type of support don't last." If anything, he warned, Puffy's "ghetto nigga" friends were just "takin' his money." They would not offer protection when Suge finally decided to strike.

"BEAT ME OUT OF MY MONEY AND I'LL KICK YOUR DRAWERS UP YOUR BEHIND"

When writer Lynn Hirschberg arrived to interview Suge for a cover story in *The New York Times Magazine*, everyone around Suge felt that accommodating her was a bad idea. Hirschberg, described by *Rolling Stone*'s Michael Azerrad as "well known for her unflattering celebrity profiles," was the journalist who accused rock singer Courtney Love of shooting heroin while pregnant: Hirschberg's profile on Love, printed in *Vanity Fair*, inspired Love's husband, Nirvana lead singer Kurt Cobain, to say, "I just decided, 'Fuck this. I don't want to be in a band anymore. It just isn't worth it. I want to kill [Hirschberg].'"

Despite warnings from everyone around him, Suge agreed to be interviewed by Hirschberg, who arrived to follow him around even as Jake Robles's murder was having a profoundly negative effect on his thinking. "You're born to die," he now felt. "Ain't nobody gonna leave here alive. Everybody is born and everybody's going to die. Period. That's the way it's played. Can't nobody change that."

When Hirschberg asked actor Warren Beatty for his opinion on Suge's intense hatred for Sean "Puffy" Combs, Beatty said, "It's hard to keep up with the apocrypha on Suge." At the time, Beatty was associating with Suge as research for a film he was preparing about the L.A. club scene. "I mean, Puff Daddy, Muff Daddy, whatever," Beatty scoffed. "I know Suge was very close to the man who died. And I know he was very upset."

Sitting in a red leather chair behind the desk in his red office, a cell phone pressed to his ear every few minutes, Suge controlled everything about the label. His office had the feel of a bunker. The walls were red, covered with framed platinum-certification platters. The red carpet featured a white Death Row logo. Instead of books, a few sports trophies in his bookshelf. Model cars sat on his desk. Piranhas in a large fish tank. Rodents occasionally tossed in to feed them.

Suge had told *Vibe* magazine that rival gang members had placed three contracts on his life; people connected to his enemies had informed him of this. Publicly, he said, "My program's the same: I'm in my office working, at my studio working." He decided to challenge his foes. "If someone wants to meet with me, they can. I'm not a person who's hiding. You can't worry about it. If you worry, you'll never get anywhere."

Despite his statements, Suge was concerned: Like his cinematic hero, the Cuban drug dealer Al Pacino portrayed in Brian De Palma's *Scarface*, Suge had workmen install surveillance cameras over every inch of Can-Am Studios: Like Pacino in the film's final reel, Suge kept six television sets behind his desk and tried to watch everything in the building. His office door was locked; strangers were never admitted. For dinner he had an assistant bring a stack of foil takeout trays containing chicken-fried steak, collard greens, corn bread, chicken rice, and macaroni and cheese. If Suge needed a nap, a small room adjoining his office contained a bed covered with maroon satin sheets.

Though a multimillionaire, he wore jeans, hooded sweatshirts, and sneakers. But he also wore a large diamond-and-ruby M.O.B. ring on one finger. Recently, Suge had purchased the ring, and eleven others from BL Diamonds, a store owned by Brian Lemberger, a friend of label accountant Steven Cantrock's. During his visit to the store (Suite 570 at 631 Olive Street) Suge purchased twelve M.O.B. rings: six with diamonds ($970 each), and six 14-karat-gold versions, priced at $480 each.

At the label, Suge distributed them to his Blood henchmen, and repeated his misogynist philosophy: Like the Tony Montana character he revered, Suge felt that real men should earn money first, *then* party with women. When *New York Times* writer Lynn Hirschberg pressed Suge to reveal what "M.O.B." stood for, he refused. Rebellious and macho—and to show Hirschberg that no woman would force him to answer questions, no matter how important her newspaper was—Suge kept muttering, "M.O.B."

Soon he was telling her that anyone could have an ugly face. "You can. I can. There are lots of dicksters out there. Beat me out of my money and I'll kick your drawers up your behind. Treat me fair and I'll treat you fair." He stood for what was right in the world, he explained. "But if you mess with me or my people, you've got a problem. If I wanted to," he added, "I could really scare the hell out of you."

"OH, SHIT, THEY SHOT ME IN THE HEAD"

A supportive friend, Tupac Shakur dropped by NBC studios in New York to watch Snoop Doggy Dogg perform on the April 2, 1994, episode of *Saturday Night Live.* In Snoop's dressing room, they smoked marijuana with pop singer Madonna Ciccone, who wanted Dr. Dre to produce songs for her next album. Occasionally, Tupac discussed the rape accusations lodged against him by nineteen-year-old Ayanna Jackson. With his own first degree murder trial coming up, Snoop was sympathetic.

Two days later, Biggie Smalls dropped by Tupac's room at the Royalton. "They had just met," claimed Dream Hampton, who recorded the meeting with Tupac's newest video camera. "I don't know where they first met. It *couldn't* have been on the *Poetic Justice* set like magazines said because Biggie didn't visit Los Angeles until *Ready to Die* happened. It must have been some other film he was doing, like *Above the*—I don't know," she said warily. "Some other film."

As usual, Biggie drank Hennessy and smoked marijuana. Eager to impress the reigning East Coast rap king, Tupac recited his newest lyrics. "They were really in sync," Dream recalled. "They were so much alike but different in this regard: Tupac used to always go around saying his rhymes. Even that day in the hotel room, he was writing and he'd say, 'Listen to this, man.' Big was more laid back. He would listen but wasn't one to just start rhyming."

After setting his lyric sheets aside, Tupac told Biggie that he was concerned about the rape accusation. He proudly displayed a new surveillance recorder, vowing to use it during upcoming dates. When Biggie left, Tupac changed his shirt, then slipped into a nice new bulletproof vest.

On November 29, 1994, a Manhattan jury convened to deliberate charges of sodomy, sexual abuse, and weapons possession against twenty-three-year-old Tupac Shakur and codefendant Charles Fuller, twenty-four. They stood accused of molesting nineteen-year-old Ayanna Jackson on November 18, 1993, in Tupac's $750-a-night suite on the thirty-eighth floor of the Parker-Meridien.

After the first day of deliberations, Tupac visited a local disc jockey's home. He traveled with his sister's boyfriend, Zayd; his old friend Randy "Stretch" Walker; and Stretch's friend, Fred Moore. At the local disc jockey's home, Tupac's beeper went off: He called the number displayed on the device and spoke with a guy named Booker, who asked him to appear on a record for a little-known Uptown recording artist named Little Shawn. "Now, *this* guy I was going to charge," Tupac said, "because I could see that they was just using me, so I said, 'All right, you give me seven gees and I'll do the song.' "

En route to the studio, Tupac stopped to purchase marijuana. His beeper sounded again. "Where you at?" Booker asked. "Why ain't you coming?"

Tupac answered, "I'm coming, man. Hold on."

"I felt nervous because this guy knew somebody I had major beef with. I didn't want to tell the police, but I can tell the world: [Jacques] had introduced me to Booker." Jacques Agnant, the Haitian-born music promoter Tupac met while filming *Above the Rim* in New York, was also a codefendant in the sex abuse case.

Nervous about meeting Booker, Tupac considered his situation: Negative publicity had led to his shows being canceled; his album royalties were barely paying his exorbitant legal costs; money he earned by appearing in films went to his dependent extended family—his mother, his sister, her baby, his aunt, and all her kids—all of whom expected him to be the breadwinner. During the sex abuse trial, he remembered, children crawled all over him. "If I don't work," he finally told a lawyer, "these kids don't eat."

Though nervous about Booker's connection to Agnant, an appearance on Little Shawn's rap record would earn Tupac a much-needed seven thousand dollars. Besides, he thought, Booker wasn't like the other street characters Biggie had introduced him to. Booker was "trying to get legitimate and all that, so I thought I was doing him a favor. But when I called him back for directions, he was like, 'I don't have the money.'"

Tupac said, "If you don't have the money, I'm not coming."

Infuriated, Booker slammed the phone down. Within minutes he called back. "I'm going to call Andre Harrell and make sure you get the money," Booker said, "but I'm going to give you the money out of my pocket."

"All right," Tupac said. "I'm on my way."

At 12:20 A.M., over an hour late, Tupac arrived at the Times Square building that housed the Quad Recording Studio. Stretch, Fred Moore, and Zayd were with him. "As we're walking up to the building, somebody screamed from up the top of the studio. It was Little Caesar, Biggie's side man. That's my homeboy. As soon as I saw him, all my concerns about the situation were relaxed."

Near the door, a man in army fatigues wore his hat low, to conceal his face. When the man didn't look up, Tupac was suspicious. "I've never seen a black man not acknowledge me one way or the other, either with jealousy or respect. But this guy just looked to see who I was and turned his face down. It didn't click because I had just finished smoking chronic."

Before entering the building, he saw another guy inside: sitting at a table, reading a newspaper, and not bothering to face them either. Tupac considered the two strangers: Both black men in their thirties, they wore army fatigues, a style favored by Brooklyn residents. He figured they must be Biggie's security guards. "But then I said, Wait a minute. Even Biggie's homeboys love me. Why don't they look up?" He pressed the elevator button, turned, and saw the men holding identical 9mm handguns. "Don't nobody move," one yelled. "Everybody on the floor. You know what time it is. Run your shit."

The men ignored Stretch. Again, Tupac's suspicion was aroused. "He was towering over those niggas," Tupac explained. "From what I know of the criminal element, if niggas come to rob you, they always hit the big nigga first. But they didn't touch Stretch. They came straight to me."

Tupac's body froze. "It wasn't like I was being brave or nothing. I just could not get on the floor." The armed bandits frisked him: The light-skinned robber ordered him to remove his jewelry. Some say this robber was Jacques Agnant. Tupac refused. The second robber, who had been waiting in the lobby with a newspaper, kept his gun aimed at Stretch and told his light-skinned cohort, *"Shoot that motherfucker! Fuck it!"*

"Then I got scared," Tupac admitted, "because the dude had the gun to my stomach. All I could think about was piss bags and shit bags. I drew my arm around him to move the gun to my side. He shot and the gun twisted and that's when I got hit the first time. I felt it in my leg. I didn't know I got shot in the balls."

He dropped to the floor and played dead. The elevator arrived and Biggie's side man, Little Caesar, stuck his head out. According to an employee at *America's Most Wanted*, the TV program, one robber yelled, "Go back upstairs!" Recognizing the bandit, Caesar complied. The elevator doors slammed shut and the robbers alternated between kicking Tupac and removing his jewelry. They snatched $5000 of Moore's jewelry, Tupac's $30,000 diamond ring, and $10,000 in gold chains. That evening Tupac was wearing the diamond-encrusted Rolex Agnant had purchased for him. Strangely, the robbers left the valuable Rolex behind.

After they fled the scene, his friends helped Tupac to his feet. "As soon as I got to the door, I saw a police car sitting there. I was like, 'Uh-oh, the police are coming and I didn't even go upstairs yet.'" Tupac limped to the elevator, entered slowly, and rode to the eighth floor, where Little Shawn's studio session continued. "When we got upstairs I looked around and it scared the shit out of me." Forty people were gathered in the room, among them, Andre Harrell, Sean "Puffy" Combs, and his old buddy, Biggie Smalls.

"All of them had jewels on," Tupac noticed. "More jewels than me. I saw Booker and he had this look on his face like he was surprised to see me. Why? I had just beeped the buzzer and said I was coming upstairs. Little Shawn burst into tears and yelled, 'Oh, my God! 'Pac, you've got to sit down!' "

Tupac Shakur was in shock. "I was feeling weird," he said, "like 'Why do they want to make me sit down?' "

He did not know the extent of his injuries. "I didn't feel nothing. I opened my pants and I could see the gunpowder and the hole in my Karl Kani drawers. I didn't want to pull them down to see if my dick was still there. I just saw a hole and went, 'Oh, shit. Roll me some weed.' I called my girlfriend and I was like, 'Yo, I just got shot. Call my mother and tell her.'

"Nobody approached me," he claimed. "I noticed that nobody would look at me. Andre Harrell wouldn't look at me." Prior to the shooting, Harrell had invited Tupac to the set of his Fox television police drama *New York Undercover* and offered him a job. "Puffy was standing back too. I knew Puffy. He knew how much stuff I had done for Biggie before he came out."

Years later, Puffy told *Rolling Stone* a different story. "Tupac was shot. I mean, that's Tupac! I immediately went to him, sat him down, calmed him, had people call the ambulance."

Eventually, people in the studio told Tupac, "Your head! Your head is bleeding!" He thought he had been pistol-whipped. An ambulance arrived, along with NYPD officers William Kelly, Joseph Kelly, and Craig McKernan, who had supervised the two Kellys in Tupac's arrest at the Parker-Meridien and recently testified at his sex abuse trial. "He had a half-smile on his face and he could see them looking at my balls," Tupac recalled. "He said, 'What's up, Tupac? How's it hanging?' "

Vibe quoted McKernan as saying, "Hey, Tupac, you hang in there."

An EMS team secured a brace around his neck; he was strapped to a board; the stretcher didn't fit in the elevator, so he was propped upright, causing blood to stream from his wounds. Outside, McKernan helped carry him past a photographer. "I can't believe you're taking my picture on a stretcher," Tupac said.

At Bellevue Hospital, the doctor faced his wounds and said, "Oh, my God." Frightened, Tupac asked, "What? What?"

The physician gathered others around him. "Look at this," he said. "This is gunpowder right here." He pointed at Tupac's head. "This is the entry wound," he said. "This is the exit wound."

Tupac felt the doctor's finger probing holes in his head. "Oh, my God," he said. "I could feel that." Between blackouts he said, "Oh, shit. They shot me in the head."

Doctors told him he was lucky: He had been shot *five* times. Tupac had remembered only the first. "Then everything went blank."

Dr. Leon Pachter, chief of Bellevue's trauma department, said, "He was hit by a low-caliber missile. Had it been a high-caliber missile, he'd have been dead."

That night and into the next morning, Tupac bled heavily. At 1:30 P.M. Dr. Pachter and a twelve-doctor team operated on a damaged blood vessel high in his right leg. At 4:00 P.M. he was out of surgery: Despite having lost a testicle, doctors reported that he would be able to reproduce. Their exploratory surgery revealed that the bullet had entered skin and left it. Same with his head. But the shooting left him with headaches. And nightmares. At 6:45 that evening, against medical advice, Tupac signed himself out of the hospital. Dr. Pachter was shocked. "I haven't seen anybody in my twenty-five-year professional career leave the hospital like this," he said.

But Tupac had his reasons. "I knew my life was in danger," he said. "The Fruit of Islam was there but they didn't have guns. I knew what type of niggas I was dealing with." His mother, Afeni, had flown to New York from Atlanta: She wheeled her heavily bandaged son out of the back door and through a mob of reporters.

The next day, November 30, 1994, Tupac woke up and was told he shouldn't attend the court proceeding. He went anyway. "I felt if the jury didn't see me, they would think I'm doing a show or some shit. Because they were sequestered and didn't know I got shot."

Mickey Rourke, his costar in the film *Bullet*, and old friend, Jasmine

Guy, of A *Different World* watched Tupac's bow-tied Fruit of Islam security guards wheel him into the Manhattan courtroom on November 30,
1994, for his sentencing. "I swear to God, the farthest thing from my
mind was sympathy," Tupac said. "All I could think of was, Stand up and
fight for your life like you fought for your life in the hospital." His Rolex
was on his right wrist. His left wrist was wrapped in gauze. His head was
bandaged and covered with a Yankee cap. He wore a black Nike jogging
suit. The judge would not meet his stare. The solemn jury entered.
Tupac sensed he would be found guilty. "Then I felt numb. I said, 'I've
got to get out of here.' "

His guards wheeled him out of the chamber. His leg felt numb. Outside, cameramen rushed him, bumping into the wounded limb. "I was
like, 'You motherfuckers are like vultures.' That made me see just the
nastiest in the hearts of men. That's why I was looking like that in the
chair when they were wheeling me away. I was trying to promise myself
to keep my head up for all my people there. But when I saw all that, it
made me put my head down. It just took my spirit."

As he secretly checked into Metropolitan Hospital Center on East 97
Street (under the name Bob Day), the jury returned with verdicts: Tupac
was found guilty of fondling Ayanna Jackson against her will and sexual
abuse, but he was not guilty on the more serious sodomy and weapons
charges. A few jurors, in fact, had voted for complete acquittal. "There
was a very strong feeling that there just was not enough evidence," one
of them told reporters.

Tupac's lawyer, Michael Warren, said he planned to appeal. Due to
Tupac's condition, sentencing was delayed and his client would be free
on $25,000 bond.

At Metropolitan Hospital, Tupac was given a phone and told, "You're
safe here. Nobody knows you're here." But the phone kept ringing. A
voice on the other end would rasp, "You ain't dead yet?" His former
friends, he realized, were merciless. Fearing for his life, he checked out of
the hospital and went to hide in actress Jasmine Guy's apartment.

There, he was able to rest and reflect on the frenzied events of the last
forty-eight hours: He had been shot five times in the head and groin; he
had undergone surgery; he had left the hospital against medical advice;
he had appeared in a courtroom; he had faced a ravenous pack of

paparazzi, then checked into a second hospital; he been found guilty of fondling a woman against her will; he had received death threats and checked out of a second hospital. He would be sentenced to time in prison. If he didn't die as a result of these injuries, which continued to hurt. Then he read the newspapers and finally caved in. "The number one thing that bothered me," he said later, "was that dude that wrote that shit that said I pretended to do it. That I had set it up, it was an act. When I read that, I just started crying like a baby, like a bitch. I could not believe it. It just tore me apart. And then the news was trying to say I had a gun and I had weed on me. Instead of saying I was a victim, they were making it like I did it."

On February 14, 1995, Tupac Shakur was sentenced to up to four and a half years and began serving time in Rikers Island, a 415-acre island in the East River that is also the largest penal colony in the world. In his cell he was forced to stop smoking dope. For two days he was jittery. "That was the hardest part. After that, the weed was out of me. Then every day, I started doing like a thousand pushups for myself. I was reading whole books in one day, and writing, and that was putting me in a peace of mind."

By day, he memorized Machiavelli's *The Prince*. At night "I wake up screaming," he said. "I've been having nightmares, thinking they're still shooting me. All I see is niggas pulling guns and I hear the dude say, 'Shoot that motherfucker!' Then I'll wake up sweaty as hell and I'll be like, Damn, I have a headache. The psychiatrist at Bellevue said that's post-traumatic stress."

In *Vibe*, Tupac admitted that this entire Thug Life image was ignorant. He was tired of rap. "I mean, in here I don't even remember my lyrics." His upcoming album, *Me Against the World*, embodied everything he wanted to tell society. "And because I already laid it down, I can be free. When you do rap albums, you got to train yourself. You got to constantly be in character." He was tired of the part he had chosen for himself. "That Thug Life shit—I did it, I put it in my work, I laid it down. But now that shit is dead. If Thug Life is real, then let somebody else represent it, because I'm tired of it. I represented it too much."

Despite his positive intentions, when inmates saw him, they yelled, "Fuck that gangsta rapper." A member of the rap group Public Enemy said, "Tupac's having a hard time. A lot of the Latin gangs in there heard rumors that the girl involved was Hispanic, so they're making it a political thing and taking it out on him."

Soon, rumors spread that Tupac had been overpowered and raped by sadistic homosexual convicts. "Kill that rumor," he said when questioned about the rape. "That got started either by some guards or by some jealous niggas. I don't have to talk about whether or not I got raped in jail. If I wouldn't lay down for two niggas with pistols, what the fuck makes you think I would bend over for niggaz without weapons?" He claimed, "That don't even fit my character."

Tupac was transferred to Clinton Correctional, a harsh prison located in Dannemora, New York—even as his single "Dear Mama" was a popular hit that would eventually be nominated for a Grammy—where he continued to suffer abuse and outright ridicule at the hands of inmates and guards. During a visit, one of his lawyers told a reporter Tupac had a rectal search while entering. "Then we spent six hours there in full view of the guards. Then the guards started saying, 'Tupac! Tupac!' in this falsetto voice, putting up their fingers with these plastic gloves, waving them. 'It's time! It's time!' Why a second rectal search when he'd been sitting there in plain view with his lawyer? why? except to humiliate him?"

"I have never had people demean me and disgrace me as they have in this jail," Tupac told an aunt. Inmates threatened to kill him; guards hounded him at every turn. The abuse continued despite the fact that on April Fool's Day his third album, *Me Against the World*, had debuted at No. 1 on *Billboard*'s Pop Chart. "That's all right," Tupac now thought when guards tormented him, "I got the number one record in the country."

His lawyers were filing appeals and Tupac should have been allowed to post bail. But the district attorney's office wanted him behind bars. The proceedings dragged on for months. Destitute, he married Keisha Morris, a woman he had known for only six months. In a deposition he wrote, "She's twenty-two, she's a Scorpio, she just graduated from John Jay College with a degree in criminal science, and she's taken a year off, she's going to law school. She's nice, she's quiet, she's a square, she's a good girl. She's my first and only girlfriend I ever had in my entire life, and now she's my wife." After the ceremony he filled her head with talk of moving to Arizona and raising kids, then accepted the small amenities she provided. (Little did Keisha Morris know—immediately upon his release Tupac would have this marriage annulled.)

In prison Tupac reflected on his shooting. Initially he did not believe Biggie was involved. How could he? When he was laid up with injuries, his road manager, Charles Fuller, reported, Biggie Smalls had come to visit. "But when Tupac was in jail," Fuller said, "he was getting letters from people saying Biggie had something to do with it. He started thinking about it. It got so out of hand. It grew. And once it got that big publicly, you had to go with it."

In an interview with *Vibe* magazine, Tupac publicly accused Sean "Puffy" Combs and Biggie Smalls of orchestrating the robbery. "I was like, 'Where the fuck is this coming from?' Puffy said. "I'm not going to rob nobody. The only reason I was at the studio was because Biggie had a session there, just like Tupac. So I wrote to Tupac in jail. I said, 'I want to come see you. I don't know if what the writer was saying in *Vibe* was true, that you really felt any of this. But whatever the situation is, I know me and Biggie want to just get it clear with you. We got nothing but love for you.' He wrote back and said, 'Well, Puff, everything's cool. It ain't no problem like that. I don't really want us to have no meeting about it like that.' "

In response to Tupac's accusations, the four-page letters-to-the-editor section in *Vibe*'s August 1995 edition featured only one note from Puffy, Biggie, and Andre Harrell: After denying each of Shakur's vengeful accusations, the trio expressed hope that the hostility between the East and West coasts (fueled by Tupac's shooting and Suge's insults at the Source Awards) would cease. "I'm still thinking this nigga's my man," Biggie Smalls said. "This shit's just got to be talk, that's all I kept saying to myself. I can't believe he would think that I would shit on him like that."

"SHE OPENED THE DOOR AND FAITH BEAT THE SHIT OUT OF HER"

At Death Row Records, Snoop Doggy Dogg pitied his old friend Tupac's plight. In the past, label CEO Suge had wanted to sign Tupac to the label. "But I kinda put the fuel to the flame and told Suge to put Tupac down with Death Row," Snoop said. "It's like an angel was talking to me when I told Suge, 'We need 'Pac on Death Row.'"

Suge agreed. Tupac was having trouble with Puffy. Now would be a good time to offer Tupac a contract. Suge made his offer. Behind bars, Tupac accepted. His friends urged him not to sign, but Tupac desperately wanted to be free. In the past, he had said, "If I have to go to jail, I don't even want to be living. I just want to cease to exist for however long they have me there, and then when I come out, I'll be reborn, you know what I'm saying?"

During a visit before Suge arrived in upstate New York, Tupac's old friend Watani Tyehimba urged him not to sign with the controversial label. Tupac hugged him, wept openly. "I know I'm selling my soul to the devil," he said.

"At that point," his mother, Afeni Shakur, claimed, "I don't think he had any choice but to sign that contract." This was not entirely true: Tupac could have decided to refuse Suge's offer and serve his time in prison—just like any other inmate.

Interscope, supportive of Tupac's decision to sign with Death Row, granted him a "verbal release." Suge's attorney, David Kenner, drafted a crude, handwritten three-page contract. Tupac scribbled his signature. Beneath it, Suge countersigned.

On October 12, 1995, Suge and Kenner chartered a private jet and flew to upstate New York. As their white limousine cruised through a small economically depressed white town, drawing stares from locals in old jeans and baseball caps, Tupac prepared to leave Dannemora. He walked out of the gray prison, past hostile guards and inmates, posed for a photo near the limousine, then quickly entered the vehicle. In the photo he looked gaunt. His stare was tentative and weak. The last few years had been rough ones, beating a limo driver in Los Angeles, attacking the Hughes brothers on the set of a video, swinging a bat at a rapper onstage at a concert in Michigan, being punched in the eye by a Crip in a convenience store, shooting two drunk off-duty cops in Atlanta, being accused of rape in New York, getting robbed and shot five times in the head and groin in Times Square, serving time in Rikers Island, then Dannemora. But the next year would be even worse. It would also be his last.

When he entered the white limo, Tupac's last album, Me Against the World, was still on the nation's pop album chart, lingering at No. 108 after twenty-six weeks. During the flight to Los Angeles and studio sessions that night, Tupac believed Suge Knight had been solely responsible for posting $1.4 million bond. Despite the fact that he had provided only $250,000—with Interscope and Time Warner paying the difference— Suge took sole credit for Tupac's release. "Whether the odds are in your favor or appear to be stacked against you," he said the next day, "the Death Row family sticks with you."

Upon signing, Tupac vowed to make Death Row the biggest label in the world. Even bigger than Snoop had made it. "Not stepping on Snoop's toes," he said, "he did a lot of work. Him, Dogg Pound, Nate Dogg, Dre, all of them. They made Death Row what it is today. I'm gonna take it to the next level."

"I saw him right when he got out of jail," said producer E Swift of the California rap trio Tha Alkaholiks. "Every time I saw him he was all love. He was so happy to be out, free. That was all he could talk about: 'Man, I'm out! I'm out! I'm happy to be alive!' He was just living for the moment."

Suge Knight, meanwhile, knew Tupac's arrival at Death Row would change the label. "It gave them a much more public profile," said author Brian Cross. "Snoop and Dre would always get press. But now there were three public stars: And at that point, with the benefit of Tupac becoming his running buddy, Suge was starting to get press. Suddenly the lights were shining on Suge and he became a player in the whole thing."

From the beginning, however, Tupac could not escape accusations that he signed to Death Row for protection. National music magazines had publicized his feud with Bad Boy, and his accusations that people connected with that label had stalked him on the East Coast. From the macho image they had promoted in his early days, when he shot off-duty white police officers, reporters now focused on the fact that Tupac had feared for his life; he had been robbed; he had lost a testicle and been left with nightmares and persistent headaches; he was rumored to have been sodomized in a New York prison. They also wrote articles emphasizing how Suge was a force powerful enough to repel any would-be assassin: He was known for brutalizing his competition and granting enemies no leniency. If anyone could keep ruthless drug dealers from killing him, reporters stressed, it was Suge Knight and his sociopathic friends in the brutal Tree Top Pirus street gang. And Tupac, they inferred, was well aware of this.

"There's nobody in the business strong enough to scare me," Tupac claimed. "I'm with Death Row 'cause they not scared either. When I was in jail, Suge was the only one who used to see me. Nigga used to fly a private plane all the way to New York and spend time with me. He got his lawyer to look into all my cases. Suge supported me, whatever I needed. When I got out of jail, he had a private plane for me, a limo, five police officers for security. I said, 'I need a house for my moms.' "

Much as Tupac supported the label, initially, former–Black Panther Afeni Shakur cheerled for generous black music mogul Suge Knight. In the past, said Tupac's aunt Yaasmyn Fula, Afeni and her brood "lived lives of scarcity, worrying about the next meal, worrying about how to pay the rent."

When Suge signed her son, he had also bought Afeni a home. When the Shakur family came to town, he put them up at the luxurious West-wood Marquis and never complained about the huge bills they ran up. "Death Row in the beginning treated us much better than Interscope had," Afeni confirmed.

By now, however, " 'Pac felt he was cursed with this dysfunctional family although he loved them," his aunt Yaasmyn later told *The New Yorker*. "And as his success grew, especially in the last year, this presence grew. They were *always* there."

Since childhood, Tupac had suffered feelings of inadequacy: His cous-ins used to tease him about his effeminate facial features; he felt "un-manly," he said. Free from prison, Tupac was now expected to return to the role he willingly abandoned during his incarceration; he was ex-pected to record "macho" gangsta rap.

Tupac regularly spent nineteen hours at a time in the studio. Though he claimed to have quit smoking and drinking, he soon picked up where he left off. High on marijuana and drunk on cheap booze, he worked on his next album. "He was released on Thursday," Afeni Shakur reported. "By Thursday night he was in the studio. By Friday he had seven songs from that double CD completed."

Like Snoop, Tupac was working to pay off legal fees Death Row had provided. To ensure that Tupac's album would sell, Suge provided Tupac with tracks that Dr. Dre had originally planned to use on his *Helter Skelter* album with Ice Cube. Suge owned every master tape used by Death Row musicians. He located a song featuring Dre and Ice Cube rhyming over a snazzy Dre production (their collaboration with funk musician George Clinton, "You Can't See Me." Without permission, Suge erased their vocals and allowed Tupac to record a generic profanity-ridden gangsta rap.

Then Suge called Johnny Jackson (producer of "Pour out a Little Liquor") into the studio. "We were very prolific," Jackson explained.

"We'd put down four to five songs a day. I saw him work with other producers, and if they took too long to lay down the music, he'd get upset. He'd say, 'You're not moving fast enough. I need you to pick up the pace.' So when me and him got together for *All Eyez on Me*, we were going at it like mad scientists.

"A typical day would go like this," Jackson continued. "After I'd been there laying down the tracks for an hour or two, he'd come in, sit right down, and write three verses in fifteen or twenty minutes. Then he'd go into the booth and deliver the vocal—and it was off to the next track. I didn't realize a rapper could write the lyrics and deliver the vocals as fast as he could. That really amazed me."

At the time, Biggie Smalls's wife was in town on business. A caramel-colored woman with bleached-blond hair, Faith Evans was born in Lakeland, Florida, in 1973. A year after her birth, she moved to her grandparents' home in Newark, New Jersey. "My mama used to sing with a white rock band," she remembered. "I don't know the name of it, but she used to take me to her shows sometime." By the age of two, Faith was singing at the Emanuel Baptist Church. An honor student at University High School, she received a scholarship to Fordham University. In 1993 she decided to begin writing songs.

Before marrying Biggie, she had been a songwriter for Mary J. Blige, Soul for Real, and Usher. Nine days after they met at a Bad Boy photo shoot on August 4, 1994, they became man and wife. "I can't explain it," Biggie said. "I just knew Faith was different. I wanted her locked down." But Faith had to deal with people assuming she was out for Biggie's money despite her songwriting credits. "Hello?" she once said. "I was already doing my own thing." A week after the wedding, she bought Biggie a green Land Cruiser. "Then he got a burgundy one," writer Dream Hampton recalled. "Then a Lexus. Then an SL."

They moved into a spacious apartment off Myrtle Street in Brooklyn, then Biggie went on tour. Faith felt terrible but focused on recording her solo album. When Biggie returned to Brooklyn, he leaped into recording an album for his protégés, Junior M.A.F.I.A. "These are my peoples," Biggie said of the group. "I grew up with them and I know how it is to come from the Ave. I wasn't going to give up the Ave. and leave my niggas out there."

A member of the group, Lil' Kim, said she loved Biggie to death. "And I mean that literally. Everybody knows. It's not a secret. I love him."

As Biggie spent time with Kim, recording her for Junior M.A.F.I.A.'s album *Conspiracy*, Faith became unhappy. "A few months after our anniversary," she told *Vibe*, "it seemed like he was getting caught up in all that 'big poppa' stuff. But I couldn't see myself being without him. He was real . . . real . . . *real*."

While Biggie toured with Kim's group, his storybook marriage to Faith Evans suffered. After a show in Virginia, a telephone conversation with Faith erupted into an argument, and Biggie hung up on her. She kept trying to call back, but he refused to answer the telephone. That night his friends invited female groupies over. One was left out, Biggie explained, so he let her sleep in his room. "It was some completely innocent shit. We weren't fucking." At eight the next morning, someone knocked on the door. Big remained in bed while his female guest went to answer. " 'Who is it?' she asked. A winsome voice replied, 'Housekeeping.'

"She opened the door," Big remembered, "and Faith beat the shit out of her. Oh, my God. Punched homegirl in the face about thirty times, then got on the next flight back to New York." It was like a scene from *Casino*. The vengeful wife strikes back. Biggie was nervous. He rushed to the airport. " 'Cause I wasn't gonna leave her buck wil'ing like that. The girl was mad cool and I felt horrible, but fuck that. I got on that plane."

Despite his marriage, Junior M.A.F.I.A. member Lil' Kim began a campaign to get Biggie back. "The whole thing between me and Faith," Kim told *Rappages*: "We don't have to be friends, but it don't need to be no beef. 'I feel your pain, but you got to feel mine. I've been there way before you. Imagine what I was going through. Imagine how I felt when y'all two got married.' "

In Los Angeles shortly after Tupac's release from prison in October 1995, Faith kept seeing Tupac at parties. Despite the fact that Tupac had accused her husband of trying to have him killed, Faith Evans felt Tupac was "mad cool." She said, "I saw him at a couple of parties and we was chillin', havin' drinks, him and my friends. And I knew Biggie always said he had mad love for Tupac."

When Tupac asked her to appear on a song, Faith agreed—pending her record company's, Bad Boy's, approval. Tupac encouraged her to record a vocal over one of his new beats. Even though Death Row Records and Bad Boy were literally at war, she complied, then returned to New York. Months later, as Death Row continued to express nothing but hate for Bad Boy, Faith's friends began to tell her they had heard her performance on Tupac's new song, "Wonda Why They Call U Bytch." Alarmed by the title, Faith was also confused. How could Death Row Records release the song when clearance forms hadn't been finalized? Bad Boy made inquiries, and Death Row insisted it wasn't Faith. Everyone was hearing Death Row's own singer Jewell, they claimed. Faith did not suspect that her associating with the maniacal Tupac would be used as ammunition against her husband and record label.

As Death Row's one-sided feud against Bad Boy continued, Bad Boy CEO Sean "Puffy" Combs continued to deny involvement in Tupac's shooting at the Quad Recording Studio, and Jake Robles's murder in Atlanta. In doing so, however, he revealed that he knew who shot Tupac. "He ain't mad at the niggas that shot him," Puffy said publicly, "he knows where they're at. He knows who shot him. If you ask him, he knows, and everybody in the street knows, and he's not stepping to them, because he knows that he's not gonna get away with that shit. To me, that's some real sucker shit."

Soon, the national media reported on the feud. But Suge tried to clarify that the battle was not between African Americans on the East and West coasts. It was "ghetto niggas and phony niggas." And Puffy, he said: "That's a phony nigga. He's frontin', tryin to be somethin' he ain't. Here's the whole thang with Puffy: They say shit to make themselves bigger. I ain't never did no interview sayin' shit about people. By sayin' shit about Death Row in magazines, they tryin' to put themselves on our level, and it ain't no muthafuckin' comparison."

The ideal solution, Suge felt, would be a boxing event that would benefit various inner-city charity organizations. "Puffy, get yo' muthafuckin' ass in the ring and fight Tupac," Suge roared. "Look at

Puffy's body! Who can he whup? How you gon' talk shit and be in a little boy's body? And I'll beat Biggie's ass all over the ring! We can do it in Vegas and give the money to the ghetto."

Puffy tried to make peace. "I'm not a gangsta and I don't have no rivalry with no person in this industry whatsoever. The whole shit is stupid—tryin' to make an East Coast/West Coast war."

Dr. Dre watched from the sidelines. "If it keeps going this way," he predicted, "pretty soon niggaz from the East Coast ain't gonna be able to come out here and vice versa."

Tha Dogg Pound (Daz and Kurupt) and Snoop arrived in New York City on December 16 to film a video for Tha Dogg Pound's single, "New York, New York." During their last visit, Daz had told the audience at the Source Awards, "Yo, from the bottom of my heart, y'all can eat this dick."

East Coast acts used their own appearances onstage to hurl a few expletives in response. Backstage, Daz claimed that when the Death Row entourage confronted them, these rappers said, " 'Oh, we ain't mean all that.' "Showin' love to us," he added, "but not in front of the public."

Following the awards ceremony, Daz claimed to harbor no malice toward the East Coast. "I got a gang of homies out there," he claimed. "I want to do an East Coast/West Coast record." Back in California, however, Tha Dogg Pound recorded a hostile, derisive cover of Grandmaster Flash and the Furious Five's "New York, New York."

"That record didn't dis no individuals, boroughs, peoples, labels, no nothing," Snoop explained. "It was just a song: 'New York, New York, big city of dreams/And everything in New York ain't always what it seems/You might get fooled if you come from out of town/But I'm down by law and I'm from the Dogg Pound.'

"That's not a *dis*," he claimed. "We *borrowed* that from Flash. *He's* the originator. And me borrowing that hook and putting it on that song? The *music* made me say that. Kurupt wrote this rap that had *nothing to do* with nobody in New York period," Snoop went on. "We had just got back from the Source Awards. Kurupt battled about three hundred MCs outside of a nightclub and he served all of them! He came home, busted a rap about how he served all these MCs.

"We had just got back from New York, so I said 'New York, New York, big city of dreams.' [Producer] Pooh threw all this shit in and it was a hit. Motherfuckers felt we dissed, but if we was dissin' we woulda said *'Fuck New York! Fuck these niggaz over here! Fuck your neighborhood! Fuck you!'* That's how we usually do. We don't ever beat around the bush or act like we wanna talk about somebody. If we got a problem, we deal with it. But that song was taken out of hand, and that's when the East/West thing started."

For the video, Tha Dogg Pound and Snoop hoped special effects would show them stomping on skyscrapers, automobiles, and theaters. By the time Tha Dogg Pound arrived in New York, however, Tupac's friend Randy "Stretch" Walker had been murdered. A year to the day of Tupac's shooting, Walker was gunned down in an execution-style drive-by shooting in Queens. During the last year, Tupac had also publicly accused Stretch of being involved in the plot to shoot and rob him. Now Stretch was dead and magazine articles published rumors that Suge may have flown killers across the country to exact revenge, though nothing ever came of them. Suge's myth as a gangster figure was at its peak.

At New York's Hot 97 radio station, Snoop and Tha Dogg Pound tried to explain that they were filming a video and welcomed New York residents to appear as extras. "But we got closed off at the radio station by the DJ," Snoop claimed. "He didn't let us explain. By the second or third day of filming, people got the wrong idea and thought maybe we were out here dissin' em. They were like, *'Well fuck it! If they ain't gonna invite us they must be dissin'.'* But it wasn't like that. We couldn't get on the radio to explain, 'Okay, this is the video we're doing.'"

Between takes on a street in Red Hook, Brooklyn, gunshots were fired at their trailer. The video crew left that location early and continued filming in less volatile parts of the city. While in New York, the Death Row camp was uncharacteristically silent about the shooting. "But like I explained myself on Hot 97," Snoop said, "those cars or buildings didn't belong to no individuals. It was a video. If you were able to do a video that expensive and creative, you woulda done it too! 'Cause you're a professional: You're entertaining your people; you're not worrying about what people are feeling. It's entertainment! And I'm *not* disrespecting. First of all: If I was gonna disrespect, I wouldn't've even came to New York and *risked my life!* I coulda made something out here in Hollywood look like New York. But I was going down there to be a part of New York and to help New York be a part of this video.

"Shit went sour but we still never said nothing about it," Snoop concluded. "We came home, put the video out, and that was that."

At the Château Le Blanc mansion in Beverly Hills, Death Row threw their 1995 Christmas party. In an upstairs room, Suge, Tupac Shakur, and a few of their boys were drinking heavily and questioning Mark Anthony Bell, an independent record promoter who worked for both Bad Boy and Death Row. They wanted Puffy's address. They also wanted Puffy's mother's address. For what, God only knew. When Bell refused to furnish that information, the goons beat him with champagne bottles. Then Suge decided to perform an ungodly jailhouse trick: To psychologically obliterate an opponent behind bars, gang members forced them to drink their urine.

Extracting his member, Suge filled a glass and forced Bell to drink every drop. Bell felt he would not survive this meeting. These drunk psychotics would kill him. He darted across the room and tried to save himself; tried to leap off the balcony, but Suge's boys grabbed his arms and shirt and dragged him back into the room. Luckily, one of Bell's friends saw him trying to fight his way out; the friend ran to a phone and called the police. When officers arrived, they saw bruises on Bell's face and arms. "I'm fine," he told them. Nearby, Suge and his entourage watched them chat. "I just fell," Bell lied. "Fell at the party."

Two days later, he filed a report about the attack; he admitted that he was reluctant to speak at the party because he feared for his life. Before matters could reach a courtroom, however, Bell received an estimated $600,000 settlement from people associated with Death Row. In return, he signed a statement saying he was "virtually certain" that Suge had nothing to do with the assault. Just as Bell stopped cooperating with authorities, label attorney David Kenner issued the standard denial of wrongdoing: Though Suge had initially been identified as the one who "lured" Bell upstairs, Suge actually had nothing to do with the incident, Kenner said. Bell, meanwhile, left the country. On a beach in sunny Jamaica, he recuperated slowly and told a friend on the phone, "I'm here till I heal. *They busted me up bad!"*

"THEM MOTHERFUCKERS WILL KILL HIM. HE AIN'T FROM THE STREET"

After Dr. Dre led the LAPD on a high-speed car chase in early 1994 (he was driving while intoxicated and didn't want the police to know this), the judge felt Dre had violated the probation he received for breaking rap producer Damon Thomas's jaw in 1992. Though David Kenner begged the judge to sentence Dre to mandatory appearance in public service announcements against drinking, the judge wanted Dre behind bars and initially offered Dre a choice as to where he would serve his time—one of the choices being the violent, gang-infested L.A. County Jail. "I told David Kenner, 'He can't go to L.A. County Jail,'" Suge said, stepping in. "'Them motherfuckers will kill him. He ain't from the street.' We made it so he did his time in a kick-back [relaxing] place, where you check in, look at TV, and check out."

During his 180 days in a Pasadena halfway house, Dre was part of a work-release program, allowing him to spend his days outside the facility and return to it at night. "When I got sentenced," Dre said, "my mom told me that jail was going to turn out to be a blessing in disguise. And she was right."

On February 6, 1996, his twenty-four-year-old friend Snoop Doggy Dogg was in L.A. Superior Court again, fighting accusations that he had participated in the August 25, 1993, murder of twenty-year-old reputed gang member Philip Woldemariam.

Snoop, who wore a black suit and tie, was free on $1 million bail. He was living with his fiancée, Chanté, and their fifteen-month-old son, Cordé, in a three-bedroom house complete with pool and basketball court. His codefendant, McKinley Lee, the twenty-five-year-old trigger man, was under electronically monitored house arrest.

During the trial, label publicist George Pryce sanitized Snoop's image. Instead of the heavy flannel shirt he wore early in the trial, Snoop now wore beige suitcoats, brown slacks, classy white dress shirts, neatly trimmed facial hair, and slicked-back braids. "Snoop Doggy Dogg always talked about 'LB' and 'Long Beach this and that,' " said gang counselor Manuel Velazquez. "But when shit hit the fan? Boy, did Death Row put out press releases! 'No! But he was in a choir!' Trying to paint this nice picture of him."

In court, Snoop occasionally turned to face supporters like Suge Knight, Jodeci producer Devante Swing, newly signed former pop-rap sensation/Kentucky Fried Chicken pitchman Hammer, and convicted sexual offender Tupac Shakur. By then a second codefendant, Snoop's friend since childhood Sean Abrams, had been acquitted of all charges. In November 1995, as jury selection began, O.J. lawyer Johnnie Cochran signed on to represent Abrams. After a pretrial hearing, Cochran told reporters, "Want me to say those famous words? If it doesn't fit, you must acquit."

Before opening statements were made on November 6, 1995, Snoop's counsel, David Kenner, publicized the fact that the Los Angeles Police Department had accidentally destroyed thirteen pieces of evidence in the case, including the victim's bloody clothes and shell casings from the crime scene.

The prosecution argued that the loss of evidence was due to a computer error; the material wasn't important; they had at least a dozen eyewitnesses to the crime. Cochran said this would be a problem. Kenner vowed to prove detectives also tried to influence key witnesses to support their theory that Woldemariam was killed in a drive-by shooting. "There was a tremendous amount of questionable police conduct in this case," Kenner said. "This shooting was done in self-defense. The [evidence loss] simply impacts on our ability to corroborate a lot of that defense."

Legal experts questioned if jurors wouldn't be swayed by a defense similar to the one Cochran had used in the O.J. Simpson case: that the LAPD was an abusive, bumbling institution. To protect against this, potential jurors were asked to fill out extensive questionnaires designed to elicit opinions on the Simpson case.

On November 6, 1995, in a courtroom adjacent to the one where Cochran had successfully defended Orenthal James Simpson, Cochran had murder charges against his twenty-six-year-old client, Sean Abrams, dropped. As the trial continued, details of Woldemariam's past emerged. He was the youngest of seven children; he came to America in 1979, at the age of six; his family relocated to this country to escape a civil war raging in Eritrea (formerly part of Ethiopia). His family was waiting until the trial ended, they said. They would be shipping his corpse to Eritrea, burying it in farmland next to the grandfather he was named after.

Defense attorneys said Woldemariam was a hotheaded gang member who had been arrested in 1992 for "negligently firing a gun."

As the trial continued, both sides agreed that Woldemariam argued with Sean Abrams on August 25, 1993, outside the Palms-district apartment building where Snoop lived. Prosecutors said they argued over a gang sign Abrams flashed as Woldemariam was driving past. Snoop's militant bodyguard Lee rushed downstairs to break it up; Woldemariam and two companions drove away. Within an hour Snoop entered the driver's seat of his Jeep; his combative bodyguard Lee was in the passenger seat; his childhood friend Sean Abrams sat in the rear. They caught up with Woldemariam and his two associates, Duchaum Lee Joseph and Jason London, eating Mexican takeout food in nearby Woodbine Park.

At this point, Snoop's lawyers claimed, Woldemariam reached for the .380 handgun he had pointed at Snoop on two prior occasions. Bodyguard McKinley Lee had to draw a gun and shoot Woldemariam in self-defense.

Deputy District Attorney Ed Nison shook his head: McKinley Lee drew first. The coroner found that Woldemariam had been shot in the back. "This was a classic gang-mentality type of case," said Nison. "You have the guys pursuing the victim to show [their] superiority." The trio chased Woldemariam, Nison stressed. How can that be self-defense?

Simple, said Woldemariam's friend Duchaum Joseph: When Snoop and his friends arrived in the park, Joseph claimed that his friend Woldemariam *did* reach for a gun. That was why Snoop's bodyguard Lee had to fire the fatal shot. As Woldemariam lay dying, Joseph revealed, he and London removed the gun from his hand. This way, Snoop would definitely be convicted for murder. The police, in fact, had confiscated the gun shortly after the shooting, from another of Woldemariam's friends during a routine traffic stop.

During closing arguments, weary prosecutors reminded jurors that they were to ignore Snoop's celebrity status when deciding his guilt or innocence. "He has to abide by the same rules and conduct that the rest of us do," said coprosecutor Ed Nison. The killing, he added, was a cold-blooded murder: No matter what anyone said, Philip Woldemariam had been shot in the back and buttocks while trying to escape a confrontation. Under these circumstances, it could not have been self-defense.

Defense lawyer David Kenner disagreed: Woldemariam, a hotheaded gang member angered by Snoop's presence in his neighborhood, was reaching for a gun in his waistband when Lee shot him from the Jeep.

Nison said, "It's clear when Phil was shot he was not facing the Jeep. If he had a gun, there would have been a gun battle."

Kenner said, "This was his turf, his neighborhood. He had to assert his dominance over anybody who dared live in his neighborhood." By flashing the gang sign, "the entire events of the day were set into motion."

Ultimately, Nison admitted that Woldemariam did have a gun on him that afternoon. "But the law doesn't say you have to be an angel to be protected," he added quickly. "Why would Philip reach for a gun knowing that the other person had a gun ready? That would be suicide."

This argument lasted for nine days. Then the jury was sent into deliberation. Six days later, Judge Paul Flynn asked for the verdict. The first not-guilty verdict for Snoop was read; Death Row supporters applauded and cried, "Thank you, Jesus!" The five-woman seven-man jury acquitted Snoop and Lee of first- and second-degree murder and on one charge each of conspiracy to commit assault. The shooter, McKinley Lee, reclined in his seat and sighed heavily; Snoop clutched his hands and bowed his head. Then they held hands and Lee turned to his attorney, Donald Re, and said, "Thank you very much."

Flanked by bodyguards outside, six-foot-four-inch Snoop held his two-year-old son, Cordé, in his arms and stopped for news cameras. At the curb, a gleaming chauffeur-driven Rolls-Royce waited for him. "They made the right decision," Snoop continued, trying to suppress a smile, "you know what I'm saying? This has been an ordeal that has affected our lives for the past two and a half years. I was just trying to figure out if I was going to be here to raise my son."

That night, at the label's haunt, Monty's Steakhouse, Suge Knight hosted a party and invited the jurors. Monty's Steakhouse was a white UCLA hangout located on the twenty-first floor of a Westwood apartment building. Usually, a television set aired a football game. Suge would enter with his artists and eight-man entourage, then head for his usual large table. Snoop would order a gin and juice. Suge would stuff his face with lobster tails, crab legs, chicken tenders, and salad. The owner would stop at his table to greet him. Suge loved the attention, and the fact that the seventeen or so people cluttered at the table saw the owner showing respect. To him, this wasn't some affordably priced steak joint that catered to casually dressed beer-chugging frat boys; this was *The Godfather*. Once the owner shuffled off, Suge would foist his latest schemes on his artists: This was where he would tell Tupac and Snoop to consider appearing in a movie as two street-smart ex-con rappers. They could base it on their lives, he would say, but emphasize the more commercial elements. Then Suge would quickly tear through his crab legs and broiled lobster tails.

At the party following Snoop's acquittal, Suge noticed that four of the jurors had shown up: They sipped champagne, gorged themselves on steak and lobster, and mingled with the label's acts and associates. Tupac Shakur celebrated the fact that *All Eyez on Me* had debuted at No. 1. Suge told his lackeys he was renaming the company: From then on, it would be known as the New and Untouchable Death Row. Tha Dogg

Pound, Hammer, and Danny Boy signed autographs for the jurors. One juror began reciting his own "rap" about the three-month-long trial. "We didn't do a rap star any favors," juror Rickey Sewell claimed. "We did what the instructors of the court told us to do. If they were guilty, I would have voted for guilty, but I always believed that they acted in self-defense."

But for Snoop, the party was over: He was a free man, but now had to deal with a reputation sullied by months of damaging media coverage. "It fucked me up 'cause a lot of people were scared to meet and do things with me," Snoop admitted. "I think that's prob'ly why I never been in movies. I think a lot of movie [studio executives] were scared of the reputation, the image. They really didn't wanna be bothered. They were thinking, 'Well, we want Snoop in the movie, but fuck that! We don't wanna deal with him or *his people*.' I guess that's what scared a lot of people away. But someday," he hoped, "we'll get movies and *everything we got coming to us*."

When Dr. Dre was released from a Pasadena jail after serving six months, he saw the world with different eyes. "You see," he began, "I got wrapped up in the Dr. Dre image and all that old Hollywood bullshit. You know what I'm saying: the clothes, the jewelry, the fly cars with the big sound systems pulling up in front of the clubs. But incarceration brought me down to earth and actually turned Dr. Dre back into Andre Young."

When he returned to Death Row, he found that artists were against him. "There started to be tension in the camp among the other writers and producers," Suge said. "The folks who really did the production and wrote stuff on *The Chronic* and Snoop's first album started complaining about credit." Daz, Suge now claimed, had produced over half of Snoop's album. In the past, Suge considered Dre a partner: He didn't mind publicly crediting Dre for Daz's ideas. "But niggas was mad. Things wasn't right by them. I can't have that."

In addition, Suge came to feel that Dre was badmouthing the label, telling Interscope executives he didn't need Snoop or any other Death Row artist on his music. Dre was a capable producer, Suge conceded.

"But Dre didn't become Dre on his own. I went out and got the *Above the Rim* soundtrack for the company; we needed something. Dre didn't do nothing on it. He did one song on *Murder Was the Case*."

While Suge objected to the fact that Dre didn't produce albums quickly, Dre, meanwhile, objected to some of Suge's opprobrious signings—first Tupac Shakur, then Stanley Kirk Burrell, alias MC Hammer.

In 1991, *Forbes* magazine estimated Hammer's worth at $33 million that year alone; he had sold 14 million albums, formed his own label (Bust It Records), constructed a mansion, and signed lucrative promotional deals with Pepsi, Taco Bell, and Kentucky Fried Chicken. Due to his lifestyle—touring with sixty performers, carrying one hundred people in his entourage, and owning seventeen exotic cars—Hammer was soon crippled by debilitating financial woes: He faced more than twenty lawsuits filed against him by friends and associates; approximately 250 creditors were claiming $13.8 million, although Hammer's assets amounted to only $9.7 million (mostly represented by a mansion in Fremont, California, which he kept trying to sell for $7 million).

When he signed to Death Row, thirty-two-year-old Hammer hoped his career would receive a much-needed boost. Suge hoped Hammer would recapture the hearts of the immense white audience that loved his single "You Can't Touch This."

Dr. Dre was disgusted by Hammer's presence on what was supposed to be a gangsta rap label. By 1996, Hammer had already achieved his flash-in-the-pan pop-rap success, then squandered it. He represented everything Dre spent a career insulting: compromising pop artists with huge egos, fancy outfits, little talent, and no spine. "It got to the point in the studio," Dre said, "where brothers were sticking their hand out like, 'Yo, what's up, we just signed to the label.' And I was like, 'I don't even know you.'"

As the relationship with Death Row soured, Dre saw Suge use subtle manipulation to sway artists to his side. Most artists were upset when they heard Suge's version of why Dre did not appear at the courtroom during Snoop's trial.

Dre said, "I don't like the fuckin' courtroom. That's my reason for not going. I don't like going up there and I never did. And I never will. I talked to the lawyers all the time and I knew he was going to get off. And if Snoop wanted to chill, he came by the 'house' and we kicked it."

But Suge told Death Row artists a different story: According to Suge, the prosecution had, at one point, claimed that Dre was present in the Jeep on the afternoon Philip Woldemariam was killed. The jury, Suge claimed, seemed to believe that. Death Row Records needed Dre to appear in court and deny that; once the prosecution's claim was disproven, "That would have saved Snoop's whole case," said Tupac Shakur. "Dre never showed up. He was too busy. When they told me that, I was like, no matter how dope he is, and Dre is one of my heroes in the music business, if he's not down for his homeboy Snoop—who brought him back when he was a relic—then I don't wanna be around him."

Despite this, Tupac's vocals appeared on Dre's music. While he was in prison, Dre discovered, Suge had erased Ice Cube's vocals from a song he planned to call "You Can't See Me." Suge left funk musician George Clinton's singing intact, but allowed Tupac Shakur to record another of his immature gangsta raps. The title had also changed, to "You Can't C Me," another insult directed at various Los Angeles Crip gangs.

But Dre decided to ignore this and focus on producing a comeback single. It had been two years since his last true hit—and that song, the Grammy-Award–winning "Gin & Juice," had been a duet with Snoop. "I decided to start on my album and 'California Love' was the first song," Dre told me.

Bored with violent gangsta rap, Dre entered a recording studio. Over a piano melody originally used by the Bronx group UltraMagnetic nearly a decade earlier, he recited harmless party-themed lyrics. Then Suge ordered Dre to include Tupac on his positive number. Even though Dre disliked Tupac. "It was just me on the song originally," Dre said. "I wanted the song to come out right then, but I didn't have a record out."

During a conversation, Suge said, "Yo, let's put this on Tupac's album since it's about to come out now."

"So what I did," Dre went on, "was take out my second verse and put in Tupac's verse and let him do some ad-libs at the end."

Dre sat behind the mixing board, watching Tupac in the recording booth. After the song's melodic bridge section, Tupac ruined the song by cursing. It was disturbing. But not as disturbing as the fact that Suge wanted Dre to stand near Tupac in a music video for the song.

Then Dre heard about Tupac's conduct one evening. "They had some type of Death Row party and he was all like, 'Fuck Dre.' Fuck that. I ain't do nothing but help Tupac."

In addition to being enraged by Dre's refusal to participate in the label's attacks against Bad Boy and East Coast rappers, Tupac also believed Suge's claim that Dre had robbed novices like Daz of their rightful production credit. "And I got tired of that," Tupac said. "He was owning the company too and he chillin' in his house; I'm out here in the streets, whoopin' niggas' asses, startin' wars and shit, droppin' albums, doin' my shit, and this nigga takin' three years to do one song! I couldn't have that." Ultimately, Suge would want Dre off Death Row, so as to totally control what had become a $300-million empire. But for now he wanted Dre to produce an album for MC Hammer: This was the final straw. Dre viewed Hammer as a contemptible jive-ass who once danced for "popcorn chicken" in a Kentucky Fried Chicken television advertisement; a has-been who wore sequined outfits onstage and spent millions of dollars on videos designed to dethrone Michael Jackson and make Hammer white America's new "king of pop."

"The nigga just kinda hid," Suge reported, "stopped callin'."

"HE CAME OUT ALL BLOODIED UP, AND TUPAC WAS A PART OF THAT"

Unknown to Suge Knight, Dr. Dre had already decided to leave Death Row Records, the company where he created *The Chronic* (which brought in an estimated $50 million in retail sales) and *DoggyStyle* ($63 million). He called Jimmy Iovine at Interscope and said, "I'm ready to bounce. Make me a deal, and I'll make you some hit records."

"That was that," Dre recalled. "Very simple. I ain't got nothing to say to nobody. I'm just out. Period. I don't like it no more. The mentality there is you have to be mad at somebody in order for yourself to feel good or make a record. They have to be mad or say something negative about a certain person, instead of just laying back, *getting off everybody's dick*, making some strong music, and going on with your life."

On March 22, when Dre announced his departure, artists' lives were immediately affected. "I didn't know he was leaving until he was gone," said Robin "Lady of Rage" Allen. "I was hurt. Because I felt Death Row was such a strong unit. We had one of the best producers, five of the best MCs, one of the best, uh, executive producers—as far as Suge gettin' shit done the way it should be done," she rationalized, "and the whole little aura around Death Row. I hated to see that happen, but there wasn't anything I could do. I mean, I could've cried and begged, 'Please don't go,' but if that's what Dre felt he had to do? That's what he had to do. I wish it wasn't like that, but that's how it happened."

"When Dre left, that was a heated situation," said Sam "Sneed" Anderson. "They might have known that he was trying to take me with him. It got to where my loyalty was questioned. They called me at home and said, 'Sam, come in. We're having an artist meeting.' I thought it was gonna be about whatever album was next and what needed to be done to put it out. But it wasn't. It was about Dre leaving and whoever was leaving with him would have problems. Suge called the meeting."

When Sam arrived at the label's Westwood offices, he was shocked to find artists watching his latest video in a conference room. "Since I had a couple of East Coast people in my video, that was a problem. By then, a lot of that East Coast/West Coast craziness was going on." That East Coast rappers appeared in his video did not mean that Sam was breaking ranks with his West Coast brethren. "It's just that, for my first video, *Recognize*, I asked all the artists to appear in my video but no one showed up. For the second video, Dre said he told all the artists about it but nobody came." Sam decided to ask rappers he met during his stint in New York, as K-Solo's producer, to appear in the video. In addition to having popular rap celebrities publicly endorsing his music, the presence of East Coast rappers would also silence claims that Death Row Records was at war with the East Coast rap industry. At the meeting, artists noted that Sam, actually, seemed to be promoting East Coast rap over Death Row's artists. "They were upset," he recalled.

Who was upset?

"I guess some of the artists and Suge."

Tupac Shakur?

"I ain't trying to go there," he groaned. "All the artists were upset. Just put 'the artists.' Everybody on Death Row. They felt I wasn't trying to be down with them, so things got crazy. They called me out. Like, 'Sam Sneed . . .' I was the first topic at the meeting. Then Suge started saying some harsh things, questioning me about why ain't I got no artists in the video and, uh, why ain't I screaming Death Row on my songs?"

Eager to prove his loyalty to the label, Tupac took the lead in haranguing Sam. He repeated Suge's query: Why didn't Sam Sneed mention Death Row on his songs?

Sam did mention the label on songs he was preparing for his solo album, but no one at Death Row expressed any interest in hearing the project. Despite this, the accusations continued. "It was petty. Just trying to find things to pick at. Then they questioned me about trying to charge Snoop a certain amount of dollars for a track—even though we never really had anything confirmed! We were gonna handle that when we both sat down with Suge."

In the studio one day, Snoop heard Sam's latest production, a mellow drum track with flourishing keyboards and lush African percussion. "Snoop was starting his own label, and he came to me and asked, 'How much for a track.' Dre had given me a nice advance for songs I did for him, so I came lower than that when I told Snoop the price. I thought it was fair. Obviously they didn't. I just gave Snoop a price off the top of my head. It didn't matter. Nigga coulda had the track for free! But at the meeting they went and made that an issue too. Like I was trying to be slick."

As the meeting began to feel more like an arraignment, "I was kinda worried, man. 'Cause I didn't know what they were gonna do to me. All the artists on Death Row were there and they made me like a sacrificial lamb. They were like, *humiliating* me. I mean, niggaz were hitting me and shit like that. Suge was saying 'verbal abuse.' "

What happened next?

"Man, it's getting real deep. I don't really wanna go into that. A few people put their hands on me and I lost respect for all of them."

Rumors swept through the industry that Sam had also been raped, but this was never corroborated.

During the course of the attack, Suge also tried to extract from Sam information he thought could turn the macho hip-hop audience away from Dre. "They tried to make Sam reveal the name of the guy Dre was fucking," a reporter at the *L.A. Times* revealed. " 'Cause Sam supposedly knew this homosexual man's name. There were a lot of reasons he was attacked, but that was one of them."

Sam would admit only to being beaten.

No one tried to break it up. Artists pummeled Sneed, punching, hitting, stomping. In vain, he tried to block his face and body. The artists surged forward; the rain of fists and footwear continued. Finally, Sam thought they would murder him. No one knew he was there. Then Suge spoke up and the beating ended. "Suge just stopped it. Told them to stop it." Sam struggled to rise to his feet, his face hurt, his body too. People he considered friends had just worked him over pretty badly. "I felt straight betrayed, played out," he said. "One artist on that label who knew Suge would never gonna put his record out was trying to sneak his little kicks in. They straight ridiculed me."

"[Sam] came out all bloodied up," said an unnamed source in *The New Yorker*. "And Tupac was a part of that. He had to show Suge what he was made of."

Sam staggered out of the office. "I was confused. Totally caught off guard. I didn't know what to do. I thought about going to Dre's house, but then Suge asked me to come to Snoop's party. He wanted to talk to me about [the beating] and I was just lost, man. Niggaz knew where I lived at. I was just kinda—I'm out my element! So Suge came to me later, saying he got love for me, love me and, um, he was saying that Dre was doing slick stuff, taking people's credit, you know. He just said, 'You don't need to be with Dre. He be taking people's credit.' That was basically it. He was like, 'Man, you know I got love for you. I ain't want that to happen, but it happened!' I just wanted to get out of there, man."

But he had to keep up appearances. He didn't want Death Row thinking he would press charges or anything. "I'm out there by myself," said Sam. "I didn't know who was watching me, you know?! I didn't know what to think. I really tried to make it seem like I wasn't trippin,' like it was cool, you know?

"After the party, I came home. First person I called was my cousin Vaughn. I told him about it and he was hurt. I was heated, man. I told my father about it and he went crazy. He's like a jailhouse lawyer and he's trying to sue and push the issue." In his prison cell back east, Anderson Sr. wrote a lengthy affidavit that detailed the beating his son received. "It went on about how Sam was sitting there and they were kicking him, and punching him in the head and giving him body blows," said one *Source* editor who read this astounding document.

After calling his father, Sam next called a travel agent and booked a flight. "A week later, I was out. When I got to where I was going, I called Suge the next day and told him I didn't appreciate what happened. Then Suge was trying to find out where I was 'cause he wanted to talk to me on another phone. I really didn't say much. I was like, 'I'm just letting you know I don't appreciate what you let go down. It was foul. Niggas *humiliate* me, you kno'msaying? And it wasn't cool.'"

After attacking Sam Sneed, Death Row Records would include Sam's music on Snoop's second album, *The DoggFather*. "'Cause we had mixed it already," said Sam. In addition, the label would continue to promise to release his solo album—despite the fact that Sam called the label months after the beating and asked to be released from his contract. During that conversation, Suge asked, "Do you still wanna put your album out?"

Sam replied, "Man, I just wanna be free."

"Well, we can arrange that," Suge said.

"And Kenner was on the phone," Sam recalled. "Those were Suge's words. 'We can arrange that.' But it never happened."

"THE OFF-DUTY COP WHO WORK FOR DRE COME OUT HOLDIN' HIS GUN AND SHIT, SCARED AND NERVOUS"

Though Dre felt Death Row was behind him, a vengeful Suge Knight appeared at his home. It happened in June, after Dre told *The Source* that he had left Death Row. By then Dre had reconciled with RBX, who stopped by his home in March, apologized, and asked to be part of Dre's new label. "From what we discussed," said RBX, "Dre was getting sick of homeboy." The relationship between Suge and Dre, Dre now revealed, had begun to deteriorate right after *The Chronic.* "Death Row's whole business was gangsta rap," RBX added. "That was a conflict right there. Dre told me, 'I'm sick and tired of drive-bys and all that shit.' Then Tupac coming to Death Row was the straw that broke the camel's back."

Dre felt it was a chain of events. "I wasn't feeling comfortable with the people I was around. Everybody wasn't professional. How can I put it? I like things to be right and positive because I'm a positive person. And the situation I was in, wasn't. Plain and simple. It was too much negativity."

After earning millions of dollars from gangsta rap, Dr. Dre no longer wanted anything to do with the genre. In fact, prior to recording Death Row's first release, *The Chronic*, he felt the same way. While he publicly played the part of unrepentant gangster, inside Dre was suffering. "I really got some deep shit to tell you," he said. "I did this song 'Fuck Tha Police' . . . I mean—I think *Straight Outta Compton* was a classic hip-hop album. But I do look back on a lot of things we were saying and doing then and think, *damn*.

"But the shit was dope at the time.

"But then—I never told nobody this in an interview. My brother got killed while I was on tour with N.W.A. He got into a fight, neck got broke, and all kinda shit." The last words his brother heard, Dre later discovered, were "Fuck Tha Police" from a nearby radio. "So it kind of fucked with me. My brother was my best friend. He was three years younger than me." He learned of the death while on the road; someone called with the bad news. "You never . . . forget that. I grew up with my brother. I mean, like I said, I'm not ashamed of anything I did with N.W.A but you know— The shit is crazy." Leaving Death Row meant finally being allowed to leave gangsta rap behind.

But it was only one of the changes Dre made: Instead of spending nights in local clubs, he stayed home. He no longer pined for singer Michel'lé, who was now rumored to be seeing Suge Knight. "As far as she goes, I have a different kind of love for her," Dre said. "She's like my sister. We don't get along. She's doing her thing and I'm doing mine. We only gotta communicate about our son."

Dre made plans to marry his newest girlfriend, Nicole, and move into a hilltop home far from old friends and associates. In the studio, he assembled a crew of producers, signed new acts, and searched for a name for his new label. At first he chose Black Market Records. But other people owned the name. He negotiated with them to purchase the rights to it, but they kept raising their price until it had risen to over $100,000.

As he worked on producing music for his label's inaugural release, he became aware that people suspected he had been attacked by his former labelmates. One source remembered Dre missing a photo shoot for *People* magazine. This person saw Dre sitting in a car outside a supermarket;

one of his friends was inside shopping for him. Dre's face was battered, bruised, and puffy. Another person said Dre had been shot in the left arm. Still another claimed he had been raped. "Just like Sam Sneed."

"It's a million fucking rumors floating around," Dre said in his *Source* interview (in the July 1996 issue). "I've gotten shot. I've gotten beat up and all this ol' shit. Ain't nothing happened to me and ain't nothing gonna happen to me."

But Dre wasn't quite certain this was true. After announcing his departure in *The Source*, Suge kept calling: Dre could leave, Suge said. But Death Row still needed those master tapes. "We was gettin' ready to put together the Death Row greatest hits album," Suge explained. "I sent somebody to Dre's house to get the masters. He called me and said, 'They don't wanna let me in.' I said, 'All right. *I'm* comin' over.' I come through the gate, knock on the door, and see motherfuckers runnin' and hidin'. What's this shit about? The off-duty cop who work for Dre come out holdin' his gun and shit, scared and nervous.

"They called the police," Suge went on, " 'bout twenty squad cars out there. But it wasn't no thang. I played a couple of games of pool, got my shit, and left. Then I read the [*Source*] interview. He's in it talkin' like he want drama. He tried to say somethin' about my little brother Tupac. That's my nigga, my little brother." (Dre told *The Source*, "And what's [Tupac] talking about, Dre jumped ship? Dre built the ship he's on right now. All that is bullshit.")

As Suge publicly told everyone this version of their meeting, Dre said Suge was lying. Someone rang his bell and claimed to be Jimmy Iovine of Interscope, Dre began. "I didn't answer the phone. Somebody else did and said, 'Jimmy Iovine? Let him in.' In comes Suge with eight or nine niggas, youkno'msayin'? Some of them I got love for. Some I don't. I opened the door. I got my four-year-old stepson, Tyler, with me and say, 'Yo w'sup fellas? Come on in.'

"Suge said, 'We trying to get the tapes,' and I go, Okay. All the tapes are being copied right now. 'Cause I want a copy of all the work that I did. He said, 'Okay. Can I talk to you for a minute?' I said, Let's go in here in my family room. Me and Suge sat down. Suge was smoking a big-ass cigar.

"He asked me for an ashtray. I said, No. You can use this motherfucking coaster. He started talking about, 'Yo, man, there's no reason for us to be beefin', we need to be making millions, getting together, this-and-that.' I'm like, Okay, that sounds good to me. I didn't say this, but I'm thinking, Long as you on some positive shit, it's all good.

"All of a sudden, out the wild blue, he starts going, 'Well, um, you should put the Death Row logo on your upcoming record.' I'm like, 'Huh? That can't happen. No way, no how. This is an insult to me and to all the people in the organization I'm building.' So I'm like, Okay. You can tell him what he wants to hear right now. I don't want no bullshit, especially in the house.

"I'm violated, disrespected. Suge can come to my house at any time by himself and he's more than welcome. There's no need to bring eight or nine motherfuckers with him. If he wants some shit I got that's his? I'll give it to him. But when he came over with all his guys, automatically I thought he's coming to bring the noise. But I ain't tripping 'cause I ain't that kinda nigga."

Days later, Dre said, they met at Gladstone's restaurant in Malibu and peacefully worked out their differences. The meeting ended with a handshake. A week later, Suge Knight posed near a Rolls-Royce for a cover of *The Source*. Inside, Suge claimed that Dre called the police on him when he dropped by to pick up the master tapes for the Death Row greatest hits album. Dre stared at the photo of Suge posing with a nervous MC Hammer, an expressionless Tupac flashing hand signs, and a dour Snoop. This would be the official story. "I ain't no playa-hater but don't be no bitch about it," Suge added. "Be a man, motherfucker! Dre know he like to go places and do thangs but now he up in the house. 'You put yourself under house arrest. What kinda shit is that?' I told him he shoulda just been a man about it instead of hiding out at home."

Turning away from the feature, Dre told himself, "Okay. That's that mentality stepping in where you got something to prove to the people around you. It's all good. I understand. I ain't that type a person. The only thing I want to do is make records, live a comfortable life, and chill with my family."

Unfortunately, the label would do their best to foil those plans. During an interview with Bay Area station KMEL's *Westside Radio* show, Tupac said, "I feel as though what's done in the dark will come to light.

It's secrets that everybody's gonna find out about that I don't have to player hate or snitch about."

In Las Vegas, Tupac met with a high-ranking *Vibe* magazine executive: He told the executive that Dre was a closet homosexual, a claim he had been repeating for months and included on two songs, his single "Toss It Up" ("Check your sexuality, it's fruity as this Alizé") and "To Live and Die in L.A." ("California Love part motherfucking two without gay ass Dre").

Dre had suspected they would resort to this. When a magazine writer arrived at his home shortly after his departure from Death Row, Dre kept him waiting, then bounded down the stairs with a bag of tapes. "Two fat carat-sized diamond earrings are in each ear," writer Frank Williams noted. " 'I was having sex with my girl,' Dre said with a laugh. 'It takes her a long-ass time to come so I was trying to time it just right.' "

During an interview in August 1996, on the eve of the release of his first new single since leaving the label, Dre alluded to the smear campaign. "Most likely, there are gonna be records coming out dissing me, dissing people I've worked with and am going to be working with," he said between sips of a Long Island iced tea. "It's just a lot of negative bullshit. So from here on out, Death Row Records don't even exist to Dre. I have nothing bad to say about anybody that's with Death Row. It's just not my vibe."

Inevitably, the rumor that Dre was a homosexual divided the L.A. rap music industry. "That was a lie," producer Chocolate said immediately. "It's like this, man: When what's-her-name, Gina from [the situation comedy] *Martin* was out there in the beginning, people said, 'Oh, she got AIDS.' That was bullshit too. It's all bullshit."

"I'm like this," said another person who knew Dre for years. "Don't playa hate a nigga just because he left. Even if a nigga was a fag, so what? That's his motherfucking preference! Whatever a nigga does is what he does. I believe it was, uh, fabricated anyway."

"They were trying to set Dre up," said a writer at *Vibe*. "They said they were going to try to 'expose' him as being homosexual. But it seems to me it's the other way around."

The rumor, Cheo Coker explained, was untrue. "In rap culture, that's the ultimate insult. I wasn't surprised to hear 'Pac and Suge popping that street and jailhouse shit 'cause it's par for the course. I don't think Dre is gay."

"Now, that's gotta be the funniest shit I've ever heard in my life," said Dre when asked about the rumor. "I can't even respond to that dumb shit. All I gotta say to that is, 'I love my wife and that's the only person I love. That's it. That's the only person I go to bed with every night."

"HE WON'T BOTHER YOU. HE'S ONLY TRAINED TO KILL ON COMMAND"

After accepting an award at the 1996 Soul Train Awards, held in Los Angeles on March 29, Biggie Smalls thanked Brooklyn. When the crowd jeered, Biggie accepted that Tupac's accusations would continue to have repercussions. Earlier, while watching Tupac arrive for the ceremony in a fancy car, Biggie felt that Tupac had become obsessed with promoting the image of a trigger-happy L.A. gang member. Where five years ago Tupac had been a political rapper, he was now indistinguishable from the other gangsta rappers signed to Death Row. "Duke came out the window fatigued out," Biggie recalled, "screaming 'Westside! Outlaws!'"

Suge's anger toward Bad Boy Records had intensified. During an interview with a *Vibe* reporter in his office at Can-Am Studios, Suge objected to the reporter's questions about his friend Jake "the Violator" Robles. Next to the reporter, Suge's German shepherd sat motionless. "That's Damu," one security guard had said. "He won't bother you. He's only trained to kill on command." The reporter asked if Suge actually believed Sean "Puffy" Combs had anything to do with Jake Robles's murder. After the interview, Suge said he had some things he wanted to discuss. The reporter was nervous. "For the first time that evening," he wrote, "Damu the dog raises up off the red carpet and turns in my direction."

Suge towered over the writer. "I didn't like them questions you was asking me about the dead."

The writer asked, "You mean the questions about Eazy-E?"

"Nah, that was my *homeboy* that was killed down there in Atlanta. I felt you was being disrespectful, and I don't forget things like that."

Suge lectured the terrified writer.

He continued his attack on Puffy and Biggie with the release of Tupac's *All Eyez on Me*, which by Thursday, February 23, had sold 566,000 copies during its first week and earned $10 million—second only to *The Beatles Anthology* in 1995. Throughout the entire two-album set, Tupac released musical attacks against his old friend Biggie, whom he still accused of being involved in his shooting. In interviews, Tupac repeated claims that he had bedded Biggie's wife, Faith Evans. As Faith denied the stories, Biggie tried hard to believe her. "If honey was to give you the pussy," he said in print, "why would you disrespect her like that? If you had beef with me, and you're like, 'Boom, I'm'a fuck his wife,' would you be so harsh on her? Like you got beef with her? That shit doesn't make sense. That's why I don't believe it."

As the attacks grew nastier, one Bad Boy insider said Puffy tried to end the feud behind the scenes. "From what I understand, [music executive] Gene Griffin and Puffy's father were supposedly friends back in the day. During this beef with Suge, Puffy brought Gene Griffin in to try to squash it. When Gene went to Suge about it, Suge supposedly said, 'Okay. Fuck it. Fuck him, whatever, it's over with.' But then Puffy never called Gene to tell him thank-you. He sent one of his boys or whatever to say it for him, had one of his boys call. So then Gene felt dissed! I mean, come on now! If you had somebody who basically saved your life, you should at least thank the motherfucker yourself."

Suge used every interview and video as an opportunity to further denigrate his opponents. Snoop Doggy Dogg, an avowed fan of East Coast rappers like Slick Rick, saw where this was heading. "So I talked to

Suge," he explained. "I said, 'Let's clean up this bad image we got, Suge. Let's make it easy on ourselves. Let's do the right thing. You know what I'm saying? Let's get out there and keep ourselves doing the right thing. 'Cause we're all righteous brothers. We all wanna do the right thing. We don't like being put in that situation where we have to overreact and do the "macho-man" type thing. Everybody knows a nigga can get crazy and do what he has to, but who wants to be living that life where we gotta be looking over our shoulders? We're makin' money. We're supposed to be up here enjoying the shit and giving back to the community; going places, traveling freely, and not worrying about shit.' "

The audience at the 1996 Soul Train Awards, infiltrated by Death Row supporters, continued to jeer. By then Death Row's feud with Bad Boy had grown to include Biggie's wife, Faith Evans, Junior M.A.F.I.A. (signed to Big Beat/Atlantic), and RCA/Loud's Mobb Deep, who recorded "L.A., L.A.," a scathing response to Tha Dogg Pound's insulting "New York, New York."

Sadly, Biggie and his crew left the stage and came face-to-face with Tupac Shakur for the first time since his shooting at the Quad Recording Studio in midtown Manhattan. "That was the first time I really looked into his face," Biggie said.

Tupac's eyes brimmed with madness, rage, and confusion.

Biggie thought, "Yo this nigga is really buggin' the fuck out."

Surrounded by goons, Suge and Tupac kept repeating, "We gonna settle this right now!" Biggie's hired security stepped forward. So did Junior M.A.F.I.A. rapper Little Caesar, who was intoxicated and yelled, "*Fuck you! Fuck you, nigga! East Coast, motherfucker!*"

"We on the West Side now!" Tupac shouted. "We gonna handle this shit!" It was like a western movie. Onlookers backed away, to give them room to draw. Both camps circled each other like prey. "Somebody pulled a gun," Biggie admitted, but it wasn't Tupac, as one local paper claimed.

At the sight of the gun, "motherfuckers start screaming, 'He got a gun, he got a gun!' " Biggie thought, "We're in L.A. What the fuck are we supposed to do, shoot out?" This run-in changed him. "That's when I knew it was on."

He couldn't knock Death Row for how they handled their business.

That's what they were, thugs and goons. But the change in Tupac shocked him. His old friend seemed to be reliving his role in the movie *Juice*. "Whatever he's doing right now," Biggie felt, "that's the role he's playing. He played that shit to a T."

By Friday, April 19, 1996, Death Row decided to establish an East Coast subsidiary. On Oakland's KMEL's *Westside Radio* rap program, Tupac Shakur announced that Death Row hoped to sign acts like Big Daddy Kane, the Wu-Tang Clan, old school rapper Melle Mel, and Eric B, who would also help run the label.

Death Row took special pride in announcing that Craig Mack had signed with them and would be working with an Oakland production unit called America's Most Wanted. Like Sam Sneed, Craig—a broad-shouldered rapper with a face scarred by eczema, a toothy grin, arrogant lyrics, and a short, dated Afro haircut—worked with the Long Island rap duo EPMD before that duo split. "I used to carry bags," said Craig. "I used to rhyme in the hotels, battling other kids that wanted to see [EPMD members] Erick and Parrish." When EPMD split up, Craig ran into Sean "Puffy" Combs.

"One night in 1993, we saw Puff inside of a club in Manhattan. We went outside in the back of the alley—up against an old garbage can—and he asked me to bust a freestyle for him. I did, and he thought it was the illest he ever heard. He was like, 'Yo, come down to the office the next morning.' We went down, talked, and he wanted to sign me. But he was getting ready to leave Uptown, so he said, 'Yo, you can get a deal with Uptown or come with me. I'm about to start a new label. I'm talking to distributors now. There are no guarantees, but if we do it, it's gonna be the dopest thing ever.' "

Craig signed to Bad Boy. "Yo, without a doubt!" he told Puffy. "You the one that picked me up and said I was dope so I'm rolling with you!"

"Craig had the song 'Flava in Your Ear,' but it didn't do as well as Big," said Cheo Coker of the *L.A. Times*. "But if Puff didn't have Biggie, then Craig would've been a good artist to have. The problem was, like most artists, Craig wasn't getting paid. And his dealings weren't really correct. When I was writing about him and trying to investigate certain things, one of the things that came up in talking to someone at Universal Records was that things got so bad for Craig, he was pumping gas in

Long Island. That's how broke he had become at one point. This was after his record came out. He was broke." Craig left Bad Boy and was soon rumored to be signing to Death Row, where he would be near Sam Sneed and rapper K-Solo, friends during the old days of touring with EPMD. "It kinda makes sense that Craig would go to the one person willing to take anything Puffy didn't want and try to blow up with it," Coker added.

"Hmm. How did I meet him?" Craig asked rhetorically. "Where was I at when I met Suge? Damn! Where was I at? I'm trying to think if I was in a club, at his house, or at a party. At a studio! We just said 'What's up' to each other but everyone else took that meeting and went crazy with it."

To this day, Craig denies ever signing to Death Row.

"According to sources at the label," Cheo Coker said, "he was very much with them. There are even ads that have 'Craig Mack' listed. If you look back through the old Death Row Records ads in various hip-hop magazines, the whole roster with twenty-six artists? Craig was on that roster."

Vibe magazine also reported on the signing.

"I know," said Craig. "They lying."

Death Row publicist George Pryce also mentioned it.

"No," Craig insisted. "It's a lie." He sighed heavily. "I just said I met Suge at a party in the studio. But that was it. I mean—you know what I'm saying?! I went by his house and that was it! Everybody else tried to blow it all crazy!" He didn't even want to discuss Death Row. "I don't have any opinions. I'm just chillin'. Getting ready for my new album!"

He was willing to discuss how he met Eric B, who was selected to run Death Row's East Coast subsidiary. "All right," Craig fumed. "Me and Eric B knew each other for a while too. And Eric B was about to start a company called Death Row East. With Suge. He knew I didn't have a label and was out there looking around for a deal—'cause I didn't have no money, I was broke, just chilling, running around. And Eric was like, 'Yo, if you wanna get down with what I'm doing, we could do it.' I said, 'Cool, I'm with it. Just let me know what the situation is; talk to my people, everything'll be cool.' Next thing I know, he told me he was gonna start it somewhere else. I was like, 'Cool, I'm still with it.' "

1994, police officers found a gun in the glove compartment of the vehicle Suge was driving. While this would have led to nothing more than a weapons charge, the gun had history. In Las Vegas, the feds had been investigating a cocaine-trafficking ring led by Suge's old friend, "music promoter" Ricardo Crockett. After the gun was found in Suge's car, federal prosecutors said the weapon was purchased illegally by an associate of Crockett's, then transported across state lines and resold to Suge. For having the gun, Suge faced federal charges. After the federal probe into Crockett's drug ring resulted in Crockett and more than a dozen people being incarcerated, the feds wondered if Suge wasn't somehow involved with drug trafficking. Ultimately Suge would receive federal probation for purchasing then transporting the gun across state lines. Drug charges would not be lodged against him, but he would become a target for federal scrutiny. Federal agents would focus on whether drug trafficking produced the "seed money" used to launch convicted felon Suge's Death Row Records.

His relationships with Michael Harris and Ricardo Crockett, both of whom were behind bars, were examined. While Suge readily admitted to knowing both during the period Death Row was formed, he denied that dirty money financed the startup. "If the government is saying that these people gave me the money to start Death Row, they couldn't be more wrong. Every penny we have put into Death Row over the past five years came from a major entertainment corporation."

In early 1996, C. Delores Tucker had complained about Death Row to the Justice Department, then announced that the FBI was investigating the sale of gangsta rap to minors. In response, the FBI quickly issued a statement denying Tucker's claim but did add that they *were* reviewing material to decide whether any additional steps should be taken.

Then, according to a reporter at *L.A. Weekly*, the feds began actively investigating the record label. Their investigation, this reporter revealed, officially began with an agent named Wayne McMullen, who was working on the Grape Street Task Force in Jordan Downs and kept hearing informants claim that a rap label was "into" drugs. After a little searching, McMullen decided the rumors were worth pursuing and formed the Death Row Task Force.

Depending on whom you speak with, the concept of Death Row East was either humorous or diabolical. A writer at *Vibe* felt it was hilarious. "Because, basically, it was gonna be run by hip-hop criminals. Nobody in the music industry wanted to be associated with Gene Griffin except for Suge. That says something about what Suge was trying to do: set up a company in New York that would intimidate the people here—the Russell Simmonses, the Andre Harrells, and the Puffys. And Suge was going about it by hiring Gene Griffin, one of those dangerous Harlem-hustler-type dudes who served time in prison and was known in the music industry for having ripped off [producer] Teddy Riley, who was his fucking godson!"

"Then you hear rumors," this reporter added. "This is what the feds are looking into: whether they were gonna set up a pipeline or cartel with Death Row East as the front, whether those cats in New York who wanted to get out of the drug game—and into a record label—would switch with forces in the drug game on the West Coast who had never been able to get any type of East Coast pipeline. Whether Death Row East was gonna be the front for that."

Then there were rumors, never proven, that Suge had been involved in the murder of a man named Bruce, owner of the Genius Car Wash off Crenshaw and 54th. Bruce, said a Rolling 60s Crip, was a member of a local Blood gang. He was also a big-time drug dealer who employed members of Crip and Blood gangs. Before Suge achieved his fame, he was said to have admired Bruce. "Bruce was 'the man' for the Bloods," this Rolling 60s Crip said. "Bruce had all the money. When Suge was coming up, he kinda envied him. Me and Bruce talked about this a few times."

In conversation, Bruce would insult Suge. This Rolling 60s Crip would ask, "Damn, Bruce, ain't you a Blood?" Bruce would continue with the insults. "Booby," he told this Rolling 60s Crip, "you know me and Suge went to school together. Man, fuck that nigga Suge. He's a punk and a pussy. That nigga ain't all that. That nigga's a buster.'"

While it was dangerous to bad-mouth Suge, Bruce wasn't worried. " 'Cause Bruce knew that karate shit, so he wasn't scared of nobody," this Rolling 60s Crip added. "This guy had so much fucking heart!"

Though Bruce was technically a rival Blood gang member, many of the Rolling 60s Crips liked him. When Bruce drove through their territory, instead of hostility, he was showered with acceptance. Bruce was allowed to stop his car, exit the vehicle, and associate with residents in the 60's territory. "Deep down in our hearts, we knew he was from a Blood gang, but it didn't matter. We got to know the person first. By the time we found out he was a Blood, it was too late: He was already our friend. We played basketball with him at Crenshaw. I just hate that that shit happened to him."

Like Suge Knight, Bruce also managed rap groups. One of his artists, a youth named Dramacydal, had recently become friendly with Suge's artist Tupac. Bruce allowed Suge to use Dramacydal on Tupac's *All Eyez on Me* album, as part of Tupac's backup group the Outlaw Immortalz. When Bruce asked for his share of the royalties, Suge said he wouldn't pay a dime. Then he said he was keeping Dramacydal.

"And Bruce confronted him at a club," the Rolling 60 said. Suge was partying with members of his all-male crew, when Bruce appeared at their table. "He rushed Suge and some of his boys and beat up three of them." Suge was roughed up a little, but three or four of his friends managed to repel Bruce. After the fight, Suge seethed with anger. He reflected on how Bruce had beaten him, had gotten the best of him in front of his friends. "I don't think Suge wanted it to end like that," said an executive at another label.

A couple of weeks later, Bruce was murdered. One person said that assassins burst into Bruce's home late one night. He went down fighting, teary-eyed gangsters reported. "The guys who came in there?" said one. "Bruce whipped the shit out of them."

Days later, his girlfriend was also murdered. Within a week, both bodies were discovered. "Him and his girlfriend were shot up and found dead in a car," said music industry executive Bigga B.

Following the double homicide, Tupac was said to have called Bruce's father to say he had nothing to do with his slaying. "Everybody knows about that," said promoter Doug Young. No charges have been brought against Suge or Tupac.

"IF YOU DON'T GET DOWN ON YOUR KNEES RIGHT NOW, BUDDY, YOU'RE GOING TO GET SHOT IN THE FUCKING HEAD AGAIN"

"At the MTV Awards you could see these [Death Row] guys walking in like they were King Tut," said one East Coast music executive. "Everybody else, including label heads, just waited in line. But these guys just walked right down the aisle."

It was September 4 and Tupac Shakur looked nervous. It had been four months since his single "Hit Em Up" attacked Biggie Smalls, Puffy, Bad Boy, and Mobb Deep. During a recent interview with *Vibe*, Puffy seemed to have lost patience with Suge and Tupac. "What it's been right now is a lot of moviemaking and a lot of entertainment drama," Puffy said. "Bad boys move in silence. If somebody wants to get your ass, you're gonna wake up in heaven. There ain't no record gonna be made about it. It ain't gonna be no interviews; it's gonna be straight up. 'Oh, shit, where am I? What are these wings on my back?'"

A *Vibe* reader, Tupac knew that Puffy had ended the "East vs. West" cover story feature by saying, "I'm ready for [this beef] to come to a head, however it gotta go down. I'm ready for it to be out of my life and be over with. I mean that from the bottom of my heart. I just hope it can end quick and in a positive way, because it's gotten out of hand."

Surrounded by security guards at the MTV Awards, Tupac also carried a walkie-talkie. His girlfriend, Kidada Jones, daughter of *Vibe* owner Quincy, reported that he was changing. "Instead of going to strip clubs," she explained, "he was cooking." He had finished recording an album (the last covered by the contract signed in prison) and told Kidada he wanted to move out of the Death-Row-leased home they inhabited and into one located in another part of town. Then they could work on having that kid they always discussed, and he could see if Warner Bros. would be interested in signing him. He also mailed David Kenner a letter, firing him.

Entering the awards show, he stopped for a film crew. Asked what would happen if Death Row met Bad Boy, he replied, "We are business-men. We are not animals. It's not like we're going to see them and rush them and jump on them. If they see us and they want drama, we're going to definitely bring it like only Death Row can bring it." By night's end, Bad Boy and Death Row did meet up, and had to be separated by the NYPD.

"The last time I talked to him," said Curtis Hall, writer-director of *Gridlock'd*, "he said to me, 'Suge told me the movie was great. I'm going to the MTV Music Awards, I'm going to Vegas to see Mike [Tyson] fight, and I'll come and see it on Monday.'" Tupac Shakur was shot that weekend.

Weary of battle, Tupac began taking steps to repair bridges he'd burned throughout his career. Some of his new songs were political. He had plans to have children with his girlfriend, two movies about to hit the-aters, hundreds of new songs recorded, and renewed relations with his estranged mom. He formed a company named Euphanasia and sifted through incoming scripts. He planned to finance a youth center, sports teams in South Central, and an 800 number for troubled youths.

On September 7, 1996, he told his live-in girlfriend he felt uneasy about attending the Mike Tyson–Bruce Seldon boxing match with Suge. Kidada advised him to wear his bulletproof vest; he said the weather would be too hot for it. Against his better judgment, he went to the fight, which was held at the MGM Grand in Las Vegas and attracted celebrities like Roseanne Arnold, Wayne Newton, Keanu Reeves, Jenny McCarthy, Charles Barkley, and Magic Johnson. After the fight ended with a quick knockout, Suge, Tupac, and other members of the Death Row entourage were in the MGM Grand lobby.

"Did you see Tyson do it 'im?" Tupac asked a film crew. "Tyson did it to 'im!" He leaped around. "Did y'all see that?" He became more agitated. "Fifty punches! I counted! Fifty punches! I knew he was gon' take him out! We bad like that. Come out of prison and now we running shit."

Having seen how Dre and Sam Sneed left the label, Tupac wanted to keep up appearances, especially with big Suge standing behind him, smiling, acting like his best friend, grabbing his thin arm, and physically leading him away.

As they walked, one of Suge's friends, a short, burly Mob Piru gang member named Travon Lane, recognized a sullen black guy standing across the lobby. "Tray" remembered him from an afternoon the past July when he decided to go to the Foot Locker store in Lakewood Mall. That afternoon Tray was wearing his diamond-covered Death Row pendant, and hanging with fellow Pirus Kevin Woods ("K.W.") and Maurice (Lil' Mo) Combs. Seven to eight Crips appeared in the store, leaped on them, and snatched Tray's Death Row chain.

This guy right across the lobby, Tray told Suge and Tupac on the night of September 7, this guy was one of the Crips involved in that robbery in the summer. Tupac approached the guy and asked, "You from the South?" Before he could answer, the Death Row entourage piled onto him, giving another of their trademark beatings. "Suge's boys beat down the Crips," said a witness. By participating, Tupac had crossed the tenuous line between rapping and gangbanging. After the assault, Suge and Tupac led the entourage through the casino like an occupying army. Hotel security approached the victim and urged him to file a report, but the guy refused and quietly left.

Tupac returned to his room at the Luxor, a hotel shaped like a giant pyramid; he was upset that his friends the Outlaw Immortalz hadn't met up with him at the fight. In his room a close friend said, "He complained of getting into a scrap with a Crip."

Despite his foul mood, Tupac rejoined the party. Outside the MGM Grand, an amateur videographer recorded Suge and Tupac waiting for their car. Tupac had changed from a silk shirt to a black basketball jersey and diamond-encrusted medallion; they were surrounded by women.

They went to Suge's house nearby.

Then at ten-thirty, Suge and Tupac entered Suge's rented black BMW 750. They turned off Boulevard onto Flamingo and headed east toward Club 662, an establishment with a name that had mainstream journalists commenting that the numbers stood for "MOB" on a telephone keypad, when more accurately the digits represent the California penal code for "Death Row."

They were most likely going to party; they would eventually get around to discussing the beating they administered at the Grand. Suge wore a colorful short-sleeve shirt, and a thick bracelet on his left wrist. In the shotgun seat, Tupac had his window down, yelling at fans, telling them to join the party. There were between six and fifteen cars in the convoy, a spectacular sight noticed by police cruisers as it left Suge's home at about 10:30 P.M. "There was a black BMW, a black Lexus 400, a white Suburban, a black BMW station wagon, a light gold Mercedes—they stood out," said Las Vegas Metro Police Sergeant Greg McCurdy.

The BMW stopped at a red light in front of the Maxim Hotel. This was where the neon of Vegas gives way to dark desert terrain. Hundreds of people walked the streets but didn't notice the late-model Cadillac with California plates pull up to the right of the rented BMW.

One of its four passengers pulled a firearm. "I heard these sounds and thought it was someone shooting in the air," an eyewitness told *Vibe*. Between ten and fifteen shots rang out. Glass shattered. "Two men got out of the [Cadillac] because the traffic was stalled," said a member of the entourage. "Then they just started spraying bullets. I could see Tupac trying to jump into the backseat. That's how his chest got exposed so much." Two bullets tore into his chest. Another through his hand.

One more in his leg. Bullet fragments grazed Suge's head. The Cadillac peeled off to the right, toward Koval Street. The group, one witness said, returned fire.

With two tires blown out and the windshield shot through, Suge floored the BMW. He threw a U-turn against oncoming traffic. Vehicles scattered. Two policemen at the Maxim heard the shots and saw the caravan making U-turns. They leaped into their car and chased Suge's BMW. Bleeding through his jersey, Tupac told himself, "Gotta keep your eyes open."

Suge stopped the car. The police arrived. Tupac stretched out on the backseat, bleeding heavily. Ambulance lights flashed. A witness said, "There was blood everywhere." Suge's face was covered with blood; he tried to tell an officer he had been shot in the head. The officer raised a shotgun. "If you don't get down on your knees right now, buddy, you're going to get shot in the fucking head again."

Suge tried to answer.

The officer kept his shotgun aimed at Suge. "*Get down!*"

"I gotta get my boy to the hospital."

"*Shut up! Get down!*"

Suge kneeled.

The white Cadillac left Las Vegas, Nevada.

"I'M DYING, I'M DYING!"

At Club 662 the mood was festive. People were dancing, having drinks, throwing up their gang signs on their fingers, and enjoying a performance of rap classics by the legendary group Run-D.M.C. "They were right in the middle of a song, when Eric B came up to me," a former Death Row employee said. "He said, 'They shot him.' I didn't know who he was talking about. I said, 'Who?' He said Tupac. I asked, Where did they take him? He didn't tell me. Wouldn't say it out loud. He took out a pen, grabbed a napkin, and wrote it down. The letters: UMC."

As Tupac was wheeled into the intensive care unit at University Medical Center, he said, "I'm dying, I'm dying!" Police accompanied Suge to the hospital but were unable to question him while he was being treated. After being released, he vanished.

Tupac, meanwhile, underwent a complicated operation in his chest area. In the waiting room, his mother, Afeni, pugilist Mike Tyson, actress Jasmine Guy, Reverend Jesse Jackson, and others waited for news. First they were told he had a fifty-fifty chance of surviving. Doctors later said his chances of survival were good: Despite a tremendous loss of blood, he was stabilizing. Rising to her feet, his mother approached a hospital chaplain and said she needed to pray. "I'm a strong believer in God," she said quietly. "And I know he'll make it."

The next day Tupac Shakur underwent another operation. Hospital spokesperson Dale Pugh told MTV, "He has been conscious." On Monday he was still in critical condition, his injuries now described as severe. During this ambush, Shakur had been shot four times—at least twice in the chest, which explained the loss of one lung. He was likely to survive, the UMC spokesperson said. The "Thug Life" tattoo on his torso had been riddled with bullets.

At eight o'clock that night, outside UMC in Vegas, Tupac's backup group, the Outlaw Immortalz, held prayer sessions with his fans. A large group gathered and rebuffed the media. One photographer across the street raised a camera; supporters rushed over and pushed his lens aside.

Fearing that Shakur's shooting would lead to more violence, the Las Vegas police had gang units patrol the area near the hospital. When these vigilant officers stopped one car to question its driver, however, things took a turn for the worse. "We had pulled up to see how things were going," said a Metro Police sergeant. "It was completely in a friendly mood. One guy misunderstood and wouldn't cooperate." The officers were shocked to see twenty of Tupac's distraught friends charge across the road. "The crowd came not knowing what was going on and got in the way and were pushing some of the officers."

Luckily, one of Tupac's female friends helped police calm the group: Four handcuffed men were released despite the fact that butts of marijuana cigarettes were found on two of them. "We let them go because they were grieving," said the sergeant. "Besides, it was such a small amount. These people are human. We detained them, hoping to get their emotions calm and logic rolling. At first they wouldn't listen, but after twenty minutes, when we explained where we were coming from, they were very easy to get along with."

There was a siege mentality inside Can-Am Studios, the Tarzana, California, facility once frequented by the Death Row family—Tupac,

Dr. Dre, Snoop, and the rest of the gang. Now Dr. Dre was busy forming his own label, and Tupac Shakur was fighting for his life at the University of Las Vegas Medical Center. It had been five days since he and Death Row CEO Suge Knight were caught in a drive-by shooting which left the label's artists, employees, and bodyguards introspective and fearful.

Nate Dogg, however, was trying to finish his collaboration on the forthcoming *Christmas on Death Row*. The potbellied vocalist wore a short-sleeve black dress shirt, beige pants, and a gold chain. His cousin, Butch, a gospel singer, was in the recording booth, fumbling with Nate's poignant lyric: "Blessed are those who receive/ all of their Xmas dreams/ I can't complain/ And I'm hoping that's the way it remains."

George Pryce, Death Row's dapper, bald, fiftysomething publicist, pulled out a long, thin Benson & Hedges Deluxe Ultra Light. He lit it, and bobbed his depilated head. A thirty-year publicity veteran, Pryce had been working overtime since the Vegas ambush, taking instructions directly from Knight, managing the crisis day by day.

The studio television caught Pryce's eye, and he leaped to his feet. "There's Suge! They're running an update on 'Pac. I gotta go see what's going on." Minutes later, Pryce returned, visibly deflated. "Seems Old Boy is getting worse."

"Nothing cool about that," Nate grimly replied.

Pryce lit another cigarette; his old hand trembled.

During a break in recording, Nate sat at a table in a large kitchen. "These days, you never know what's gonna happen. Perfect example. Not to bring this, but, uh . . . Tupac just got shot. It had to be, what, five, ten off-duty police officers around him? I been with these same guards before, and I had my little gun and I'm, like, 'I'm taking it with me.' They like, 'Naw, don't! We got you, we got you.' Makes me wonder. Did Tupac say that that night?

"We're fucked up," he continued, his voice rising. "We need help bad. That's my feeling. We run around killing motherfuckers, shooting all them people that's our same color. We got to be fucked up. I think everybody just lost hope. Just, 'Fuck it. No matter what, we end up dead or in jail so I'm'a just go out here and act the fucking fool.' Only comment at this time I can say about anything is pray for Tupac. That's about it. The rest of it don't seem to make no sense right now."

On Friday, September 13, 1996, at 4:03 P.M., a report aired on L.A.'s Channel 7: After six days in critical condition at University Medical Center, twenty-five-year-old Tupac Shakur was pronounced dead from respiratory failure and cardiopulmonary arrest.

George Pryce answered his phone on the first ring.

"It's true," he said quietly. "He's gone. I'm trying to talk to Suge, to prepare a statement. I spoke with Snoopy: He's back from Vegas. I told him we'd come by the studio, but I don't think we'll do it tonight. I'm very busy now. Okay?"

University Medical Center was still and silent. More than one hundred and fifty people stood out front. After asking doctors to unplug Tupac from a respirator, his mother rushed from the trauma unit. A member of Tupac's Outlawz group emerged, glared at a hospital employee, then shrieked, "Why the fuck you let him die, yo?! Why the fuck you let him die?!"

Singer Danny Boy appeared in front of the hospital. He wore tube socks and slippers and sobbed behind his trademark glasses. He fell to one knee as if in prayer. Three shining cars appeared. Suge left a black Lexus, his head wound barely noticeable. The mere sight of him hushed the crowd. "He enters the trauma center hugging Danny Boy around the neck and talking quietly with members of Tupac's family," a reporter wrote. Minutes later, puffing on a cigar, Suge left.

In Los Angeles, Kierdis Tucker, a spokesperson for Dre's Aftermath Entertainment label, said Dre had no comment on the death. "You know Dre ain't trying to get wrapped up in all this. Nothing personal, but he doesn't want anyone from Aftermath saying anything about it."

RBX, however, who left Death Row three years before and recently signed with Dre, was eager to discuss the situation. He was long gone by the time Suge signed Tupac. Still, he knew his friend Dre was having problems with Tupac. RBX was preparing an answer before he learned Shakur had been shot. "I felt it was gonna happen," he revealed sadly.

"Rappers can't keep talking trash. You ain't really out there gangbanging, so why you gonna promote that shit? You got to grow up. If you're thirty and still talking like you're sixteen, you might be retarded. You might need to get your shit checked."

RBX said he thought the shooting would, at worst, force Tupac to retire. "Then I heard TUPAC SHAKUR DEAD and was like, Aw, no. That's crazy. The little beef I had with him? I squashed it. When he passed, he stepped over. He's with the Father, he's on my team now. He's my brother. I'll give him a 'Rest in peace' and go about my business."

Dressed entirely in black, George Pryce rose from his seat at Death Row's Beverly Hills offices. Rows of framed portraits by Pryce's computer said a lot about his role at the label: Suge's son, the spitting image of his dad, held a cell phone to his ear, Snoop's wife sits in profile with their smiling son on her lap.

Pryce was under stress. Snoop was high in the studio and not returning calls. Phones rang incessantly. Receptionists said over and over, "We'll be issuing a statement." Everyone needed to know when Tupac's memorial would be held, and where. Pryce was having difficulty locating a venue. One place would have been perfect, but some numbskull blurted out that he represented Death Row. Sighing heavily, Pryce lit a cigarette. "I'm trying to book the memorial at the Santa Monica Civic Auditorium," he said. "The police station is right across the way. They have this parking lot where people can mingle—for anyone who's upset about not getting in. I'm also trying to do it in the morning so we won't attract people who like to ride," said Pryce, hoping for a violence-free affair. Then he added, half jokingly, "But Suge loves that shit."

That afternoon Pryce told reporters the memorial service would be held at 11:30 A.M. on Thursday, September 19, at the Wilshire-Ebell Theater. A few days later, the memorial would be indefinitely postponed.

"DO YOU KNOW THAT A DEPUTY DISTRICT ATTORNEY IS RENTING HIS HOME TO A KNOWN CRIMINAL?"

On September 17, 1996, District Attorney Larry Longo was removed from Suge's case but allowed to continue working in the Beverly Hills courthouse. In the past, Longo had helped Suge avoid a nine-year prison sentence for his attack on the Stanley brothers; Longo urged Judge John Ouderkirk to cut that down to five years probation. Though Ouderkirk felt the arrangement was "rather unusual," he approved the deal.

On January 2, 1996, at the district attorney's office, Longo had received a phone call from his daughter, Gina, who was negotiating a recording contract with Death Row. "We're going to sign the contract," Gina told him. "We're all going to this restaurant in the Valley."

"It was kind of a last-minute thing," Longo explained.

That night Suge Knight and his attorney, David E. Kenner, sat at a table in Benihana on Ventura Boulevard in Encino. District Attorney Longo was also there with most of his immediate family: his wife, Aelina;

his son, Frank; Frank's fiancé; his daughter, Gina; and her boyfriend. Everyone was present to witness Gina sign to Death Row Records.

Her association with the praetorian label began in June 1995, when her brother, Attorney Frank Longo, met with David Kenner to discuss an Eazy-E film project. During that meeting, Frank told Kenner about his eighteen-year-old sister: She was a singer; she wanted to be a performer since the age of six; she mostly liked classic rock, but publicly claimed that Otis Redding, Aretha Franklin, and Billie Holiday were influences. Some people even felt she sounded like Teena Marie or Celine Dion. When Frank passed David Kenner her demo tape, Gina was living in Santa Barbara and taking summer classes at the University of California.

A month later, Frank Longo was told that Death Row wanted Gina to audition for the label's CEO. Ecstatic, Frank took her to Suge's office at Can-Am Studios and introduced her. "I was very nervous," Gina said. "But I sang a song I'd been singing for years—'The Greatest Love of All.' There was a great piano player, so it just came natural, and with emotion."

She knew Death Row was a rap label. "I just assumed it was a record company, and record companies have all different kinds of music. I was excited. Who wouldn't be?"

At audition's end, Suge Knight clapped his giant hands. A short, thin white girl who dresses in baggy jeans, Gina beamed with pride. Her "voice and look" were impressive, Suge claimed: She could work with his producers and record a few tunes. If he enjoyed what he heard, and felt it had star quality to equal that of his beloved Danny Boy, then he would sign her. "I'm no Milli Vanilli," she claimed. "The reason I'm on Death Row has nothing to do with my dad. I got my deal because I can sing. I know the perception out there is that everything was just handed to me on a silver platter, but that's not the way it went down. I'm my own person and I got my own contract."

At Benihana on January 2, 1996, Suge brought the recording contract out. The deal Frank Longo negotiated with Kenner granted Gina the standard new artist royalty—twelve percent of the suggested retail record price, a dollar per album—$25,000 upon signing, and another $25,000 when her album was recorded and accepted. When Gina signed it, her father, Larry Longo, felt uneasy: He oversaw Suge's probation and now his daughter was signing to Suge's label; an outsider might consider this a conflict-of-interest situation, with Suge using this recording deal as a front to funnel a payment to Longo in exchange for a complaisant probation experience.

David Kenner, meanwhile, looked on with approval: He had negotiated the deal and felt that Gina's being signed to the label would cause Larry Longo to do his best to see that Suge remained free. If Gina's label CEO were imprisoned, then her recording contract and career—a lifelong dream—might be in danger. Kenner didn't think Longo would want to hurt his daughter's chances of stardom.

After the contract was signed, the festivities continued. "Everybody was laughing, saying, 'Isn't this wonderful?'" District Attorney Larry Longo recalled. "There was a toast to a successful contract."

Gina was in heaven. "It is a night I will never forget." The contract meant no more performing in small-time neighborhood holiday shows, rinky-dink banquets, or at Malibu's Colin McEwen College Preparatory School, where she graduated a year ahead of her class as 1994 valedictorian. Thanks to Suge Knight, Gina Longo would be the only Caucasian act at one of the most successful black-run labels in North America.

With a straight face, and with his associates watching, Suge Knight claimed that this young white girl had the voice of a Billie Holiday—but in a white woman's body! This was why he signed her, he said with a slightly forced smile.

Gina noticed that Suge had become a bit distant. "I'm sure to Suge Knight it was more business," she said. "For my family and me it was a big moment."

Throughout the evening, as Longo studied his charge Suge's mannerisms, suspicion crept in. Leaning over, he told Suge not to expect any preferential treatment. Suge replied, Don't worry about it. Gina was a genuine talent. He would even announce her signing at that year's Grammy Awards ceremony.

Billed simply as "Gina" in a Death Row magazine ad, she had spent much of the year training with a vocal coach and recording demo tracks at a studio rented by the company. Suge and David Kenner, meanwhile, worked to strengthen the bond between them and D.A. Longo. When

Suge wanted an oceanfront residence, Kenner approached Longo—father of their latest signing. Kenner asked to rent Longo's home in the exclusive Colony section of Malibu, home to movie stars and entertainment moguls seeking refuge from inner city crime.

Believing Kenner would be the tenant, Longo agreed to rent it to Kenner. A deal was negotiated. Despite the fact that he could have asked for $30,000 to $50,000 per month, Longo gave Kenner a bargain: $19,000 a month. During Memorial Day weekend 1996, Suge moved in.

What Suge didn't know was that the home had a troubled history. In December 1994, Longo and his wife appeared before the Malibu City Council with plans and needs for variances and permits. "He was building this really oversized house [4900 square feet], way bigger than most of his neighbors'," one neighbor told *Buzz* magazine. "He was being unneighborly. He's a very unpleasant person. He intimidates everyone. He's this chap in black. Black hair, black suit, and he's just gross."

Longo and his wife argued with many neighbors, who opposed plans for the home. "The whole problem was that he was building a house that the neighbors didn't like," said a Colony real estate agent. "Particularly the height and size. And they tried to get together and stop him and they couldn't because his house was totally legal."

By Memorial Day, the beach house had become a hideous three-story stucco structure with a red tile roof. "I rented the house to David Kenner and he was allowed to rent it to whoever he wanted," said Larry Longo. "When I found out Suge was there, I felt a little uneasy about it."

After lugging his belongings in, Suge immediately threw a boisterous party. Neighbors were appalled. They tried calling the house to ask them to hold it down. The parties continued, the calls were ignored, and the Malibu Colony Association mailed Suge's landlord, Larry Longo, a letter urging him to order Suge to be quiet. Longo responded by threatening to sue the entire board of directors. "And simply because we suggested to his tenants what the rules of the Colony are," one Canadian neighbor whined. "Like, you're supposed to be quiet after ten o'clock. You know, normal, good-neighborly business."

Except for a short period of time when former Motown singer Diana Ross lived there, the Colony had a history of being all white. Neighbors repeatedly called the security guards at the Colony gate to complain about the noisy new tenants, and to alert them to the fact that the tenants had armed guards at the Longo house. The Colony's private security guards kept out of it. Undeterred, the neighbors called the sheriff to complain. "When you hear people talking outside your window," the Canadian neighbor said, "even if it is three houses away, it's disturbing."

Though the sheriff's office documented every complaint, responding officers felt they weren't merited. To them, white homeowners were harassing the black occupants of the Longo house. "Upon close monitoring of this property," one sheriff wrote, "I have yet to witness any noise, except for two people having a conversation on the balcony, not to a level of disturbance. The waves are louder than any voices. Mr. Knight apologized for any disturbance to neighbors."

When Tupac Shakur began renting a house in the Colony, one white woman kept calling the police on him. If his car wasn't parked within marked lines, she reached for her phone. "It got to be so ridiculous, he just couldn't stand being there," said Longo's wife, Aelina. "No matter what he did, the lady next door called the cops on him every day."

Following Tupac's death, Caucasian residents began to fear that other shootings would follow, and that they would occur in their idyllic lily-white enclave. One Colony homeowner decided to take action: On September 17, the neighbor called Longo's office, asked for his boss, Gil Garcetti, then asked Garcetti, "Do you know that a deputy district attorney is renting his home to a known criminal?"

Removed from Suge's case, Longo was allowed to continue working in the Beverly Hills courthouse. In an October 24, 1996, interview with the L.A. Times, he acknowledged that, initially, he did pursue Suge's case aggressively. "He is a thug," Longo once told Newsweek, "and he gets the charges pushed back because he has money."

But over the years he had formed a different opinion of the man. He had said, "Marion Knight is one of the few guys I have ever prosecuted who I actually believe can turn his life around and really change the community from where he came. I have never seen a guy transform as much as this guy has since he was first booked. It's remarkable."

His family's financial relationships with Suge never affected his decisions about the case during the four years he supervised it, Longo claimed. "Why should Suge Knight bother to sign [Gina] if she doesn't have any talent?" he asked. "What was he going to gain? I told Suge Knight before he signed her to the label that he was not going to get any special treatment from me. That's all there is to it. My daughter is an adult. She does what she wants."

Unfortunately, his superiors didn't want to hear it. On October 25, 1996, when Longo arrived for work at the Beverly Hills courthouse, superiors told him to go home. In the office that morning, the phones were ringing nonstop. Reporters kept calling to ask about Longo's relationship with Suge, the rental of the beach house, and Gina Longo's record deal even though Frank Longo said, "My father had nothing to do with either deal. I negotiated both of them."

Before it even started, Gina Longo's career as an R&B singer looked to be over. When Tupac was shot, she was working hard on what she hoped would be her first album: She had recorded a duet with Danny Boy and completed recording her eighth song. "I wrote another song and tried to get in to record it but never got the [studio] time," she said. "And then, of course, this thing happened with my dad."

Then CEO Suge Knight was arrested and Death Row stopped taking her calls. (Today, Death Row declines to comment on the status of her album.) "I feel angry," she said. "But even more than that, I feel hurt. I can barely believe this is actually happening. It's like when you're watching one of those movies where some innocent guy is put on trial for a crime he didn't commit. My dad is a great person. I am a talented singer. Why would the media want to take this and twist it into something that it's not?"

"SOMEONE JUST DROVE UP ALONGSIDE AND BLASTED HIM"

On September 9, 1996, in the economically depressed, gang-infested city of Compton, a young black man named Darnell Brim entered a convenience store located at 2430 East Alondra Boulevard. Near the intersection of Alondra and Atlantic Avenue, Brim felt confident. Though close to various Blood neighborhoods, he was still technically in Crip territory. Despite this, the door to the store opened and a rival Blood with a gun rushed in. The murderous Blood raised a gun and opened fire. Brim heard the shots, then felt the burning sensation. As he fell, he heard a bloodcurdling scream. The shooter approached his fallen, bleeding body and took aim. After years of membership in the Southside Crips, Brim knew what would happen next: The shooter would finish him off, send him to whatever there was after life on earth. But the shooter didn't fire. His eyes had landed on a movement underneath his target's body. In horror, the shooter realized that Brim had leaped to cover a ten-year-old girl's wounded form: One of his bullets had inadvertently struck the innocent child in the back. The shooter paused, deciding Brim's fate, then left without firing.

The next day in Compton, Crips retaliated. They crossed Compton Boulevard, one of two streets that separate the Southside Crips from the 'hood [territory] of the Lueders Park Piru gang. At 713 North Bradfield, a Lueders Park Piru hangout, Piru members George Mack and Johnny Burgie didn't see the Crips until it was too late. The Crips shouted the name of their gang to let everyone know who was behind what would follow, then raised their weapons. Shots rang out. Wounded, Mack and Burgie fell to the pavement.

That same day, Compton Crips entered deeper into the neighboring Lynwood section of town, which was entirely controlled by Blood gangs. Gary Williams was outside near the intersection of Pine and Bradfield. His brother George worked as one of Death Row's security guards. This made Gary Williams a target. The Crips drove by and opened fire. Gary Williams fell to the ground: He would survive. But the Southside Crips had sent yet another message to their long-standing mortal enemies, the Blood gang next door to their territory: No one shoots a Southside Crip and gets away with it.

The next morning, Wednesday, September 11, thirty-year-old Bobby Finch dropped off his ten-year-old daughter at 1513 South Mayo, his mother's home in Compton. The home was located in the south end of the Southside Crips' known territory: Finch also felt safe. The violence of the past few days would not affect him. Besides, it was too early. Most gang members were awake till all hours of the night. Their mornings were spent snoring, or recovering from hangovers caused by forty-ounce bottles of cheap malt liquor.

Sitting behind the wheel of his new Acura, Finch looked forward to a workout at the gym, where he planned to spend his morning. At some point during the day, he would contact other members of his gang, the Southside Crips, and hear about the latest developments in this feud with the Bloods. A Honda Civic hatchback pulled up. "Someone just drove up alongside and blasted him," said an LAPD homicide detective. Taken to Martin Luther King Jr. General Hospital, Finch was pronounced dead at 9:53 A.M. "This was a case of mistaken identity," said a relative. "Bobby wasn't no gangbanger. Look, if you live in an area, you know people. Around here, if somebody in a neighborhood does some-thin' wrong, the entire neighborhood will suffer the consequences. The whole neighborhood is at risk. When the gangs do shit like this, they go after the ballers. They aim to take out the money first. Because Bobby had a nice car, they assumed he was a baller. He was a bodyguard but he didn't work for none of them rappers. He had nothing to do with any of this."

A Compton resident told the L.A. Times, "This is only the beginning. The gang shit is about to be on."

Unknown to the mainstream media (CNN, Prime Time Live, The Jenny Jones Show) suddenly canvassing L.A. for the "truth behind Tupac's shooting," local street gangs were blaming the Compton-based Southside Crips gang for shooting Tupac and grazing Suge. A gang war was beginning: Crip and Blood gangs chose sides. Southside joined forces with other Crip gangs like Kelly Park, Atlantic Drive, and Neigh-borhood Crips: Their long-standing enemies, the Mob Piru Blood gang teamed with the Lueders Park Piru gang and the Elm Lane Pirus.

Two days before suspected Southside Crip Bobby Finch was murdered outside his mother's Compton home, the Compton Police Department received an anonymous tip about the white limousine used during the Las Vegas ambush on Tupac and Suge: A Southside Crip named Jerry "Monk" Bonds was seen driving a late-model white Cadillac into an automotive shop at White and Alondra in Compton, deep in the terri-tory of the Southside Crips. A day after receiving the tip, police began surveillance on Monk and his friend Orlando Anderson: The suspects entered a car and drove to 1315 Glencoe Avenue, a known Southside Crip safe house.

That Tuesday afternoon, police officers raided the duplex. But Monk's cohort Orlando Anderson had vanished. The police officers were stunned: They recovered seven ski masks, an assault rifle, Smith & Wes-son .40-caliber rounds, photos of gang members, and a duffel bag with a Southwest Airlines baggage tag bearing a Vegas address. Asked to iden-tify Crip members in the photographs, Monk complied. But he lied about his friend Orlando Anderson: He stared at his good friend's face in one of the photos but didn't say he knew him. The police kept asking about Anderson. Then they told Monk they knew he and Anderson were associates. When they asked why Monk didn't tell them, or identify Anderson in the photos, Monk said, "Because he's my cousin."

On the night of September 11, Compton police received another anonymous tip: Members of the Southside Crips gang were loading guns at a house, the caller reported. The police arrived and spotted Orlando Anderson standing with four other Crips in the front yard. When Anderson spotted the officers, he immediately ran into the home. The officers gave chase, subdued Anderson, and confiscated another gruesome arsenal of weapons: an AK-47 assault rifle, a .38 revolver, two shotguns, a 9mm M-11 pistol, and assorted ammunition. Officers asked who lived in this house. Anderson said he didn't know. He lived next door, he explained, with his uncle, Dwayne Keith Davis. The police nodded: Dwayne Keith Davis was known to them as Southside Crip Keefee D. And despite Anderson's convincing delivery, Argus-eyed officers noticed his name on a high school diploma hanging on a wall in the room.

On Friday, September 13, two more victims (Tyrone Lipscomb and David McKulin) were wounded at 802 South Ward: This attack occurred directly on the border between Crip and Blood territory. A member of the Southside Crips thought they were Bloods and opened fire. The pair were not members of any gang. They were simply in the wrong place at the wrong time. The *L.A. Times* sought to explain why this current war between Crips and Bloods had erupted. "The theory involving the Compton slayings was that local gang members had gone gunning for Knight and Shakur as part of a long-simmering gang feud that had worsened after some acquaintances of Knight allegedly stomped a man to death at a party hosted by Death Row in February."

Now Bloods and Crips were at one another's throats.

The minor war continued at 12:18 P.M., when two Blood members were repairing a car in the carport of a run-down complex on North Burris Avenue. Though Bloods, Fruittown Piru member Marcus Duron Childs and Elm Lane Piru member Timothy Flanagan were west of Long Beach Boulevard, the street that separated Bloods from Crips. Aware of the war raging on the streets of Compton and neighboring Lynwood, they were distracted by the problems under the hood of the car they were repairing. Spotting opportunity, a Southside Crip quietly approached on foot, raised the handgun he was carrying, and methodically opened fire. Both victims were killed instantly, and a thirty-seven-year-old bystander was wounded by a stray bullet. "I know my nephew wasn't affiliated with any gang," Wanda Childs, relative of one victim, claimed. "I doubt he knew those people either. He wasn't into any particular rap artist or anything. But I've been hearing those rumors since day one, and who knows what's possible in the world of rap and all that? All I know is my nephew was quiet and didn't mess with anybody. He fixed old cars, basically, has never been involved in a gang, and was getting ready to have a baby next month."

At 4:03 P.M. that afternoon, Tupac Shakur was pronounced dead at UMC in Las Vegas. In Compton the war would continue, and the body count was higher than the one reported in local newspapers. "War is an understatement," a Neighborhood Crip said that afternoon. "Six Crips from over here died and five Bloods over there died. They got my boy the other day, coming out his house in the morning at eight o'clock and I'm still fucked up by that. One day the nigga was here, the next he's not. Because of that Tupac thing. One of my boys went out and got four of them Bloods himself. One of them was innocent though, just putting some stereo speakers in his car. And there was a drive-by.

"The feeling out here about Tupac's murder is that it's one of two things: that it was the Southside Crips—'cause Biggie would kick it in Southside when he was out here—or that it was Suge himself, which doesn't make sense. From what I understand, he and Tupac were good friends. And even if he was treatin' him like a trick and just making money off him, why is a nigga who's making so much money gonna be in the same car with the nigga he wants killed? He could get killed too.

"But it's crazy, dog. I gotta go to work in the morning and sneak out the 'hood early, while niggaz are sleeping. Then at night, to come home, I gotta call my [gang-member] homies beforehand and bargain with them so they'll be waiting at my job when I get out. That's the only way I can get back into the 'hood.

"Shit is crazy. I ain't trying to die. I just wanna find myself a lady that's right and settle down with her—so that when my career jumps off again, she'll be there to take my back."

Initially, Captain Steven Roller of the Compton P.D. denied that

Tupac's death had touched off a gang war. "First of all, there's been no connection to indicate that any of these killings are related to the killing of Tupac Shakur," Roller claimed. "As we do in all homicide investigations, all leads will be investigated. I'm sorry to say it, but gang members do get killed. To say they're killed over this murder would be inaccurate. We've heard the rumors, but we have no control over them, as we didn't in the case of the O.J. Simpson trial. If someone's saying differently, we encourage any person with information that can help solve this double homicide to step forward.

"We have actually noticed a decrease in gang activity this year," Roller continued. "And for us to 'pay a special attention to the groups'? We are vigilant in our duties throughout the year. We also have our own intelligence sources and they have not given us any information to indicate that these killings are in any way connected to the murder of Tupac Shakur in Nevada."

Within weeks, Captain Roller would admit that as many as a dozen shootings—three of them fatalities—may have been linked to Shakur's murder. Before dawn on Wednesday, October 2, acting on rumors heard on the streets of Compton, over three hundred officers from eleven law enforcement agencies convened. Clad in black masks, helmets, and bulletproof vests, the agents planned to sweep through Compton, Long Beach, Lakewood, Paramount, and unincorporated county areas. At some locations, agents set off flash-bang diversionary devices; they kicked in doors at thirty-seven houses, and rousted suspects from their beds. At a booking center set up in the Compton police parking lot, police asked the twenty-three people they arrested (and countless suspects), "Who killed Tupac?"

When the gang sweep reached Orlando Anderson's home, two Las Vegas detectives were present. They watched police kick Anderson's door in and take him into custody. Identified as a member of the Southside Crips, Anderson was being arrested for an unrelated murder in April and one of the retaliatory shootings. As police led Anderson away, someone claiming to be his brother accused them of "scapegoating" him. "Tupac Shakur, the talented musical genius, fell at the hands of a violent, cruel drive-by shooter," the man told a nearby reporter. "That person, however, is not Orlando."

Neighborhood Crip member Magic Mike said, "There were actually *two* types of sweeps. The first: They swept and got all guns. The second raid started at three in the morning. Bam! Everybody was just getting picked up. They picked people up a block or so to the right, which was the Southside, then picked up over here"—another direction—"which was the M.O.B. Pirus.

"Anybody they felt was 'affiliated' was served with a warrant. At first everybody thought these warrants were for some traffic tickets. But the police were takin' everybody down to Compton station and askin' questions like, 'Ay, how you know about Tupac's shooting?' They raided people's houses and found guns and drugs. But in the newspaper stories about the raids, they mashed the two raids together and said, 'Ay, we raided today and this is what we picked up!' But they picked the guns up a week before. And people around here were the only ones who knew that."

When the raids were over, police announced the seizure of an assortment of rifles and handguns, three bulletproof vests, $17,000 in cash, and two pounds of cocaine, methamphetamine, and marijuana. They also captured Orlando Anderson, who retained counsel and fought accusations that he murdered Tupac Shakur. Anderson, his lawyer, Edi Faal, reminded reporters, was the victim of a beating at the MGM Grand. "At the time he was being attacked, he did not know his attacker was Mr. Shakur. He believes he is a victim of Tupac." Ultimately, no charges were brought and Anderson was released.

"I'LL SIGN ANYTHING YOU WANT! JUST DON'T LET THE FIRM OR MY WIFE KNOW!"

Suge was furious. Steven Cantrock had gone too far.

During his college days, Cantrock had been a Haight-Ashbury hippie who listened to drowsy music, associated with pot-smoking longhairs, and dreamed of a world without suit-and-tie capitalists. When he started with the informal Gelfand, Rennert & Feldman accounting agency in 1986, firm founder Irwin Rennert let Cantrock adopt some of his clients. Soon Cantrock was representing heavy metal bands like Slaughter and White Zombie. An aggressive business manager, Cantrock went from partying with clients backstage to developing his own taste for Porsches, double-breasted suits, and socializing with the rich and famous. "Steve wasn't poring over the books," a coworker told *The Wall Street Journal*. "I never saw a piece of paper on his desk. His persona was the salesman, the hustler going out to get the business."

In 1989, accounting giant Coopers & Lybrand had become interested in the entertainment field. A conservative New York–based firm that generated $6.8 billion in worldwide annual revenue, Coopers had a client list that included AT&T and Ford. While its employees were buttoned down and formal, Coopers decided to acquire Gelfand. As parent company, it allowed Gelfand to keep its own name on the door and run things as they saw fit.

By 1992, Irwin Rennert considered Steven Cantrock a protégé: Like many hippies, Cantrock had become everything he once claimed to despise. He wore double-breasted suits, drove a Porsche, and spent every day thinking about money. But he wanted more.

After failing his certified public accounting exam twice, aspiring firm-partner Cantrock was named a "principal," allowed to enjoy partner status while not certified, and allowed to run the "Cantrock division," an autonomous sector that included musical groups as clients.

In November 1992, Cantrock's mentor, firm founder Irwin Rennert, introduced Cantrock to Marion "Suge" Knight. Suge needed someone to manage the financial end of Death Row. Firm founder Rennert passed the account to Cantrock.

Though Death Row Records had received $1 million from Sony (for the rights to Dre's publishing), that money had been used to finance recording of Dre's *The Chronic*. Then Interscope and Time Warner gave another $1.5 million, but that money was spent just as quickly. "A startup record label can cost millions to get off the ground," the *L.A. Times* reported. "The company has to pay all the costs of recruiting talent, recording costs, and setting up a company infrastructure before any revenue comes in."

With his staff, Cantrock was responsible for managing the label's remaining capital, paying its bills, haggling with its suppliers, handling its income taxes, and advising Suge and David Kenner on investments. But Cantrock was not your ordinary accountant. During his tenure with Gelfand, Rennert & Feldman, Cantrock had handled rowdy heavy-metal groups such as Slaughter and White Zombie: Backstage at their concerts, he partied with these longhairs; soon he developed his own taste for luxury cars, fine clothing, and famous friends.

Initially, Cantrock maintained a professional distance from his new client, Suge, who took his money very seriously. As Death Row's de facto controller, Cantrock had sole authority to write checks for the company, and Suge—an intimidating giant with eight convictions to his name—kept a watchful eye on him.

But as time passed, Suge came to trust him. He decided to let Cantrock handle his own personal finances as well as those of his label's biggest stars.

Soon they were partying outside the office. But Cantrock came to see another side of this gentle giant. On the night of May 25, 1993, they went to Prince's club, Glam Slam. Suge had a few henchmen with him, and before night's end had argued with security guard Roderick Lockett and pounded him to a pulp. But Cantrock felt he was safe. He would never give Suge a reason to dislike him.

As the label generated millions of dollars in sales on records and merchandise, Cantrock signed off on Suge's purchases: When Suge wanted to buy luxury cars, expensive Rolex watches, yachts, and jewelry, Cantrock said fine. When Suge demanded that on the road, stretch limousines be lined up outside their five-star luxury hotels twenty-four hours a day, against his better judgment Cantrock agreed. It was, after all, Suge's money. But he knew of ways to help him spend less: He prevailed on Suge to frequent BL Diamonds, a jewelry wholesaler located at 631 Olive Street, which was owned by his friend Brian Lemberger and ultimately sold the label over $1 million in merchandise.

But then Death Row's name kept appearing on overdraft reports. The reports circulated among Gelfand partners. Despite having received millions from Interscope, Time Warner, and Sony, Death Row's checks would begin to bounce. Gelfand partners were unhappy that Death Row was constantly on overdraft for large amounts. So, it seemed, were executives at Interscope, who constantly reprimanded Cantrock during meetings and listened as Cantrock continued to claim, "We're getting it all under control."

At this point, Suge later claimed, he was unaware of the label's overdraft problems. According to Suge, Cantrock always said, "Everything is fine."

To keep Death Row's checks from bouncing, Cantrock asked City National Bank in Beverly Hills to allow Death Row to be overdrawn within certain limits.

For his service, and silence, Suge rewarded him with a brand-new green Jeep Cherokee, which prompted Cantrock to retire his aging Porsche and make the scene in his new gift. Instead of notifying his superiors at the Gelfand firm or their parent company, Coopers & Lybrand, or refusing to accept the Jeep (since accountants were not supposed to accept gifts from clients due to potential conflicts of interest), Suge saw Cantrock accept the gift and keep his mouth shut. Since Cantrock was willing to bend the rules, Suge introduced him to a rogue corporate culture unlike any Cantrock had ever known. "Cash was king," *The Wall Street Journal* noted, "and disputes frequently turned violent." At this point, Cantrock's subordinates at Gelfand claimed, he would brag that he was "running Death Row."

When Suge wanted to open a nightclub in Las Vegas, Cantrock worked with David Kenner to negotiate with a number of shady characters: They spoke with the wife of Carl Thomas, who had been convicted in the early 1980s for helping Chicago-based mob figures skim money from the Stardust Hotel. With Carl in jail, his wife held a long-term lease on the building.

Cantrock introduced Suge to Robert Amira, fondly remembered by mobster Michael Franzese for helping him pull his "most enjoyable scams in Las Vegas."

In 1982, Robert Amira was indicted with New York Mafia figures Joseph Colombo Jr. and Alphonse "the Whale" Merolla for helping to defraud the Dunes Hotel-Casino in an airline junket ticket scam. But the case was dismissed when the judge claimed he saw the prosecutor and jury foreman communicating in an improper manner.

After Cantrock brought Amira into Suge's life, Club 662 finally opened.

But the FBI would investigate the club, and a paper trail that linked Suge to organized crime figures. According to investigators, Suge had paid $800,000 over the last sixteen months to East Coast crime families: The payments were meant to buy a stake in the club, renovate it, and install a management team capable of getting a liquor license. As time passed, Suge suspected that Amira and others had robbed him.

On June 4, 1996, at 11:00 P.M., Suge appeared at Steven Cantrock's home in the Los Angeles suburb of Calabassas. Accompanied by David

Kenner and the label's security chief, Reginald Wright, he entered Cantrock's living room and, between sips from a can of Diet Coke, asked for
details about money Cantrock had handled in two Las Vegas deals with
Robert Amira. In both deals, Suge felt cheated. Then he asked about a
$25,000 down payment for a house he decided not to buy. According to
Wright, Cantrock cried, made up stories, then confessed to having stolen
the $25,000. Then Suge asked why Cantrock didn't account for money
Amira had been given for Club 662, and Cantrock said he had been
distracted by accusations of sexual harassment made against him by a
subordinate at Gelfand. Here, Wright claimed, Suge said, "Just stop
stealing, pay me back, and get on the ball with putting business in
order." That meeting ended with Suge trying to assist Cantrock with his
sexual harassment defense.

But Suge no longer trusted Cantrock: He sent his brother-in-law, Norris Anderson, to Cantrock's office to obtain financial records detailing
the label's transactions. Suge also continued to feel that Cantrock and
his furtive Vegas contacts were defrauding him. His partners in the 662
deal denied wrongdoing, said they didn't owe Suge a penny, and noted
that Cantrock and Kenner had represented him during every business
transaction—maybe he should speak with them. Suge was confused but
angry. "I paid a lot of money to people who made a lot of promises and
all I ended up was getting taken advantage of," he felt. "I'm the victim
here. These people stole my money and I want it back."

Cantrock, meanwhile, did not suspect that Suge mistrusted him.

During the holiday season in 1995, he continued acting like one of the
gang and no longer tried to rein in his client Suge's spending habits. For
their Christmas party that year, Suge rented the Château Le Blanc mansion in Beverly Hills and spent a small fortune on champagne. During
the party, Cantrock became so inebriated, Norris Anderson claimed
"people were literally holding the guy up. We were like, 'Can you believe
our accountant is at an industry party and smashed like this?'"

When forty-three-year-old Cantrock arrived at Death Row singer Michel'lé Toussaint's Woodland Hills home on the night of October 11, he
found Suge Knight; attorney David Kenner; Suge's brother-in-law, Norris
Anderson; Death Row "associate" Kevin Tubbs; the label's travel agent,
Jim Rodman; Rodman's assistant, John Bell; and Michel'lé waiting in the

backyard. Cantrock was confused as to why a meeting had been called. Suge—whose eyes were like a shut door—had his reasons.

In addition to the money in the Club 662 deal, Suge blamed Cantrock for some of the high charges listed on a bill he and Kenner had received from American Express at the end of September.

From June 1996 to September, the firm reminded them, Death Row credit card expenditures totaled $1,574,991.82. On September 4 and 17, Kenner chartered several private jets: Jetwest International charged him $42,279.86. For refueling, Spirit Aviation charged $23,041.88. For each limousine in the label's convoy, CLS Transportation charged $95 per hour, as well as costs for driver lodging, per diem, a twenty percent gratuity, and per-mile charges ($1.95). The total was $160,000.

Next, Kenner repeatedly used the credit card at Bel Air Travel, a Los Angeles firm unlisted in directory assistance: On September 10 he charged $122,303.44; nine days later he charged another $108,294.95. Both transactions, American Express reported, used the same reference code but listed no airline, passenger, destination, or hotel information.

At the Luxor in Las Vegas, meanwhile, Suge Knight booked twenty-seven separate rooms for $50 each (placing $1,584.21 on his card), then spent an astounding $666.45 on fancy cigars at the Tinder Box smoke shop. On September 12 they gave CLS Limousines another $50,000. The final "unknown" charge, made on September 21, was for $2,738.82 at the Beverly Hills Hotel. In addition, American Express was billing a delinquency charge of $25,787.43.

After receiving the bill, Suge and Kenner admitted to American Express that the expenses *were* Death-Row related, but had been placed on the credit cards without authorization by their rogue accountant, Steven Cantrock.

In Michel'lé's backyard, everyone finished eating takeout food. Cantrock was still confused. Why had Suge called him over there? When Suge began the conversation with a joke, Cantrock relaxed. But then Suge began to discuss the many occasions that Cantrock had made unwanted overtures to women. After mentioning Michel'lé's name, Suge said, "All right, cut the bullshit. Steve, how much did you steal from me and Death Row?"

Before Cantrock could respond, Suge demanded that he kneel on the grass. When he refused, Suge's huge fist hit him. Cantrock burst into tears and kneeled before the giant. While crying, he heard Suge say he wanted a confession. He wanted Cantrock to admit to having embezzled four and a half million dollars from Death Row during the last four years.

On the sidelines, David Kenner hastily drafted a handwritten document. Suge handed it to Cantrock and demanded his signature. Fearing for his life, Cantrock accepted a pen. In horror, he realized it was an IOU/confession. Suge demanded that he sign it. The frightened accountant obeyed, trying to keep his hand from trembling.

The next day Steven Cantrock called a superior and notified him of the previous evening's horrifying encounter with Suge Knight: When he arrived at Michel'lé Toussaint's home in the Valley, Suge assaulted him, then forced him to his knees. Then they forced him to sign a trumped-up IOU. The coerced statement, which said he had embezzled four million from Death Row, was false and absurd. Coopers & Lybrand would stand behind him, Cantrock learned. But they had to act. Now that the document existed, Cantrock might be in jeopardy. If he were to suddenly vanish, who would dispute the document's authenticity? Suge and Kenner would be absolved of the $4-million debt. But Cantrock should not worry. They had a plan.

At the office, a security guard was posted in the lobby, and assistants were ordered to tell clients, "Steven Cantrock is away on 'stress leave.' " By sunset, Cantrock and his family were said to have left the country. State and federal prosecutors knew about the IOU and were said to be delighted: Their investigation had run into a number of obstacles, but Cantrock looked to be a credible insider who would provide damning details about Death Row.

The label denied Cantrock's claim that he had been physically assaulted. Suge, they claimed, simply asked how much was stolen. In their version, Cantrock replied, "About four and a half million dollars, sir." Then Suge supposedly said, "I trusted you. How could you do this to me? How could you do this to Death Row?"

"I'm sorry, sir," Cantrock was quoted as saying. "I was stupid."

According to everyone present that evening, Suge insisted on a guarantee that Cantrock would repay the debt; Cantrock stopped crying long enough to suggest that they produce an IOU. He said he would be able to pay Suge back quickly; he would confess the theft to his partners at Gelfand, who would pay the debt to protect their good name. *"I'll do anything you want!"* Michel'lé quoted him as saying. *"I'll sign anything you want! Just don't let the firm or my wife know!"*

Then, everyone but Cantrock added, the accountant was too flustered to draft up the document. Suge asked David Kenner to do it. Michel'lé went upstairs with the signed IOU, made photocopies, and returned to find everyone talking about sports. "Rodman was into fishing, so we went from this heavy conversation to how we should all go fishing," Suge's relative, Norris Anderson, claimed.

Michel'lé said she handed one copy of the IOU to Death Row, then another to Cantrock. After that, everyone left. Kenner and Suge denied there was an assault. "After I caught him stealing millions of dollars and confronted him, he started crying," Suge claimed. "He said, 'Please, just give me time to get you all your money back. . . .' I said, 'Okay, Steve, don't get so bent out of shape.'"

Travel agent Jim Rodman agreed. "At no time from the time I entered the home until we all left was Mr. Cantrock or Mr. Knight out of my sight," he wrote in a statement. "At no time do I recall seeing or hearing any abusive behavior."

Federal investigators didn't believe Death Row and the people they conducted business with. They believed Cantrock's friends and business associates. "They say he was threatened by Knight at an after-hours meeting attended by a handful of the rap mogul's closest associates at a San Fernando Valley residence," the *L.A. Times* reported. "They have told federal investigators that Cantrock was forced to his knees and feared for his life before agreeing to sign the two-page confession drafted on the spot by Knight's attorney, David Kenner—an accusation that both Knight and Kenner deny." Coopers & Lybrand kept Cantrock in hiding. Cantrock and the Coopers & Lybrand firm eventually provided federal agents with documents detailing the label's financial dealings over the last three years.

As witnesses were being subpoenaed to give testimony before a federal grand jury in L.A., Suge said he was baffled. Later, he would wonder why he was in jail while the people who "took him for a ride" were free: He would accuse the government of harassing his small, black-owned business and ignoring what he called the "giant white-owned" Coopers & Lybrand (whose accountant, he maintained, had ripped him off for millions). "I'm just a fall guy here," he would say as the federal probe continued. "It's the saddest thing in the world to me that everybody is trying to find so much wrong with Death Row. I busted my ass to build this company." The government, he finally realized, would work just as hard to shut it down.

"HE SHOULDN'T BE AFRAID OF ME. I COULD MAKE HIM A STAR"

"Some say he's the most dangerous man in music, a convicted felon with his own record company."

With these words, ABC-TV's *Prime Time Live* began its attack on Death Row Records, entitled "The Gangsta's Rap." It was November 6, 1996, and Suge Knight was in a jail cell at the L.A. County Jail.

On October 15, 1996, Suge failed to appear for a court-ordered drug test.

On October 17 he failed to appear for another drug test. Suge had already violated the three years' probation he received for a separate federal weapons case: He had tested positive for marijuana in late August and was scheduled to appear in federal court at the end of October. Superior Court Judge John Ouderkirk—who agreed to Suge receiving a "rather unusual" grant of probation for his attack on the Stanley brothers—had discovered that Suge had tested positive and ordered him to be tested by federal probation agents *and* the county Probation Department. By missing two drug tests that Judge Ouderkirk had ordered, Suge now violated the probation he received for attacking the Stanley brothers on July 13, 1992.

Tired of reiterating his order that Suge be tested for drug use by the county Probation Department, Judge John Ouderkirk said, "He's going to test just like every other person who is on probation. He's been given many warnings already."

But he's not in the country, a probation officer told the judge. Suge had left the country, to travel to the Bahamas without permission. Enraged, Ouderkirk issued an arrest warrant. But he would rescind the order if Suge appeared in his court the following Tuesday. Unknown to Ouderkirk, Suge was in the United States. In fact, he was less than an hour away, moving his possessions out of Larry Longo's Malibu beach house. "That morning," a Colony neighbor told the *L.A. Times*, "the biggest furniture van you've ever seen pulled up. By five P.M. they were gone."

Kenner told Judge Ouderkirk that Suge would appear. "He's here."

That Tuesday, October 22, Suge wore a brown pinstripe three-piece suit and swaggered by news cameras in front of the courthouse. "He became Suge Knight the Don," said a former label employee. After telling reporters "It's in God's hands," he entered the chamber with Kenner.

Inside, Ouderkirk said he had repeatedly given Suge the benefit of the doubt. To let him walk free would be an embarrassment. Looking down from his bench, he read a long list of Suge's failures to make appointments for drug tests and court appearances. "Mr. Knight has run out of that string of excuses as far as this court is concerned." Bailiffs surrounded Suge's chair as Ouderkirk ordered him held in jail until the following Monday—October 28's bail hearing.

In closing, Ouderkirk brought up the fact that during the 1992 attack on the Stanley brothers, Suge had pointed a gun and said, "When I say do something, you do it."

"Apparently," Ouderkirk quipped, "Mr. Knight likes to make those rules. He doesn't like to follow those rules."

Rising to his feet, Suge casually removed his credit cards and cash from a pocket, handed the bundle to Kenner, then walked into the courtroom lockup. "When Suge was taken into custody," said *America's Most Wanted* reporter Lena Nozizwe, "his wife Sharitha got up and said, sort of loud-voiced to the judge, 'Well, can he see his daughter?' Because she was standing there with their cute daughter in the court. That was the emotion *du jour*."

Outside the chamber Kenner protested Ouderkirk's decision. "I thought what happened this morning in court was inappropriate. Mr. Knight came back to court as he was requested to do. He came back to test as he was requested to do." The Probation Department's reports to the court, he claimed, said Suge should remain on probation; Suge was blameless for having missed drug tests on the sixteenth and eighteenth; he was in the Bahamas and bad weather complicated flight schedules to L.A.; Suge informed federal officials of his whereabouts but didn't notify county officials because he didn't know he was expected to.

For violating probation, Suge remained in jail. He was still in jail in November: Just as his bail hearing was scheduled, District Attorney Larry Longo was accused of conflict of interest. It was revealed that his daughter, Gina, had been signed to Death Row, and that Suge had moved into his Malibu beach house after Memorial Day.

On November 4, two days before his appearance on *Prime Time Live*, probation officer David S. Crowley urged new judge Stephen Czuleger to keep Suge in jail: Crowley had shown Judge Czuleger a written report that highlighted Suge's involvement in the brawl at the MGM Grand. In person, Crowley explained that Suge appeared in footage shot by a surveillance camera, which was very compelling evidence. Kenner, meanwhile, called Crowley's allegations "meritless."

On the night of November 6, 1996, close to a month after Tupac Shakur had been shot in Las Vegas, *Prime Time* reporter Brian Ross began his "investigation." Since 1980, when he broke the Abscam story, Ross was viewed as a fearless reporter. When Tupac was shot and Suge was imprisoned, Ross knew he was on to what Sam Donaldson's script called "a shocking story about violence in the music industry."

The story began with Robert Van Winkle, also known as Vanilla Ice, simulating drum sounds with his voice, chuckling, then saying, "Yeah, I did that." A voice-over explained that five years ago, Vanilla had the number-one song in America. With "Ice Ice Baby" playing faintly, Vanilla reminisced about his glory days. "My record was selling over a million copies a week. The fastest-selling record in history. I was like, 'Oh, my God.' I was just blown away by the whole thing. I said, Oh, I can't believe this." Ross's voice-over explained that now "for what Rob Van Winkle says is good reason, he has moved far away from the recording studios of Los Angeles, as far away as he can."

"Because I'm scared. That's why."

After explaining how Suge coerced Eazy-E to sign forms releasing Dr. Dre from Ruthless Records in mid-1991, Eazy's former attorney, Jerry Heller, pulled a small pistol from a bedside drawer and showed it to Brian Ross. Years after the incident, Heller said he was still frightened for his life.

"The reason for all the fear," Ross's voice-over explained, "involves the world of this man, the man getting out of the limousine—" The camera zoomed in on Suge exiting a luxurious rental car; he was heading to see Judge Ouderkirk and stood still while behind him, a driver pulled his brown jacket over his huge shoulders. "Six-foot-three, three-hundred-and-thirty-five-pound Marion Knight," Ross said, "known by the nickname of Suge, short for Sugar."

Heller appeared onscreen again, saying, "I think the guy is a serious major gangster."

Then the screen was filled with footage of Suge purposefully entering the courthouse. "At the age of only thirty, and with a lengthy criminal record including three felony convictions, Suge Knight has managed to become the head of a hundred-million-dollar record company and one of the most powerful and feared men in the American music industry," Ross explained.

From Suge entering the courthouse, the story moved to Suge sitting in a visiting area in prison. He wore county blues. "All these allegations are lies," he said.

"Lies?" Ross asked.

"Lies."

"For the last few weeks," the voice-over explained, "Knight has been running his empire from a cell in the Los Angeles County Jail. While he awaits a hearing on charges he violated his probation from a particularly vicious assault case."

"You're six foot three," Ross reminded him, "three hundred and thirty-five pounds."

"Uh-hm."

"You're a big guy and there are people who are afraid of you. You know that, don't you?"

"There's probably people afraid of you."

Following Tupac's death, curiosity about Suge was at its peak. In September he failed to appear for an interview with worried Las Vegas detectives. Police officers had accompanied him to the University Medical Center immediately after the shooting, but were told by doctors that they could not question him while he received treatment. After being treated, Suge vanished. On Monday, September 9, police were searching for him, but he stayed on the move; that day he was sighted at Death Row's Beverly Hills offices and at his home in Vegas.

His attorney, David Kenner, finally promised Las Vegas police Suge would appear for questioning the next day. But that didn't happen. A day after that he appeared with three attorneys and a fruitless narration. "We was at the light," he told detectives. "We was havin' a conversation; heard some gunshots. We looked to the right of us. Tupac was tryin' to get in the backseat. I grabbed him and pulled him down. It was about fifteen gunshots."

Now Brian Ross and Suge were on television, sitting in Suge's cell at the L.A. County Jail, and Ross was asking, "What did you see?"

"Heard shots."

"Heard shots?"

"Yeah."

"And then what'd you see?"

Suge smiled and arched his eyebrows. "Blood," he slurred.

After the voice-over explained that Suge had been struck in the head with a bullet—onscreen, he smiled, bowed his head, and pointed at the wound—it implied that he was being uncooperative with police.

"If you knew who killed Tupac," Ross began, "would you tell the police?"

"Absolutely . . . not!"

"Why not?!" Ross whined.

" 'Cause it's not my job. I don't get paid to solve homicides. I don't get paid to tell on people."

"If you knew, you wouldn't tell."

"No."

Suge said, "The first year of Death Row Records, we came out, we generated a billion dollars."

"How much?"

"A billion dollars."

"One billion?!"

"Yeah, for the first year."

Ross was uninterested in Suge's self-aggrandizing "successful black businessman" shtick. He returned to the subject of craven white rapper Vanilla Ice. The lens zoomed in on Vanilla describing his first meeting with Suge at the Palm restaurant in L.A.: Suge entered with his men, sat at his table, and said, "How you doing?"

"Uninvited?" Brian Ross asked.

"Totally uninvited. I didn't even know them."

"See them again?"

Months later, Suge and his men approached; Suge said hello; the group withdrew; Vanilla began thinking, "Wow, this guy knows where I'm at at all times. How does he know where I'm at? You know? What's going on here?"

Ross's voice-over explained. "What was going on was the beginning of an effort by Suge Knight to get rich off of Vanilla Ice's hit song, to get Van Winkle to sign over a percentage of the profits, or the points, to an associate of Suge Knight's, who Knight claims actually wrote the song. Knight told us, before he knew we had talked to Van Winkle, that it was all very friendly."

"He agreed to everything," Suge said in prison, "it wasn't a problem."

"He agreed?"

"I mean, you know, he said the guy wrote the song. He didn't have a problem with it—"

"That's not what he says at all."

Vanilla was onscreen again, describing how Suge and his men appeared at his hotel room one night: After Suge's armed bodyguards roughed up his entourage, Suge asked Vanilla Ice out onto the balcony.

"On the balcony?" Brian Ross asked.

"On the balcony."

"High above . . ."

"Like fifteen floors. He had me look over the edge, showed me how high I was up there."

"Were you scared?"

Vanilla implied that he lost control of his bodily functions. He needed to wear a diaper on that day.

"On the balcony," the voice-over explained, "Van Winkle says Suge Knight told him to sign over points on the song to a man named Mario Lavelle Johnson."

"Who is Mario Lavelle Johnson?" Ross asked.

"That's the guy Suge Knight brought over there that was an acquaintance of mine *that had nothing to do with that song!*"

"You signed over the rights."

"I signed over the rights to him so Suge and them can get paid for it."

"So Mario Lavelle Johnson didn't write that song."

"No way."

"How much were those points worth?"

"About four million, three million, anywhere between there. Three or four million dollars."

"And you just signed them—"

"I signed them. And walked away alive."

In the cell, Ross leaned forward in his seat. "He says you had a number of men there with guns." Suge laughed. "You then took him out to the balcony—" Suge said, Hm-hm. "And you said, 'You're gonna sign over the rights.' Did you do that?"

"No, I did not."

"It never happened?"

"Never happened."

"You didn't take him out to the balcony—"

"How that sound?"

"It sounds like what all the other police reports involving you again and again—"

"Come on, man. That's not true."

"But in our *Prime Time* investigation," the voice-over added, "we found one court case after another in which Knight has pleaded guilty, involving vicious assaults, beatings, a pistol whipping, and on and on."

Seconds later Suge was shown sitting in the cell, holding a piece of paper and pretending to scribble on it with one hand. "If you force somebody to sign something, it'll be all like—" His hand gestured wildly.

"How do you know that?" Ross asked.

" 'Cause . . ."

"Have you done it before?"

"No, I never done it before. It's common sense."

"But did you force him to sign it?"

"Never."

"You did not?"

"I did not."

Ross brought up Larry Longo, the beach house, and the record deal, calling it "the Suge Knight way of doing business."

"Did you think you were trying to influence him?" Ross asked in the cell.

"I don't gotta influence nobody."

"Trying to bribe him?"

"What's bribe?"

Vanilla appeared onscreen one final time, to explain that he was terrified. *"The only reason why I'm telling this story now is because you guys already knew the story! I would never get on a witness stand and go against that guy! 'Cause you put a target on my forehead."* He aimed a finger at Ross. *"I sleep good at night. I had nightmares for a long time over this thing, you know. It's very scary for me."*

Suge sat in his cell, a half-smile on his face. "You know what he needs to do? He needs to come find me, say, 'You know what, Suge Knight—?' "

"He's afraid of you," said Ross.

"He shouldn't be afraid of me. I could make him a star."

"You could make him a star."

"Exactly," Suge said, then laughed.

"THE FBI IS LOOKING AT DEATH ROW FROM THE TOP TO THE BOTTOM"

After **Prime Time Live** labeled Suge "the most dangerous man in music," his lawyers had to devise an imaginative defense. With their accountants gone, Death Row's bills had begun to pile up. The company was already behind in payments for the old Carolco building, a property acquired with help from its former owner (*Hustler* and *Rappages* publisher Larry Flynt). Then Can-Am Studios asked the label to leave. Neighbors had called police to complain about noise and gang-related activities, the studio claimed, and every once in a while police officers made an arrest there: police officers, Suge learned, that were cooperating with the federal investigation against the label.

Though FBI spokesman John Hoos would neither confirm nor deny that a probe was under way, an unidentified law enforcement source told the *New York Post*, "The FBI is looking at Death Row from the top to the bottom."

In court on Thursday, November 7, the bailiffs brought Suge into the chamber; he faced the rows of seats reserved for visitors, until he spotted his mother, Maxine. Then he flashed a reassuring smile: He wanted his mother to know that he would be back on the streets any minute now. Near him at a table in the front of the courtroom, Suge's six unpaid lawyers produced a copy of the videotape probation officer David S. Crowley mentioned in his written report to Judge Czuleger. Filmed by a surveillance camera in the MGM Grand hotel, the videotape detailed Orlando Anderson being attacked by Tupac Shakur and members of Death Row's entourage. Suge's attorneys tried to lessen its impact on the court by claiming that Suge was not a participant in the beating. He was trying to stop the fight. After watching the tape twice, Judge Czuleger disagreed. "Looks like he's getting a last lick in, that's what it looks like to me."

Czuleger decided to hold a hearing: A week from now, he said, they would discuss the extent of Suge's involvement in the fight. He also wanted to discuss other possible probation violations, including Suge's drug tests in August showing a positive for marijuana.

Death Row Records had fallen behind in meeting deadlines to deliver five albums to Interscope, which hoped to have them in stores during the lucrative holiday season. If they failed to deliver the albums, Death Row might find itself having to pay back millions of dollars in advances. Before his imprisonment, Suge had been able to complete only two of the five albums: a Tupac album issued under the pseudonym Makaveli (and released earlier that week) and Snoop's sophomore work *The DoggFather*.

Since Suge was closely involved with production and mastering of all Death Row albums, defense attorney Marcia Morrissey explained, Suge wanted to get out and finish Nate's album, *G-Funk Classics Volume I*, the label's compilation *Christmas on Death Row*, and *Death Row's Greatest Hits*. That's why bail until next Thursday's hearing was imperative, Morrissey continued: If Suge remained behind bars, "production is in some danger."

Deputy District Attorney William Hodgman detailed Knight's criminal record, eight convictions he described as "a history replete with assaultive behavior, violence, and weapons."

After Hodgman's adamant disquisition, Judge Czuleger thought it over: To him, Suge assaulting Orlando Anderson was the most climacteric allegation. If he did it, he violated probation. If he violated probation, he deserved to be in jail. "He's had every reason to believe things would work out," Czuleger said. "He's been given a lot of breaks. No one's said, 'Enough's enough. That's it.' " He denied bail.

Word on the street and in the county jail was that Suge was in danger. When he bought out the prison commissary and began giving gifts to other inmates, it was seen as a desperate move to buy friends. "He's paying motherfuckers to watch his back," said music industry executive Bigga B. "He got everybody living lovely off of him. Taking care of all the Bloods."

On November 14, Suge's supporters wore yellow ribbons to signify love and unity with Suge. Gathered in the hallway outside the courtroom, they yelled, "Keep the faith!" After having spent close to a month in jail, Suge was allowed to appear in court without handcuffs. The videotape from the MGM Grand was shown. Everyone in the courtroom saw a flock of gang members attack Anderson, who wore a white football jersey with the number thirteen. "But Knight is not sharply in focus," the *L.A. Times* initially claimed.

Dressed entirely in blue, Anderson took the witness stand. Before the session began, he had spoken with Suge's lawyer, David Kenner, and refused to speak with prosecutors. Suge, he now claimed, had not been an aggressor that evening. When Tupac and seven other men attacked him, Suge was a peacemaker coming to his rescue. "I seen him pulling people off of me." Suge was the only one yelling, *"Stop this stuff!"*

Deputy District Attorney Bill Hodgman waited, then asked Anderson if he was a Crip. Anderson pleaded the Fifth. Hodgman asked if he went by the name Baby Lane. Anderson pleaded the Fifth. Hodgman asked if Anderson or his "associates" had ever attacked Blood members in a Lakewood-area Foot Locker store in August 1996. Anderson pleaded the Fifth.

Cradling his shaved head in his left arm, Suge watched the prosecution put two police officers on the stand: Both said Orlando gave a different story last month. Compton police officer Ray Richardson said he interviewed Anderson on October 2. "He basically said he had been jumped by some Bloods. Also Suge and Tupac."

Brent Becker, a Las Vegas police detective, added, "He made the comment that Tupac and Knight beat him up pretty good."

Then Annette Machuca, the MGM Grand's security manager, said she had seen Suge kick Orlando three times. Suge's lawyers pounced: Since the kicks didn't appear in the ten-second videotape of the fight, they felt Machuca was not credible. David Kenner cross-examined her, and got her to admit that her recall was not clear. In fact, Kenner stressed, it was so hazy, she could not remember "what she thought she saw and what she really recalls."

After court, Suge returned to his cell in the county jail, where he had to listen to inmates perform cellblock auditions and use a pay phone in his cell to continue running Death Row and get another two albums completed.

Testimony resumed the next day. Motionless and silent, Suge watched prosecutors push to have his probation revoked; they kept saying they wanted him in state prison for nine years. When his lawyers scored points, he turned and smiled at his audience. His legal arsenal decided to bring in their karate expert, Kent Moyer, who said he choreographed fight scenes for action movies and was "good friends" with Steven Seagal. After watching the video one hundred times, Moyer concluded that anyone studying a frame-by-frame breakdown of the first three seconds would be able to see that Suge's hands were in a defensive posture. "He's trying to stop the activity from [going] any further."

Czuleger called a recess that afternoon, saying Moyer could return to the stand during the next hearing on November 25, the next day Czuleger was available. Suge's mother, Maxine, was devastated. "I want him home for Thanksgiving," she told a reporter.

On November 21, Snoop's *The DoggFather* was reported to have sold 479,000 copies in its first week. While the figure was lower than the 803,000 first-week copies the Dre-produced *DoggyStyle* sold, it was still the third best-selling rap debut in 1996: behind Tupac's *All Eyez on Me* (566,000 first-week copies) and his chart-topping, posthumous Makaveli album (664,000 copies).

From his cell, Suge instructed Death Row employees to prepare for their fourth annual Thanksgiving turkey giveaway. He wanted the birds distributed to the poor families that would appear at the Compton Fashion Center parking lot at 11:30 the next morning. "Even with the tragic loss of Tupac Shakur and Mr. Knight's present inconveniences," Compton Councilwoman Marcine Shaw said, clearly moved, "this shows that their concerns are still with the community."

On Monday, November 25, two dozen of Suge's supporters gathered in the hallway outside the courtroom to hold hands and join in a prayer led by Danny Boy, who said they should pray for Suge and "our enemies."

Everyone said, "Amen."

"The entourage was always there," said *America's Most Wanted* reporter Lena Nozizwe. "Big-time. At every single hearing there was extra security to get into his courtroom. It was always filled with recording artists, bodyguards, people from back in the 'hood, at least a half dozen of California's best lawyers lined up at a table, and his mother, who was wearing a tight red sweatshirt."

Suge appeared in county blues and took the stand in his own defense, to clarify that he didn't punch or kick anyone that night at the MGM Grand. He was trying to "break up the rumble." He couldn't remember details about who did what when the fight broke out but knew he had no idea why it happened. Even though he never came forward to give hotel security, Las Vegas police, or his L.A. County probation officer details of the incident, he had "nothing to hide." He said, "It all happened so fast. It was like a bad dream."

The night Orlando Anderson was attacked, he and Tupac were walking through the hotel after the Tyson fight. Then, he stressed, Tupac ran ahead of him and started "a physical confrontation with a guy on the ground." It looked like he was participating, he explained, only because of his new alligator shoes: They had wood soles and made him slip on the hotel carpet, then onto the pile of people. When he tried to break up the fight, people grabbed his legs, but he pulled himself away and led everyone out of the casino.

"Did you punch anyone in that altercation?" Kenner asked.

"No, sir."

"Did you kick anyone in that altercation?"

"Absolutely not."

The video showed one of Death Row's employees, thirty-year-old Alton McDonald of Compton, trying to stomp Anderson out. Then a man in black jumped in. Asked about the guy, believed to be a close friend, Suge said he couldn't identify him. All he knew was he tried to end the fight. People grabbed for his legs, but he pulled himself away and left the hotel with Tupac.

Under cross-examination, prosecutor Bill Hodgman asked what made Tupac charge Anderson. "I don't recall exactly who was doing anything," Suge answered. "I don't want to be incarcerated. I definitely want to be on the streets."

The videotape was played in court. During the scene where Suge and Tupac led a crew of people out of the hotel, Judge Czuleger turned to Suge and asked, "Are you smiling there?"

"No. I was tired. And upset."

The next day, when Dr. Dre planned to release his Aftermath compilation, Death Row released its *Greatest Hits* album: While Dre had produced the majority of the label's biggest hits, from *DoggyStyle* to Tupac's "California Love," the CD booklet barely acknowledged him. The label printed a blurry photo, gave a brief mention, and included songs that attacked him (including Ice Cube's "No Vaseline," which he recorded for Priority, and newcomer J-Flex's acerbic "Who Been There, Who Done That," which accused Dre of hogging payment and credit for songs unknown rapper J-Flex now claimed he wrote: "Keep Their Heads Ringin'," "Natural Born Killers," and "California Love").

In court that day, Judge Czuleger ruled that Suge was an "active participant" in the attack on Anderson. The ruling changed everything. Suge now faced nine years in prison and would be forbidden from running the label.

Judge Czuleger was inclined to sentence him to the full nine years but needed a full report on Suge's background: After three months in state custody, where a diagnostic evaluation would be conducted, the judge wanted Suge back in court for sentencing. "He has a history of violence," Czuleger sighed. "I am concerned about those people in the community who are potential victims."

What happened next shocked everyone. "At the hearing, when the judge was saying he was gonna send Suge to prison, I heard this high-pitched cry," said an editor at *Rappages* magazine. "I thought it was a girl, you know? You ever see that movie *Friday?* when DJ Pooh gets his chain stolen and runs across the street? Well, it was like that. Well, I turned around, expecting to see a girl, and see Danny Boy crying! Leaving the courtroom like a bitch!"

Throughout Death Row's short history at the top of the charts, every aspect of Marion "Suge" Knight's public image had centered on how he loved being a real man. He told *The New York Times*, "A lot of guys are not men. Even if they have money or success, they are just males."

After Danny Boy's outbursts in the courtroom, rumors surfaced that he and Danny were having a relationship. "Somebody told me that when Suge got sentenced to his years in jail, Danny Boy was crying and needed to be consoled or some shit," said a record label executive. "Then the person who told me was like, Man, it looked like that type of shit, like . . . your woman would cry for you. Like, *Oh shit!* You kno'msaying? I don't know how true it was but I thought it was funny. If he did do that, that's got to be some classical 'funny' shit to me. Now I'm wondering what the hell is going on."

During her visit to California, *New York Times* reporter Lynn Hirschberg had seen seventeen-year-old Danny Boy at Can-Am Studios. "He's usually wherever Suge is," she noted. Despite the fact that singers Nate Dogg, Michel'lé, and Jewell were dying to work on albums of their own, Suge explained that he had been searching for an R&B singer to round out the label. "I wanted a guy with Michael Jackson status," Suge had said. "Not the hair and the skin, but that same kind of star quality. Like Snoop. Snoop is a star. And I wanted that in a singer."

He did research, he told Hirschberg, and since he didn't trust tapes, an audition had been arranged. After hearing thirty singers, he personally selected Danny Boy. "I wanted a guy under my wing who was sexy," Suge added. "I met Danny Boy. He's from Chicago. I met him when he was fifteen and he was right."

"Danny Boy, who is handsome in a teen-idol sort of way, beams at Suge's remark," Hirschberg wrote. "He is wearing a black and white ensemble—black sweats, black and white sneakers, white sweatshirt— and around his neck hangs his Christmas present from Suge, a gold medallion that spells Danny with the male sex sign across it in diamonds."

Danny Boy's glasses were going to be his gimmick, Suge crowed. The lenses were split horizontally; the upper half of the left lens was dim, as was the bottom half of the right lens. His spectacles would be worn low on his nose so Danny could peer over the frames and look wide-eyed and innocent.

When Danny Boy first arrived in L.A., Suge remembered, he rented him a room at the Peninsula, a posh luxury hotel in Beverly Hills. He also gave Danny the use of a Rolls-Royce limousine and a charge card for incidentals. But things got out of hand. "He had girls coming over for manicures and pedicures and Cristal and whatever!" Suge fumed. "And then I get this bill. I said, 'Don't be Hollywood.' And he stopped. I told him, 'Fans will always love you but that Hollywood shit is a problem.'"

Since then, Suge reported, Danny Boy had been a "model son" who strove to make him proud. With Hirschberg present, Suge said, "Sing something, Danny Boy. Sing." On command, Danny crooned a few syrupy notes. "When he's finished," Hirschberg reported, "he smiles at Suge and sort of rocks from side to side. Suge doesn't say anything." Within seconds, Suge predicted that Danny Boy would be a major star. Exhilarated, Danny Boy agreed, saying, "I think it's gonna happen."

"Suge," Hirschberg noticed, "just fixes him with that look of his. He doesn't think it's gonna happen. He knows." Apparently, Suge had decided that Nate Dogg and his other singers would have to wait. To Suge, Danny Boy came first.

The *L.A. Times* was polite when reporting on Danny's shocking outburst in the courtroom. "As Czuleger announced his decision, a *handful* of Knight's supporters, including top Death Row newcomer Danny Boy, bolted from the courtroom in tears." Asked for an opinion about Danny's wailing, producer Sam Sneed said, "I can't even speak on that. I know he's always with Suge. I guess that's 'Suge's little nigga' and he's just schooling him on the industry. That's what *I* thought it was. 'Cause Danny Boy's young!"

Producer Chocolate said, "You know what? I guess I been away, to be honest with you. 'Cause I ain't heard nothing about [Suge's] homosexuality. Only thing I've read is that he made some guys strip."

"It's funny that all this shit is coming out now," said an editor at *Rappages.* "I got people coming out the woodwork, claiming, 'Well, this happened to me too!'"

"It's kind of hard to believe about Suge unless he got 'turned-out' [persuaded to sleep with homosexual men] since he got all that money and shit," said artist manager Lamont Bloomfield. "With the bitches I used to see him bringing around, I'm thinking, 'Hell naw.'"

As the rumor spread, quicker than the one the late Tupac started about Dr. Dre, Suge's supporters grew furious. "Who's telling you that?" one of them asked. "Are you serious with all that? Naw, hell no. That's shocking to me. Shocking. I've *seen* Danny Boy. The funny thing about Danny Boy is DJ Black found him in Chicago. At that time, a kid named Shorty had him, he had a tape of him and another girl group on the flip side. But DJ Black hooked him up with Suge . . ." This man's voice slowed to a crawl. ". . . and I *did* see Danny at that Loud/TNT party . . ." His voice filled with suspicion. ". . . and there *was* a kind of '*feminineness*' [sic] about him when we spoke."

"You got a lot of prison motherfuckers who just *like* that shit," said an executive at another label. " 'Cause they actually got some sexual tendencies like that, youkno'msayin'? That might be it. Suge might be a little 'funny,' but he's probably just caught up in that jailhouse way of thinking."

The rumors were cruel.

They were also untrue, said Cheo Coker of the *L.A. Times.* "Danny Boy always saw Suge as a father figure," Coker quickly explained. "A lot of folks had love for Suge, and Danny was certainly one of them: Suge basically saved Danny from a life of extreme poverty and, um, was helping Danny, you know, make his dreams come true."

"WHY DON'T YOU LET THEM SEE THE SUGE I SEE?"

Prime Time Live *'s Suge Knight* update ran on February 5, weeks before Suge was scheduled to appear in court for sentencing on four probation violations, including an assault and smoking marijuana. This time, reporter Brian Ross focused on Tupac Shakur's mother, Afeni Shakur. Onscreen, the recovering crack addict wore a bandanna tied around her head, resembling the son she ordered unplugged from life support; she sat in her lawyer's office and discussed what really troubled her. "He absolutely thought he was quite rich," she said, "and that his family would, you know, be rich for . . . ever."

Teary-eyed, Ross sat and listened intently.

Afeni continued accusing Death Row of robbing her son. Her campaign against the label began as early as September 1996, when the label tried to organize a Tupac memorial at the Wilshire-Ebell Theater despite her protests. In November, she hired New York attorney Richard Fischbine, and threatened to bar the release of Tupac's posthumous release as Makaveli. "When Afeni brought her lawyer," said a high-ranking Interscope executive, "Jimmy told Suge to handle this. But Suge kept saying no. Jimmy said, 'You have to. Why don't you let them see the Suge I see?' Suge wouldn't listen, and that was the one time he had to act. But Jimmy stepped in and paid everyone to stop them from attacking each other. He wanted to be able to move forward."

On November 1, 1996, Afeni and her attorney, Fischbine, attended a meeting at Interscope's West Coast office. Suge and Kenner were not present. "It was Jimmy Iovine who took the lead in getting the ball rolling to straighten this mess out," said Fischbine. "Nothing would have happened if it wasn't for him. Death Row never even came to the table to have a discussion."

In addition to a $3-million "nonrefundable" advance, Interscope attorneys said the label would pay Afeni an additional $2 million in advances before April; they would also provide an upgrade in royalties (from twelve percent to eighteen percent) and allowed the new rate to apply to Tupac's earlier releases. As for the $4.9 million Death Row Records claimed Tupac owed? Interscope would forgive close to fifty percent of the debt, Fischbine claimed.

But Afeni was not finished with the label: On Friday, December 13, 1996, with Fischbine (who had been appointed co-administrator of Shakur's estate), Afeni decided to sue Death Row for fraud. The *All Eyez on Me* album contained an ad and order form for unauthorized merchandise, her lawsuit noted. Due to the advertising, thousands of baseball caps, T-shirts, and sweatshirts with Tupac's image had been sold: According to the suit, Death Row, a company called Globex, Cronies-Reproductive Images, and David E. Kenner had robbed Tupac of $1 million from sales of unauthorized merchandise. Though Kenner said the suit lacked merit, by December 24, Afeni had succeeded in preventing the label from continuing to profit from the items. A judge ordered that the company discontinue production of the items. Then, on January 22, federal judge William Matthew Byrne ruled that Death Row had to stop selling Tupac merchandise and pay Afeni eighteen percent of the gross moneys earned in 1996—$500,000 in back revenues.

Next, Afeni questioned why, despite his albums earning over $60 million, Death Row Records continued to assert that Tupac still owed them

$4.9 million. "Tupac was one of the most successful artists in the music business and yet, somehow—on the day he died, he had absolutely nothing," said Fischbine.

An auditor was hired to conduct an independent accounting, but Death Row wouldn't provide the necessary books. Though *All Eyez on Me* had sold five million copies, Fischbine noted, "He was paid less than a million dollars as far as we can see. They've never opened the books so that we can see." They continued to file lawsuits accusing the label of wrongly billing Tupac's account for others' expenses in a "pattern of fraud and deception involving millions of dollars."

In response, Death Row blamed Tupac's extravagant spending habits for the huge debt: Tupac used his large advances to buy several cars and a home for Afeni. Then he stuck the label with lease payments for three homes, a $300,000 tab at the Peninsula, hundreds of thousands of dollars in invoices for furniture, jewelry, security, and limo services, and over $2 million in recording and video costs.

Although many industry executives felt Afeni was premature in accusing Death Row of robbing her son, she continued her crusade against the label. Former Death Row employee Doug Young said, "First of all, Death Row put down that million-dollar bond, meaning Tupac owed him a million. A lot of people not in this business have to understand that Tupac would have gotten his royalties a year and a half after *All Eyez on Me* came out. And that's after the label recouped what they spent on his videos, recording costs, a million-dollar bond, and the car and house Suge bought him. It was nowhere near a year and a half after the album came out, and Suge still had to recoup before Tupac's account could actually turn a profit."

When Afeni appeared on *Prime Time Live*, she and Richard Fischbine had already begun to question Tupac's actual contract, a three-page document Fischbine said was unlike anything he had ever seen. "It's nothing but toilet paper," he scoffed.

Wiping tears from her eyes, Afeni continued telling sympathetic white reporter Brian Ross that Death Row Records had defrauded her late son. "Please remember that my great-grandmother was a slave, my grandmother was a sharecropper, my mother was a factory worker, and I was a legal worker, do you understand? And so this represents the first time in our lives, in our memory, ever, that we have been able to enjoy the American dream, and that's what Tupac brought to this family.

"I discovered he had next to zero, next to nothing," she continued. "I discovered that the home that he had thought that he had just bought was not his."

By segment's end, accusations of impropriety had been leveled at David Kenner, the contract Tupac signed was called "a joke," and Suge was accused of withholding royalties and underpaying Tupac. "And now," Ross intoned, "Tupac's mother says not only is her son's money missing but, more important, the master recordings of the some two hundred songs he wrote and sang, potentially worth hundreds of millions of dollars."

"We don't know where the masters are because we can't get an accounting—ha!—from Death Row Records," Afeni said.

"You don't know where they are?"

"We don't know where they are," she whispered.

The label also had to deal with the lawsuit American Express Travel Related Services filed in January 1997: The credit card company was suing Suge and Kenner for nonpayment, accusing them and Kenner's wife of running up $1,574,000 in bills. "And AmEx isn't gonna hold anyone at gunpoint to get it," *The Phoenix New Times* reported. "It's gonna do it the old-fashioned way." In a suit filed in L.A. Superior Court, the company wanted payment in full, plus court costs, attorneys' fees, and prejudgment interest. "Unfortunately for AmEx," *The New Times* added, "with the FBI, DEA, ATF, and IRS scrutinizing Death Row and Knight's Club 662 in Las Vegas under the RICO statutes, the credit card company may have to get in line for a piece of the action."

Then producer Johnny Jackson filed suit against Death Row, Interscope, and MCA: As Johnny J, he had produced eleven songs on Tupac's *All Eyez on Me*, including the Grammy-nominated "How Do U Want It." Suge promised to pay $10,000 per song, plus royalties. Since he wouldn't pay, Jackson was claiming "unspecified compensatory and punitive damages for alleged breach of contract and fraud."

Suge also faced a horde of creditors who claimed the company owed them millions for goods and services. A $75-million lawsuit sought to have the label put into receivership to protect its assets. Then Suge's former mentor, Solar Records' Dick Griffey, and disgruntled rapper the DOC filed a $125-million breach-of-contract suit against Death Row: When Solar released the *Deep Cover* soundtrack, Griffey and the DOC claimed they were original partners in Death Row. But they were squeezed out by Suge, Dr. Dre, and Interscope Records. Now Griffey and the DOC wanted a court-appointed receiver to take over Death Row, to make sure, in the words of former Solar president Virgil Roberts, that "the company doesn't go away, which in Death Row's case is a distinct possibility."

David Kenner refused to comment on any of the lawsuits.

The words L.A. COUNTY JAIL were stenciled on the back of his county-issue blue shirt. His glacial stare arced over the throng his sentencing hearing had attracted. It was February 28 and Suge hoped he would be going home. During the last court session, Judge Czuleger said he would send him to jail; Danny Boy bolted from the courtroom in tears; Deputy District Attorney Bill Hodgman reminded the judge that Suge had never appealed the original sentence—Czuleger was now bound by law to impose the entire nine-year sentence.

Wearing an ill-fitting black suit with a red tie, David E. Kenner tried to look like a no-nonsense lawyer. But his eyes had bags under them; his voice was frail; he looked unhealthy. He sat to Suge's left and turned his head when someone in the audience stifled a cough.

So far, the judge had denied their motion for a stay. Kenner rose to his feet and explained why more time was needed. Czuleger cut him off again. But Kenner persisted, explaining that he wanted to subpoena the people who had prepared these supplemental reports. Prosecutors accused the defense of stalling for time. These reports were good enough. "Are you able to say if there's an ongoing criminal investigation?" the judge asked.

A blonde from the attorney general's office said yes.

The judge reclined in his black leather seat, rocked back and forth, and pointed a finger. "Any last words, Mr. Kenner?"

Kenner wanted Suge to testify.

"Shouldn't this have been addressed in a 1203.03?"

The defense filed a subpoena, Kenner explained.

Czuleger wanted a 1203.03. "Motions to quash both of them are granted," he said.

Kenner frowned at pages scattered on the defense table.

Another of Suge's lawyers, a stone-faced blonde, accused police officers of perjury; she demanded that the probation violation be thrown out. The judge disagreed, then denied a motion of discovery.

The morning recess finally arrived. Aggrieved Death Row supporters wandered down corridors. Snoop arrived in a flashy blue pinstripe suit, his braids slicked back. Somber label supporters relayed the morning's events. Taciturn, Snoop nodded and stroked the fiendish pointed goatee hanging from his chin.

That afternoon in court, David Kenner rose to his feet. "I think again we need to have a hearing. I ask the court to reconsider its denial of hearing."

"Anything else?"

"I'm boring you."

"You're not boring me, Mr. Kenner. It's my job to move things along."

Ten minutes later, Kenner repeated that Suge truly did require a hearing. Another defense lawyer said all Suge did was slightly kick someone described by the court as "a perjurous gangbanger." Pointing at Suge, this lawyer said, laughably, "A *man's freedom is at stake!*"

This case was based on testimony from a Nevada cop who had perjured himself in court, Kenner claimed. "*Will you let that happen?!*" And another crooked cop also guilty of perjury. In fact, to Kenner's eyes, the issue wasn't whether Suge violated probation by kicking Orlando Anderson. It was that the district attorney continued to pursue this case because his office had trouble "convicting celebrities."

Deputy District Attorney Bill Hodgman accused the defense of trying to stall for time.

"*They can be insulted, offended, whatever! I don't care! I'm here for one reason. To help Mr. Knight get out of here. His life is at stake! We need a hearing about this, your honor.*" Even Orlando Anderson denied that Suge was involved in attacking him, the lawyer calmly noted.

With annoyance, Czuleger shook his head. To him, Anderson was so patently unbelievable while trying to exculpate Mr. Knight that his testimony was useless. After dismissing everything, Czuleger mentioned that he was ready for sentencing.

One last lawyer, a pallid, tight-lipped man named Hersh, requested permission to put two witnesses on the stand. Czuleger agreed, but only if they addressed the 1203.03.

The first witness, Dr. Coburn, was introduced as a "board certified psychiatrist." While launching into his credentials on the stand, the judge cut him off. "I'm sorry," he said. "Right now we're dealing with the sentencing matter."

Coburn discussed a report on Suge's mental health. The report had been prepared by a correctional officer, a staff psychiatrist (with a Ph.D.), and the associate warden, who summarized what the other two had concluded. It detailed the psychiatric evaluation, whether Knight should receive probation or prison time, and had been critical of Suge: According to its authors, Suge portrayed himself as a victim; he refused to accept responsibility for his actions; he had a "proclivity toward physical action" and associated with violent rappers. He was "criminally oriented," "unsuitable for probation," and harbored a "negative attitude toward probation." Since his past and recent history involved violent activity, its authors predicted that his "problematic behavior" would continue in the future.

After noting that he had read hundreds of these reports, Coburn said he disagreed with this one's findings. The judge rocked in his seat, checked through notepads, or shuffled loose pages. To Dr. Coburn, Suge was not "a marginal candidate for reinstatement of probation." Shaking his head, he claimed Suge was, in fact, pro-social: He had no propensity for violence, no adult antisocial behavior, no psychological impairments. And no "pattern of dangerous behavior." "He's not a violent person. He's not a dangerous person."

Marion Knight was a good businessman with benevolent intentions, Coburn reported: He shared his good fortune with those around him; he had a good support system with his family and welcomed "feedback regarding his irresponsible behavior." Though the report said "Mr. Knight's arrests would involve serious assaultive behavior and violent offenses," Coburn pointed out that in the last five years there had been nothing but a potential kick: no gun wounds, broken jaws—

Prosecutor Bill Hodgman's questions established that Dr. Coburn was paid ("in part") $1500 as a flat fee for the first exam—then $250 an hour. In fact, Death Row Records still owed him $2500. Wasn't that right? Reluctantly, Coburn nodded. And how much time did Dr. Coburn spend actually reviewing these materials? "An hour or two," he admitted.

With a firm nod, Hodgman summarized Suge's criminal history: In 1987 Suge pleaded guilty to battery with a deadly weapon; on September 19, 1990, he pleaded guilty to violating Penal Code 242, battery, in Beverly Hills; on October 31, 1990, he pleaded nolo contendere to violating 242, battery, in Hollywood, and received twenty-four months summary probation. "This was his second grant of probation," Hodgman noted.

On December 24, 1990, Suge pleaded guilty to violating Penal Code 415—disturbing the peace—in Van Nuys; on December 4, 1991, he violated Penal Code 12025 sub A—carrying a concealed weapon—and attempted to give a phony name, identifying himself as "Richard Chappin." On November 24, 1992, in Clark County, Nevada, he was found guilty of assault with the use of a deadly weapon as a felony and placed on probation again: On January 19, 1993, he was granted probation for an indeterminate term not to exceed three years. On January 18, 1995, in federal court in Vegas, he was charged with conspiracy to illegally possess a firearm (18 U.S. Code 371) and granted a supervised release program. On February 9, 1995, he pleaded guilty to two counts of assault with a firearm and again received probation. After a breath, Hodgman said Suge had lied to Dr. Coburn.

Coburn replied that he would entrust his family to Suge.

Ignoring him, Hodgman told the judge he would like to introduce five photographs. The defense were up in arms, chairs scraping, raised voices, protest. With a groan, Czuleger said the court would recess for lunch. He left the chamber with his black robe billowing like a cape.

During the recess, singer Nate Dogg led his girlfriend away from the courtroom and onto an elevator. MC Hammer, in what seemed to be his only suit (the threadbare gray one with the Nehru collar worn for every magazine photo session) left with other Death Row employees. Snoop and his friends crossed a parking lot and loitered in front of their luxury cars. Four teenage girls involved in the so-called "free Suge" march spotted him and yelled, "Ooh!" They quickened their step, reduced to chasing his car for autographs. The lunch recess ended and with it, Snoop's appearance at the sentencing hearing.

In the courtroom, Kenner stood near Suge's five other lawyers and watched Suge enter with more pep in his step. This time his cold stare lingered on the media section. Label publicist George Pryce appeared in a somber black suit and sat directly behind Suge's legal arsenal. Judge Czuleger assumed his post and listened to Kenner object to the five photographs prosecutor Hodgman wanted to introduce.

Czuleger asked to see them. "The court tells me there are only four."

As Czuleger considered the photographs, Hodgman attempted to introduce a transcript of a conversation between Suge and a prison guard named Charles Brittin on the subject of whether Suge should be placed in a gang module. "This is not a gang case," Czuleger said with a frown.

On the witness stand again, Dr. Coburn was now presented as a psychologist who had interviewed innumerable gang members. As Coburn stared at the four photographs, prosecutor Hodgman asked if he would recognize people flashing gang signs. To the crowd's delight, Coburn replied, *"I have trouble doing the handshake!"*

Look at these photos, he said firmly. Wouldn't it seem that Suge and these Death Row people were throwing up gang-identifying hand signals? Yes or no.

"This is not a gang case," Czuleger repeated.

Coburn looked relieved.

On redirect, Suge's wan lawyer, Hersh, pointed out that of the five probation grants Suge had received, two were successfully completed without incident. Then he called the next witness, Dr. Fairstein, a professor of psychology at UCLA who had testified in 250 court cases. Fairstein also disagreed with the report: This report did not state the "underlying facts," that Suge's positives outweighed his negatives. At this, a reporter laughed out loud and publicist George Pryce turned his bald head as if to say, Who dares?

Next, Suge's team of lawyers were allowed to call Rahiem Jenkins to the stand. Forty-seven-year-old Jenkins, who worked with a Washington,

D.C.,–based group called the Righteous Men Commission, wore a pea-green suit; his hair was clean-cut; his chin was covered with a three-day growth and a thick goatee. Suge's lawyers passed Czuleger his résumé. Jenkins beamed. On the stand he detailed how he wanted a national peace treaty signed by the gangs on Father's Day. Since Suge had a "powerful impact" on American youth, Suge could help. Defense lawyer Milton Grimes, who had previously defended Rodney King, asked Jenkins, How can you use Mr. Knight?

"That goes without saying. Through his funding. That's the bottom line."

How is Suge different from other rich men?

"His record company." Death Row employed Bloods and Crips; these rival gang members worked in peace. Hopefully, Knight could share his peacekeeping techniques with the Righteous Men Commission. If the judge allowed Knight to go free, Jenkins would force Suge to take a "hands-on" approach to this national gang truce. Suge, Jenkins added, had emerged as a "Berry Gordy, head of Motown."

Only now did Suge pay attention to his character witness.

Suge could use his influence and fame to help steer kids away from gangs, Jenkins added. Even C. Delores Tucker, sitting in a back row, knew that. And Tucker, Jenkins wanted everyone to know, was in the courtroom today. Despite the fact that in early 1996 Suge decided to retaliate against her for attacks she had made against his label.

Back then Tucker had spent most of her time giving depositions for a civil suit Death Row had filed against her. Suge accused her of having an economic motive for criticizing rap music. According to the lawsuit, Tucker had tried to persuade Suge to relinquish creative and financial control of Death Row during the summer of 1995; she asked Suge to sign a document appointing her Death Row's exclusive representative during negotiations with Time Warner for a new "clean" rap venture they would finance. Tucker, the suit claimed, had offered Suge two choices—work with her or see her organization use its "power to cause the government to go after Knight" and his artists, several of whom were on probation. According to Death Row's lawsuit, C. Delores Tucker was guilty of contractual interference, extortion, and unfair business practices.

After the label hired San Francisco detective firm Palladino & Sutherland to sift through her past, Suge openly challenged Tucker's credibility. In interviews with national music magazines, Suge accused her of misrepresenting her education—Tucker, he revealed, derived her title from honorary degrees issued by Sumter S.C.'s Morris College and Erie, Pa.'s Villa Maria College. "Delores Tucker is a hoax," Suge added. "She pretends to care about the black community, but if you look into her history, you find she was a slumlord. She pretends to want to help young black males, but she's trying to destroy a company owned and run by them. She pretends to be a doctor. But, hey, she's about as much of a doctor as Dr. Dre is."

Sixty-seven-year-old Tucker had called the lawsuit nonsense. "Sure, we talked with Suge Knight, but the allegations in the suit are just lies. They want me to back off, but I won't. It's important to pay attention to who is dredging up all these charges. Remember: These are the same people who are out there pimping pornography to your children. Their record, and records, speak for them. I've been an activist all my life. My record speaks for itself." As of this writing, nothing has come of Death Row's lawsuit against Tucker.

But now Tucker was in the courtroom, Rahiem Jenkins noted once more: And if Tucker could forgive Suge, then the courts should also "embrace" him. In response, Suge nodded like a churchgoer.

Defense lawyer Milton Grimes asked Jenkins to explain the rift between Tucker and Suge, and the significance of her presence at this hearing. But Judge Czuleger interrupted: He knew all about the debate over gangsta rap lyrics. Move on.

As Jenkins spoke of wanting to save young black lives, a gloom drifted over spectators. This was what gangsta rap was supposed to accomplish. But it had all gone wrong. A rapper had been killed gangland style on the streets of Las Vegas, a CEO was facing nine years, and the feds were probing a record label's activities. Jenkins's words brought a sad political tone to the hearing. "We have a real responsibility to do what's right in this case and put pressure on Mr. Knight," he concluded. "Right now he's a captive audience—"

As Jenkins left the stand, Suge's pale lawyer, Hersh, beamed with confidence. Then the next witness, Melba Jackson Carter, took the stand. For fifteen years she had been working to help young black males learn job skills that would put them on "an equal plane." And she was surprised when, a month ago, Suge's lawyers told her Suge Knight wanted to help.

Her testimony seemed to be an attempt to expunge Suge's bad reputation. As she spoke about finding jobs for black youth, rebuilding their self-esteem, and giving them real opportunities, Suge nodded his head in agreement. "We see him as a wonderful ambassador," Carter said before adding that Suge would actually have to work for her program or answer to her.

Finally, Danny J. Blakewell of the Brotherhood Crusade took the stand. A black man who appeared to be in his forties, Blakewell had a thick beard and hairstyle that evoked country singer Kenny Rogers. Without delay he called Suge "a compassionate man, a strong black man . . ." Blakewell listed Suge's many contributions to the black community: Mother's Day events, toy giveaways, donating artists to benefit concerts—

Before Tupac's death, Suge had donated $50,000 for a "family time" concert and met with one hundred gang members in his Death Row office: He urged them to exercise their right to vote and work with the Brotherhood Crusade to improve their communities. As Blakewell spoke, Suge drooped in his seat.

"I'd like to hear from the prosecution," the judge said, "then the defense counsel, then from the defendant himself."

On his feet again, prosecutor Hodgman tried to introduce the photos that clearly showed Suge and his friends promoting the "M.O.B. and Piru gangs." Czuleger sighed. "Doesn't get anywhere. My kids throw gang signs."

As everyone laughed, Hodgman requested that Suge receive the full nine years. The bargain reached on February 9, 1995, had been: Stay clean or face this sentence. "He has to accept responsibility for his fate . . ." During his "criminal career," Suge received six grants of probation. "How many bites of the probation apple will this defendant receive? Six counts of probation are enough."

After Hodgman's grim presentation, David Kenner stood behind the podium and in his most gentle tone said he wanted to speak his heart and mind: Everyone was after Suge because he was famous, and the nine-year sentence was repugnant. Suge had been in jail five months already, spending time in "Palm Hall," the Administrative Segregation Unit, shackled hand and foot, deprived of benefits and allowed no time in the yard or outdoors.

At L.A. County Jail, Kenner explained, Suge was in a "high-profile module, or area." With shackles and cuffs. "These five months have been severe, shocking, draconian." If the court wanted to teach Suge a lesson, these last five months had accomplished just that. "It's not appropriate for there to be a state prison sentence of any sort. There's not any inherent risk or danger to the community." His suggestion? Grant Suge probation. To do otherwise would amount to treating him as a "political prisoner."

Finally Suge raised his chin and faced the judge. He wanted to speak on his own behalf. In a voice that wavered between remorse and quiet menace, Suge said, "I'm not here to try and sugar-coat my life and say I've been the most perfect guy in the world." At his side, Kenner looked uncomfortable. "But this is my life," Suge added, "and I feel I should speak about my life. I've learned a lot from being incarcerated. I've gotten closer to God and I've read the Bible inside out. I've learned that my role in the community is important as far as kids and the elders. I do a lot of good in the community and I don't do it for publicity or fame. The stuff I've done has come from the heart.

"I know in the past, when I was working security in the music business, a few times I had fights. These were fights with my hands. I'm guilty for those fights, and I got punished for them.

"When I walk through this courtroom, I see the D.A. say everybody hates me; I'm a bad guy; I'm this monster. And I don't see it. 'Cause if I was that type of person, these guys wouldn't keep following me around, coming to the studio wanting to work with me, coming to jail to visit with me.

"I'm not trying to be a politician. I believe in the community 'cause that's all I've ever had. I've seen mayors, even the president, give speeches and say they gonna give back to the community, that they'll hire people from the community. And we never see it. When I was growing up, it never happened.

"So when—thanks to God—I was able to make a little money and do these things, I done them. But instead of someone giving me applause, they slandered my name. A few times, I was treated like a wild animal. And the way you treat a wild animal is: You either catch him and hunt him down or throw him in a cage. Or kill him.

"I've been in a cage for five months, where they feed me when they want to feed me, and they give me water when they feel I should have water. And I was 'this-close' to being dead 'cause I still got the bullet in my head," he claimed, despite having only been grazed by one shot.

"Being in prison," he added, "has made me realize I definitely don't want to do my life behind bars. But if it's more positive for the community by me being incarcerated, I'm willing to sacrifice. I'm willing to give my life for a friend or for kids. I really feel I'm more positive now.

"I'd like to take out time to thank Dr. Tucker for coming down. It was a surprise because we always been on different sides of the fence. I know Dr. Tucker argued with me a lot about some of our lyrics, but I've made my own decision that any album I put out, the artist can never use the word, 'nigger.' After being in County, I can't put out a record just to say 'anything' anymore.

"So I don't agree with all the things that's being brought against me right now as far as my reputation. I am a man, your honor, and I have a family and kids and loved ones. And I would like them to know the truth.

"I been through a lot this year. I lost my best friend. A lot of people don't realize how it is to lose a best friend. I always wanted a little brother, and now he's not here. Besides all that, I'm not mad, but I'm disappointed at Tupac's mother. While I'm incarcerated, people tell her that the songs I paid for and marketed is her songs. And she made statements saying that he never got any money. I got signed documents where he received over $2.5 million, even before he was supposed to receive money. And beyond all that, when he was incarcerated, I gave his mother $3 million. But when the media gets it, it turns around that I left him for dead, I left him with zero and that I'm this monster.

"Whether it's my competition or prosecution, they made me look like Frankenstein. And if I look like Frankenstein, even though Frankenstein could be the nicest creature on earth, when he failed or when he died, everybody applauded. They clapped instead of cried.

"And as far as the situation with the fight, I'm not trying to open up the case or go back to the incident in Vegas, but I wanna stipulate on that because it's important to me. 'Cause I gotta live with this. When Anderson came up to testify, I'd be the first to say, he's not a friend of mine. And to be honest, I felt that this guy could play with the truth and go against me just to lie. But since he was under oath, I felt he told the truth.

"Your honor, I *was* breakin' up the fight. I knew I was on probation. I put my freedom and my life on the line. And I feel if I wouldn't have stopped that fight—I'm not saying the person who came and shot us later was these type of people, but if they was—instead of me getting shot in my head and one person dead, it could have been thirty people dead in Vegas at the MGM.

"And even at the end, your honor, when everybody say 'It was a kick,' it wasn't a kick. I admit that I was breaking up a fight, and I admit I was frustrated. But at the same time, it wasn't no nine-year kick. This guy wasn't harmed, wasn't anything broke on him. If you ask anybody that seen me fight, your honor, the first thing they'd tell you is 'That guy wouldn't be standing there giving statements.' When I fight, sir, I fight.

"But I've changed my life to get away from fighting. And I wanna enlighten not just you, but the courtroom, because my family is here. And it might be the last time I speak to my family. I could go to jail and anything could happen. But I'm not here for the judge to feel pity for me. I'm just speaking from my heart.

"When I was at Chino, one of the counselors asked me what if one of the conditions for getting out of jail was 'You can't be involved with Death Row Records.' I told him, 'I love Death Row. I love the music business.' Because I was lucky enough that God found something for me to do, to be successful and help people. That was the only calling I had. Everything happened so fast, I never had nobody to consult with me, I never had anybody to help me, because each person I met in this business, they always wanted to take, take, take.

"I'm not gonna waste any more of the court's time, but I just thought it was important that I get this off my chest and address the court the way I feel."

Suge's lawyer Milton Grimes leaped to his feet. "It wasn't one of those 'vicious' kicks," he said. "*You need him! I need him! Our families need him!*"

Emotionless, Czuleger called for a ten-minute recess.

Led back into the courtroom, Suge saw the prosecutors staring with hard faces. His lawyer Hersh stepped in front of him, blocking the view; with a confident smile Hersh slapped his arms. Unfortunately, during his speech, Suge Knight had chosen to label the Stanley brothers "the aggressors," and stressed that he never pleaded guilty to assaulting them; he also boasted of owning his master tapes, a claim not even Prince could make.

Czuleger rushed in and told everyone to sit. Three armed officers positioned themselves behind Suge's chair. Everyone faced Suge, searching for signs of criminality. Czuleger said he felt Suge had squandered benefits and advantages. "You blew it. I really hate to say it, but you really did. You really had everything going for you. Unfortunately, you found yourself in either a certain environment or atmosphere that has resulted in violent conduct." Suge tried to interrupt. "Let me finish, Mr. Knight."

Suge's eight convictions and refusal to "accept responsibility for his acts" led Czuleger to see only two options: return him to probation or sentence him to state prison. Shaking his head, he said, "I can't trust you. I wish I could." He sentenced him to nine years. As Suge nodded, Czuleger calculated that he had already served 375 days. Rising to his feet, Suge gave David Kenner a firm handshake. Then he allowed the guards to lead him away.

After the verdict, the label called a press conference on the twelfth floor of the court building. "This was not proper," David Kenner said. "This was inappropriate. We will be filing appeals and we will do what is necessary to correct what this clearly is, which is a miscarriage of justice." Death Row was a movement, he explained, that would continue to function under Suge's direction.

Danny Boy, who came to the label at age fifteen after his dying mother allowed Suge to become his legal guardian, reassured the media that Death Row would remain in business. "Suge Knight is the brain of

Death Row, but we are his thoughts. I'm here with Death Row until the world blows up. I'm here at Death Row because we are not going anywhere."

A tearful Maxine Knight said, "Death Row is moving on, even if I have to run it."

Outside, Suge's thirty-four-year-old brother-in-law, Norris Anderson, smoked a Marlboro. When Knight was jailed the year before, Anderson, who met Knight's sister during the 1970s and married her a decade later, went from answering phones to acting as general manager. But he soon realized he was nothing but a figurehead. "Suge was still the man at the controls. I was in contact with him. He made the decisions and I made sure they were carried out."

Anderson said he hated the present circumstances. "We have a whole lot of adversity ahead. There's still federal investigations going on. There's still the shock of this decision. Everybody here is not like brother and sister. We have our arguments and disagreements too."

Many of the attacks against the label, he knew, were due to its image. But everyone had the wrong impression of Death Row. "When I first started working there, I used to hear all the stories," he recalled. "And people would come to our office and they would walk in scared. They had heard the music and they had made up their own minds what they were going to see when they got here. But when they would come out of a meeting with Mr. Knight, you would have thought they shot heroin, they were so relaxed and happy."

"ALL OF A SUDDEN I HEARD ABOUT FIVE OR SIX SHOTS: POW, POW, POW, POW, POW,

Thanks to hip-hop's woes, the 1997 Soul Train Awards ceremony, held in Los Angeles, was rife with tension. Behind a podium
onstage a little over a week after Suge was sentenced, rapper Biggie
Smalls had barely finished announcing the nominees, when the embit-
tered crowd released a chorus of boos. "What's up, Cali?" Biggie yelled
in response, then handed an award to R&B singer Toni Braxton.

"Puffy thought it was all calmed down out here," an unidentified
industry source told *Vibe*. "But at Soul Train, there were boos and they
were throwin' up Westside from the balcony." Fingers curled to resemble
a **W**. "That should have been a sign right there."

Using a cane to support the leg he had broken during a recent car
accident, six-foot-three, three-hundred-pound Biggie left the brightly lit
stage.

Holed up in his posh $275-a-night suite at the Westwood Marquis
Hotel in Beverly Hills, Biggie reflected on his life. Thanks to his former

friend Tupac Shakur, the West Coast disliked him and also believed that his wife, Faith Evans, was pregnant with Tupac's child.

During a guest appearance on Brooklyn rapper Jaÿ-Z's song "Brooklyn's Finest," Biggie addressed the rumor. "If Fay has twins, she'll probably have two pacs," he rapped. "Get it? Tu . . . Pac's." All he could do was laugh: When 'Pac first claimed he slept with Faith, Biggie confronted her. You fucked him? She said, No. Since Tupac was dead, Biggie couldn't ask him. "So am I gonna hate her for the rest of her life thinking she did something? Or am I gonna be a man about the situation? If she did it, she can't do it no more, so let's just get on with our lives."

Though he and Faith had decided to separate, Biggie still thought about her. "I married her after knowing her eight days and I was happy," he said in his final interview. "That was my baby. At the same time, with us being so spontaneous, we did it backward. Maybe she won't admit it, but I will. We should have got to know each other and then got married. The relationship kind of dissolved, but we're still going to be friends. I love her. We have a baby together, and we're always gonna love our kids. Who knows? Ten years from now we might even get back together."

The next night, at the Petersen Automotive Museum in the Wilshire district, *Vibe* magazine threw a party to celebrate the eleventh annual Soul Train Awards. Don Cornelius, executive producer of *Soul Train*, said the weekly dance show had nothing to do with the event. For close to a year, Quincy Jones's national monthly had been reporting on the so-called feud between the coasts. One employee said, "I truly believe *Vibe* is responsible. I refuse to let them off the hook. But not just *Vibe*. *The Source*, all of them—they celebrated this feud every month like it was fun and games instead of real people with real guns and bullets. *Vibe* and *The Source* blew it up to the point where they added fuel to the fire."

Vibe's party attracted rapper Busta Rhymes, entertainment mogul Russell Simmons, Uptown Records artist-turned-executive Heavy D, rapper/*Vibe* columnist Yo-Yo, Snoop-clone Da Brat, Dre-clone Jermaine Dupri, comedian Keenen Ivory Wayans, MTV-creation Jenny McCarthy, and basketball player Grant Hill.

Believing it to be a closed affair, for industry executives only, Sean "Puffy" Combs decided it would be safe to attend. During their business trip to California, they had been careful about public appearances. Though many people thought it unwise for them to travel to California so soon after Tupac's murder, Combs wanted superior production values for Biggie's videos: He envisioned overblown, extravagant epics that would rival the big-budget action films Hollywood produced. Biggie, meanwhile, thought the trip would be an opportunity to appear on West Coast radio stations and proclaim his love for California.

At the *Vibe* party, Puffy and Biggie made a reserved entrance. At a table in a dark corner, Biggie took a seat, set his walking cane aside, and watched the crowd dance to current rap hits. Entertainment mogul Russell Simmons, who shared their table, said, "I was throwin' paper at him, tellin' him how much I liked his record. These girls were dancin' for him and he was just sittin' there, not even movin' his cane. I told him I wanted to be like him. He was so cool; so funny and calm."

During the trip, Biggie had spent much of his time thinking about his former friend Tupac's murder. "You be thinking that when a nigga is making so much money that his lifestyle will protect him," Biggie said in his final interview, "that a drive-by shooting ain't supposed to happen."

But he had nothing to fear at the peaceful *Vibe* party. The audience seemed weary of the animosity between the East and West coasts. "I was right up in there," said videographer Matt McDaniel, "having a ball and loving it. Matter of fact, other people were saying, 'Is it me or is this party fun? This is kinda nice.'"

When the DJ premiered Biggie's new funk rap "Going Back to Cali," the crowd cheered. By then the room was filled to capacity. Some party-goers decided to light marijuana cigarettes: Others drank heavily and raised their voices. By 12:35 A.M. the air was so clouded with marijuana smoke, someone stepped onstage to address the crowd. "Please stop smoking blunts," this person said. "The fire marshal's gonna turn the party out!"

Within thirty minutes, partygoers were drained: The chamber was brimming with heavy smokers; the air was stifling; the mood changed; the party now felt like it was winding down. People began to crowd the coat check area.

Using his cane, Biggie headed for the exit. Junior M.A.F.I.A. rapper Little Caesar and Puffy stood near him, in case he needed help. "Biggie had a broken leg at the time, so it took us a while to get out," Puffy explained. They finally made it outdoors. The air was cool. Attendees milled about, waiting for their valet-parked cars. It was a quarter to one. Biggie chatted with his label head, unaware that undercover officers from New York were in the vicinity, part of a federal investigation of criminals allegedly affiliated with Bad Boy, which the Justice Department, the LAPD, and the NYPD refused to comment on.

At the curb, Biggie and Puffy debated about whether to attend another party or call it a night and return to their suites at the Marquis Hotel. "It's time to leave," Puffy decided, then entered his car.

After entering the rented GMC Suburban parked behind Puffy's car, Biggie began to showcase his new double album, *Life After Death*. Faith Evans, who had recently named her newborn son Christopher Wallace Jr., was nearby; fans leaned in to read the sticker attached to the wheel of the Suburban: To promote his new album, the label printed up stickers reading THINK B.I.G. MARCH 25TH.

Behind both vehicles, bodyguards sat in a third car. One police officer and as many as six acted as security guards for Biggie and may have witnessed what happened next. But none came forward to say they were present, including the one off-duty cop who sat directly behind Biggie in the GMC Suburban. "If they were there all that time before, it just seems impossible to me that they didn't see the incident," Biggie's old friend Damion Butler would say later. "Where did they go? They had to see it."

As Puffy drove away, Biggie settled into the GMC's front passenger seat and watched his friends Little Caesar and Damion enter. After driving out of the museum parking lot, the trio made a right turn. The automotive museum was still in view; hundreds of people stood around and socialized; Biggie's estranged wife, Faith, watched the caravan leave.

From his car up ahead, Puffy watched the GMC. One after the other, the vehicles stopped at a red light. They did not see the dark green vehicle driving erratically, stopping on the GMC's right side, discharging passengers. "All of a sudden I heard about five or six shots," said a security guard across the street. "Pow, pow, pow, pow, pow."

Everyone in Puffy's car stooped to avoid being hit. Someone yelped that Biggie's GMC was under attack. The shooters hastily reentered their dark green vehicle and drove away. Puffy threw his door open, left the moving car, and ran toward the bullet-riddled GMC Suburban. He knew Biggie's leg was broken. "There's no way he could have made it out of the car."

Puffy opened the door, saw Biggie hunched over the dashboard, and tried to speak with him. But Biggie was still and silent. Turning to a security guard, Puffy said, Jump in and get us to the nearest hospital.

The Suburban headed for Cedars-Sinai Medical Center, where Eazy-E had spent his final days. They were speeding; fans joined the caravan. Puffy kept trying to talk to Biggie, who still didn't respond. Frightened, Puffy began to pray over his body. At the hospital, people leaped out of their cars and helped carry the fallen rapper onto a stretcher. Inside, doctors rushed him into surgery. Everyone dropped to their knees and prayed. Within minutes, Christopher ("Biggie Smalls") Wallace was pronounced dead.

By the end of business hours on March 10, a rumor spread across North America. In retaliation for Biggie's death, an inmate had attacked Death Row CEO Marion "Suge" Knight in prison. "They ran up on him in jail," a source at *Rappages* magazine claimed. "He got stabbed like eleven times with a chicken bone."

Death Row had to issue a statement: After offering condolences to Biggie's family, they wrote, "In addition, Death Row Records would like to dispel all rumors and speculation of a prison stabbing incident involving Knight, CEO, Death Row Records. Mr. Knight has not been a part of any type of attack and is doing fine."

After an initial spurt of optimism, the investigation into Biggie's death also slowed to a crawl. Originally, Lieutenant Ross Moen of the LAPD told reporters that Biggie's assassin had been lying in wait. While no one had been arrested, as many as two hundred people had witnessed the killing. Some witnesses fled the scene or refused to speak, but most were cooperating. The killer, police reported, was a young black male in his early twenties. But they weren't overlooking the possibility that the killing was payback for Tupac's murder last fall.

Twenty LAPD homicide detectives were on the case; they contacted two hundred people. Across America, Lou Savelli of the NYPD's Citywide Anti-gang Enforcement Unit said, "The information we're getting is that it's connected. The murder of Biggie Smalls is connected to revenge, and all indications are that Biggie Small's murder was retaliation for Tupac Shakur's murder."

Then Lieutenant Ross Moen said the LAPD was looking at other murders and trying to tie them to Biggie's death. "We're looking at those as a possible connection. We can't eliminate the fact of those other murders in . . . rap music. Yes, we think there may be a possible connection."

By March 12, 1997, the LAPD said witnesses were unable to provide quick and complete descriptions of suspects. "The realization that we have to believe is that when somebody's shooting at you, the first reaction is not to get a description of the shooter," said Lieutenant Moen. "It's to take cover and duck, close your eyes and get out of there."

Within days, the *L.A. Times* reported that Biggie's murder may have stemmed from a personal dispute with a Compton gang member. While authorities tried to pin his death on the East Coast/West Coast rivalry, the *Times* felt the suspect was a Crip who acted independently, not on behalf of the gang. To date, no one has been arrested. The police have not been able to produce a suspect involved in the coastal feud.

The *Times*, meanwhile, reported that the shooter was a member of the same Crip gang Biggie hired to protect him during trips to Los Angeles—the same Southside Crips accused of killing Tupac. As weeks passed, descriptions of the murder changed: What happened, newspapers now reported, was that a man walked up to Biggie's GMC and struck up a friendly conversation. Biggie was rolling the window down to "give him five," when the man pulled a gun and opened fire. The shooter then leaped back into a dark sedan, and while speeding off, unleashed a volley of shots at the GMC. Lieutenant Ross Moen said, "There are a lot of people saying different things, but we're not going into that."

The new description seemed to support the position that Biggie's killer was a Southside Crip. While Bad Boy denied ever hiring Crips to act as security, an affidavit prepared to obtain search warrants in the October 1996 gang sweep asserted that Bad Boy Entertainment did in fact employ Southside Crips as security. A week after Tupac was shot, Southside Crips in Compton were bragging about having received money from an undisclosed source on the East Coast; tips poured in that the gang was going to use this payment to buy guns.

The relationship with the gang, police revealed, began in 1995, when Biggie hired Southside Crips to accompany him to the 1995 Soul Train Awards show. Members of the gang were also with him when Biggie encountered Tupac backstage at the Shrine Auditorium. It had been a Southside Crip who saw one of Tupac's goons pull a gun, who responded by drawing his own weapon and getting into a scuffle.

Before being shot at the *Vibe* party, Biggie had spent his final day associating with Southside Crip members, first in a Compton park, then at a basketball tournament at Cal State Dominguez Hills that afternoon, where these Crips were acting as part of his security team. The man who killed Biggie, the *L.A. Times* reported, believed he had been short-changed in an undisclosed financial transaction several months before. Members of the gang had been warning Biggie for weeks that his life would be in danger if he didn't pay this guy.

Puffy denied everything. "We've never hired Crips or any other gang faction to do security for us. But the misconception is that because we're young and we're black, we're not handling business like anybody else. We're trying our best to handle our business just like any other business-man in the world. And it would be extremely unintelligent to hire gangs to do security for you. We have never . . . never hired gangs for secu-rity. As a matter of fact, when we were out there, we had off-duty Cali-fornia police officers as security with us that night. We always have bonded security professionals with us."

To date, no one has been apprehended for Biggie's murder.

Tupac's murder.

Rolling 60 Crip Kelly Jamerson's murder.

Jake Robles's murder.

Randy "Stretch" Walker's murder.

Genius-Car-Wash-owner Bruce's murder.

His girlfriend's murder.

"The chief has given us a gag order," said Lieutenant Sneed of the Compton Police Department. "We can't say anything about Death Row Records. There are so many open investigations . . . we don't want to jeopardize any other agency's investigation."

On March 19, 1997, Biggie returned to New York City. He was laid out in a double-breasted white suit and matching hat. Held on Manhattan's Upper East Side, his funeral service was attended by Dr. Dre, Flavor Flav, Treach, Spinderella, Pepa, Latifah, and Mary J. Blige, who left in tears and had to be consoled by other mourners. Faith Evans sang, and Puffy eulogized him. "It was a peaceful event," said one attendee. "It wasn't all sorrow. Everybody was hugging and kissing, just like Biggie would have wanted."

Then Biggie's body was driven through the Brooklyn streets, where he went from crack dealer to hip-hop superstar. Thousands of mourners lined the streets, numbly watching as the procession of black limousines passed. Some cheered as he made his final trip; some left empty forty-ounce beer bottles, photos, candles, and a copy of *Ready to Die* at a makeshift shrine. Then the New York police moved in and skirmishes formed. To disperse the group, the police used pepper spray. Ten people were arrested on disorderly conduct charges; one was a *New York Times* freelance writer who asked a policeman why he used pepper spray on her and found herself being handcuffed; seven officers suffered minor injuries. Three children stood on the roof of a car and raised a cardboard sign that read WE LOVE YOU B.I.G. STOP THE VIOLENCE. FROM FUTURE STARS OF TOMORROW.

After his death, Biggie Smalls graced the covers of most American rap magazines. For *Rappages*, he had posed against a red background and worn a crown. While being interviewed for a segment on *America's Most Wanted*, Biggie's mother, Voletta Wallace, told the film crew to wait. Biggie's young daughter had burst into tears. Hysterical with grief, she screamed, "Where's my daddy? I want my daddy!" The child had seen his face on a poster advertising the *Rappages* issue.

When *Vibe* magazine put Biggie on its cover near the words "When Will It End?" one *Vibe* employee felt, "You motherfuckers are full of shit!

"Nobody ever wants to take responsibility," the employee added. "*No one* was doing anything to stop the violence. Not *Vibe*, *The Source*, or *Rappages*. And they still aren't! They may be thinking, 'Oh, my God! Tupac and Biggie are dead. *We gotta say something!*' But why the fuck didn't you say something a year ago? *Huh?!*"

"DID YOU GET EVERYTHING YOU WANTED?"

Suge began serving his nine-year sentence at the California Men's Colony in San Luis Obispo, where he was barred by law from running Death Row, saw half of the label's staff get laid off, and watched creditors like American Express continue demanding payment. Immediately after his imprisonment, he noticed, the Death Row family disbanded. Where the label once promoted a united front, artists had scattered to the four winds.

After the label's next release (the Lady of Rage's *Necessary Roughness*) entered the bottom of the sales charts, then quickly vanished, Rage became disillusioned with the label. "I only see the changes now that Suge isn't here," she said. "He was the backbone, so naturally things won't be the same. And Dre's gone. You know." She paused. "Snoop, Daz, and Kurupt—we all used to hang out together. Now we don't. Everybody's off doing their own thing right now. And that's what I have to do. I have to survive. Sink or swim."

Dogg Pound rapper Kurupt returned to Philadelphia. For years he believed his album would assure his fortune. "But here comes *Dogg Food* and he's still broke," said his former manager Lamont Bloomfield. "And I asked Kurupt, 'Did you get everything you wanted?' That's what woke him up: thinking he would get major money then being broke after *Dogg Food.*"

They had a meeting, Bloomfield explained: "Me, him, Suge, my attorney, their attorney. And we brought that up. 'So, Kurupt, shouldn't you be owed some money on your album?' Suge was like, *'Wait a minute! I spent all this money! I still didn't recoup things. Matter of fact, he owes a million six with me!'* Kurupt gave him this look. Only I knew what it meant. Five days after that, hearing he was a million six in the hole, Kurupt left Death Row Records for good. Grabbed all his shit and moved back to Philly."

Despite his claim that he would remain with Death Row "until the world blows up," singer Danny Boy returned to Chicago.

Belligerent Dogg Pound member Dat Nigga Daz was in Los Angeles, but not calling the office as much. He had finished recording a solo single for the *Gang-Related* soundtrack.

Snoop Doggy Dogg prepared to tour and told reporters about his upcoming reunion album with Dr. Dre *(Break Up to Make Up).*

MC Hammer was still trying to sell his mansion for a fraction of what he paid for it; he appeared in a film for the Showtime cable network (a sentimental drama about a has-been rapper finding it difficult to cope with life) and finished recording an album. "It's actually a gospel type of record, but, uh, it's also a mainstream type of record," he told *HardCopy.* The new album would be on his own label.

Gina Longo's brother, Frank, said she couldn't give an interview without the label's permission. Death Row publicist Greg Howard said her album wasn't a priority right now. He couldn't really say when her album, if ever, would see release.

Attorney David Kenner underwent triple bypass heart surgery. "Some of Knight's associates even go so far as to privately blame Kenner for giving Knight legal advice that they feel may have put the rap entrepreneur and his company in jeopardy," reporter Chuck Philips wrote.

Sharitha Knight decided to file suit against Snoop for alleged breach of contract, seeking unspecified compensatory damages: As president of

Knightlife Management, she was his manager from 1993 to 1996, she explained, and Snoop never fired her. But he refused to pay her twenty percent of the estimated $20 million he earned during the term of their contract—$1.6 million. She wanted a judge to place his salary into a trust because Snoop had a price on his head. "In other words," *L.A. Weekly* reported, "Sharitha Knight wants her money before Snoop gets shot—or spends all his money to avoid getting shot."

"The defendant presently owns and oftentimes travels in an armored van equipped with gun ports," the lawsuit claimed. "Death threats have been reported against the defendant. The defendant's life appears to be in jeopardy."

Snoop, she claimed, was also spending "large sums of money on frivolous items and objects," and "twenty-four-hour armed security and a large entourage." After filing suit, Sharitha was said to be pursuing a book deal. "She can't even speak English," a former employee said. "So how the fuck can she write it?"

Despite her attempt to try to write a tell-all book about her estranged husband, Suge, and her lawsuit against artist Snoop—Sharitha was appointed to run Death Row Records.

By now the label was knee-deep in litigation. On July 2, 1997, Dick Griffey's $75-million suit reached L.A. Superior Court and Judge Gregory O'Brien ordered Suge to turn over documents to Griffey and Tracy "the DOC" Curry.

Then Death Row filed a $7.1-million countersuit against Tupac's estate, demanding reimbursement for money advanced to him for cars, homes, jewelry, and recording and video costs. But Afeni Shakur and Richard Fischbine responded with another $17-million lawsuit that accused the label of failing to pay royalties and cheating Tupac of millions. In addition, they sought to invalidate the handwritten contract Tupac signed in prison, and asked that 152 unreleased Tupac songs be ordered into court-appointed receivership. This latest suit, Fischbine would explain, was in response to "the deafening silence from Death Row."

Then C. Delores Tucker, after appearing at Suge's sentencing hearing, included Death Row in a $10-million lawsuit against Tupac's estate, Interscope, Time Warner, Seagram Co., Tower Records, and seven other individuals: sixty-seven-year-old Tucker claimed defamatory lyrics on

Tupac's *All Eyez on Me* had caused her to undergo "great humiliation, mental pain, and suffering." She contended that due to Tupac's lyrics, her husband, William, did not want to have sex with her. She suffered a "loss of advice, companionship, and consortium." In fact, she complained, five million people now considered her "an object of scorn."

As the label continued its downward spiral, artists' efforts to leave were affected. "Man, I'm just trying to get off," producer Sam Sneed explained. "And if Suge's a thorough nigga, he'll let me go. I don't know what's going on. I mean, I asked him to release me, and he said, 'Cool. We can arrange that.' But we never got down to making it happen. It's sickening. Let's just part."

"THE SHIT'S ABOUT TO HIT THE FAN"

"At first it didn't matter much that some of the guys behind Death Row were real-life thugs, complete with criminal records and ties to L.A. gangs, or that their cronies brought guns and drugs into Interscope's headquarters," *Fortune* magazine reported.

By May 31, however, agents from the FBI, IRS, and the Bureau of Alcohol, Tobacco and Firearms had conducted interviews with West Coast music executives about Suge's relationship with imprisoned drug lord Michael Harris. Despite trying to distance itself from Death Row, Interscope was being involved.

"Seventeen months ago," the *L.A. Times* reported, "Harris sent a letter to Interscope Records executives, contending in an unfiled lawsuit that Harris had helped fund Death Row. The letter threatened to take legal action against Interscope and Death Row. Sources said Interscope eventually paid [his wife] Lydia Harris about $300,000 to resolve the matter."

Interscope's sales had risen from $125 million to a projected $325 million; its hit albums helped MCA increase its market share to twelve percent. But Jimmy Iovine feared that the federal investigation into Death Row might endanger Interscope's deal with MCA. "Universal [executives] are up in arms about it," one source told reporters. "How did [Interscope] not know Death Row was being run this way?"

At this point, MCA had already come under attack for its association with Death Row. In December 1996, conservative watchdog William Bennett said, "Their word is not worth anything. Seagram/MCA is peddling filth for profit and reneging on a moral commitment."

Interscope, half owned by MCA, wanted to sell the remaining half to Seagram's CEO Edgar Bronfman Jr. (who owned eighty percent of MCA). Instead of shock-value groups like Marilyn Manson, Interscope began to focus on nonthreatening acts like R&B producer R. Kelly, soul group BLACKstreet, pop rockers No Doubt and God's Property, a fifty-member gospel youth choir whose album debuted at No. 3 on the *Billboard* charts.

Interscope also decided not to distribute Death Row's next two releases (Nate Dogg's *G-Funk Classics* and the *Gang-Related* soundtrack), and urged Suge to grant Afeni Shakur ownership of any unreleased Tupac material Death Row may release.

Despite Interscope's sanitized image, the Death Row controversy continued to affect Bronfman at MCA, and Seagram. In August 1997, investors for two state pension funds (Texas and Maryland) threatened to pull out of Seagram's—due to Seagram's involvement with MCA and Death Row. "Politically, Death Row is causing Mr. Bronfman some discomfort," *The New York Observer* revealed. "Financially, it isn't doing him much good. And esthetically, as one financial analyst put it, 'Edgar's a songwriter whose specialty is love ballads. I doubt if rap is really his thing.'"

After mortgaging his beloved Death Row master tapes to Iovine, and receiving millions of dollars to keep the label afloat in 1997, Suge felt that Interscope was abandoning him. "We know that there has been a lot of pressure around Death Row," an unnamed source at Interscope told the *L.A. Times*. "We've been grappling for months with how to deal with this issue."

It was Bronfman who made the decision. When Grand Met and

Guinness, two of Seagram's competitors, considered a merger that would lead to them controlling fifty-four percent of the world's Scotch market, Bronfman realized he might have to ask the government to prevent what he felt was an anticompetitive merger. When he did, he would need friends in Congress and the White House.

As Suge sat in his prison cell, Bronfman decided that MCA/Universal would not be involved with any recording issued by Death Row Records. "Bronfman is getting rid of Interscope and Interscope is getting rid of Death Row," said an Interscope insider. "Bronfman has been under pressure from his own shareholders and regulators, and he doesn't need to be near gangs and thugs and murderers."

Federal agents conducted a second round of interviews with West Coast music executives; agents from the FBI, IRS, BATF, and DEA also approached the label's accountant and reviewed documents. Michael Harris, serving a twenty-eight-year sentence in Lancaster Prison, continues to maintain that he put up $1.5 million to launch Death Row, then was cheated out of millions. "David [Kenner] is a real piece of work," he told a television program. "The shit's about to hit the fan."

The probe, now said to be in its final stage, is focusing on the relationship between Suge, attorney David Kenner, Michael Harris, and another imprisoned drug dealer named Patrick Johnson.

Suspected of being a silent partner in the label, Johnson went from growing up in Suge's neighborhood to operating one of the nation's largest PCP rings during the 1980s and laundering millions through real estate and other legitimate Compton-based businesses.

The tie between the drug dealers and Suge, agents knew, was lawyer David Kenner: In 1991 Kenner represented Suge; he helped negotiate a thirty-year plea bargain for Johnson and accompanied Suge to numerous visits with another client, Michael Harris. Though some reporters predicted that Kenner would escape unscathed, earlier in the year he had been subpoenaed to turn over documents related to the investigation. Agents are now trying to determine if Kenner's involvement in the label extended beyond his role as its chief attorney.

In mid-1997, a grand jury was convened in Los Angeles to hear allegations that the company was financed by drug lords, and that employees were involved in racketeering and money laundering. Michael Harris was moved to a cell in the Metro Detention Center in Los Angeles, and said to be cooperating with federal agents. Harris would be testifying before the grand jury, an *L.A. Weekly* reporter said. "If he hasn't already."

Suge Knight remains in prison. Lawyers are filing appeals and trying to get him released. If the federal investigation proves Death Row Records was funded by drug money, federal agents may seize the company. Suge will also face additional charges and time in prison. As the investigation enters its final stage, defense lawyer Milton Grimes has been hired to represent him. "It is our understanding that the government is spending a lot of time seeking out individuals who will say that Mr. Knight authorized or approved of criminal activities such as assault," Grimes said, "and that is simply not true. Mr. Knight never authorized, approved, or participated in any such crime."

Once the probe concludes, indictments will be handed down.